LABORATORY TECHNIQUES
IN ARCHAEOLOGY

GARLAND REFERENCE LIBRARY
OF SOCIAL SCIENCE
(VOL. 110)

LABORATORY TECHNIQUES IN ARCHAEOLOGY
A Guide to the Literature, 1920–1980

compiled by
Linda Ellis

GARLAND PUBLISHING, INC. • NEW YORK & LONDON
1982

Library of Congress Cataloging in Publication Data

Ellis, Linda.
  Laboratory techniques in archaeology.

  (Garland reference library of social science ; v. 110)
  Includes indexes.
    1. Archaeology—Methodology—Bibliography.   2. Antiq-
uities—Analysis—Bibliography. I. Title. II. Series.
Z5131.E43   1982   [CC75]   016.9301   81-43361
ISBN 0-8240-9272-4

Printed on acid-free, 250-year-life paper
Manufactured in the United States of America

CONTENTS

v

INTRODUCTION

Terms such as "science in archaeology," "archaeological science," "archaeometry," or a host of specialized terms including "archaeological chemistry," "paleoethnobotany," "zooarchaeology," etc. have all had one purpose, i.e., to designate the interrelationship of the physical and biological sciences with archaeology. This marriage of disciplines, with roots going back to the last century, has flourished to the extent that a major problem now confronts many scholars—finding literature pertinent to specific scientific and archaeological interests. This is, of course, not a new problem for any discipline, and bibliographies were created to meet this need. However, the problem does become quite acute concerning this "alloy" of science and archaeology, since, on the one hand, there is a well-established repertoire of archaeological periodical literature and, on the other hand, the physical and biological sciences also have their own literature with highly specialized journals in a multitude of subdisciplines. Then consider the archaeologist, the natural scientist, or an "archaeometrist"—each wanting to search the literature. These people are automatically confronted with a global archaeological literature that is by no means *consistent* in its publishing of articles dealing with the *applications of science in archaeology*, together with an elaborately computerized and abstracted scientific literature which often appears as a maze to anyone not utilizing these resources on a regular basis.

Fortunately, a number of journals have been designed to act as a forum for communication between the sciences and archaeology—*Archaeometry, Archaeo-Physika, Journal of Archaeological Science, Prospezioni Archeologiche, MASCA Newsletter* (now *MASCA Journal*), *Tree-Ring Bulletin, Newsletter of Computer Archaeology, PACT, Ossa, Studies in Conservation, Berliner Beiträge zur Archäometrie, Science and Archaeology, Archäologie und Natur-*

wissenschaften. These journals, therefore, have been thoroughly indexed for this bibliography. However, these journals—excluding *Archaeometry, Tree-Ring Bulletin*, and *Studies in Conservation*— began publishing in the late 1960s and 1970s and, therefore, cannot possibly reflect current publications much less the vast literature that existed prior to 1960. Hence, there is a need for a bibliography that covers an appreciable time span as well as a vast number of other archaeological and scientific publications.

This bibliography encompasses the use of the biological, physical, and mathematical sciences in archaeology. The time period is 1920 to 1980—the beginning date of 1920 was chosen since much material published prior to that date was found to be of limited usefulness, considering the technical advances that have been made, or was too difficult or impossible to locate even when using interlibrary services. Articles and books published in one of the six major European languages—English, German, French, Italian, Spanish, and Russian—are included in the original language. In accordance with the policy of the Tozzer Library, Harvard University, all German and Russian titles have been translated into English. Journal titles are given in full. Up to three authors are listed for books and articles; for articles having more than three authors, the listing will be under the first author's name.

The bibliography has been organized on the basis of subject, as opposed to an alphabetical listing by author, in order to facilitate the searching of literature pertinent to specific problems. The subject divisions were chosen on the basis of questions asked in archaeology which cannot be answered by standard excavation methods alone, i.e., the application of laboratory techniques used in the biological, physical and mathematical sciences to solve archaeological problems: (1) how to locate prehistoric settlements and objects, (2) how to date these finds, (3) how to reconstruct the natural environmental and ecological conditions in the past, (4) how to characterize organic and inorganic materials, and finally (5) how to organize and manipulate large volumes of data. There are six major sections devoted to General Works, Remote Sensing, Chronometry, Environmental Reconstruction, Materials Analysis, and Data Management. The sections on Remote Sensing, Chronometry, and Materials Analysis are further subdivided by method. The section on Environmental Reconstruction is divided by discipline, i.e., soil science, climatology, zoology, botany, medicine, etc. Data Management consists of two sections dealing with general studies and specific applications of computer programming and statistics.

In order to facilitate the search for specific references, four indexes have been provided for geographical location, method of analysis, type of material analyzed, and authorship. The geographical index should prove particularly useful for archaeologists. A method index is included, since each article is listed only once and many articles deal with multiple methods of analysis. The materials index is perhaps most useful when used in conjunction with the sections on Chronometry and Materials Analysis, since, quite obviously, some methods and instrumentation can only be used for certain types of materials. The author index includes the names of both main and joint authors.

For all sections, comprehensiveness has been the main objective. However, some brief comments about specific sections are needed in order to explain the principles guiding the development of the bibliography.

For radiocarbon dating, it must be agreed that since the 1950s the instrumentation itself has undergone a remarkable evolution. In fact, radiocarbon dating demonstrates a classic problem for bibliographic work in the sciences: At which point is bibliographic comprehensiveness useful when older scientific technology is useless? Older literature, therefore, has been de-emphasized for maximum practicable utility. In addition to this problem are two others: The publishing of date lists and the continuing dialogue among archaeologists over specific C-14 results. It is assumed that professional archaeologists are familiar with the journal *Radiocarbon*, whose main purpose is to publish date lists and that archaeologists are also familiar with the specific dates for their respective geographic interests as well as the archaeological and historical implications of those dates.

For analysis of faunal remains found at archaeological sites, over 450 references are offered here. It was thought that some further organization of the material might be useful, perhaps on the basis of Genus, Family or Order; however, this proved too cumbersome. When reviewing the literature, it was then found that research interests rested in three main areas: theoretical and methodological problems; the history of domestication; and the problems of identifying elusive and fragmentary materials mainly consisting of insects and fish. The material, therefore, has been classified accordingly as method/theory, mammalia, and non-mammalia, together with a small section on the analysis of "animal by-products."

The sub-section on paleopathology presented other problems. Four types of studies were recognized in the medical-archaeological literature: The analysis of mummified remains, the analysis of bone for evidence of disease, the documentation of culturally dictated skull deformation ("head binding"), and the documentation of prehistoric skull surgery ("trepanation"). Considering the fact that paleopathology was most appropriately included under Environmental Reconstruction and that skull deformation and surgery do not necessarily reflect environmental stress, disease, and nutrition imbalances but are based more on cultural aesthetics and traditional healing practices, respectively—usually for little-known or understood reasons—it was thought best to include material on mummified remains ("soft-tissue research") and on the evidence for disease and diet on human bone. The analysis of soft-tissue, although from very limited geographic regions, was included because of its vast potential for the documentation of diseases which would not leave traces on bone and for its potential in paleodietary research.

For the section on Materials Analysis, the emphasis is on the chemical and physical analysis of archaeological materials. Broad and generalized histories of technology and experiments in replicating ancient manufacturing techniques have *not* been included here, since many of these studies are based on information derived from published chemical and microscopic investigations.

Other published bibliographies concerned with the applications of science in archaeology are few in number and are quite limited in scope. The most comprehensive is a three-volume bibliography (#2732) published between the years 1967 and 1971. This bibliography, compiled by Rolf-Dieter Bleck, has both advantages and serious limitations and appears to have been primarily designed for the field of conservation and museum studies. The advantages of this three-volume set are its inclusion of a considerable amount of older and nineteenth-century material, material published in languages other than those found here, and its broad coverage of the conservation literature. An alphabetical listing of authors is used but with no attempt to organize the material chronologically among the three volumes, so one has to search all three volumes to find one article. Abbreviations of journal titles are used throughout from which full titles are not readily derivable. The presentation of article titles is inconsistent—all too often, titles in English, Russian, Polish, and other languages are translated into German or French without giving the titles as they appeared in the journal, while other titles are presented in their original language. There is only one index provided, based on materials and their conservation, but most articles are annotated.

A few more specialized bibliographies are available. The oldest (1940) is E. Schulman's bibliography (#1197) on dendrochronology; this bibliography is still useful for archaeology in the southwestern United States and has excellent coverage of the formative years of tree-ring research. An attempt at bibliographic compilation in paleoethnobotany has been made by J. Schultze-Motel (# 2345–2351 and 2353) in a series of journal articles published between 1968 and 1974. S.M. Borgognini-Tarli (#2471) published a short bibliography in 1979 on paleoserology. And G.J. Armelagos et al. (#2460) published an excellent bibliography on paleopathology in 1971. The Armelagos bibliography has a thorough coverage of the subject, including much material on cultural skull deformation and skull surgery. A considerable amount of older material from the nineteenth century and the early decades of the twentieth century is also to be found in this work, and a complete list of journal abbreviations, with full titles given, is included.

From the foregoing discussion, it is obvious that a more comprehensive and well-organized bibliography for the applications of science in archaeology is necessary. This bibliography has been designed for the disciplines of archaeology and the physical, biological, and mathematical sciences. The Materials Analysis section should also prove useful for conservation and museology.

This bibliography is the culmination of six years of careful thought and time-consuming work. Since there are so few existing bibliographies and none that are truly comprehensive in their coverage of the subject matter of "archaeometry," this bibliography is in many ways an experiment, especially in format and in the types of material included. It is hoped that this experiment will prove to be beneficial to those working in the many fields represented here.

LABORATORY TECHNIQUES IN ARCHAEOLOGY

I. GENERAL WORKS

0001 Aitken, M. J. (1974) Physics and archaeology. Second edition. Oxford, England: University Press.

0002 Berger, R., ed. (1971) Scientific methods in medieval archaeology. Berkeley, California: University of California Press.

0003 Brill, R. H., ed. (1971) Science and archaeology. Cambridge, Massachusetts: MIT Press.

0004 Brothwell, D. and Higgs, E., eds. (1969) Science in archaeology. Second edition. London: Thames and Hudson.

0005 Davidson, D. A. and Shackley, M. L., eds. (1976) Geoarchaeology. London: Duckworth.

0006 Goffer, Z. (1980) Archaeological Chemistry. New York: J. Wiley.

0007 Heizer, R. F. and Cook, S. F., eds. (1960) The application of quantitative methods in archaeology. Viking Fund publications in anthropology, no. 28. New York.

0008 Hrouda, B., ed. (1978) Methoden der Archäologie. (The methods of archaeology). München: Verlag C. H. Beck.

0009 Kolčin, B. A., ed. (1965) Arkheologija i estestvennye nauki. (Archaeology and the natural sciences). Moskva: Akademija Nauk SSSR.

0010   Rudenko, S. I., ed. (1963) Novye metody v
       arkheologičeskikh issledovanijakh. (New methods in
       archaeological investigations). Moskva: Akademija
       Nauk SSSR.

0011   Tite, M. S. (1972) Methods of physical examination in
       archaeology. New York: Academic Press.

II. REMOTE SENSING

A. General studies

0012 Aitken, M. J. (1962) Physics applied to archaeology, part I. Contemporary physics 3(3):161.

0013 Aitken, M. J. (1962) Physics applied to archaeology, part II. Contemporary physics 3(5):333.

0014 Bass, F. G. and Katzev, M. L. (1968) New tools for underwater archaeology. Archaeology 21(3):164-173.

0015 Fowler, G. N. (1967) Physics in archaeology. Physics education 2:65-72.

0016 Frantov, G. S. (1965) Primenenie geofiziceskikh metodov razvedki v arkheologii. (The application of geophysical methods of reconnaissance in archaeology). Materialy i issledovanija po arkheologii SSSR 129:244-251.

0017 Frantov, G. S. and Pinkevič, A. A. (1966) Geofizika v arkheologii. (Geophysics in archaeology). Leningrad: Akademija Nauk SSSR. 212p.

0018 Hesse, A. (1966) Prospections géophysiques à Faible Prefondeur. Applications à l'archéologie. Paris: Dunod. 149p.

0019 Lauterbach, R. (1962) Geophysik in der Vor- und Frühgeschichte. (Geophysics in prehistory and early history). Geophysik und Geologie 4:123.

3

4

0020 Lauterbach, R. and Olszak, G. (1964) Archäologie und
     Geophysik. (Archaeology and geophysics).
     Ausgrabungen und Funde 9:280-287.

0021 Lerici, C. M. (1955) Prospezioni archeologiche.
     Rivista di geofisica applicata 16:7-31.

0022 Lerici, C. M. (1956) La scienza al servizio dell'-
     archeologia. La ricerca scientifica 26(4):1044-1075.

0023 Lerici, C. M. (1958) Aspetti economici ed organizza-
     tivi. La prospezioni geofisica nella ricerca
     archeologica. VII Convegno internazionale di
     archeologia classica. Milano, 64-69.

0024 Lerici, C. M. (1958) La prospezioni geofisica nella
     ricerca archeologica. La prospezioni geofisica nella
     ricerca archeologica. VII Convegno internazionale di
     archeologia classica. Milano, 8-10.

0025 Lerici, C. M. (1958) Le applicazioni geofisiche nella
     ricerca archeologica. Studi etruschi 26:297-301.

0026 Lerici, C. M. (1961) Alla scoperta delle civiltà
     Sepolte--I. Nuovi metodi di prospezione archeologica.
     Milano. 415p.

0027 Lerici, C. M. (1961) Methods used in the archaeological
     prospecting of Etruscan tombs. Studies in
     conservation 6(1):1-8.

0028 Lerici, C. M. (1962) New archaeological techniques and
     international cooperation in Italy. Expedition
     4(3):5-10.

0029 Linington, R. E. (1961) Physics and archaeological
     salvage. Archaeology 14:287-289.

0030 Linington, R. E. (1963) The application of geophysics
     to archaeology. American Scientist 51(1):48-70.

0031 Lyons, T. R., comp. (1976) Remote sensing experiments
     in cultural resource studies. Chaco Center series
     no. 3. Albuquerque, New Mexico: Chaco Center.

0032 Lyons, T. R. and Mathien, F. J., eds. (1980) Cultural
     resources remote sensing. Washington, D.C.:
     National Park Service.

0033 Lyons, T. R. and Avery, T. E. (1977) Remote sensing. Washington, D.C.: National Park Service.

0034 Musty, J. (1968) The Ancient Monuments Laboratory geophysical programme 1967: review and assessment. Prospezioni archeologiche 3:123-126.

0035 Rainey, F. G. and Ralph, E. K. (1966) Archaeology and its new technology. Science 153(3743):1481-1491.

0036 Rainey, F. G. and Stirling, M. W. (1960) Electronics and archaeology. Expedition 2:19-29.

0037 Scott-Elliott, J. (1958) Archaeological detection. Journal of the British society of dowsers 14:338-339.

0038 Solaini, L. (1958) Avvenire delle prospezioni geofisiche in archeologia. La prospezione geofisica nella ricerca archeologica. VII Convegno internazionale di archeologia classica. Milano, 11-14.

0039 Sunčugašev, JA. I. and Zakharov, E. P. (1964) Opyt primenenija geologičeskikh poiskovykh metodov v arkheologičeskoj razvedke. (Experiment in the application of geological methods in archaeological prospection). Sovetskaja arkheologija 1:295-298.

0040 Swain, P. H. and Davis, S. M., eds. (1978) Remote sensing. New York: McGraw-Hill.

0041 Uspenskij, A. (1967) Gde iskat' Nineviju ili fizika v arkheologii. (Where to find Nineveh or physics in archaeology). Nauka i religija 6:76-79.

0042 Vecchia, O. (1958) Condizione geologiche per la ricerca geofisica in archeologia. La prospezione geofisica nella ricerca archeologica. VII Convegno internazionale di archeologia classica. Milano, 15-22.

B. Electrical resistivity surveying

0043 Al Chalabi, M. M. and Rees, A. I. (1962) An experiment on the effect of rainfall on electrical resistivity anomalies. Bonner Jahrbücher 162:266-271.

0044 Appel, H. J. (1965) Elektronische Steuerung einer chemischen Anlage: Deionisierungsanlage zur Entsalzung von Bodenfunden. (Electronic steering of chemistry: deionization tendency to desalinization of buried finds). Archaeo-Physika 1:123-174.

0045 Aspinall, A. and Pickard, K. (1971) A direct-reading earth resistance meter. Prospezioni archeologiche 6:21-23.

0046 Atkinson, R. J. C. (1962) Méthodes électriques de prospection en archéologie. In: A. Laming, ed., La découverte du passé. Paris: Picard, 59-70.

0047 Åström, P. (1967) Electrical prospecting at Calatia, Caserta. Prospezioni archeologiche 2:81-83.

0048 Blundell, D. J., Garside, A. W., and Wilton, T. J. (1974) Geophysical surveys across the centre of the Roman fort at Watercrook, Kendal. Prospezioni archeologiche 9:35-45.

0049 Braissant, P. and Chapellier, D. (1971) Le potentio-mètre Braissant. Prospezioni archeologiche 6:25-27.

0050 Brancaleoni, F. and Linington, R. E. (1974) Pros-pezione elettrica a S. Vincenzino, Cecina. Prospezioni archeologiche 9:75-82.

0051 Burian, J., Hrdlička, L. and Tykva, B. (1968) The geophysical exploration of St. George's Square, Prague Castle. Prospezioni archeologiche 3:45-53.

0052 Burnez, C. and Hesse, A. (1967) Prospections géo-physiques sur les sites archéologiques de la Charante. Bulletin de la société préhistorique française. Études et travaux 64(2):299-304.

0053 Burnez, C. and Hesse, A. (1971) Prospection électrique --le site gaulois de la Croix-des-Sables à Mainxe (Charente). Bulletin de la société préhistorique française 68:468-469.

0054 Carabelli, E. (1958) Metodi elettrici ed elettro-
magnetici di prospezioni geofisica per finalità
archeologiche. La prospezioni geofisica nella
ricerca archeologica. VII Convegno internazionale di
archeologia classica. Milano, 37-42.

0055 Carabelli, E. (1961) Ricerca archeologica sperimentale
eseguita ad Aniba (Nubia Egiziana). La ricerca
scientifica 4/5:129-145.

0056 Carabelli, E. (1967) Ricerca sperimentale dei dis-
positivi piú adatti alla prospezioni elettrica di
cavità sotterranee. Prospezioni archeologiche 2:9-21.

0057 Carabelli, E. and Brancaleoni, F. (1968) Rilievo
elettrico di tombe a camera con dispositivo a doppio
dipolo. Prospezioni archeologiche 3:55-60.

0058 Clark, A. J. (1968) A square array for resistivity
surveying. Prospezioni archeologiche 3:111-114.

0059 Clark, A. J. (1975) Archaeological prospecting: a
progress report. Journal of archaeological science
2(4):297-314.

0060 Dabrowski, K. and Stopiński, W. (1962) The application
of the electric-resistivity method to archaeological
investigations illustrated on the example of an early
medieval hillfort Zawodzie in Kalisz. Archaeologia
Polona 5:21-30.

0061 Dabrowski, K., Stopiński, W. and Stupnicka, E. (1962)
Issledovanie arkheologičeskikh pamjatnikov metodom
opredelenija veličiny èlektrosoprotivljaemosti
grunta. (Investigations of archaeological monuments
by the determination of electrical resistivity of the
earth). Sovetskaja arkheologija 3:105-115.

0062 Di Ceglie, S. and Mosetti, F. (1957) Applicazioni dei
metodi geoelettrici alla esplorazione archeologica.
Bollettino di geodesia e scienze affini 16:367-381.

0063 Dunk, A. J. (1962) An electrical resistance survey over
a Romano-British villa site. Bonner Jahrbücher
162:272-276.

8

0064 Glazunov, V. V. (1978) Arkheologo-geofizičeskoe
      izučenie gorodišča Kamno. (Archaeo-geophysical study
      of the ancient site of Kamno). Kratkie soobščenija
      instituta arkheologii 152:82-92.

0065 Glazunov, V. V. (1978) Opyt vyjavlenija detal'nogo
      plana postrojki metodom elektrorazvedki. (Experiment
      of exposure of detailed construction schemes by the
      method of electrical resistance). Kratkie
      soobščenija instituta arkheologii 152:68-73.

0066 Goell, T. (1968) Geophysical survey of the Hierothesion
      and tomb of Antiochus I, Commagene, Turkey. National
      geographic society research reports. 1963 Projects,
      83-102.

0067 Hampl, F. and Fritsch, V. (1959) Geoelektrische
      Messungen in ihrer Anwendung für die Archäologie.
      (Geoelectrical measurements in their application for
      archaeology). Technische Beiträge zur Archäologie
      1:116.

0068 Hesse, A. (1962) Contribution des mesures de résis-
      tivité à la connaissance du site du 'Petit Vaux' à
      Champs (Yonne). Appendix to: M. Brezillon,
      Néolithique danubien et Bronze récent à Champs
      (Yonne). Gallia préhistoire 5:169-172.

0069 Hesse, A. (1962) Geophysical prospecting for archaeol-
      ogy in France. Archaeometry 5:123-125.

0070 Hesse, A. (1962) Mesures de résistivités électriques
      sur une coupe stratigraphique de gisement pré-
      historique. Comptes rendus des séances de l'académie
      des sciences 254:525-527.

0071 Hesse, A. (1966) The importance of climatologic ob-
      servations in archaeological prospecting. Prospezioni
      archeologiche 1:11-13.

0072 Hesse, A. (1966) Perfectionnement des applications
      archéologiques de la prospection électrique. Bulletin
      de la société préhistorique française 63(1):xv-xix.

0073 Hesse, A. and Renimel, S. (1979) Can we survey the
      limits of an archaeological site? The example of St.
      Romain en Gal (France). Archaeo-Physika 10:638-646.

0074 Hesse, A. and Spahos, Y. (1979) The evaluation of
Wenner and dipole-dipole resistivity measurements
and the use of a new switch for archaeological field
work. Archaeo-Physika 10:647-655.

0075 Homilius, J. (1963) Geoelektrische Tiefensondierungen
zur Untersuchung verdeckter archäologischer Befunde
bei Xanten. (Geoelectrical depth probing for the
investigation of hidden archaeological finds by
Xanten). Bonner Jahrbücher 163:167-187.

0076 Iciek, A. et al (1974) Prospections géophysiques à
Carthage. Prospezioni archeologiche 9:61-74.

0077 Lenkiewicz, T. and Stopiński W. (1969) The application
of an electric resistivity method to archaeological
research in towns. Archaeologia Polona 11:173-197.

0078 Lerici, C. M. (1960) Esplorazione geofisica nella zona
archeologica di Sibari. La ricerca scientifica
30(8):1107-1145.

0079 Lerici, C. M., Carabelli, E. and Segre, E. (1958)
Prospezioni geofisiche nella zona archeologica di
Vulci. Quaderni di geofisica applicata 11:47p.

0080 Linington, R. E. (1961) Étude de la résistivité des
sols. Appendix to: C. Burnez and H. Case, Les
camps néolithiques des Matignons à Juillac-le-Coq.
Gallia préhistoire 9:198-200.

0081 Linington, R. E. (1962) Relazione sulle campagne di
prospezione archeologica a Tarquinia, Cerveteri,
Veio, Sibari. Quaderni di geofisica applicata
22:113p.

0082 Linington, R. E. (1967) A short geophysical campaign
carried out at Bolonia, Cadiz. Prospezioni
archeologiche 2:49-68.

0083 Linington, R. E. (1967) An electrical resistivity
survey at Les Matignons. Prospezioni archeologiche
2:91-93.

0084 Linington, R. E. (1968) The search for the supposed
obelisk under Via Giustiniani, Rome. Prospezioni
archeologiche 3:77-81.

10

0085 Martinaud, M. and Colmont, G. (1971) Intérêt de l'étude des sols par mesure de résistivité et carottages mécaniques. Prospezioni archeologiche 6:53-60.

0086 Palmer, L. S. (1960) Geoelectrical surveying of archaeological sites. Proceedings of the prehistoric society 26:64-75.

0087 Peschel, G. (1967) A new favourable combination of resistivity sounding and profiling in archaeological surveying. Prospezioni archeologiche 2:23-28.

0088 Peschel, G. and Freess, W. B. (1963) Geophysikalischer Nachweis prähistorischer Gruben in Canitzer Urnengräberfeld. (Geophysical survey of prehistoric graves in the Canitz urnfield). Ausgrabungen und Funde 3:117-119.

0089 Peschel, G. and Freess, W. B. (1966) Geoelektrische Untersuchungen im jungbronzezeitlichen Urnengräberfeld von Canitz bei Wurzen. (Geoelectrical investigations in the late Bronze Age cemetry of Canitz by Wurzen). Arbeits- und Forschungsberichte zur Sächsischen Bodendenkmalpflege 14/15:75-94.

0090 Rees, A. I. (1962) Electrical prospecting methods in archaeology. Antiquity 36:131-134.

0091 Rees, A. I. and Wright, A. E. (1969) Resistivity surveys at Barnsley Park. Prospezioni archeologiche 4:121-124.

0092 Schwarz, G. T. (1959) Geo-elektrische Bodenuntersuchungen als Hilfsmittel der Archäologie: Testversuche in Aventicum. (Geo-electrical surveying as an aid to archaeology: a test in Aventicum). Jahrbuch der Schweizerischen Gesellschaft für Urgeschichte 47:96-102.

0093 Schwarz, G. T. (1961) The 'Zirkelsonde': a new technique for resistivity surveying. Archaeometry 4:67-70.

0094 Scollar, I. (1959) Einführung in die Widerstandsmessung, eine geophysikalische Methode zur Aufnahme von archäologischen Befunden unter der Erdoberfläche. (Introduction of resistivity measurement, a geophysical method to detect archaeological finds under the earth surface). Bonner Jahrbücher des Rheinischen Landesmuseums in Bonn 159:284-313.

0095 Sieveking, G. de G. et al. (1973) A new survey of Grime's Graves, Norfolk--first report. Proceedings of the Prehistoric Society 39:182-218.

0096 Šilik, K. K. (1967) Opyt êlektrorazvedki metodom simmetričnogo profilirovanija. (Electro-prospecting experiment by the method of symmetrical profiling). Sovetskaja arkheologija 3:205-211.

C. Magnetic surveying

0097 Abrahamsen, N. (1967) Some archaeomagnetic investigations in Denmark. Prospezioni archeologiche 2:95-97.

0098 Aitken, M. J. (1958) Magnetic prospecting: I--The Water Newton survey. Archaeometry 1:24-29.

0099 Aitken, M. J. (1959) Dowsing and magnetism. Archaeometry 2:58-59.

0100 Aitken, M. J. (1959) Magnetic prospecting: II (Surveys). Archaeometry 2:32-36.

0101 Aitken, M. J. (1959) Magnetic prospecting: IV--The proton magnetometer. Archaeometry 2:40-44.

0102 Aitken, M. J. (1959) Magnetic prospecting--an interim assessment. Antiquity 33:205-207.

0103 Aitken, M. J. (1960) Magnetic prospecting: the proton gradiometer. Archaeometry 3:38-40.

0104 Aitken, M. J. (1960) The magnetic survey. Appendix to: S. S. Frere, Excavations at Verulamium 1959, 5th. interim report. Antiquaries journal 40:21-24.

0105 Aitken, M. J. (1961) The magnetic survey. Appendix to: S. S. Frere, Excavations at Verulamium 1960, 6th. interim report. Antiquaries journal 41:83-85.

0106 Aitken, M. J. (1961) Magnetic location in Britain.
Archaeometry 4:83-84.

0107 Aitken, M. J. (1961) The magnetic survey. Appendix to:
I. M. Stead, Excavations at Arras. Antiquaries
journal 41:58-59.

0108 Aitken, M. J. (1964) The proton magnetometer and its
relationship to aerial photography. Colloque
international d'archéologie aérienne. Paris: École
Pratique des Hautes Études, 255-258.

0109 Aitken, M. J. and Alldred, J. C. (1964) A simulator-
trainer for magnetic prospection. Archaeometry
7:28-35.

0110 Aitken, M. J. and Alldred, J. C. (1966) Prediction of
magnetic anomalies by means of a simulator.
Prospezioni archeologiche 1:67-72.

0111 Aitken, M. J. and Tite, M. S. (1962) A gradient
magnetometer, using proton free-precession. Journal
of scientific instruments 39:625-629.

0112 Aitken, M. J. and Tite, M. S. (1962) Proton
magnetometer surveying on some British hill-forts.
Archaeometry 5:126-134.

0113 Aitken, M. J., Webster, G. and Reeds, A. (1958)
Magnetic prospecting. Antiquity 32:270-271.

0114 Alldred, J. C. (1964) A fluxgate gradiometer for
archaeological surveying. Archaeometry 7:14-19.

0115 Alldred, J. C. and Aitken, M. J. (1966) A fluxgate
gradiometer for archaeological surveying.
Prospezioni archeologiche 1:53-60.

0116 Becker, H. (1977/1978) Vorläufiger Bericht über eine
magnetische Prospektion des Demircihüyük
(Nordwestanatolien). (Preliminary report on magnetic
prospection of Demircihüyük, northwest Anatolia).
Istanbuler Mitteilungen 27/28:32-44.

0117 Becker, H. (1979) Magnetic prospecting with a differ-
ence-protonmagnetometer with an automatic data-record
on a digital cassette. Archaeo-Physika 10:633-637.

0118 Bevan, B. (1975) A magnetic survey at Les Forges du Saint-Maurice. MASCA newsletter 11(2):1.

0119 Black, G. A. and Johnston, R. B. (1962) A test of magnetometry as an aid to archaeology. American antiquity 28:199-205.

0120 Breiner, S. (1965) The rubidium magnetometer in archaeological exploration. Science 150(3693): 185-193.

0121 Breiner, S. and Coe, M. D. (1972) Magnetic exploration of the Olmec civilization. American scientist 60(5):566-575.

0122 Chevallier, R. and Roguet, R. (1968) Prospections géophysiques à Izernore (Ain), France. Prospezioni archeologiche 3:61-76.

0123 Colani, C. and Aitken, M. J. (1966) Utilisation of magnetic viscosity effects in soils for archaeological prospection. Nature 212:1446-1447.

0124 Dabrowski, K. (1963) The application of geophysical method to archaeological research in Poland. Archaeometry 6:83-88.

0125 Dabrowski, K. and Linington, R. E. (1967) Test use of a proton magnetometer near Kalisz, Poland. Prospezioni archeologiche 2:29-42.

0126 Danilenko, V. N., Dudkin, V. P. and Kruts, A. V. (1967) Arkheologo-magnitnaja razvedka v Kievskoj oblasti. (Archaeo-magnetic survey in the Kiev district). Arkheologičeskie issledovanija na Ukraine 1(1965-1966):209-215.

0127 Fischer, P. M. (1980) Geophysical prospecting at Hala Sultan Tekke, Cyprus. Journal of field archaeology 7(4):479-484.

0128 Fowler, P. J. (1959) Magnetic prospecting: III--archaeological note. Archaeometry 2:37-39.

0129 Graham, I. D. G. and Scollar, I. (1976) Limitation on magnetic prospection in archaeology imposed by soil properties. Archaeo-Physika 6:1-124.

0130 Green, J. N. (1970) A new sea-going magnetometer detector head. Archaeometry 12(2):167-172.

0131 Groševoj, G. V., Galkin, L. L. and Zajončkovskij, M. A. (1967) Arkheologičeskaja razvedka magnitometrom napravlennogo dejstvija. (Archaeological survey by magnetometry). Sovetskaja arkheologija 3:191-204.

0132 Hall, E. T. (1962) Some notes on the design and manufacture of detector heads for proton magnetometers. Archaeometry 5:139-145.

0133 Hall, E. T. (1966) The use of the proton magnetometer in underwater archaeology. Archaeometry 9:32-44.

0134 Harknett, M. R. (1969) A proton magnetometer with solid state switching. Archaeometry 11:173-177.

0135 Hesse, A. (1967) Mesures et interprétation en prospection géophysique des sites archéologiques du Nil. Prospezioni archeologiche 2:43-48.

0136 Hesse, A. (1978) Reconnaissance géophysique du site. Memoires et travaux du Centre de recherches préhistoriques français de Jerusalem 2:83-89.

0137 Johnston, R. B. (1961) Archaeological application of the proton magnetometer in Indiana (U.S.A.). Archaeometry 4:71-72.

0138 Johnston, R. B. (1964) Proton magnetometry and its application to archaeology. An evaluation at Angel site. Indiana historical society, prehistorical research series 4(11):45-140.

0139 Kermorvant, A. and Masson, J. (1979) Bilan d'activité de l'unité de prospection archéologique de l'université de Tours (France). Archaeo-Physika 10:669-673.

0140 Langan, L. (1966) Use of new atomic magnetometers in archaeology. Prospezioni archeologiche 1:61-66.

0141 Le Borgne, E. (1955) Susceptibilité magnétique anormale du sol superficiel. Annales de géophysique 11:399-419.

0142 Le Borgne, E. (1960) Influence du feu sur les propriétés magnétiques du sol. Annales de géophysique 16:159-195.

0143 Le Borgne, E. (1965) Les propriétes magnétiques du sol. Applications à la prospection des sites archéologiques. Archaeo-Physika 1:1-20.

0144 Lerici, C. M. (1961) Archaeological surveys with the proton magnetometer in Italy. Archaeometry 4:76-82.

0145 Linington, R. E. (1964) The use of simplified anomalies in magnetic surveying. Archaeometry 7:3-13.

0146 Linington, R. E. (1966) An extension to the use of simplified anomalies in magnetic surveying. Archaeometry 9:51-60.

0147 Linington, R. E. (1966) Further examples of the use of simplified theoretical anomalies in magnetic surveying. Prospezioni archeologiche 1:73-80.

0148 Linington, R. E. (1967) Magnetic survey at La Civita, Tarquinia. Prospezioni archeologiche 2:87-89.

0149 Linington, R. E. (1969) The prospecting campaign undertaken in Czechoslovakia in July-August 1969. Prospezioni archeologiche 4:131-138.

0150 Linington, R. E. (1970) A brief test survey at Passo di Corvo near Foggia. Prospezioni archeologiche 5:85-87.

0151 Linington, R. E. (1972/1973) A summary of simple theory applicable to magnetic prospecting. Prospezioni archeologiche 7/8:9-59.

0152 Linington, R. E. (1972/1973) Topographical and terrain effects in magnetic prospecting. Prospezioni archeologiche 7/8:61-84.

0153 Linington, R. E. (1972/1973) The magnetic survey at Metapontum, Italy. Prospezioni archeologiche 7/8:135-149.

0154 Linington, R. E. (1974) Magnetic, electrical and coring surveys at Colle del Forno, Montelibretti 1970-1973. Prospezioni archeologiche 9:47-59.

0155 Linington, R. E. (1974) The magnetic disturbances caused by DC electric railways. Prospezioni archeologiche 9:9-20.

0156 McGovern, P. (1979) The Baqcah Valley, Jordan: a cesium magnetometer survey. MASCA journal 1(2):39-41.

0157 Magnetometer survey at Malkata, Egypt. (1973) MASCA newsletter 9(2):3-5.

0158 Morrison, F., Clewlow, C. W. and Heizer, R. F. (1970) Magnetometer survey of the La Venta Pyramid. Contributions of the University of California archaeological research facility 8:1-20.

0159 Mudie, J. D. (1962) A digital differential proton magnetometer. Archaeometry 5:135-138.

0160 Mullins, C. E. (1974) The magnetic properties of the soil and their application to archaeological prospecting. Archaeo-Physika 5:145-161.

0161 Munro, M. A. R. and Papamarinopoulos, S. (1979) The investigation of an unusual magnetic anomaly by combined magnetometer and soil susceptibility surveys. Archaeo-Physika 10:675-680.

0162 Proton magnetometer survey at Buccino, Italy. (1973) MASCA newsletter 9(2):3.

0163 Rainey, F. G. et al. (1967) The search for Sybaris 1960-65. Roma: Lerici Editori.

0164 Ralph, E. K. (1964) Comparison of a proton and a rubidium magnetometer for archaeological prospecting. Archaeometry 7:20-27.

0165 Ralph, E. K., Morrison, F. and O'Brien, D. P. (1968) Archaeological surveying utilizing a high sensitivity difference magnetometer. Geoexploration 6:109-122.

0166 Schenk, H. (1978) Archaeological prospecting at Valley Forge. MASCA journal 1:16-17.

0167 Schulze, R. and Scollar, I. (1960) Magnetische Unter-
      suchungen bei archäologischen Forschungen. (Magnetic
      investigations beside archaeological research).
      Conti Elektro Berichte 4:2-4.

0168 Schwarz, G. T. (1967) Prospecting without a computer
      in southern Switzerland. Prospezioni archeologiche
      2:73-80.

0169 Scollar, I. (1961) Magnetic prospecting in the
      Rheinland. Archaeometry 4:74-75.

0170 Scollar, I. (1963) Proton precession magnetometer with
      diurnal variation correction. Electronic
      engineering 35:177-179.

0171 Scollar, I. (1965) A contribution to magnetic pros-
      pecting in archaeology. Archaeo-Physika 1:21-92.

0172 Scollar, I. (1966) Recent developments in magnetic
      prospecting in the Rheinland. Prospezioni
      archeologiche 1:43-51.

0173 Scollar, I. (1968) Automatic recording of magnetometer
      data in the field. Prospezioni archeologiche
      3:105-110.

0174 Scollar, I. (1969) Some techniques for the evaluation
      of archaeological magnetometer surveys. World
      archaeology 1:77-89.

0175 Scollar, I. (1970) Magnetic methods of archaeological
      prospecting. Advances in instrumentation and
      evaluation techniques. Philosophical transactions of
      the royal society of London 268(1193):111-121.

0176 Scollar, I. (1970) A wide range, differential proton
      magnetometer with direct readout in gammas.
      Prospezioni archeologiche 5:59-66.

0177 Scollar, I. (1971) A magnetometer survey of the
      Colonia Ulpia Trajana near Xanten, West Germany.
      Prospezioni archeologiche 6:83-89.

0178 Scollar, I. (1972) Magnetic mapping of buried
      archaeological sites. Endeavour 31(112):34-40.

18

0179 Šilik, K. K. (1965) Opyt primenenija magnitorazvedki
      na dreverusskom gorodišče. (Experiment in the use of
      magnetic surveying for ancient Russian towns).
      Materialy i issledovanija po arkheologii SSSR
      129:252-256.

0180 Stanley, J. M. (1979) The application of geophysical
      methods to hunter/gatherer prehistory in Australia.
      Archaeo-Physika 10:692-699.

0181 Tite, M. S. (1961) Alternative instruments for
      magnetic surveying: comparative tests at the Iron
      Age hill-fort at Rainsborough. Archaeometry 4:85-90.

0182 Tite, M. S. (1966) Magnetic prospecting near to the
      geomagnetic equator. Archaeometry 9:24-31.

0183 Tite, M. S. (1967) The magnetic survey. Appendix to:
      M. Avery, J. E. G. Sutton and J. W. Banks,
      Rainsborough, Northants, England--excavations
      1961-5. Proceedings of the prehistoric society
      33:296-300.

0184 Tite, M. S. (1970) Magnetic survey at Dragonby,
      Lincolnshire. In: Scritti di archeologia ed arte in
      onore di C. M. Lerici. Stockholm, 35-38.

0185 Tite, M. S. (1972) The influence of geology on the
      magnetic susceptibility of soils on archaeological
      sites. Archaeometry 14(2):229-236.

0186 Tite, M. S. and Mullins, C. (1970) Magnetic properties
      of soils. Prospezioni archeologiche 5:111-112.

0187 Tite, M. S. and Mullins, C. (1971) Enhancement of the
      magnetic susceptibility of soils on archaeological
      sites. Archaeometry 13(2):209-219.

0188 Tite, M. S. and Linington, R. E. (1975) Effect of
      climate on the magnetic susceptibility of soils.
      Nature 256(5518):565-566.

0189 Weymouth, J. (1979) Technical developments and results
      of the 1977 season of the Great Plains magnetic
      surveying program. Archaeo-Physika 10:710-717.

0190 Whitwell, J. B. and Wood, K. F. (1969) Three pottery kiln sites in Lincolnshire, located by proton gradiometer (Maxbleep) survey and confirmed by excavation. Prospezioni archeologiche 4:125-129.

0191 Wilson, A. E. (1970) A winter survey with proton magnetometers of an underwater site. Prospezioni archeologiche 5:89-93.

D. Electromagnetic surveying

0192 Connah, G. (1962) An archaeological experiment with the '4c' mine detector. Antiquity 36(144):305-306.

0193 Howell, M. (1966) A soil conductivity meter. Archaeometry 9:20-23.

0194 Howell, M. (1968) An electro-magnetic technique for the location of anomalous soil features. Bulletin of the Bristol archaeological research group 3(2):32-34.

0195 Howell, M. (1968) The soil conductivity anomaly detector (SCM) in archaeological prospection. Prospezioni archeologiche 3:101-104.

0196 Laming, A. (1962) Le détecteur électro-magnétique. In: A. Laming, ed., La découverte du passé. Paris, 71-75.

0197 Musson, C. R. (1968) A geophysical survey at South Cadbury Castle, Somerset, using the Howell soil conductivity anomaly detector (SCM). Prospezioni archeologiche 3:115-121.

0198 Parchas, C. and Tabbagh, A. (1979) Simultaneous measurements of electrical conductivity and magnetic susceptibility of the ground in electromagnetic prospecting. Archaeo-Physika 10:682-691.

0199 Renimel, S. and Tabbagh, A. (1973) Un atout pour la prospection archéologique: la détection électromagnétique. La recherche 30:82-84.

0200 Scarani, R. (1953) Esperimenti con il detector elettromagnetico. Rivista di scienze preistoriche 8:99-104.

0201 Schioler, T. (1971) An attempt to locate lead pipes in Ostia Antica. Prospezioni archeologiche 6:93-94.

0202 Scollar, I. (1962) Electromagnetic prospecting methods in archaeology. Archaeometry 5:146-153.

0203 Tabbagh, A. (1972/1973) Méthode de prospection électromagnétique S.G.D. utilisation de deux sources. Prospezioni archeologiche 7/8:125-133.

0204 Tabbagh, A. (1974) Définition des caractéristiques d'un appareil électromagnétique classique adapte à la prospection archéologique. Prospezioni archeologiche 9:21-33.

0205 Tabbagh, A. (1974) Méthodes de prospection électromagnétique applicables aux problèmes archéologiques. Archaeo-Physika 5:351-437.

0206 Tite, M. S. and Mullins, C. (1969) Electromagnetic prospecting: a preliminary investigation. Prospezioni archeologiche 4:95-102.

0207 Tite, M. S. and Mullins, C. (1970) Electromagnetic prospecting on archaeological sites using a soil conductivity meter. Archaeometry 12(1):97-104.

E. Metal detection

0208 Colani, C. (1966) A new method and wide range apparatus for locating metal objects in the ground, fresh water and salt water. Prospezioni archeologiche 1:15-23.

0209 Colani, C. (1966) A new type of locating device I--the instrument. Archaeometry 9:3-8.

0210 Colani, C. and Aitken, M. J. (1966) A new type of locating device II--field trials. Archaeometry 9:9-19.

0211 Foster, E. J. (1968) Further developments of the pulse induction metal detector. Prospezioni archeologiche 3:95-99.

0212 Foster, E. J. (1970) A diver-operated underwater metal detector. Archaeometry 12(2):161-166.

0213 Foster, E. J. and Hackens, T. (1969) Decco metal detector survey on Delos. Archaeometry 11:165-172.

0214 Green, J. N. (1971) Cape Andreas: a survey of a tile wreck. Prospezioni archeologiche 6:61-64.

0215 Green, J. N., Hall, E. T. and Katzev, M. L. (1967) Survey of a Greek shipwreck at Kyrenia, Cyprus. Archaeometry 10:47-56.

0216 Green, J. N. and Martin, C. (1970) Metal detector survey at Dun on Oir. Prospezioni archeologiche 5:101-104.

0217 Green, J. N. and Martin, C. (1970) Metal detector survey of the wreck of the armada ship the Santa Maria de la Rosa. Prospezioni archeologiche 5:95-100.

F. Aerial, balloon and satellite photographic surveying

0218 Adamesteanu, D. (1964) Note per una carta delle zone archeologiche. Colloque international d'archéologie aérienne. Paris: École Pratique des Hautes Études, 283-288.

0219 Agache, R. (1962) Detection aérienne et au sol sur terrains san végétation. Revue archéologique de l'est et du centre-est 13(3):177-191.

0220 Agache, R. (1964) La prospection aérienne sur sols nus et l'inventaire archéologique de la Somme. Colloque international d'archéologie aérienne. Paris: École Pratique des Hautes Études, 49-58.

0221 Alfieri, N. (1964) Topografia antica e aerofotografia a Spina. Colloque international d'archéologie aérienne. Paris: École Pratique des Hautes Études, 155-160.

0222 Alvisi, G. (1964) L'utilità dei vecchi rilevamenti
nella ricerca archeologica. Colloque international
d'archéologie aérienne. Paris: École Pratique des
Hautes Études, 277-281.

0223 Alvisi, G. (1974) Note sulle applicazioni delle equi-
densità di colore nella fotointerpretazioni
archeologica. Prospezioni archeologiche 9:85-88.

0224 Andrianov, B. V. (1965) Dešifirovanie aérofotosnimkov
pri izučenii drevnikh orositel'nykh sistem. (The
deciphering of aerial photographs for the study of
ancient irrigation systems). Materialy i issledovanija po arkheologii SSSR 129:261-267.

0225 Andrianov, B. V. (1967) Kartografirovanie drevnej
irrigatsii na osnove aérofotos"ëmki. (Cartography of
ancient irrigation on the basis of aerial photographic surveying). Aérometody 1:17-18.

0226 Aston, M. and Rowley, T. (1974) Landscape archaeology:
an introduction to fieldwork techniques on post-
Roman landscapes. Newton Abbot, England: David &
Charles.

0227 Bailloud, G. and Chombart de Lauwe, P. (1962) La
photographie aérienne. In: A. Laming, ed., La
découverte du passé. Paris, 45-58.

0228 Baisley, H. K. (1937) Aerial photography. Annual report
of the Smithsonian Institution for 1936, 383-390.

0229 Bandi, H.-G. (1942) Luftbild und Urgeschichte. (Air
photography and prehistory). Jahrbuch der
Schweizerische Gesellschaft für Urgeschichte
33:145-153.

0230 Bermond-Montanari, D. G. (1964) Le ricerche aerofoto-
grafiche nella zona di Classe. Colloque
international d'archéologie aérienne. Paris: École
Pratique des Hautes Études, 161-170.

0231 Betti, L. (1964) Le tracce nella fotoarcheologia.
Colloque international d'archéologie aérienne. Paris:
École Pratique des Hautes Études, 59-75.

0232 Bradford, J. S. (1957) Ancient landscapes; studies in
field archaeology. London: G. Bell. 297pp.

0233 Brongers, J. A. (1964) Photo-archeology in Holland. Colloque international d'archéologie aérienne. Paris: École Pratique des Hautes Études, 141-142.

0234 Bruder, J. S., Large, E. G. and Stark, B. L. (1975) A test of aerial photography in an estuarine mangrove swamp in Veracruz, Mexico. American antiquity 40(3):330-336.

0235 Burger, A. (1964) La pérennité des tracés urbains. Colloque international d'archéologie aérienne. Paris: École Pratique des Hautes Études, 191-196.

0236 Cazzaniga, A. (1964) Caratteristiche tecniche ed impiego dei mezzi aerei (velivolo ed elicottero) per la ricerca archeologica. Possibilità e limitazioni. Colloque international d'archéologie aérienne. Paris: École Pratique des Hautes Études, 29-38.

0237 Chevallier, R. (1964) Détections aériennes dans le sud du département de l'Aisne. Colloque international d'archéologie aérienne. Paris: École Pratique des Hautes Études, 95-108.

0238 Chevallier, R. (1964) L'avion à la découverte du passé. Paris: Fayard.

0239 Chevallier, R. (1964) Photographie aérienne carte archéologique et sauvegarde du patrimoine historique. Colloque international d'archéologie aérienne. Paris: École Pratique des Hautes Études, 293-300.

0240 Chevallier, R. (1965) La révélation des paysages ensevelis. Archeologia (Paris) 3:31-37.

0241 Chevallier, R. (1978) Archéologie spatiale et traitement electronique des images. Archeologia (Paris) 124:19-21.

0242 Clos-Arceduc, A. (1964) La métrique des voies gallo-romaines et ses rapports avec leur recherche. Colloque international d'archéologie aérienne. Paris: École Pratique des Hautes Études, 213-217.

0243 Crawford, O. G. S. (1923) Air survey and archaeology. Geographical journal 61:342-360.

0244 Crawford, O. G. S. (1933) Some recent air discoveries. Antiquity 7:290-296.

0245 Crawford, O. G. S. (1938) Air photography, past and future. Proceedings of the prehistoric society 4:233-238.

0246 Crawford, O. G. S. (1954) A century of air-photography. Antiquity 28(112):206-210.

0247 Cresswell, R. (1976) Photographies aériennes obliques. Outils d'enquête et d'analyse anthropologiques. Paris: François Maspero, 49-50.

0248 Darsy, R. P. F. (1964) Le limes de la Provincia et les ouvrages défensifs en Bas-Vivarais. Colloque international d'archéologie aérienne. Paris: École Pratique des Hautes Études, 197-198.

0249 Dassié, J. (1967) Nouveaux sites archéologiques en Saintonage. Compte rendu de prospections photographiques aérienne. Bulletin de la société préhistorique française 64(3):819-830.

0250 Dassié, J. (1973) Archéologie aérienne en Charente-Maritime: découverte de la protohistoire saintongeaise. Archéologie 1:46-57.

0251 Dassié, J. (1978) Manuel d'archéologie aérienne. Paris: Éditions Technip.

0252 Deuel, L. (1969) Flights into yesterday; the story of aerial archaeology. New York: St. Martin's Press.

0253 Dollar, C. D. (1962) Aerial archaeology in search of a pilot site for Arkansas. Arkansas archaeologist 3(3):1-7.

0254 Dubois, J. (1980) La photographique aérienne en ballon aerostatique. Archeologia (Paris) 139:41-46.

0255 Ebert, J. I., Lyons, T. R. and Drager, D. L. (1979) Comments on "Application of orthophoto mapping to archaeological problems". American antiquity 44(3):341-345.

0256 Ertlé, R. (1964) Etat de la recherche archéologique
par photographie aérienne dans la zone Marne-
Ardennes. Colloque international d'archéologie
aérienne. Paris: École Pratique des Hautes Études,
109-115.

0257 García de León, P. (1977) Recuperación de datos y
fotografía aérea (aeroarqueología). Revista
Mexicana de estudios antropologicos 23(1):97-122.

0258 Garlick, G. F. J., Steigman, G. A. and Lamb, W. E.
(1974) A device for display of degree of optical
polarisation in a scene or surface. Prospezioni
archeologiche 9:89-91.

0259 Goessler, P. (1929) Das Flugzeug im Dienste der
Archäologie. (The airplane in the service of
archaeology). Prähistorische Zeitschrift 20:291-292.

0260 Goguey, R. (1964) Avion, stéréoscope ou projecteur?
Colloque international d'archéologie aérienne.
Paris: École Pratique des Hautes Études, 77-85.

0261 Grütter, H. (1964) La photographie aérienne au service
des recherches archéologiques en Suisse. Colloque
international d'archéologie aérienne. Paris: École
Pratique des Hautes Études, 143-145.

0262 Guy, M. (1964) L'apport de la photographie aérienne à
l'étude de la colonisation antique de la province
de Narbonnaise. Colloque international d'archéologie
aérienne. Paris: École Pratique des Hautes Études,
117-124.

0263 Harp, E. (1968) Optimum scales and emulsions in air
photo archaeology. 8th. International congress of
anthropological and ethnological sciences. Tokyo,
3:163-165.

0264 Igonin, N. I. (1965) Primenenie aérofotos"ëmki pri
izučenii arkheologičeskikh pamjatnikov. (The use of
aerial photographic survey for the study of
archaeological monuments). Materialy i issledovanija
po arkheologii SSSR 129:256-260.

0265 Jalmain, D. (1964) Cinq années de prospection aérienne sur la Bassée. Colloque international d'archéologie aérienne. Paris: École Pratique des Hautes Études, 125-130

0266 Jones, R. J. A. and Evans, R. (1975) Soil and crop marks in the recognition of archaeological sites by air photography. In: D. R. Wilson, ed., Aerial reconnaissance for archaeology. London: Council for British archaeology, research report no. 12, 1-11.

0267 Jones, R. J. A. (1979) Crop marks induced by soil moisture stress at an Iron Age site in Midland England, UK. Archaeo-Physika 10:656-668.

0268 Kapps, R. (1964) De la détection des sites archéologiques à leur inscription sur le plan cadastral. Colloque international d'archéologie aérienne. Paris: École Pratique des Haute Études, 131-133.

0269 Lebel, P. (1952) Détection aérienne de vestiges archéologiques. Revue archéologique de l'est et du centre-est 3:251-255.

0270 Lerici, C. M. (1964) Prospection aérienne et prospection géophysique appliquées à la recherche archéologique. Colloque international d'archéologie aérienne. Paris: École Pratique des Hautes Études, 249-254.

0271 Lyons, T. R. and Hitchcock, R. K. (1977) Aerial remote sensing techniques in archaeology. Reports of the Chaco center no. 2. Albuquerque, New Mexico: Chaco Center.

0272 Manneke, P. (1974) Aerial photography of 'Celtic fields' on Gotland. Norwegian archaeological review 7:33-38.

0273 Mertens, J. (1964) La prospection aérienne en Belgique et quelques problèmes archéologiques. Colloque international d'archéologie aérienne. Paris: École Pratique des Hautes Études, 135-140.

0274 Miller, W. C. (1957) Uses of aerial photographs in archaeological field work. American antiquity 23:46-62.

0275 Nicolardot, J.-P. (1964) Prospection aérienne et au sol en trois dimensions. Colloque international d'archéologie aérienne. Paris: École Pratique des Hautes Études, 87-92.

0276 Palmer, R. (1976) Interrupted ditch enclosures in Britain: the use of aerial photography for comparative studies. Proceedings of the prehistoric society 42:161-186.

0277 Palmer, R. (1978) Aerial archaeology and sampling. Sampling in contemporary British archaeology. British archaeological reports, British series 50:129-148.

0278 Parrington, M. (1979) Geophysical and aerial prospecting techniques at Valley Forge National Historic Park, Pennsylvania. Journal of field archaeology 6(2):193-201.

0279 Quann, J. (1977) The pyramids from 900 kilometers. MASCA newsletter 13(1/2):12-14.

0280 Reeves, D. M. (1936) Aerial photography and archaeology. American antiquity 2:102-107.

0281 Reichstein, J. (1974) Schwarz-Weiss-Infrarotphotographie als Hilfsmittel für die Analyse schwer beobachtbarer Funde. (Black-white-infrared photografy as an aid for the analysis of hard-to-observe features). Offa 31:108-125.

0282 Rendic Miocevic, D. (1964) La photographie aérienne. Colloque international d'archéologie aérienne. Paris: École Pratique des Hautes Études, 187-190.

0283 Richards, D. G. (1980) Water-penetration aerial photography. International journal of nautical archaeology and underwater exploration 9(4):331-337.

0284 Riley, D. R. (1946) The technique of air archaeology. Archaeological journal 101:1-16.

0285 Riley, T. J. (1979) Air photography based on Sheffield. Current archaeology 66:219-222.

28

0286 Schleiermacher, W. (1964) Aus der Kinderstube des
archäologischen Luftbildes. Der römische Limes in
der Dobrudscha. (From the children's room of
archaeological air photographs. The Roman limes in
the Dobrogea). Colloque international d'archéologie
aérienne. Paris: École Pratique des Hautes Études,
199-201.

0287 Schmidt-Kraepelin, E. (1964) Photographie aérienne et
archéologie agraire en Allemagne. Colloque international d'archéologie aérienne. Paris: École
Pratique des Hautes Études, 235-238.

0288 Scollar, I. (1964) Physical conditions tending to
produce crop sites in the Rhineland. Colloque
international d'archéologie aérienne. Paris: École
Pratique des Hautes Études, 39-47.

0289 Scollar, I. (1975) Transformation of extreme oblique
aerial photographs to maps or plans by conventional
means or by computer. In: D. R. Wilson, ed., Aerial
reconnaissance for archaeology. London: Council for
British archaeology, research report no. 12, 52-59.

0290 Seel, K. A. (1964) Luftbild und Altflurforschung. (Air
photography and ancient field research). Colloque
international d'archéologie aérienne. Paris: École
Pratique des Hautes Études, 239-245.

0291 Siškin, K. V. (1966) Primenenie aérofotos"ëmki dlja
issledovanija arkheologičeskikh pamjatnikov. (The
use of aerial photographic survey for the investigation of archaeological monuments). Sovetskaja
arkheologija 3:116-121.

0292 Solecki, R. S. (1957) Pratical aerial photography for
archaeologists. American antiquity 22:337-351.

0293 Soyer, J. (1964) Les fortifications circulaires des
bas-fonds marécageux. Colloque international
d'archéologie aérienne. Paris: École Pratique des
Hautes Études, 203-206.

0294 Szafranski, W. (1964) La photographie aérienne
archéologique en Pologne. Colloque international
d'archéologie aérienne. Paris: École Pratique des
Hautes Études, 147-149.

0295 Tolstov, S. P. et al. (1948) Opyt primenenija aviatsii v arkheologičeskikh rabotakh Khorezmskoj èkspeditsii. (Experiment in the use of aviation in the archaeological work of the Khorezm expedition). Vestnik akademii nauk SSSR, no. 6.

0296 Tolstov, S. P., Andrianov, B. V. and Igonin, N. I. (1962) Ispol'zovanie aèrometodov v arkheologičeskikh issledovanijakh. (The use of aerial methods in archaeological investigations). Sovetskaja arkheologija 1:3-15.

0297 Verhoeve, A. (1964) Formes circulaires en Basse-Belgiques, faits naturels ou archéologiques? Colloque international d'archéologie aérienne. Paris: École Pratique des Hautes Études, 207-210.

0298 Webster, G. and Hobley, B. (1965) Aerial reconnaissance over the Warwickshire Avon. Archaeological journal 121:1-22.

0299 Whittlesey, J. H. (1972/1973) A multi-band camera for archaeology. Prospezioni archeologiche 7/8:153-154.

0300 Whittlesey, J. H. (1970) Tethered balloon for archaeological photos. Photogrammetric engineering magazine, February, 181-186.

0301 Wilson, D. R., ed. (1975) Aerial reconnaissance for archaeology. London: Council for British archaeology, research report no. 12.

G. Photogrammetry and stereoscopy

0302 Bonneval, H. (1964) Applications de la photogrammétrie aux levés architecturaux et archéologiques. Colloque international d'archéologie aérienne. Paris: École Pratique des Hautes Études, 269-275.

0303 Green, J. N. et al. (1971) Simple underwater photogrammetric techniques. Archaeometry 13(2):221-232.

0304 McFadgen, B. G. (1971) An application of stereophotogrammetry to archaeological recording. Archaeometry 13(1):71-81.

0305 Nylen, E. (1978) The recording of unexcavated finds:
X-ray photography and photogrammetry. Field
techniques and research design. World archaeology
10(1):88-93.

0306 Rivett, L. J. (1980) The photogrammetric recording of
rock art in the Kakadu National Park, Australia.
Australian archaeology 10:38-51.

0307 Schwarz, G. T. (1964) Stereoscopic views taken with an
ordinary single camera--a new technique for
archaeologists. Archaeometry 7:36-42.

0308 Turpin, S. A. et al. (1979) Stereophotogrammetric
documentation of exposed archaeological features.
Journal of field archaeology 6(3):329-337.

0309 Wittlesey, J. (1966) Photogrammetry for the excavator.
Archaeology 19(4):273-276.

                    H. Sonar and radar surveying

0310 Bevan, B. and Kenyon, J. (1975) Ground-penetrating
radar for historical archaeology. MASCA newsletter
11(2):2-7.

0311 Carabelli, E. (1966) A new tool for archaeological
prospecting: the sonic spectroscope for the
detection of cavities. Prospezioni archeologiche
1:25-35.

0312 Carabelli, E. (1968) Ricerca delle cavità superficiali
con l'impiego di vibratori: primi esperimenti.
Prospezioni archeologiche 3:55-60.

0313 Dubrov, E. F. and Šilik, K. K. (1965) Primenenie
metoda zvukovoj geolokatsii dlja poiskov i
issledovanija ob"ektov, pogrebennykh gruntami na dne
vodoemov. (The use of sound in geoprospecting for the
search and investigation of objects buried at the
bottom of a reservoir). Materialy i issledovanija po
arkheologii SSSR 129:279-281.

0314 Hall, E. T. (1966) A sea-going sonar position-fixing system. Archaeometry 9:45-50.

0315 Hranicky, W. J. (1977) Use of radar in archaeological field surveying. The Chesopeian 15(1/2):10-14.

0316 Hrdlička, L. and Lukašová, M. (1969) Geophysical survey of the Royal Oratory in the Cathedral of St. Vitus, Prague Castle. Prospezioni archeologiche 4:111-119.

0317 Kenyon, J. L. and Bevan, B. (1977) Ground-penetrating radar and its application to a historical site. Historical archaeology 11:48-55.

0318 Linington, R. E. (1970) Prospezioni soniche ed elettriche a S. Maria in Stelle, Verona. Prospezioni archeologiche 5:77-84.

0319 Michael, H. N. and Vickers, R. S. (1979) Subsurface radar probing for detection of buried bristlecone pine wood. In: Radiocarbon dating. Berkeley, California: University of California Press, 520-531.

0320 Ozawa, K. and Matsuda, M. (1979) Computer assisted techniques for detecting underground remains based on acoustic measurement. Archaeometry 21(1):87-100.

0321 Vickers, R. S. and Dolphin, L. T. (1975) A communication on an archaeological radar experiment at Chaco Canyon, New Mexico. MASCA newsletter 11(1):6-8.

I. Other surveying methods

0322 Alldred, J. C. and Shepherd, A. (1963) Trial of neutron scattering for the detection of buried walls and cavities. Archaeometry 6:89-92.

0323 Aspinall, A. and Lynam, J. (1968) Induced polarization as a technique for archaeological surveying. Prospezioni archeologiche 3:91-93.

0324 Aspinall, A. and Lynam, J. (1970) An induced polarization instrument for the detection of near surface features. Prospezioni archeologiche 5:67-75.

0325 Carson, H. H. (1962) A seismic survey at Harpers Ferry. Archaeometry 5:119-122.

0326 Cassinis, R. (1958) Metodi sismici nelle prospezioni archeologiche. La prospezioni geofisica nella ricerca archeologica. VII Convegno internazionale de archeologia classica. Milano, 23-33.

0327 Chapellier, D. (1974) Une méthode sismique au service de l'archéologie. Prospezioni archeologiche 9:93-95.

0328 Hrdlička, L. (1969) Apparatus for the investigation of inaccessible underground cavities. Prospezioni archeologiche 4:103-109.

0329 Linington, R. E. (1966) Test use of a gravimeter on Etruscan chamber tombs at Cerveteri. Prospezioni archeologiche 1:37-41.

0330 Linington, R. E. (1971) Prove eseguite con il periscopio-distanziometro. Prospezioni archeologiche 6:33-41.

0331 Parenti, G. (1958) Il periscopio Nistri per explorazione archeologica. La prospezioni geofisica nella ricerca archeologica. VII Convegno internazionale de archeologia classica. Milano, 51-55.

0332 Parenti, G. (1971) Nuovo dispositivo distanziometrico per il periscopio Nistri. Prospezioni archeologiche 6:29-31.

0333 Tabbagh, A. (1973) Essai sur les conditions d'application des mesures thermiques à la prospection archéologique. Annales de géophysique 29(2):179-188.

0334 Tabbagh, A. (1976) Les proprietes thermiques des sols. Premiers résultats utilisables en prospection archéologique. Archaeo-Physika 6:128-148.

0335 Tabbagh, A. (1977) Sur la détermination du moment de mesure favorable et l'interprétation des résultats en prospection thermique archéologique. Annales de géophysique 33(1):243-253.

0336 Tabbagh, A. (1979) Prospection thermique aéroportée
      du site de Prépoux (Villeneuve-la-Guyard, Yonne).
      Revue archéologique de l'est et du centre-est
      30(1/2):101-104.

0337 Tabbagh, A. (1979) Thermal airborne prospection of the
      Lion en Beauce township (Loiret, France). Archaeo-
      Physika 10-700-709.

III. CHRONOMETRY

A. General studies

0338 Bishop, W. W. and Miller, J. A. (1972) Calibration of hominoid evolution. Edinburgh: Scottish Academic Press.

0339 Fleming, S. (1976) Dating in archaeology. London: J. M. Dent.

0340 Fleming, S. (1977) Dating in archaeology: a guide to scientific techniques. New York: St. Martin's Press.

0341 Hedges, R. E. M. (1979) Radioisotopic clocks in archaeology. Nature 281(5726):19-24.

0342 Ivanova, I. K. et al., eds. (1963) Absoljutnaja geo-khronologija četvertičnogo perioda. (Absolute chronology of the Quaternary period). Moskva: Akademija Nauk SSSR.

0343 Michael, H. N. and Ralph, E. K. (1971) Dating techniques for the archaeologist. Cambridge, Massachusetts: MIT Press.

0344 Michaels, J. W. (1973) Dating methods in archaeology. New York: Seminar Press.

0345 Oakley, K. P. (1969) Frameworks for dating fossil man. Third edition. Chicago: Aldine.

B. Radiometric methods

1. Radiocarbon dating

0346 Alessio, M. et al. (1976/1977) Carbon-14 dating of bone collagen from Upper Paleolithic Palidoro deposit. Quaternaria (Roma) 19:181-186.

0347 Arnold, J. R. and Libby, W. F. (1949) Age determination by radiocarbon content. Checks with samples of known age. Science 110:678-680.

0348 Artem'ev, V. V. et al. (1961) Rezul'taty opredelenija absoljutnogo vozrasta rjada arkheologičeskikh i geologičeskikh ob"ektov po radiouglerodu (C-14). (Results of absolute age determination of a series of archaeological and geological objects by radiocarbon, C-14). Sovetskaja arkheologija 2:3-11.

0349 Barker, H. (1958) Radiocarbon dating: its scope and limitations. Antiquity 32:253-263.

0350 Barker, H. (1967) Radiocarbon dating of bone. Nature 213:415.

0351 Barker, H. (1970) Critical assessment of radiocarbon dating. Philosophical transactions of the royal society of London A269:37-45.

0352 Barker, H. (1972) The accuracy of radiocarbon dates. Journal of African history 13:177-187.

0353 Baur, W. H. (1972) An example of hard-water error in radiocarbon dating of vegetable matter. Nature 240(5382):460-461.

0354 Baxter, M. S. (1974) Calibration of the radiocarbon time-scale. Nature 249:93.

0355 Baxter, M. S. and Walton, A. (1970) Radiocarbon dating of mortars. Nature 225:937-938.

0356 Baxter, M. S. and Walton, A. (1971) Fluctuations of atmospheric carbon-14 concentrations during the past century. Proceedings of the royal society of London A321:105-127.

0357 Beaumont, P. B. and Vogel, J. C. (1972) On a new radiocarbon chronology for Africa south of the equator. African studies 31:65-89, 155-182.

0358 Becker, B. (1979) Holocene tree ring series from southern Central Europe for archaeologic dating, radiocarbon calibration, and stable isotope analysis. In: Radiocarbon dating. Berkeley, Calif.: Univ. of California Press, 554-565.

0359 Beer, J. et al. (1979) The contribution of the Swiss lake-dwellings to the calibration of radiocarbon dates. In: Radiocarbon dating. Berkeley, Calif.: Univ. of California Press, 566-584

0360 Bennett, C. L. et al. (1977) Radiocarbon dating using electrostatic accelerators: negative ions provide the key. Science 198:508-510.

0361 Bennett, C. L. et al. (1978) Radiocarbon dating with electrostatic accelerators: dating of milligram samples. Science 201:345-347.

0362 Berger, R. (1970) Ancient Egyptian radiocarbon chronology. Philosophical transactions of the royal society of London A269:23-36.

0363 Berger, R. (1972) Tree-ring calibration of radiocarbon dates. Proceedings of the eighth international conference on radiocarbon dating. Lower Hutt City, New Zealand, 1:A97-A103.

0364 Berger, R. (1976) Radiocarbon dating in the prehistoric past: accuracy and limitations. Colloque I. IX Congrès, Union internationale des sciences préhistoriques et protohistoriques. Nice, 21-38.

0365 Berger, R. (1979) Annual radiocarbon in the strato- sphere. In: Radiocarbon dating. Berkeley, Calif.: Univ. of California Press, 309-312.

0366 Berger, R. (1979) Radiocarbon dating with accelerators. Journal of archaeological science 6(1):101-104.

0367 Berger, R. et al. (1972) Radiocarbon dating of parchment. Nature 235(5334):160-161.

38

0368 Berger, R., Horney, A. G. and Libby, W. F. (1964) Radiocarbon dating of bone and shell from their organic components. Science 144:999-1001.

0369 Berger, R., Taylor, R. E. and Libby, W. F. (1966) Radiocarbon content of marine shells from the California and Mexican west coast. Science 153:863-866.

0370 Betancourt, P. P., Michael, H. N. and Weinstein, G. A. (1978) Calibration and the radiocarbon chronology of Late Minoan IB. Archaeometry 20(2):199-203.

0371 Betancourt, P. P. and Weinstein, G. A. (1976) Carbon-14 and the beginning of the Late Bronze Age in the Aegean. American journal of archaeology 80:329-348.

0372 Beukens, R. P. (1979) Carbon-14 dating of milligram samples using a Tandem Accelerator. Archaeo-Physika 10:388-394.

0373 Bray, J. R. (1967) Variation in atmospheric carbon-14 activity relative to a sunspot-auroral solar index. Science 156:640-642.

0374 Brenninkmeijer, C. A. and Mook, W. G. (1979) The effect of electronegative impurities on CO_2 proportional counting: an on-line purity test counter. In: Radiocarbon dating. Berkeley, Calif.: Univ. of California Press, 185-196.

0375 Broecker, W. S., Olson, E. A. and Bird, J. (1969) Radiocarbon measurements on samples of known age. Nature 183(4675):1582-1584.

0376 Brooks, S. T., Heglar, R. and Brooks, R. H. (1979) Radiocarbon dating and paleoserology of a selected burial series from the Great Cave of Niah, Sarawak, Malaysia. Asian perspectives 20(1):21-31.

0377 Brothwell, D. and Burleigh, R. (1977) On sinking Otavalo Man. Journal of archaeological science 4:291-294.

0378 Brothwell, D. and Burleigh, R. (1980) The human cranium from Punin, Ecuador, with particular reference to morphology and dating. Journal of archaeological science 7(1):97-99.

0379 Bucha, V. (1970) Influence of the Earth's magnetic field on radiocarbon dating. In: I. U. Olsson, ed., Radiocarbon variations and absolute chronology. Stockholm: Almqvist & Wiksell; New York: J. Wiley, 502-510.

0380 Bucha, V. (1979) Causal mechanisms in climatic and weather changes as revealed from paleomagnetic investigations of samples dated by the C-14 method and from geomagnetic variations. In: Radiocarbon dating. Berkeley, Calif.: Univ. of California Press, 670-690.

0381 Burleigh, R. (1974) Radiocarbon dating: some practical considerations for the archaeologist. Journal of archaeological science 1(1):69-87.

0382 Burleigh, R. (1980) Radiocarbon dating of animal remains from Egypt. MASCA journal 1(6):188-189.

0383 Burleigh, R. and Hewson, A. (1976) Evidence for short term atmospheric C-14 variations about 4000 yr B.P. Nature 262:128-130.

0384 Burleigh, R. and Hewson, A. (1979) Archaeological evidence for short-term natural C-14 variations. In: Radiocarbon dating. Berkeley, Calif.: Univ. of California Press, 591-600.

0385 Burleigh, R. and Zivanovic, S. (1980) Radiocarbon dating of a Cro-Magnon population from Padina, Yugoslavia, with some general recommendations for dating human skeletons. Zeitschrift für Morphologie und Anthropologie 70(3):269-274.

0386 Butomo, S. V. (1965) Radiouglerodnoe datirovanie i postroenie absoljutnoj khronologičeskoj škaly arkheologičeskikh pamjatnikov. (Radiocarbon dating and the construction of absolute chronological scales for archaeological monuments). Materialy i issledovanija po arkheologii SSSR 129:28-34.

0387 Butzer, K. W. et al. (1972) Radiocarbon dating of East African lake levels. Science 175(4027):1069-1076.

0388 Cain, W. F. (1979) C-14 in modern American trees. In: Radiocarbon dating. Berkeley, Calif.: Univ. of California Press, 495-510.

0389 Campbell, J. A., Baxter, M. S. and Harkness, D. D. (1978) Radiocarbon measurements on a floating tree-ring from north-east Scotland. Archaeometry 20(1):33-38.

0390 Clark, J. D. (1979) Radiocarbon dating and African archaeology. In: Radiocarbon dating. Berkeley, Calif.: Univ. of California Press, 7-31.

0391 Clark, R. M. (1975) A calibration curve for radio-carbon dates. Antiquity 49:251-266.

0392 Clark, R. M. (1978) Bristlecone pine and ancient Egypt: a re-appraisal. Archaeometry 20(1):5-17.

0393 Clark, R. M. and Renfrew, C. (1973) The tree-ring calibration of radiocarbon and the chronology of ancient Egypt. Nature 243:266-270.

0394 Coleman, D. D. (1979) The origin of drift-gas deposits as determined by radiocarbon dating of methane. In: Radiocarbon dating. Berkeley, Calif.: Univ. of California Press, 365-387.

0395 Costin, A. B. and Polach, H. A. (1969) Dating soil organic matter. Atomic energy in Australia 12(4):13-17.

0396 Craig, H. (1961) Mass-spectrometer analyses of radiocarbon standards. Radiocarbon 3:1-3.

0397 Crowe, C. (1958) Carbon-14 activity during the past 5000 years. Nature 182:470.

0398 Currie, L. A., Noakes, J. E. and Breiter, D. N. (1979) Measurement of small radiocarbon samples: power of alternative methods for tracing atmospheric hydrocarbons. In: Radiocarbon dating. Berkeley, Calif.: Univ. of California Press, 158-175.

0399 Damon, P. E. (1970) Climatic versus magnetic pertur-bation of the atmospheric C14 reservoir. In: I. U. Olsson, ed., Radiocarbon variations and absolute chronology. Stockholm: Almqvist & Wiksell; New York: J. Wiley, 571-593.

0400   Damon, P. E., Long, A. and Grey, D. C. (1966) Fluc-
       tuations in atmospheric C-14 during the last six
       millennia. Journal of geophysical research
       71(4):1055-1063.

0401   Damon, P. E., Long, A. and Grey, D. C. (1970) Arizona
       radiocarbon dates for dendrochronologically dated
       samples. In: I. U. Olsson, ed., Radiocarbon
       variations and absolute chronology. Stockholm:
       Almqvist & Wiksell; New York: J. Wiley, 615-618.

0402   Damon, P. E., Long, A. and Wallick, E. I. (1972)
       Dendrochronological calibration of the radiocarbon
       timescale. Proceedings of the eighth international
       conference on radiocarbon dating. Lower Hutt City,
       New Zealand, 2:A29-43.

0403   Donner, J. and Jungner, H. (1979) The use of marine
       shells in dating land/sea level changes. In:
       Radiocarbon dating. Berkeley, Calif.: Univ. of
       California Press, 397-403.

0404   Edwards, I. E. S. (1970) Absolute dating from
       Egyptian records and comparison with carbon-14
       dating. Philosophical transactions of the Royal
       Society of London A269:11-18.

0405   Erlenkeuser, H. (1979) Environmental effects on
       radiocarbon in coastal marine sediments. In:
       Radiocarbon dating. Berkeley, Calif.: Univ. of
       California Press, 453-469.

0406   Erlenkeuser, H. (1979) A thermal diffusion plant for
       radiocarbon isotope enrichment from natural samples.
       In: Radiocarbon dating. Berkeley, Calif.: Univ.
       of California Press, 216-237.

0407   Ermolova, N. M. (1980) Laboratorija arkheologičeskoj
       tekhnologii LOIA. (Laboratory for archaeological
       technology at the Leningrad department of the
       Institute of Archaeology). Kratkie soobščenija
       Instituta Arkheologii 163:76-80.

0408   Fletcher, J. (1968) Radiocarbon dating for medieval
       timber buildings. Antiquity 42:230-231.

0409 Folk, R. L. and Valastro, S. (1979) Dating of lime mortar by C-14. In: Radiocarbon dating. Berkeley, Calif.: Univ. of California Press, 721-732.

0410 Francke, H. W., Münnich, K. O. and Vogel, J. S. (1961) Die Radiokohlenstoff Datierung von Kalkabscheidung. (Radiocarbon dating of lime precipitation). Atompraxis 7(8):298-300.

0411 Freundlich, J. C. (1979) Fossil fuel exhaust-gas admixture with the atmosphere. In: Radiocarbon dating. Berkeley, Calif.: Univ. of California Press, 388-393.

0412 Geyh, M. A. (1979) C-14 routine dating of marine sediments. In: Radiocarbon dating. Berkeley, Calif.: Univ. of California Press, 470-491.

0413 Geyh, M. A., Merkt, J. and Muller, H. (1970) C14-Datierung limnischer Sedimente und die Eichung der C14-Zeitskala. (C14 dating of limnological sediments and the calibration of the C14 timescale). Naturwissenschaften 57(12):564.

0414 Geyh, M. A. and Morgenrath, G. (1970) A fast separation technique of humic acids from peat to be dated by radiocarbon method. International journal of applied radiation and isotopes 21(9):566.

0415 Gillespie, R. and Polach, H. A. (1979) The suitability of marine shells for radiocarbon dating of Australian prehistory. In: Radiocarbon dating. Berkeley, Calif.: Univ. of California Press, 404-421.

0416 Godwin, H. (1962) Half-life of radiocarbon. Nature 195:984.

0417 Godwin, H. (1969) The value of plant materials for radiocarbon dating. American journal of botany 56(7):723-731.

0418 Graham, J. J. and Berger, R. (1977) Fechamientos por radiocarbono provenientes de Copan. Yaxkin 2(2):117-120.

0419 Grootes, P. M. (1978) Carbon-14 time scale extended: comparison of chronologies. Science 200:11-15.

0420 Gulliksen, S. and Nydal, R. (1979) Further improvement of counter background and shielding. In: Radiocarbon dating. Berkeley, Calif.: Univ. of California Press, 176-184.

0421 Haas, H. (1979) Specific problems with liquid scintillation counting of small benzene volumes and background count rate estimation. In: Radiocarbon dating. Berkeley, Calif.: Univ. of California Press, 246-255.

0422 Håkanssan, S. (1979) Radiocarbon activity in submerged plants from various south Swedish lakes. In: Radiocarbon dating. Berkeley, Calif.: Univ. of California Press, 433-443.

0423 Harbottle, G., Sayre, E. V. and Stoenner, R. W. (1979) Carbon-14 dating of small samples of proportional counting. Science 206(4419):683-685.

0424 Haring, A., Vries, A. E. de and Vries, H. de (1958) Radiocarbon dating up to 70,000 years by isotope enrichment. Science 128:472-473.

0425 Harkness, D. D. and Burleigh, R. (1974) Possible carbon-14 enrichment in high altitude wood. Archaeometry 16:121-127.

0426 Hassan, A. A. and Ortner, D. J. (1977) Inclusions in bone material as a source of error in radiocarbon dating. Archaeometry 19(2):131-135.

0427 Haynes, C. V. (1968) Radiocarbon analysis of inorganic carbon of fossil bones and enamel. Science 161: 687-688.

0428 Hendy, C. H. (1970) The use of C14 in the study of cave processes. In: I. U. Olsson, ed., Radiocarbon variations and absolute chronology. Stockholm: Almqvist & Wiksell; New York: J. Wiley, 419-442.

0429 Ho, T. Y., Marcus, L. F. and Berger, R. (1969) Radiocarbon dating of petroleum-impregnated bone from tar pits at Rancho La Brea, California. Science 164:1051-1052.

0430   Hood, S. (1978) Discrepancies in C-14 dating as
       illustrated from the Egyptian New and Middle
       Kingdoms and from the Aegean Bronze Age and
       Neolithic. Archaeometry 20(2):197-199.

0431   Houtermanns, J., Suess, H. E. and Munk, W. (1967)
       Effect of industrial fuel combustion on the
       carbon-14 level of atmospheric CO_2. Radioactive
       dating and methods of low-level counting. Vienna:
       International Atomic Energy Agency, 57-68.

0432   Houtermanns, J., Suess, H. E. and Oeschger, H. (1973)
       Reservoir models and production rate variations of
       natural radiocarbon. Journal of geophysical research
       78:1897-1908.

0433   Jansen, H. S. (1970) Secular variations of radiocarbon
       in New Zealand and Australian trees. In: I. U.
       Olsson, ed., Radiocarbon variations and absolute
       chronology. Stockholm: Almqvist & Wiksell; New York:
       J. Wiley, 261-271.

0434   Johnson, F. and Willis, E. H. (1970) Reconciliation of
       radiocarbon and sidereal years in Meso-American
       chronology. In: I. U. Olsson, ed., Radiocarbon
       variations and absolute chronology. Stockholm:
       Almqvist & Wiksell; New York: J. Wiley, 93-104.

0435   Kalil, E. K. (1979) Climate controlled uranium
       distribution in Atlantic Ocean core V29-179. In:
       Radiocarbon dating. Berkeley, Calif.: Univ. of
       California Press, 95-101.

0436   Kedar, B. Z. and Mook, W. G. (1978) Radiocarbon dating
       of mortar from the city-wall of Ascalon. Israel
       exploration journal 28(3):173-176.

0437   Keith, M. L. and Anderson, G. M. (1963) Radiocarbon
       dating; fictitious results with mollusk shells.
       Science 141:634-637.

0438   Kigoshi, K. and Hasegawa, H. (1966) Secular variations
       of atmospheric radiocarbon concentration and its
       dependence on geomagnetism. Journal of geophysical
       research 71(4):1065.

0439 Kigoshi, K., Tezuka, A. and Mitsuda, H. (1979) Comparison of C-14 ages and ionium ages of corals. In: Radiocarbon dating. Berkeley, Calif.: Univ. of California Press, 733-739.

0440 Krueger, H. W. (1965) The preservation and dating of collagen in ancient bones. Proceedings of the sixth international conference on radiocarbon and tritium dating. Washington, 332-337.

0441 Labeyrie, J., Delibrias, G. and Duplessy, J. C. (1970) The possible origin of natural carbon radioactivity fluctuations in the past. In: I. U. Olsson, ed., Radiocarbon variations and absolute chronology. Stockholm: Almqvist & Wiksell; New York: J. Wiley, 539-546.

0442 Lal, D. and Venkatavaradan, V. S. (1970) Analysis of the causes of C14 variations in the atmosphere. In: I. U. Olsson, ed., Radiocarbon variations and absolute chronology. Stockholm: Almqvist & Wiksell; New York: J. Wiley, 549-567.

0443 La Marche, V. C. and Harlan, T. P. (1973) Accuracy of tree-ring dating of bristlecone pine for calibration of the radiocarbon time scale. Journal of geophysical research 78:8849-8858.

0444 Lambert, G. E. and Orcel, C. (1979) Dendrochronology of Neolithic settlements in western Switzerland: new possibility for prehistoric calibration. In: Radiocarbon dating. Berkeley, Calif.: Univ. of California Press, 585-590.

0445 Law, R. G. (1975) Radiocarbon dates for Rangitoto and Motutapu, a consideration of the dating accuracy. New Zealand journal of science 18:441-451.

0446 Lerman, J. C. (1972) Carbon-14 dating: origin and correction of isotope fractionation errors in terrestrial living matter. Proceedings of the eighth international conference on radiocarbon dating. Lower Hutt City, New Zealand, H16-H28.

0447 Lerman, J. C. et al. (1969) Carbon-14 in Patagonian tree rings. Science 165(3898):1123-1125.

0448 Lerman, J. C., Mook, W. G. and Vogel, J. C. (1967)
Effect of the Tunguska meteor and sunspots on
radiocarbon in tree rings. Nature 216:990-991.

0449 Lerman, J. C., Mook, W. G. and Vogel, J. C. (1970)
C14 in tree rings from different localities. In:
I. U. Olsson, ed., Radiocarbon variations and
absolute chronology. Stockholm: Almqvist &
Wiksell; New York: J. Wiley, 275-299.

0450 Libby, L. M. and Lukens, H. R. (1973) Production of
radiocarbon in tree rings by lightning bolts.
Journal of geophysical research 78(26):5902.

0451 Libby, L. M. and Pandolfi, L. J. (1979) Isotopic tree
thermometers: anticorrelation with radiocarbon. In:
Radiocarbon dating. Berkeley, Calif.: Univ. of
California Press, 661-669.

0452 Libby, W. F. (1952) Radiocarbon dating. First edition.
Chicago: Univ. of Chicago Press. 175p.

0453 Libby, W. F. (1967) History of radiocarbon dating.
Radioactive dating and methods of low-level counting.
Vienna: International Atomic Energy Agency, 3-25.

0454 Libby, W. F. (1970) Radiocarbon dating. Philosophical
transactions of the royal society of London
A269:1-10.

0455 Libby, W. F., Anderson, E. C. and Arnold, J. R. (1949)
Age determination by radiocarbon content, world-wide
assay of natural radiocarbon. Science 109:227-228.

0456 Lingenfelter, R. E. and Ramaty, R. (1970) Astrophysical
and geophysical variations in C14 production. In:
I. U. Olsson, ed., Radiocarbon variations and
absolute chronology. Stockholm: Almqvist & Wiksell;
New York: J. Wiley, 513-535.

0457 Long, A. et al. (1979) Radial translocation of carbon
in bristlecone pine. In: Radiocarbon dating.
Berkeley, Calif.: Univ. of California Press,
532-537.

0458 Long, A. and Rippeteau, B. (1974) Testing contem-
poraneity and averaging radiocarbon dates. American
antiquity 39(2):205-215.

0459 Longin, R. (1971) New method of collagen extraction for radiocarbon dating. Nature 230:241-242.

0460 Lowden, J. A. (1970) Carbon-isotope fractionation during dry combustion of oxalic acid. Radiocarbon 12(2):347-349.

0461 McKerrell, H. (1971) Some aspects of the accuracy of carbon-14 dating. Scottish archaeological forum 3:73-84.

0462 May, I. (1955) Isolation of organic carbon from bones for C-14 dating. Science 212:508-509.

0463 Meeks, S. (1979) Evaluation of total variability in radiocarbon counting. In: Radiocarbon dating. Berkeley, Calif.: Univ. of California Press, 619-630.

0464 Merwe, N. J. van der (1969) The carbon-14 dating of iron. Chicago: Univ. of Chicago Press.

0465 Michael, H. N. and Klein, J. (1979) An international calibration for radiocarbon dates. MASCA journal 1(2):56-57.

0466 Michael, H. N. and Ralph, E. K. (1970) Correction factors applied to Egyptian radiocarbon dates from the era before Christ. In: I. U. Olsson, ed., Radiocarbon variations and absolute chronology. Stockholm: Almqvist & Wiksell; New York: J. Wiley, 109-120.

0467 Michael, H. N. and Ralph, E. K. (1972) Discussion of radiocarbon dates obtained from precisely dated sequoia and bristlecone pine samples. Proceedings of the eighth international conference on radio-carbon dating. Lower Hutt City, New Zealand, 1:A11-27.

0468 Mościcki, W. (1979) Examination of counting efficiency during measurements of natural C-14. In: Radiocarbon dating. Berkeley, Calif.: Univ. of California Press, 197-201.

0469 Münnich, K. O. (1957) Messungen des C14-Gehaltes von hartem Grundwasser. (Measurements of C14 content of hard groundwater). Naturwissenschaften 44:32.

0470 Muller, R. A. (1977) Radioisotopic dating with a cyclotron. Science 196:489-494.

0471 Muller, R. A., Stephenson, E. J. and Mast, T. S. (1978) Radioisotopic dating with an accelerator: a blind measurement. Science 201:347-348.

0472 Nelson, D. E., Korteling, R. G. and Stott, W. F. (1977) Carbon-14: direct detection at natural concentrations. Science 199:507-508.

0473 Neustupný, E. (1968) Absolute chronology of the Neolithic and Aeneolithic periods in central and southeastern Europe. Slovenska archeologia 16:19-60.

0474 Neustupný, E. (1970) The accuracy of radiocarbon dating. In: I. U. Olsson, ed., Radiocarbon variations and absolute chronology. Stockholm: Almqvist & Wiksell; New York: J. Wiley, 23-30.

0475 Neustupný, E. (1970) A new epoch in radiocarbon dating. Antiquity 44:38-55.

0476 Neustupný, E. (1970) Radiocarbon chronology of central Europe from c. 6450 B.P. to c. 3750 B.P. In: I. U. Olsson, ed., Radiocarbon variations and absolute chronology. Stockholm: Almqvist & Wiksell; New York: J. Wiley, 105-107.

0477 Nydal, R., Lövseth, K. and Gulliksen, S. (1979) A survey of radiocarbon variation in nature since the test ban treaty. In: Radiocarbon dating. Berkeley, Calif.: Univ. of California Press, 313-323.

0478 Oeschger, H. et al. (1979) Recent progress in low level counting and other isotope detection methods. In: Radiocarbon dating. Berkeley, Calif.: Univ. of California Press, 147-157.

0479 Oeschger, H. and Siegenthaler, U. (1979) Prognosis for the expected CO_2 increase due to fossil fuel combustion. In: Radiocarbon dating. Berkeley, Calif.: Univ. of California Press, 633-642.

0480 Olsson, I. U., ed. (1970) Radiocarbon variations and absolute chronology. Proceedings of the 12th Nobel symposium. Stockholm: Almqvist; New York: J. Wiley.

49

0481 Olsson, I. U. (1979) The importance of the pretreatment of wood and charcoal samples. In: Radiocarbon dating. Berkeley, Calif.: Univ. of California Press, 135-146.

0482 Olsson, I. U. (1979) The radiocarbon contents of various reservoirs. In: Radiocarbon dating. Berkeley, Calif.: Univ. of California Press, 613-618.

0483 Olsson, I. U. et al. (1974) A comparison of different methods for pretreatment of bones I. Geologiska föreningens i Stockholm förhandlingar 96:171-181.

0484 Otlet, R. L. (1979) An assessment of laboratory errors in liquid scintillation methods of C-14 dating. In: Radiocarbon dating. Berkeley, Calif.: Univ. of California Press, 256-267.

0485 Ottaway, B. and Ottaway, J. H. (1972) The Suess calibration curve and archaeological dating. Nature 239(5374):513-514.

0486 Otvos, E. G. (1980) Age of Tunica Hills (Louisiana-Mississippi) quaternary fossiliferous creek deposits: problems of radiocarbon dates and intermediate valley terraces in coastal plains. Quaternary research 13(1):80-92.

0487 Pavlish, L. A. and Banning, E. B. (1980) Revolutionary developments in carbon-14 dating. American antiquity 45(2):290-297.

0488 Pearson, G. W. (1979) Precise C-14 measurement by liquid scintillation counting. Radiocarbon 21(1):1-21.

0489 Pearson, G. W. et al. (1977) Absolute radiocarbon dating using a low altitude European tree-ring calibration. Nature 270:25-28.

0490 Peng, T. H., Goddard, J. G. and Broecker, W. S. (1978) A direct comparison of C-14 and Th-230 ages at Searles Lake, California. Quaternary research 9(3):319-329.

0491 Polach, H. A. (1969) Optimisation of liquid scintillation of radiocarbon age determinations and
reporting of ages. Atomic energy in Australia
12(3):21-28.

0492 Polach, H. A. (1972) Cross checking of NBS oxalic acid
and secondary laboratory radiocarbon dating
standard. Proceedings of the eighth international
conference on radiocarbon dating. Lower Hutt City,
New Zealand, 2:688-717.

0493 Polach, H. A. (1976) Radiocarbon dating as a research
tool in archaeology: hopes and limitations. In:
N. Barnard, ed., Scientific methods of research in
the study of ancient Chinese and Southeast Asian
metal artefacts: a symposium. Melbourne: National
Gallery, 255-298.

0494 Polach, H. A. (1979) Correlation of C-14 activity of
NBS oxalic acid with Arizona 1850 wood and ANU
sucrose standards. In: Radiocarbon dating. Berkeley,
Calif.: Univ. of California Press, 115-124.

0495 Protsch, R. R. (1979) New absolute dates on upper
Pleistocene fossil hominids from America. In:
Radiocarbon dating. Berkeley, Calif.: Univ. of
California Press, 69-75.

0496 Radnell, C. J., Aitken, M. J. and Otlet, R. L. (1979)
In situ C-14 production in wood. In: Radiocarbon
dating. Berkeley, Calif.: Univ. of California
Press, 643-657.

0497 Rafter, T. A. and Grant-Taylor, T., eds. (1972)
Proceedings of the eighth international conference
on radiocarbon dating. Lower Hutt City, New Zealand.
Two volumes. Royal Society of New Zealand.

0498 Rafter, T. A. and O'Brien, B. J. (1970) Exchange rates
between the atmosphere and the ocean as shown by
recent C14 measurements in the South Pacific. In:
I. U. Olsson, ed., Radiocarbon variations and
absolute chronology. Stockholm: Almqvist & Wiksell;
New York: J. Wiley, 355-374.

0499 Rafter, T. A. and Stout, J. D. (1970) Radiocarbon measurements as an index of the rate of turnover of organic matter in forest and grassland ecosystems in New Zealand. In: I. U. Olsson, ed., Radiocarbon variations and absolute chronology. Stockholm: Almqvist & Wiksell; New York: J. Wiley, 401-415.

0500 Ralph, E. K. (1972) A cyclic solution for the relationship between magnetic and atmospheric C-14 change. Proceedings of the eighth international conference on radiocarbon dating. Lower Hutt City, New Zealand, 1:A76-84.

0501 Ralph, E. K. and Klein, J. (1979) Composite computer plots of C-14 dates for tree-ring dated bristlecone pines and sequoias. In: Radiocarbon dating. Berkeley, Calif.: Univ. of California Press, 545-553.

0502 Ralph, E. K. and Michael, H. N. (1967) Problems of the radiocarbon calendar. Archaeometry 10:3-11.

0503 Ralph, E. K. and Michael, H. N. (1970) MASCA radiocarbon dates for sequoia and bristlecone pine samples. In: I. U. Olsson, ed., Radiocarbon variations and absolute chronology. Stockholm: Almqvist & Wiksell; New York: J. Wiley, 619-623.

0504 Ralph, E. K. and Michael, H. N. (1974) Twenty-five years of radiocarbon dating. American scientist 62:553-560.

0505 Ralph, E. K., Michael, H. N. and Han, M. C. (1973) Radiocarbon dates and reality. MASCA newsletter 9(1):1-20.

0506 Ralph, E. K., Michael, H. N. and Han, M. C. (1976) Tree rings and carbon-14 scale. Colloque 1. IX Congrès, Union internationale des sciences préhistoriques et protohistoriques. Nice, 101-128.

0507 Ralph, E. K. and Stuckenrath, R. (1960) Carbon-14 measurements of known age samples. Nature 188:185-187.

0508 Read, D. W. (1979) The effective use of radiocarbon dates in the seriation of archaeological sites. In: Radiocarbon dating. Berkeley, Calif.: Univ. of

52

California Press, 89-94.

0509   Renfrew, C. (1970) New configurations in Old World
       archaeology. World archaeology 2(2):199-211.

0510   Renfrew, C. (1971) Carbon-14 and the prehistory of
       Europe. Scientific American 225(4):63-72.

0511   Renfrew, C. and Clark, R. M. (1974) Problems of the
       radiocarbon calendar and its calibration.
       Archaeometry 16(1):5-18.

0512   Renfrew, C, Harkness, D. and Switsur, R. (1976)
       Quanterness, radiocarbon and the Orkney cairns.
       Antiquity 50:194-204.

0513   Robinson, S. W. (1979) Radiocarbon dating at the U.S.
       Geological Survey, Menlo Park, California. In:
       Radiocarbon dating. Berkeley, Calif.:   Univ. of
       California Press, 268-273.

0514   Säve-Söderbergh, T. and Olsson, I. U. (1970) C14
       dating and Egyptian chronology. In: I. U. Olsson,
       ed., Radiocarbon variations and absolute chronology.
       Stockholm: Almqvist & Wiksell; New York: J. Wiley,
       35-53.

0515   Scharpenseel, H. W. (1979) Soil fraction dating. In:
       Radiocarbon dating. Berkeley, Calif.:   Univ. of
       California Press, 277-283.

0516   Schell, W. R., Fairhall, A. W. and Harp, G. D. (1967)
       An analytic model of carbon-14 distribution in the
       atmosphere. Radioactive dating and methods of low-
       level counting. Vienna: International Atomic Energy
       Agency, 79-92.

0517   Schove, D. J. (1955) The sunspot cycle between 649 B.C.
       to 2000 A.D. Journal of geophysical research
       60:127-146.

0518   Schwabedissen, H. (1978) Konventionelle oder
       kalibrierte C14-Daten? (Conventional or calibrated
       C14 dates?). Archäologische Informationen 4:110-117.

0519   Selkirk, A. R. L. S. (1970) The radiocarbon revolution.
       Current archaeology 18:180-184.

0520 Sellstedt, H., Engstrand, L. and Gejvall, N.-G. (1966) New application of radiocarbon dating to collagen residue in bones. Nature 212(5062):572-574.

0521 Sheppard, J. C., Ali, S. Y. and Mehringer, P. J. (1979) Radiocarbon dating of organic components of sediments and peats. In: Radiocarbon dating. Berkeley, Calif.: Univ. of California Press, 284-305.

0522 Shotton, F. W. (1972) An example of hard-water error in radiocarbon dating of vegetable matter. Nature 240:460-461.

0523 Smith, P. E. L. (1964) Radiocarbon dating of a late Paleolithic culture from Egypt. Science 145:811.

0524 Spaulding, A. C. (1958) The significance of differences in carbon-14 dates. American antiquity 23:309-311.

0525 Stickel, E. G. and Berger, R. (1979) The Neolithic chronology of Switzerland by underwater archaeological methods. In: Radiocarbon dating. Berkeley, Calif.: Univ. of California Press, 102-111.

0526 Stuiver, M. (1961) Variations in radiocarbon concentration and sunspot activity. Journal of geophysical research 66:273-276.

0527 Stuiver, M. (1967) Origin and extent of atmospheric C-14 variations during the past 10,000 years. Radioactive dating and methods of low-level counting. Vienna: International Atomic Energy Agency, 27-40.

0528 Stuiver, M. (1970) Long-term C14 variations. In: I. U. Olsson, ed., Radiocarbon variations and absolute chronology. Stockholm: Almqvist & Wiksell; New York: J. Wiley, 197-213.

0529 Stuiver, M. (1970) Tree ring, varve and carbon-14 chronologies. Nature 288:454-455.

0530 Stuiver, M. (1978) Radiocarbon time scale tested against magnetic and other dating methods. Nature 273:271-274.

0531 Stuiver, M., Robinson, S. W. and Yang, I. C. (1979)
C-14 dating to 60,000 years B.P. with proportional
counters. In: Radiocarbon dating. Berkeley, Calif.:
Univ. of California Press, 202-215.

0532 Stuiver, M. and Suess, H. E. (1966) On the relationship between radiocarbon dates and true sample ages.
Radiocarbon 8:534.

0533 Suess, H. E. (1954) Natural radiocarbon measurements
by acetylene counting. Science 120:1-3.

0534 Suess, H. E. (1955) Radiocarbon concentration in
modern wood. Science 122:415-417.

0535 Suess, H. E. (1965) Secular variations of the cosmic-
ray-produced carbon 14 in the atmosphere and their
interpretations. Journal of geophysical research
70:5937-5952.

0536 Suess, H. E. (1967) Bristlecone pine calibration of
the radiocarbon time scale from 4100 B.C. to 1500
B.C. Radioactive dating and methods of low-level
counting. Vienna: International Atomic Energy
Agency, 143-151.

0537 Suess, H. E. (1967) Zur Chronologie des alten Ägypten.
(On the chronology of ancient Egypt). Zeitschrift
für Physik 202:1-7.

0538 Suess, H. E. (1970) Bristlecone-pine calibration of
the radiocarbon time-scale 5200 B.C. to the present.
In: I. U. Olsson, ed., Radiocarbon variations and
absolute chronology. Stockholm: Almqvist & Wiksell;
New York: J. Wiley, 303-309.

0539 Suess, H. E. (1970) The three causes of the secular
C14 fluctuations, their amplitudes and time con-
stants. In: I. U. Olsson, ed., Radiocarbon
variations and absolute chronology. Stockholm:
Almqvist & Wiksell; New York: J. Wiley, 595-604.

0540 Suess, H. E. (1976) A calibration curve for radiocarbon dates. Antiquity 50:61-62.

0541 Suess, H. E. (1979) A calibration table for conventional radiocarbon dates. In: Radiocarbon dating. Berkeley, Calif.: Univ. of California Press, 777-784.

0542 Suess, H. E. (1979) The C-14 level during the fourth and second half of the fifth millennium B.C. and the C-14 calibration curve. In: Radiocarbon dating. Berkeley, Calif.: Univ. of California Press, 538-544.

0543 Suess, H. E. (1979) Were the Allerod and Two Creeks substages contemporaneous? In: Radiocarbon dating. Berkeley, Calif.: Univ. of California Press, 76-82.

0544 Switsur, V. R. (1973) The radiocarbon calendar recalibrated. Antiquity 47:131-137.

0545 Switsur, V. R., Berger, R. and Hammond, N. (1979) A second millennium B.C. radiocarbon chronology for the Maya lowlands. In: Radiocarbon dating. Berkeley, Calif.: Univ. of California Press, 83-88.

0546 Switsur, V. R. and Jacobi, R. M. (1979) A radiocarbon chronology for the early post-glacial stone industries of England and Wales. In: Radiocarbon dating. Berkeley, Calif.: Univ. of California Press, 41-68.

0547 Tamers, M. A. (1972) Radiocarbon dating of kill sites. Archaeometry 14(1):21-26.

0548 Tamers, M. A. (1979) Radiocarbon transmutation mechanism for spontaneous somatic cellular mutations. In: Radiocarbon dating. Berkeley, Calif.: Univ. of California Press, 355-364.

0549 Tamers, M. A. and Pearson, F. J. (1965) Validity of radiocarbon dates on bone. Nature 208(5015):1053-1055.

0550 Tans, P. P. and Mook, W. G. (1979) Design, construction and calibration of a high accuracy carbon-14 counting set up. Radiocarbon 21(1):22-40.

0551 Tauber, H. (1979) C-14 activity of Arctic marine
      mammals. In: Radiocarbon dating. Berkeley, Calif.:
      Univ. of California Press, 447-452.

0552 Taylor, R. E. and Berger, R. (1967) Radiocarbon con-
      tent of marine shells from the Pacific coast of
      Central and South America. Science 158:1180-1182.

0553 Taylor, R. E. and Berger, R. (1968) Radiocarbon
      dating of the organic portion of ceramic wattle-and-
      daub house construction materials of low carbon
      content. American antiquity 33:363-366.

0554 Taylor, R. E. and Slota, P. S. (1979) Fraction studies
      on marine shell and bone samples for radiocarbon
      analyses. In: Radiocarbon dating. Berkeley, Calif.:
      Univ. of California Press, 422-432.

0555 Thommeret, J. (1976) Difficultés d'interprétation des
      dates C14 mésurées à partir des coquilles marines.
      Colloque 1. IX Congrès, Union internationale des
      sciences préhistoriques et protohistoriques. Nice,
      160-169.

0556 Thurber, D. L. and Broecker, W. S. (1970) The behavior
      of radiocarbon in the surface waters of the Great
      Basin. In: I. U. Olsson, ed., Radiocarbon vari-
      ations and absolute chronology. Stockholm: Almqvist
      & Wiksell; New York: J. Wiley, 379-398.

0557 Vinogradov, A. P. et al. (1963) Opredelenie absoljut-
      nogo vozrasta po C-14. (The determination of
      absolute age by C-14). Geokhimija 9:795-812.

0558 Vogel, J. C. (1969) Radiocarbon dating at Bushman
      Rock Shelter, Ohrigstad district. South African
      archaeological bulletin 24:56.

0559 Vogel, J. C. (1969) Remarks on the C14 method.
      Helinium 9:19-27.

0560 Vogel, J. C. (1970) C14 trends before 6000 B.P. In:
      I. U. Olsson, ed., Radiocarbon variations and
      absolute chronology. Stockholm: Almqvist & Wiksell;
      New York: J. Wiley, 313-320.

0561 Vogel, J. C. and Beaumont, P. B. (1972) Revised radiocarbon chronology for the Stone Age in South Africa.
Nature 237:50-51.

0562 Walton, A. et al. (1967) Carbon-14 concentrations in
environmental materials and their temporal fluctuations. Radioactive dating and methods of low-
level counting. Vienna: International Atomic Energy
Agency, 41-47.

0563 Ward, G. K. and Wilson, S. R. (1978) Procedures for
comparing and combining radiocarbon age determinations: a critique. Archaeometry 20:19-31.

0564 Watkins, T., ed. (1975) Radiocarbon calibration and
prehistory. Edinburgh: Univ. of Edinburgh Press.
147p.

0565 Weinstein, G. A. and Michael, H. N. (1978) Radiocarbon
dates from Akrotiri, Thera. Archaeometry 20(2):203-
209.

0566 Wendland, W. M. and Donley, D. L. (1971) Radiocarbon
calendar-age relationship. Earth and planetary
science letters 11:135.

0567 Wendorf, F. et al. (1975) Dates for the Middle Stone
Age of East Africa. Science 187:940-942.

0568 Wendorf, F., Schild, R. and Said, R. (1970) Problems
of dating the Late Paleolithic age in Egypt. In:
I. U. Olsson, ed., Radiocarbon variations and
absolute chronology. Stockholm: Almqvist & Wiksell;
New York: J. Wiley, 57-77.

0569 White, L. T. (1979) An appeal from the consumer. In:
Radiocarbon dating. Berkeley, Calif.: Univ. of
California Press, 37-40.

0570 Whitehouse, R. D. (1978) Italian prehistory, Carbon 14
and the tree-ring calibration. British archaeological reports, supplementary series 41(1):71-91.

0571 Willis, E. H., Tauber, H. and Münnich, K. O. (1960)
Variations in the atmospheric radiocarbon concentration over the past 1300 years. Radiocarbon 5:1-4.

0572 Willkomm, H. (1970) Möglichkeiten der C14-Datierung.
      (Possibilities of C14 dating). Germania 48:98-109.

0573 Wilson, H. W. (1979) Possibility of measurement of C14
      by mass spectrometer techniques. In: Radiocarbon
      dating. Berkeley, Calif.: Univ. of California
      Press, 238-245.

0574 Winter, J. (1972) Radiocarbon dating by thermo-
      luminescent dosimetry. Archaeometry 14(2):281-286.

2. Potassium-argon dating

0575 Bishop, W. W., Miller, J. A. and Fitch, F. J. (1969)
      New potassium-argon age determinations relevant to
      the Miocene fossil mammal sequence in East Africa.
      American journal of science 267:669-699.

0576 Breton, N. R. (1970) Corrections for interfering
      isotopes in the Ar-40/Ar-39 dating method. Earth and
      planetary science letters 8:427-433.

0577 Curtis, G. H. (1975) Improvements in potassium-argon
      dating: 1962-1975. World archaeology 7(2):198-209.

0578 Dalrymple, G. B. (1969) Ar-40/Ar-39 analyses of
      historic lava flows. Earth and planetary science
      letters 3:47-55.

0579 Dalrymple, G. B. and Lanphere, M. A. (1969) Potassium-
      argon dating: principles, techniques and applica-
      tions to geochronology. San Francisco: Freeman.
      258p.

0580 Dalrymple, G. B. and Lanphere, M. A. (1971) Ar-40/
      Ar-39 technique of K-Ar dating: a comparison with
      the conventional technique. Earth and planetary
      science letters 12:300-308.

0581 Drake, R. E. et al. (1980) KBS tuff dating and geo-
      chronology of tuffaceous sediments in the Koobi Fora
      and Shungura formations, East Africa. Nature
      283(5745):368-372

0582 Evernden, J. F. and Curtis, G. H. (1965) The
      potassium-argon dating of Late Cenozoic rocks in
      East Africa and Italy. Current anthropology 6:343-
      385.

0583 Evernden, J. R. et al. (1964) Potassium-argon dates
      and Cenozoid mammalian chronology of North America.
      American journal of science 262:145-198.

0584 Findlater, I. C. et al. (1974) Dating of the rock
      succession containing fossil hominids at East
      Rudolf, Kenya. Nature 251:213-215.

0585 Fitch, F. J. and Miller, J. A. (1970) Radioisotopic
      age determinations of Lake Rudolf artefact site.
      Nature 226:226-228.

0586 Fitch, F. J. and Miller, J. A. (1971) Atmospheric
      argon correction in the K/Ar dating of young vol-
      canic rocks. Journal of the geological society,
      London 127:277-280.

0587 Fitch, F. J. and Miller, J. A. (1971) Potassium-argon
      radioages of Karroo volcanic rocks from Lesotho.
      Bulletin volcanologique 35:64-84.

0588 Grasty, R. L. and Miller, J. A. (1965) The omegatron:
      a useful tool for argon isotope investigation.
      Nature 207:1146-1148.

0589 Grasty, R. L. and Mitchell, J. G. (1966) Single sample
      potassium-argon ages using the omegatron. Earth and
      planetary science letters 1:121-122.

0590 Hayatsu, A. and Carmichael, C. M. (1970) K-Ar isochron
      method and initial argon ratios. Earth and planetary
      science letters 8:71-76.

0591 Hooker, P. J. and Miller, J. A. (1979) K-Ar dating of
      the Pleistocene fossil hominid site at Chesowanja,
      North Kenya. Nature 282(5740):710-712.

0592 Koenigswald, G. H. R. von, Gentner, W. and Lippolt,
      H. J. (1961) Age of the basalt flow at Olduvai, East
      Africa. Nature 192:720-721.

0593 Langley, K. M. (1978) Dating sediments by a K-Ar method. Nature 276(5683):56-57.

0594 Leakey, L. S. B., Curtis, G. H. and Evernden, J. F. (1962) Age of basalt underlying Bed I, Olduvai. Nature 194:610-612.

0595 Leakey, L. S. B., Evernden, J. F. and Curtis, G. H. (1961) Age of Bed I, Olduvai Gorge, Tanganyika. Nature 191:478-479.

0596 McDougall, I. et al. (1980) K-Ar age estimate for the KBS tuff, East Turkana, Kenya. Nature 284(5753): 230-234.

0597 Mitchell, J. G. (1968) The argon-40/argon-39 method for potassium-argon age determination. Geochimica et cosmochimica acta 32:781-790.

0598 Mussett, A. E. and Dalrymple, G. B. (1968) An investigation of the source of air Ar contamination in K-Ar dating. Earth and planetary science letters 4:422-426.

0599 Schaeffer, O. A. and Zähringer, J. (1966) Potassium argon dating. New York: Springer Verlag. 234p.

0600 Stoenner, R. W., Schaeffer, O. A. and Katcoff, S. (1965) Half-lives of Argon-37, Argon-39. Science 148:1325-1328.

3. Uranium decay series dating

0601 Cherdyntsev, V. V., Kazachevskii, I. V. and Kuzmina, E. A. (1965) Dating of Pleistocene carbonate formations by the thorium and uranium isotopes. Geochem. international 2:794-801.

0602 Cherdyntsev, V. V., Senina, N. and Kuzmina, E. A. (1975) Die Alterbestimmung der Travertin von Weimar-Ehringsdorf. (Über das Alter des Riss-Würm-Interglazials). (The age determination of the travertine of Weimar-Ehringsdorf. On the age of the Riss-Würm interglacial). Abhandlungen, Zent. Geol. Inst. Paläontologie 23:7-14.

0603 Fornaca-Rinaldi, G. (1968) Th-230/Th-234 dating of cave concretions. Earth and planetary science letters 5:120-122.

0604 Hansen, R. O. and Begg, E. L. (1970) Age of Quaternary sediments and soils in the Sacramento area, California, by uranium and actinium series dating of vertebrate fossils. Earth and planetary science letters 8:411-419.

0605 Hennig, G. J. and Bangert, U. (1979) Dating of Pleistocene calcite formations by disequilibria in the uranium decay series. Archaeo-Physika 10:464-476.

0606 Howell, F. C. et al. (1972) Uranium-series dating of bone from the Isimila prehistoric site, Tanzania. Nature 237(5349):51-52.

0607 Kaufman, A. et al. (1971) The status of U-series methods of mollusk dating. Geochimica et cosmochimica acta 35:1155-1183.

0608 Kaufman, A. and Broecker, W. (1965) Comparison of Th-230 and C-14 ages for carbonate materials from Lakes Lahontan and Bonneville. Journal of geophysical research 70:4039-4054.

0609 Sakanoue, M. and Yoshioka, M. (1974) Uranium-series dating of bone samples from the Amud Cave site. Quaternary research 13:220-224.

0610 Schwarcz, H. P. (1980) Absolute age determination of archaeological sites by uranium series dating of travertines. Archaeometry 22(1):3-24.

0611 Schwarcz, H. P. et al. (1979) Uranium series dating of travertine from archaeological sites, Nahal Zin, Israel. Nature 277(5698):558-560.

0612 Schwarcz, H. P. and Debenrath, A. (1979) Datation absolue des restes humains de la Chaise-de-Vouthon (Charente) au moyen du déséquilibre des séries d'Uranium. Comptes rendus de l'académie des sciences 288:1155-1157.

0613 Szabo, B. J. (1979) Dating fossil bone from Cornelia, Orange Free State, South Africa. Journal of archaeological science 6(2):201-203.

62

0614　Szabo, B. J. and Butzer, K. W. (1979) Uranium-series
　　　 dating of lacustrine limestones from pan deposits
　　　 with final Acheulian assemblage at Rooidam, Kimberly
　　　 district, South Africa. Quaternary research 11(2):
　　　 257-260.

0615　Szabo, B. J. and Collins, D. (1975) Ages of fossil
　　　 bones from British Interglacial sites. Nature
　　　 254:680-682.

0616　Szabo, B. J., Malde, H. E. and Irwin-Williams, C.
　　　 (1969) Dilemma posed by uranium-series dates on
　　　 archaeologically significant bones from
　　　 Valsequillo, Puebla, Mexico. Earth and planetary
　　　 science letters 6:237-244.

0617　Szabo, B. J. and Rosholt, J. N. (1969) Uranium-series
　　　 dating of Pleistocene molluscan shells from southern
　　　 California--an open system model. Journal of
　　　 geophysical research 74:3253-3260.

0618　Turekian, K. K. and Nelson, E. (1976) Uranium decay
　　　 series dating of the travertines of Caune de l'Arago
　　　 (France). Colloque 1. IX Congrès, Union interna-
　　　 tionale des sciences préhistoriques et protohis-
　　　 toriques. Nice, 171-179.

0619　Volchok, H. L. and Kulp, J. L. (1957) The ionium
　　　 method of age determination. Geochimica et cosmo-
　　　 chimica acta 11:219-246.

4. Fission-track dating

0620　Brill, R. H. (1964) Applications of fission-track
　　　 dating to historic and prehistoric glasses.
　　　 Archaeometry 7:51-57.

0621　Brill, R. H. et al. (1964) The fission-track dating of
　　　 man-made glasses: preliminary results. Journal of
　　　 glass studies 6:151-155.

0622　Durrani, S. A. et al. (1971) Obsidian source
　　　 identification by fission track analysis. Nature
　　　 233:242-245.

0623　Fleischer, R. L. (1975) Advances in fission track
　　　 dating. World archaeology 7(2):136-150.

0624 Fleischer, R. L. (1976) Fission tracks and archaeology. Colloque 1. IX Congrès, Union internationale des sciences préhistoriques et protohistoriques. Nice, 82-100.

0625 Fleischer, R. L. et al. (1965) Fission-track dating of Bed I, Olduvai Gorge. Science 148:72-74.

0626 Fleischer, R. L. et al. (1965) Fission-track dating of a Mesolithic knife. Nature 205:1138.

0627 Fleischer, R. L. and Price, P. B. (1964) Glass dating by fission fragment tracks. Journal of geophysical research 69:331-339.

0628 Fleischer, R. L. and Price, P. B. (1964) Techniques for geological dating of minerals by chemical etching of fission fragment tracks. Geochimica et cosmochimica acta 28:1705-1714.

0629 Fleischer, R. L. and Price, P. B. (1964) Uranium contents of ancient man-made glass. Science 144:841-842.

0630 Fleischer, R. L., Price, P. B. and Walker, R. M. (1965) Effects of temperature, pressure and ionization on the formation and stability of fission tracks in minerals and glasses. Journal of geophysical research 70:1497-1502.

0631 Fleischer, R. L., Price, P. B. and Walker, R. M. (1965) Tracks of charged particles in solids. Science 149:383.

0632 Fleischer, R. L., Price, P. B. and Walker, R. M. (1975) Nuclear tracks in solids. Berkeley, Calif.: Univ. of California Press.

0633 Garrison, E. G., McGimsey, C. R. and Zinke, O. H. (1978) Alpha-recoil tracks in archaeological ceramic dating. Archaeometry 20(1):39-46.

0634 Gleadow, A. J. W. and Lovering, J. F. (1974) The effect of weathering on fission track dating. Earth and planetary science letters 22:163-168.

0635 Huang, W. H. and Walker, R. M. (1967) Fossil alpha-particle recoil tracks: a new method of age determination. Science 155:1103-1106.

64

0636 Hurford, A. J. (1974) Fission track dating of a vitric
      tuff from East Rudolf, North Kenya. Nature
      249:236-237.

0637 Lakatos, S. and Miller, D. S. (1972) Evidence for the
      effect of water content on fission-track annealing
      in volcanic glass. Earth and planetary science
      letters 14:128-130.

0638 Lakatos, S. and Miller, D. S. (1972) Fission track
      stability in volcanic glass of different water con-
      tents. Journal of geophysical research 77:6990-6993.

0639 Lakatos, S. and Miller, D. S. (1973) Problems of
      dating mica by the fission-track method. Canadian
      journal of earth science 10:403-407.

0640 McDougall, D. and Price, P. B. (1974) Attempt to date
      early South African hominids by using fission tracks
      in calcite. Science 46:943.

0641 Mark, E., Pahl, M. and Mark, T. D. (1972) Fission
      track annealing behaviour of apatite. Transactions
      of the American nuclear society 15:126-127.

0642 Maurette, M., Pellas, P. and Walker, R. M. (1964)
      Étude des traces de fission fossiles dans le mica.
      Bulletin de la société française de mineralogie et
      cristallographie 87:6-17.

0643 Mantovani, M. S. M. (1974) Variations of characteris-
      tics of fission tracks in muscovites by thermal
      effects. Earth and planetary science letters 24:
      311-316.

0644 Menta, P. P. and Rama (1969) Annealing effects in
      muscovite and their influence on dating by fission
      track method. Earth and planetary science letters
      7:82-86.

0645 Naeser, C. W. and Fleischer, R. L. (1975) The age of
      apatite at Cerro de Mercado, Mexico: a problem for
      fission track annealing corrections. Geophysical
      research letters 2:67-70.

0646 Nishimura, S. (1971) Fission track dating of
      archaeological materials from Japan. Nature
      230(5291):242-243.

0647 Reimer, G. M. (1974) Effect of progressive etching on
      fission track ages. Transactions of the American
      nuclear society 18:87.

0648 Scott, B. C. (1976) The possible application of
      fission track counting to the dating of bloomery
      slag and iron. Historical metallurgy 10:87.

0649 Suzuki, M. (1969) Fission track identification of
      geologic source of obsidian artefacts collected from
      the Sone Site. Archaeological journal 36:12-15.

0650 Wagner, G. (1976) Radiation damage dating of rocks and
      artifacts. Endeavour 35:3.

0651 Wagner, G. and Storzer, D. (1970) Die Interpretation
      von Spaltspurenalten (fission track ages) am
      Beispiel von Naturliehen Gläsern, Apatiten und
      Zirkonen. (The interpretation of fission track ages,
      for example, of natural glasses, apatites and
      zircons). Ecologae geologicae helvetiae 63(1):
      335-344.

0652 Watanabe, N. and Suzuki, M. (1969) Fission track dating
      of archaeological glass materials from Japan. Nature
      222:1057-1058.

0653 Wolfman, D. and Rolniak, T. M. (1979) Alpha-recoil
      track dating: problems and prospects. Archaeo-
      Physika 10:512-521.

5. Thermoluminescence dating

0654 Agrawal, D. P., Bhandari, N. and Singhvi, A. K. (1979)
      Thermoluminescence dating--an Indian perspective.
      Man and environment 3:78-82.

0655 Aitken, M. J. (1965) Thermoluminescence. Science
      journal 1(4):32-38.

0656 Aitken, M. J. (1968) Thermoluminescence dating in
      archaeology. In: D. J. McDougall, ed., Thermo-
      luminescence of geological materials. New York:
      Academic Press, 369-378.

66

0657 Aitken, M. J. (1969) Thermoluminescent dosimetry of environmental radiation on archaeological sites. Archaeometry 11:109-114.

0658 Aitken, M. J. (1974) Thermoluminescent dating. In: Recent advances in science and technology of materials. New York: Plenum Press, 3:191-203.

0659 Aitken, M. J. (1976) Thermoluminescence in archaeology. Colloque 1. IX Congrès, Union internationale des sciences préhistoriques et protohistoriques. Nice, 7-20.

0660 Aitken, M. J. (1976) Thermoluminescent age evaluation and assessment of error limits: revised system. Archaeometry 18(2):233-238.

0661 Aitken, M. J. (1977) Thermoluminescence and the archaeologist. Antiquity 51(201):11-19.

0662 Aitken, M. J. (1978) Dose-rate evaluation. PACT 2:18-34.

0663 Aitken, M. J. (1978) Radon loss evaluation by alpha counting. PACT 2:104-114.

0664 Aitken, M. J. (1979) Interlaboratory calibration of alpha and beta sources. PACT 3:443-447.

0665 Aitken, M. J. (1979) Pre-dose dating: predictions from the model. PACT 3:319-324.

0666 Aitken, M. J. (1979) Pre-dose dating: high So sherds. PACT 3:345-355.

0667 Aitken, M. J. et al. (1968) Thermoluminescence study of lavas of Mt. Etna and other historic flows: preliminary results. In: D. J. McDougall, ed., Thermoluminescence of geological materials. New York: Academic Press, 359-366.

0668 Aitken, M. J. et al. (1968) Elimination of spurious thermoluminescence. In: D. J. McDougall, ed., Thermoluminescence of geological materials. New York: Academic Press, 133-142.

0669 Aitken, M. J. et al. (1970) Thermoluminescent dating of pottery. In: I. U. Olsson, ed., Radiocarbon variations and absolute chronology. Stockholm: Almqvist & Wiksell; New York: J. Wiley, 129-138.

0670 Aitken, M. J. et al. (1974) Age determination by TL; a review of progress at Oxford. Proceedings of the fourth international conference on luminescence dosimetry. Krakow, 1005-1019.

0671 Aitken, M. J. and Alldred, J. C. (1972) The assessment of error limits in thermoluminescent dating. Archaeometry 14(2):257-267.

0672 Aitken, M. J. and Bowman, S. G. E. (1975) Thermoluminescent dating: assessment of alpha particle contribution. Archaeometry 17(1):132-138.

0673 Aitken, M. J. and Fleming, S. J. (1972) Thermoluminescence dosimetry in archaeological dating. In: Topics in radiation dosimetry. New York: Academic Press, supplement 1:1-78.

0674 Aitken, M. J., Moorey, P. R. S. and Ucko, P. J. (1971) The authenticity of vessels and figurines in the Hacilar style. Archaeometry 13(2):89-142.

0675 Aitken, M. J., Tite, M. S. and Reid, J. (1963) Thermoluminescence dating: progress report. Archaeometry 6:65-75.

0676 Aitken, M. J., Tite, M. S. and Reid, J. (1964) Thermoluminescent dating of ancient ceramics. Nature 202:1032-1033.

0677 Aitken, M. J. and Wintle, A. G. (1977) Thermoluminescence dating of calcite and burnt flint: the age relation for slices. Archaeometry 19(1):100-105.

0678 Aitken, M. J., Zimmerman, D. W. and Fleming, S. J. (1968) Thermoluminescent dating of pottery. Nature 219:442-445.

0679 Bailiff, I. K., Bowman, S. G. E. and Aitken, M. J. (1974) Measurement of internal beta dose-rate by TLD: utilization in TL dating. Proceedings of the fourth international conference on luminescence dosimetry. Krakow, 1043-1052.

0680   Bangert, U. and Hennig, G. J. (1979) Effects of sample
        preparation and the influence of clay impurities on
        the TL-dating of calcite cave deposits. PACT
        3:281-289.

0681   Bell, W. T. (1976) The assessment of the radiation
        dose-rate for thermoluminescence dating.
        Archaeometry 18(1):107-111.

0682   Bell, W. T. (1977) Thermoluminescence dating: revised
        dose-rate data. Archaeometry 19(1):99-100.

0683   Bell, W. T. (1979) Thermoluminescence dating:
        radiation dose-rate data. Archaeometry 21(2):243-245.

0684   Bell, W. T. and Zimmerman, D. W. (1978) The effect of
        HF acid etching on the morphology of quartz in-
        clusions for thermoluminescent dating. Archaeometry
        20(1):63-65.

0685   Benkö, L. (1977) Contribution à la datation des
        céramiques par thermoluminescence. Acta
        archaeologica (Budapest) 29(1/2):203-207.

0686   Bøtter-Jensen, L. and Bundgaard, J. (1978) An auto-
        mated reader for thermoluminescent dating. PACT
        2:48-56.

0687   Bowman, S. G. E. (1975) Dependence of supralinearity
        on pre-dose: some observations. Archaeometry 17(1):
        129-132.

0688   Bowman, S. G. E. (1979) Phototransferred TL in quartz
        and its potential use in dating. PACT 3:381-400.

0689   Bowman, S. G. E. and Seeley, M. A. (1978) The British
        Museum flint dating project. PACT 2:151-164.

0690   Bronson, B. and Han, M. C. (1972) A thermoluminescence
        series from Thailand. Antiquity 46:322-326.

0691   Burleigh, R. and Seeley, M. A. (1975) Use of a wire
        saw for slicing certain sample materials for thermo-
        luminescence dating. Archaeometry 17(1):116-119.

0692   Cairns, T. (1976) Archaeological dating by thermo-
        luminescence. Analytical chemistry 48(3):266A.

0693 Carpenter, R. J. and Ryan, K. (1975) TL dating of burnt soil. MASCA newsletter 11(2):7.

0694 Carriveau, G. W. (1974) Annealing threshold and thermoluminescent dating of ceramic material. MASCA newsletter 10(1):3.

0695 Carriveau, G. W. (1974) Dating of 'Phoenician' slag from Iberia using thermoluminescence techniques. MASCA newsletter 10(1):1-2.

0696 Carriveau, G. W. and Harbottle, G. (1979) Direct measurement of the fraction of radon loss in ceramics by gamma-ray spectroscopy. Archaeo-Physika 10:423-427.

0697 Carriveau, G. W. and Nievens, M. (1979) Guatemalan obsidian source characterization by thermoluminescence. PACT 3:506-509.

0698 Carriveau, G. W. and Troka, W. (1979) Annual dose rate calculations for thermoluminescence dating. Archaeo-Physika 10:406-422.

0699 Chen, R. (1979) Saturation of sensitization of the 110°C TL peak in quartz and its potential application in the pre-dose technique. PACT 3:325-335.

0700 Chen, R. and Bowman, S. G. E. (1978) Supralinear growth of TL due to competition during irradiation. PACT 2:216-230.

0701 Christodoulides, C. and Fremlin, J. H. (1971) Thermoluminescence of biological materials. Nature 232:257-258.

0702 Courtois, L. et al. (1977) Thermoluminescent dating of archeological pottery from the Marajó Island (Brazil). Fifth international conference on luminescence dosimetry. São Paulo, Brazil, 459-468.

0703 Daniels, F., Boyd, C. A. and Saunders, D. J. (1953) Thermoluminescence as a research tool. Science 117:343-349.

0704 Desai, V. S. and Aitken, M. J. (1974) Radon escape from pottery: effect of wetness. Archaeometry 16(1):95-97.

70

0705 Driver, H. S. T. (1979) The preparation of thin slices
of bone and shell for TL. PACT 3:290-297.

0706 Drover, C. E. et al. (1979) Thermoluminescence determinations of early ceramic materials from coastal
southern California. American antiquity 44(2):285-
295.

0707 Early Thai bronzes. (1973) MASCA newsletter 9(2):3.

0708 Fagg, B. E. B. and Fleming, S. J. (1970) Thermoluminescent dating of a terracotta of the Nok
culture, Nigeria. Archaeometry 12(1):53-55.

0709 Félszerfalvi, J. et al. (1979) Dy concentration,
grain size and TL sensitivity of CaSo4:Dy. PACT
3:311-314.

0710 Fleming, S. J. (1966) Study of thermoluminescence of
crystalline extracts from pottery. Archaeometry
9:170-173.

0711 Fleming, S. J. (1968) Thermoluminescence age studies
in mineral inclusions separated from ancient
pottery. In: D. J. McDougall, ed., Thermoluminescence of geological materials. New York:
Academic Press, 431.

0712 Fleming, S. J. (1970) Thermoluminescent dating:
refinement of the quartz inclusion method.
Archaeometry 12(2):133-145.

0713 Fleming, S. J. (1971) New techniques of thermoluminescent dating of ancient pottery: II. The
predose method. In: V. Mejdahl, ed., Proceedings
of the third international conference on
luminescence dosimetry. Risø: Danish Atomic Energy
Commission, Risø report no. 249:895-929.

0714 Fleming, S. J. (1971) Thermoluminescence dating--
principles and application. Naturwissenschaften
58:333-338.

0715 Fleming, S. J. (1971) Thermoluminescent authenticity
testing of ancient ceramics: the effects of
sampling by drilling. Archaeometry 13(1):59-70.

0716 Fleming, S. J. (1972) Thermoluminescence authenticity
      testing of ancient ceramics using radiation-
      sensitivity changes in quartz. Naturwissenschaften
      59:145-151.

0717 Fleming, S. J. (1973) The pre-dose technique: a new
      thermoluminescent dating method. Archaeometry
      15(1):13-30.

0718 Fleming, S. J. (1973) Thermoluminescence and glaze
      studies of a group of T'ang Dynasty ceramics.
      Archaeometry 15(1):31-52.

0719 Fleming, S. J. (1974) Thermoluminescent authenticity
      studies of unglazed T'ang Dynasty ceramic tomb
      goods. Archaeometry 16(1):91-95.

0720 Fleming, S. J. (1975) Supralinearity corrections in
      fine-grain thermoluminescence dating: a re-
      appraisal. Archaeometry 17(1):122-129.

0721 Fleming, S. J. (1978) The quartz inclusion method.
      PACT 2:125-130.

0722 Fleming, S. J. (1978) Thermoluminescent dating: MASCA
      date-list I, quotation of results. MASCA journal
      1:12-13.

0723 Fleming, S. J. (1979) Of Igueghae and the
      Iguneromwon. MASCA journal 1(2):48-49.

0724 Fleming, S. J. (1979) Pre-dose method: basic elements.
      PACT 3:315-318.

0725 Fleming, S. J. (1979) Revival of Pollajuolo's combat
      of nude men. MASCA journal 1(2):35-36.

0726 Fleming, S. J. and Fagg, B. E. B. (1977) Thermo-
      luminescent dating of the Udo bronze head.
      Archaeometry 19(1):86-88.

0727 Fleming, S. J., Jucker, H. and Riederer, J. (1971)
      Etruscan wall-paintings on terracotta: a study in
      authenticity. Archaeometry 13(2):143-167.

0728 Fleming, S. J., Moss, H. M. and Joseph, A. (1970)
      Thermoluminescent authenticity testing of some Six
      Dynasties' figures. Archaeometry 12(1):57-66.

0729 Fleming, S. J. and Roberts, H. S. (1970) Thermoluminescent authenticity testing of a Pontic
amphora. Archaeometry 12(2):129-131.

0730 Fleming, S. J. and Sampson, E. H. (1972) The
authenticity of figurines, animals and pottery
facsimiles of bronzes in the Hui Hsien style.

0731 Fleming, S. J. and Stoneham, D. (1971) New techniques
of thermoluminescent dating of ancient pottery: I.
The subtraction method. In: V. Mejdahl, ed.,
Proceedings of the third international conference
on luminescence dosimetry. Risø: Danish Atomic
Energy Commission, Risø report no. 249:880-894.

0732 Fleming, S. J. and Stoneham, D. (1973) The subtraction
technique of thermoluminescent dating. Archaeometry
15(2):229-238.

0733 Fleming, S. J. and Stoneham, D. (1973) Thermoluminescent authenticity study and dating of
Renaissance terracottas. Archaeometry 15(2):239-247.

0734 Fleming, S. J. and Thompson, J. (1970) Quartz as a
heat-resistant dosimeter. Health physics 18:567-568.

0735 Fornaca-Rinaldi, G. (1968) $^{230}TL/^{234}TL$ dating of cave
concretions. Earth and planetary science letters
5:120-122.

0736 François, H., McKerrell, H. and Mejdahl, V. (1977)
Thermoluminescence dating of ceramics from Glozel.
Proceedings of the fifth international conference on
luminescence dosimetry. São Paulo, Brazil, 469-479.

0737 Fremlin, J. H. and Srirath, S. (1964) Thermoluminescent dating: examples of non-uniformity of
luminescence. Archaeometry 7:58-62.

0738 Gallois, B. et al. (1979) Datation par TL de corraux
fossiles des Caraïbes: observation et interprétation de méchanismes inhabituels de TL. PACT
3:493-505.

0739 Gillot, P. Y., Valladas, G. and Reyss, J. L. (1978)
Dating of lava flow using a granitic enclave:
application to the Laschamp magnetic event. PACT
2:165-173.

0740 Göksu, H. Y. et al. (1974) Age determination of burned flint by a thermoluminescent method. Science 183:651-654.

0741 Göksu, H. Y. (1979) The TL age determination of fossil human footprints. Archaeo-Physika 10:455-462.

0742 Göksu, H. Y. and Fremlin, J. H. (1972) Thermoluminescence from unirradiated flints: regeneration thermoluminescence. Archaeometry 14(1):127-132.

0743 Göksu, H. Y. and Turetken, N. (1979) Source identification of obsidian tools by TL. PACT 3:356-359.

0744 Goerler, J. (1964) Die Thermolumineszenz und ihre Anwendung zur Alterbestimmung von Keramikscherben. (Thermoluminescence and its use for age determination of ceramic sherds). Bonner Jahrbücher 164:189-201.

0745 Grögler, N. von, Houtermans, F. G. and Stauffer, H. (1960) Über die Datierung von Keramik und Ziegel durch Thermolumineszenz. (On the dating of ceramics and tile by thermoluminescence). Helvetica physica acta 33:595-596.

0746 Groom, P. J. et al. (1978) The dose-rate dependence of thermoluminescence response and sensitivity in quartz. PACT 2:200-210.

0747 Han, M. C. (1975) Effects of alpha and X-ray doses and annealing temperatures upon pottery dating by thermoluminescence. MASCA newsletter 11(1):1-3.

0748 Han, M. C. and Ralph, E. K. (1971) Some uncertainties in thermoluminescence dating. In: V. Mejdahl, ed., Proceedings of the third international conference on luminescence dosimetry. Risø: Danish Atomic Energy Commission, Risø report no. 249:948-959.

0749 Hedges, R. E. M. and McLellan, M. (1976) On the cation exchange capacity of fired clays and its effect on the chemical and radiometric analysis of pottery. Archaeometry 18(2):203-207.

0750 Hütt, G., Smirnov, A. and Tale, I. (1979) On the application of TL of natural quartz to the study of geochronology of sedimentary deposits. PACT 3:362-373.

74

0751 Huntley, D. J. and Bailey, D. C. (1978) Obsidian source identification by thermoluminescence. Archaeometry 20(2):159-170.

0752 Huntley, D. J. and Wintle, A. G. (1978) Some aspects of alpha counting. PACT 2:114-119.

0753 Huxtable, J. H. et al. (1972) Thermoluminescent dates for Ochre Coloured Pottery from India. Antiquity 46:62-63.

0754 Huxtable, J. et al. (1976) Dating a settlement pattern by thermoluminescence: the burnt mounds of Orkney. Archaeometry 18(1):5-17.

0755 Huxtable, J. (1978) Fine grain dating (F.G.D.). PACT 2:7-11.

0756 Huxtable, J. and Aitken, M. J. (1978) Thermoluminescence dating of sherds from Sham Wan. Journal monograph--Hong Kong archaeological society 3:116-124.

0757 Huxtable, J., Aitken, M. J. and Weber, J. C. (1972) Thermoluminescent dating of baked clay balls of the Poverty Point culture. Archaeometry 14(2):269-275.

0758 Ichikawa, Y. and Nagatomo, T. (1978) Thermoluminescence dating of burnt sandstones from Senpukuji Cave. PACT 2:174-175

0759 Ichikawa, Y., Nagatomo, T. and Hagihara, N. (1978) Thermoluminescent dating of Jomon pattern pottery from Taishaku Valley. Archaeometry 20(2):171-176.

0760 Jasińska, M. and Niewiadomski, T. (1970) Thermoluminescence of biological materials. Nature 227:1159-1160.

0761 Kalef-Ezra, J. and Horowitz, Y. S. (1979) Electron backscattering corrections for beta dose-rate estimations in archaeological objects. PACT 3:428-438.

0762 Keisch, B. et al. (1967) Dating and authenticating works of art by measurement of natural alpha emitters. Science 155(3767):1238-1242.

0763 Kelly, J. C. (1978) Defects in quartz and thermo-luminescence dating. PACT 2:120-124.

0764 Kelly, J. C. and Smith, A. (1978) A new high efficiency thermoluminescence apparatus. PACT 2:66-69.

0765 Kennedy, G. C. and Knopff, L. (1960) Dating by thermo-luminescence. Archaeology 13:147-148.

0766 Levy, P. W. (1979) TL studies having applications to geology and archaeometry. PACT 3:466-480.

0767 Liritzis, Y. and McKerrell, H. (1979) Some TL dates and neutron activation analysis of Greek Neolithic pottery. Archaeo-Physika 10:486-498.

0768 Liritzis, Y. and Thomas, R. (1980) Paleointensity and thermoluminescence measurements on Cretan kilns from 1300 to 2000 B.C. Nature 283(5742):54-55.

0769 McKeever, S. W. S. et al. (1978) TL sensitivity: dependence upon irradiation temperature. PACT 2:211-215.

0770 McKerrell, H. et al. (1974) Thermoluminescence and Glozel. Antiquity 48:262-272.

0771 Malik, S. R., Durrani, S. A. and Fremlin, J. H. (1973) A comparative study of the spatial distribution of uranium and of TL-producing minerals in archaeolog-ical materials. Archaeometry 15(2):249-253.

0772 Mazess, R. B. and Zimmerman, D. W. (1966) Pottery dating from thermoluminescence. Science 152:347-348.

0773 Meakins, R. L., Dickson, B. L. and Kelly, J. C. (1978) The effect of thermoluminescent dating of dis-equilibrium in the uranium decay chain. PACT 2:97-103.

0774 Meakins, R. L., Dickson, B. L. and Kelly, J. C. (1979) Gamma ray analysis of K, U and Th for dose-rate estimation in thermoluminescent dating. Archaeometry 21(1):79-86.

0775 Mejdahl, V. (1969) Thermoluminescence dating of ancient Danish ceramics. Archaeometry 11:99-104.

0776   Mejdahl, V. (1970) Measurement of environmental
       radiation at archaeological excavation sites.
       Archaeometry 12(2):147-159.

0777   Mejdahl, V. (1972) Progress in TL dating at Risö.
       Archaeometry 14(2):245-256.

0778   Mejdahl, V. (1978) Measurement of environmental
       radiation at archaeological sites by means of TL
       dosimeters. PACT 2:70-83.

0779   Mejdahl, V. (1978) Thermoluminescence dating: a
       thermoluminescence technique for beta-ray dosimetry.
       PACT 2:35-47.

0780   Mejdahl, V. (1979) Thermoluminescence dating: beta-
       dose attenuation in quartz grains. Archaeometry
       21(1):61-72.

0781   Mejdahl, V. and Winther-Nielsen, M. (1978) Dating of
       Danish ceramics by means of the quartz inclusion
       technique. PACT 2:131-140.

0782   Mobbs, S. F. (1979) Phototransfer at low temperatures.
       PACT 3:407-413.

0783   Moreno Moreno, A. and Espinosa, G. (1978) Choice of
       photomultiplier tube light coupling transmission
       and electronic instrumentation for thermo-
       luminescence dating. PACT 2:57-65.

0784   Murray, A. S., Bowman, S. G. E. and Aitken, M. J.
       (1978) Evaluation of the gamma dose-rate contri-
       bution. PACT 2:84-96.

0785   Murray, A. S. and Wintle, A. G. (1979) Beta source
       calibration. PACT 3:419-427.

0786   Namby, K. S. V. (1979) Influence of rare earth im-
       purities on TL characteristics. PACT 3:298-310.

0787   Nicklin, K. and Fleming, S. J. (1980) A bronze
       "carnivore skull" from Oron, Nigeria. MASCA journal
       1(4):104-105.

0788   Ralph, E. K. and Han, M. C. (1966) Dating of pottery
       by thermoluminescence. Nature 210:245-247.

0789 Ralph, E. K. and Han, M. C. (1969) Potential of thermoluminescence in supplementing radiocarbon dating. World archaeology 1(2):157-169.

0790 Rappolt, J. P. (1975) Analyses and thermoluminescent dating of a 'Chung'. MASCA newsletter 11(1):11.

0791 Rottländer, R. C. A. (1978) Thermolumineszenz. (Thermoluminescence). Archäologische Informationen 4:120-130.

0792 Sampson, E. H., Fleming, S. J. and Bray, W. (1972) Thermoluminescent dating of Colombian pottery in the Yotoco style. Archaeometry 14(1):119-126.

0793 Sasidharan, R., Sunta, C. M. and Namby, K. S. V. (1979) Phototransfer method of determining archaeological dose of pottery sherds. PACT 3:401-406.

0794 Sears, D. W. (1978) TL dating of meteorites. PACT 2:231-239.

0795 Seeley, M. A. (1975) Thermoluminescent dating in its application to archaeology: a review. Journal of archaeological science 2(1):17-43.

0796 Shaplin, P. D. (1978) Thermoluminescence and style in the authentication of ceramic sculpture from Oaxaca, Mexico. Archaeometry 20(1):47-54.

0797 Simon, K. H. (1976) Ergebnisse der archäologischen Altersbestimmung mittels Thermolumineszenz. (Results of archaeological age determination by means of thermoluminescence). Naturwissenschaftliche Rundschau 29(5):167-168.

0798 Singhvi, A. K. and Zimmerman, D. W. (1979) The luminescent minerals in fine-grain samples from archaeological ceramics. Archaeometry 21(1):73-77.

0799 Skupinska-Lovset, I. and Fleming, S. J. (1979) A Scythian figurine from Beth Shean. MASCA journal 1(3):76-77.

0800 Srirath, S. and Fremlin, J. H. (1968) Non-uniformity in the thermoluminescence of "pot boilers". In: D. J. McDougall, ed., Thermoluminescence of geological materials. New York: Academic Press, 427-429.

78

0801 Sunta, C. M. and Kathuria, S. P. (1978) Factors in-
fluencing the kinetics of glow-peaks. PACT 2:189-199.

0802 Sutton, S. R. and Zimmerman, D. W. (1976) Thermoluminescent dating using zircon grains from
archaeologic ceramics. Archaeometry 18(2):125-134.

0803 Sutton, S. R. and Zimmerman, D. W. (1978) Thermoluminescence dating: radioactivity in quartz.
Archaeometry 20(1):67-69.

0804 Tite, M. S. (1966) Thermoluminescent dating of ancient
ceramics: a reassessment. Archaeometry 9:155-169.

0805 Tite, M. S. and Waine, J. (1962) Thermoluminescent
dating: a reappraisal. Archaeometry 5:53-79.

0806 Turetken, N. et al. (1979) TL and electron spin
resonance studies of stalactites from a cave in the
southern part of Turkey. PACT 3:266-280.

0807 Valladas, H. (1977) On the magnetic separation of
quartz for the thermoluminescence dating of an
ancient kiln. Archaeometry 19(1):88-95.

0808 Valladas, G. (1978) Thermoluminescence dating of burnt
stones from a prehistoric site. PACT 2:180-184.

0809 Valladas, G. (1979) A gamma ray irradiator. PACT
3:439-442.

0810 Valladas, G. (1979) A problem encountered in dating
quartz by thermoluminescence. Archaeo-Physika
10:499-505.

0811 Valladas, G. and Gillot, P. Y. (1978) Dating of the
Olby lava flows using heated quartz pebbles: some
problems. PACT 2:141-150.

0812 Valladas, G., Gillot, P. Y. and Guerin, P. (1979)
Dating plagioclases. PACT 3:251-257.

0813 Valladas, G. and Valladas, H. (1979) High temperature
thermoluminescence. Archaeo-Physika 10:506-510.

0814 Varma, M. N. and Garriveau, G. W. (1979) A precise
alpha source calibration for TL dating. PACT 3:414-8.

0815 Vaz, J. E. and Cruxent, J. M. (1975) Determination of the provenience of Majolica pottery found in the Caribbean area using its gamma-ray induced thermoluminescence. American antiquity 40(1):71-82.

0816 Visocekas, R. (1979) Miscellaneous aspects of artificial TL of calcite: emission spectra, athermal detrapping and anomalous fading. PACT 3:258-265.

0817 Wagner, G. A. and Bischof, H. (1977) Echtheitstests mittels Thermolumineszenz an altchinesischen Keramikplastiken. (Authenticity tests by means of thermoluminescence on ancient Chinese ceramic objects). Archäologie und Naturwissenschaften 1:20-41.

0818 Warren, S. E. (1978) Thermoluminescence dating of pottery: an assessment of the dose-rate from rubidium. Archaeometry 20(1):71-72.

0819 Watson, J. R. (1976) Thermoluminescent dating of Florida flint artifacts--recent developments. MASCA newsletter 12(2):3-4.

0820 Whittle, E. (1975) Thermoluminescent dating of Egyptian Predynastic pottery from Hemamieh and Qurna-Tarif. Archaeometry 17(1):119-122.

0821 Whittle, E. and Arnaud, J. M. (1975) Thermoluminescent dating of Neolithic and Chalcolithic pottery from sites in central Portugal. Archaeometry 17(1):5-24.

0822 Willett, F. and Fleming, S. J. (1976) A catalogue of important Nigerian copper-alloy castings dated using thermoluminescence. Archaeometry 18(2): 135-146.

0823 Wintle, A. G. (1973) Anomalous fading of thermoluminescence in mineral samples. Nature 245:143-144.

0824 Wintle, A. G. (1978) Anomalous fading. PACT 2:240-244.

0825 Wintle, A. G. and Aitken, M. J. (1977) Thermoluminescence dating of burnt flint: application to a Lower Palaeolithic site, Terra Amata. Archaeometry 19(2):111-130.

0826 Wintle, A. G. and Huntley, D. J. (1979) TL dating of sediments. PACT 3:374-380.

0827 Wintle, A. G. and Murray, A. S. (1977) Thermoluminescent dating: reassessment of the fine grain dose-rate. Archaeometry 19(1):95-98.

0828 Wintle, A. G. and Oakley, K. P. (1972) Thermoluminescent dating of fired rock-crystal from Bellan Bandi Palassa, Ceylon. Archaeometry 14(2):277-279.

0829 Wright, D. A. (1979) Pre-dose thermoluminescence measurements at Durham. PACT 3:336-344.

0830 Zimmerman, D. W. (1971) Thermoluminescent dating using fine grains from pottery. Archaeometry 13(1):29-52.

0831 Zimmerman, D. W. (1971) Uranium distributions in archaeological ceramics: dating of radioactive inclusions. Science 174:818-819.

0832 Zimmerman, D. W. (1978) Introduction to basic procedures for sample preparation and thermoluminescence measurement of ceramics. PACT 2:1-6.

0833 Zimmerman, D. W. (1979) TL dating using zircon grains. PACT 3:458-465.

0834 Zimmerman, D. W. and Huxtable, J. (1969) Recent applications and developments in thermoluminescent dating. Archaeometry 11:105-108.

0835 Zimmerman, D. W. and Huxtable, J. (1970) Some thermoluminescent dates for Linear Pottery. Antiquity 44:304-305.

0836 Zimmerman, D. W. and Huxtable, J. (1971) Thermoluminescent dating of Upper Palaeolithic fired clay from Dolní Věstonice. Archaeometry 13(1):53-58.

0837 Zimmerman, D. W., Yuhas, M. P. and Meyers, P. (1974) Thermoluminescence authenticity measurements on core material from the bronze horse of the New York Metropolitan Museum of Art. Archaeometry 16(1):19-30.

C. Non-radiometric methods

1. Archaeomagnetic dating

0838 Abrahamsen, N. (1973) Archaeomagnetic tilt correction on bricks. Archaeometry 15(2):267-274.

0839 Aitken, M. J. (1958) Magnetic dating--I. Archaeometry 1:16-20.

0840 Aitken, M. J. (1960) Magnetic dating. Archaeometry 3:41-44.

0841 Aitken, M. J. (1964) Archaeomagnetic results: some geophysical implications. Archaeometry 7:43-46.

0842 Aitken, M. J. (1964) Remanent magnetism in ancient ceramics and pottery kilns. Proceedings of the British ceramic society 2:143-149.

0843 Aitken, M. J. and Harold, M. R. (1959) Magnetic dating--II. Archaeometry 2:17-20.

0844 Aitken, M. J., Harold, M. R. and Weaver, G. H. (1964) Some archaeomagnetic evidence concerning the secular variation in Britain. Nature 201:659-660.

0845 Aitken, M. J. and Hawley, H. N. (1966) Magnetic dating--III: further archaeomagnetic measurements in Britain. Archaeometry 9:187-197.

0846 Aitken, M. J. and Hawley, H. N. (1967) Archaeomagnetic measurements in Britain--IV. Archaeometry 10:129-135.

0847 Aitken, M. J. and Hawley, H. N. (1971) Archaeomagnetism: evidence for magnetic refraction in kiln structures. Archaeometry 13(1):83-85.

0848 Aitken, M. J., Hawley, H. N. and Weaver, G. H. (1963) Magnetic dating: further archaeomagnetic measurements in Britain. Archaeometry 6:76-80.

0849 Aitken, M. J. and Weaver, G. H. (1962) Magnetic dating: some archaeomagnetic measurements in Britain. Archaeometry 5:4-22.

0850   Aitken, M. J. and Weaver, G. H. (1965) Recent archaeo-
       magnetic results in England. Journal of geomagnetism
       and geoelectricity 17(3/4):391.

0851   Athavale, R. N. (1966) Intensity of the geomagnetic
       field in India over the past 4000 years. Nature
       210:1310-1312.

0852   Athavale, R. N. (1969) Intensity of the geomagnetic
       field in prehistoric Egypt. Earth and planetary
       science letters 6:221-224.

0853   Barbetti, M. (1976) Archaeomagnetic analyses of six
       Glozelian ceramic artifacts. Journal of
       archaeological science 3:137-151.

0854   Barbetti, M. (1979) Determination of ancient geo-
       magnetic strengths from specimens with multi-
       component magnetizations. Journal of
       archaeological science 6(2):195-199.

0855   Barbetti, M. et al. (1980) Archaeomagnetic results
       from late Pleistocene hearths at Etiolles and
       Marsangy, France. Archaeometry 22(1):25-46.

0856   Barbetti, M. et al. (1980) Palaeomagnetism and the
       search for very ancient fireplaces in Africa:
       results from a million-year-old Acheulian site in
       Ethiopia. Anthropologie (Brno) 18(2/3):299-304.

0857   Barbetti, M. and McElhinny, M. (1972) Evidence of a
       geomagnetic excursion 30,000 yr B.P. Nature
       239(5371):327-330.

0858   Barraclough, D. R. (1974) Spherical harmonical analy-
       sis of the geomagnetic field for eight epochs
       between 1600 and 1910. Geophysical journal of the
       royal astronomical society 36:497.

0859   Becker, H. (1979) Archaeomagnetic investigations in
       Anatolia from prehistoric and Hittite sites (first
       preliminary results). Archaeo-Physika 10:382-387

0860   Belshé, J. C., Cook, K. and Cook, R. M. (1963) Some
       archaeomagnetic results from Greece. The annual of
       the British school of archaeology at Athens 58:8.

0861 Bock, R. and Franz, L. (1937) Ein naturwissenschaftliches Hilfsmittel zur vorgeschichtlichen Chronologie. (A scientific aid to prehistoric chronology). Nachrichtenblatt für deutsche Vorzeit 13(4):65.

0862 Bonhommet, N. and Zähringer, J. (1969) Paleomagnetism and potassium-argon age determinations of the Laschamp geomagnetic polarity event. Earth and planetary science letters 6:43-46.

0863 Brice, W. et al. (1976) A manuscript confirmation of archaeomagnetic determinations in the Mediterranean region. Archaeometry 18(2):228-229.

0864 Brock, A. and Isaac, G. (1974) Palaeomagnetic stratigraphy and chronology of hominid-bearing sediments east of Lake Rudolf, Kenya. Nature 249:344-348.

0865 Brock, A. (1977) Magnetic dating methods in prehistory. South African archaeological bulletin 32(125):5-13.

0866 Bucha, V. (1965) Results of archaeomagnetic research in Czechoslovakia for the epoch from 4400 B.C. to the present. Journal of geomagnetism and geoelectricity 17(3/4):407-412.

0867 Bucha, V. (1967) Archaeomagnetic and palaeomagnetic study of the magnetic field of the earth in the past 600,000 years. Nature 213:1005-1007.

0868 Bucha, V. (1967) Intensity of the Earth's magnetic field during archaeological times in Czechoslovakia. Archaeometry 10:12-22.

0869 Bucha, V. et al. (1970) Geomagnetic intensity: changes during the past 3000 years in the western hemisphere. Science 168:111-114.

0870 Bucha, V. and Mellaart, J. (1967) Archaeomagnetic intensity measurements on some Neolithic samples from Çatal Hüyük (Anatolia). Archaeometry 10:23-25.

0871 Bucha, V. and Neustupný, E. (1967) Changes of the Earth's magnetic field and radiocarbon dating. Nature 215:261.

84

0872 Burlatskaja, S. P. (1961) Drevnee magnitnoe pole Zemli
v rajone g. Tbilisi po arkheomagnitnym dannym. (The
ancient magnetic field of the Earth in the region of
Tbilisi according to archaeomagnetic data).
Geomagnetizm i aëronomija 1(5):803.

0873 Burlatskaja, S. P. (1962) O datirovanii arkheologičeskikh ob"ektov arkheomagnitnym metodom. (On the
dating of archaeological objects by the archaeomagnetic method). Sovetskaja arkheologija 3:99-104.

0874 Burlatskaja, S. P. (1963) Datirovanie arkheologičeskikh ob"ektov arkheomagnitnym metodom. (The
dating of archaeological objects by the archaeomagnetic method). Sovetskaja arkheologija 4:115-121.

0875 Burlatskaja, S. P. (1965) Arkheomagnetizm. Issledovanie
magnitnogo polja Zemli v prošlye ëpokhi. (Archaeomagnetism. Investigation of the magnetic field of
the Earth in former epochs). Moskva: Akademija
Nauk SSSR. Institut fiziki Zemli. 128p.

0876 Burlatskaya, S. P. et al. (1970) Archaeomagnetic
research in the U.S.S.R.: recent results and
spectral analysis. Archaeometry 12(1):73-85.

0877 Burlatskaya, S. P. and Braginsky, S. I. (1978) The
comparison of archaeomagnetic data with the
analytical representation of the geomagnetic field
for the last 2000 years. Archaeometry 20(1):73-83.

0878 Burlatskaja, S. P. and Nečaeva, T. B. (1965)
Datirovanie arkheologičeskikh ob"ektov arkheomagnitnym metodom. (The dating of archaeological
objects by the archaeomagnetic method). Materialy i
issledovanija po arkheologii SSSR 129:50-61.

0879 Burlatskaja, S. P. and Nečaeva, T. B. (1968)
Datirovanie obraztsov Černjakhovskoj kul'tury arkheomagnitnym metodom. (The dating of samples of the
Černjakhovskaja culture by the archaeomagnetic
method). Sovetskaja arkheologija 4:258-263.

0880 Burlatskaja, S. P., Nečaeva, T. B. and Petrova, G. N.
(1966) Čto takoe arkheomagnetizm? (What is archaeomagnetism?). Zemlja i vselennaja 3:42-50.

0881 Burlatskaya, S. P., Nechaeva, T. B. and Petrova, G. N. (1969) Some archaeomagnetic data indicative of the westward drift of the geomagnetic field. Archaeometry 11:115-130.

0882 Burlatskaja, S. P. and Petrova, G. N. (1961) Arkheomagnitnyj metod izučenija izmenenij geomagnitnogo polja v prŏslom. (The archaeomagnetic method of the study of the changes in the geomagnetic field in the past). Geomagnetizm i aeronomija 1(1):111.

0883 Burlatskaja, S. P. and Petrova, G. N. (1961) Pervye rezul'taty izučenija geomagnitnogo polja v prošlom arkheomagnitnym metodom. (The first results of a study of the geomagnetic field in the past by the archaeomagnetic method). Geomagnetizm i aeronomija 1(2):262.

0884 Burlatskaja, S. P. and Petrova, G. N. (1961) Vosstanovlenie kartiny izmenenija magnitnogo polja Zemli v prošlom s pomošč'ju arkheomagnitnogo metoda. (A reconstruction of a picture of the changes in the magnetic field of the Earth in the past with the help of the archaeomagnetic method). Geomagnetizm i aeronomija 1(3):426.

0885 Burnham, R. J. P. and Tarling, D. H. (1975) Magnetization of shards as an assistance to the reconstruction of pottery vessels. Studies in conservation 20(3):152-157.

0886 Clarke, D. L. and Connah, G. (1962) Remanent magnetism and Beaker chronology. Antiquity 36:206-209.

0887 Collinson, D. W., Creer, K. M. and Runcorn, S. K., eds. (1967) Methods in palaeomagnetism. Amsterdam: Elsevier.

0888 Cook, R. M. (1958) Intensity of remanent magnetization of archaeological remains. Nature 181:1421-1422.

0889 Cook, R. M. and Belshé, J. C. (1958) Archaeomagnetism: a preliminary report on Britain. Antiquity 32:167-178.

0890 Cox, A. (1969) Geomagnetic reversals. Science 163:237-246.

0891 Cox, A., Hillhouse, J. and Fuller, M. (1975) Paleo-
       magnetic records of polarity transitions, excursions
       and secular variation. Transactions of the American
       geophysical union 13(3):185-189.

0892 Creer, K. M. and Kopper, J. S. (1974) Paleomagnetic
       dating of cave paintings in Tito Bustillo Cave,
       Asturias, Spain. Science 168:348-350.

0893 DuBois, R. L. (1971) Archeomagnetic dating of
       archeological sites. Newsletter of the Oklahoma
       anthropological society 19(2):7-9.

0894 DuBois, R. L. (1975) Secular variation in the south-
       western United States as suggested by archeo-
       magnetic studies. In: R. F. Fisher et al., eds.,
       Proceedings of the Takesi Nagata conference.
       Greenbelt: Goddard Space Flight Center, 133-144.

0895 DuBois, R. L. and Watanabe, N. (1965) Preliminary
       results of investigations made to study the use of
       Indian pottery to determine the paleointensity of
       the geomagnetic field for the United States 600-1400
       A.D. Journal of geomagnetism and geoelectricity
       17:417-423.

0896 Eighmy, J. L., Sternberg, R. S. and Butler, R. F.
       (1980) Archaeomagnetic dating in the American
       Southwest. American antiquity 45(3):507-517.

0897 Griffiths, D. H. (1957) The remanent magnetism of
       varved clays from Sweden. Nature 179:4549.

0898 Harold, M. R. (1960) Magnetic dating: kiln wall
       fall-out. Archaeometry 3:45-46.

0899 Harold, M. R. (1960) Magnetic dating: the spinning
       magnetometer. Archaeometry 3:47-49.

0900 Hartley, B. R. (1962) Archaeological dating evidence
       for Romano-British pottery kilns. Archaeometry 5:1-3.

0901 Hawley, H. N. (1964) Magnetic dating: the use of
       compass readings for orientation marking.
       Archaeometry 7:47-50.

0902 Hurst, J. G. (1962) Post-Roman archaeological dating and its correlation with archaeomagnetic results. Archaeometry 5:25-27.

0903 Hurst, J. G. (1963) Post-Roman archaeological dating and its correlation with archaeological results. Archaeometry 6:81-82.

0904 Hurst, J. G. (1966) Post-Roman archaeological dating and its correlation with archaeomagnetic results. Archaeometry 9:198-199.

0905 Kawai, N. et al. (1972) Archaeomagnetism in Iran. Nature 236(5344):223-224.

0906 Kitazawa, K. (1970) Intensity of the geomagnetic field in Japan for the last 10,000 years. Journal of geophysical research 75:7403-7411.

0907 Kitazawa, K. and Kobayashi, K. (1968) Intensity variation of the geomagnetic field during the past 4000 years in South America. Journal of geomagnetism and geoelectricity 20(1):7-19.

0908 Koenigsberger, I. (1932) Zu Folgheraiters Bestimmungen des magnetischen Erdfeldes aus der Magnitisierung gebrannter Tongegenstande. (On Folgheraiter's determinations of the magnetic field of the Earth from the magnetization of fired clay objects). Gerlands Beiträge zur Geophysik 35(1):51-54.

0909 Kopper, J. S. and Creer, K. M. (1973) Cova dets Alexandres: paleomagnetic dating and archeological interpretation of its sediments. Caves and Karst 15:13-20.

0910 Kopper, J. S. and Creer, R. M. (1976) Paleomagnetic dating and stratigraphic interpretation in archeology. MASCA newsletter 12(1):1-3.

0911 Kopper, J. S. and Papamarinopoulos, S. (1978) Human evolution and geomagnetism. Journal of field archaeology 5(4):443-452.

0912 Kovacheva, M. (1969) Inclination of the earth's magnetic field during the last 2000 years in Bulgaria. Journal of geomagnetism and geoelectricity 21(3):1-5.

0913 Kovacheva, M. (1972) Upon the intensity of the ancient magnetic field during the last 2000 years in southeastern Europe. Earth and planetary science letters 17(1):199-206.

0914 Kovacheva, M. (1976) Archaeomagnetic investigations of some prehistoric sites in Bulgaria. Archaeometry 18(1):99-106.

0915 Kovacheva, M. (1979) Archaeomagnetic investigations in Bulgaria. Archaeo-Physika 10:477-485.

0916 Kovacheva, M. and Veljovich, D. (1977) Geomagnetic field variations in southeastern Europe between 6500 and 100 years b.c. Earth and planetary science letters 37:131-138.

0917 Nagata, T., Arai, Y. and Momose, K. (1963) Secular variation of the geomagnetic total force during the last 5000 years. Journal of geophysical research 68(18):5277-5281.

0918 Nagata, T., Kobayashi, K. and Schwarz, E. J. (1965) Archaeomagnetic intensity studies of southern and central America. Journal of geomagnetism and geoelectricity 17:399-405.

0919 Nodia, M. Z. et al. (1966) O metodike izučenija vekovykh variatsij magnitnogo polja Zemli do našej ery. (On a method of studying the secular variations of the magnetic field of the Earth up to our era). Geomagnetizm i aëronomija 3:613-614.

0920 Pucher, R. (1978) Methode und Möglichkeiten paläomagnetischer Untersuchungen in der Archäologie. (Methods and possibilities of paleomagnetic investigations in archaeology). Nachrichten aus Niedersachsens Urgeschichte 46:127-145.

0921 Rogers, J., Fox, J. M. W. and Aitken, M. J. (1979) Magnetic anisotropy in ancient pottery. Nature 277(5698):644-646.

0922 Rusakov, O. M. and Zagniy, G. F. (1973) Archaeomagnetic secular variation study in the Ukraine and Moldavia. Archaeometry 15(1):153-157.

0923 Rusakov, O. M. and Zagniy, G. F. (1973) Intensity of
the geomagnetic field in the Ukraine and Moldavia
during the past 6000 years. Archaeometry 15(2):
275-285.

0924 Sasajima, S. (1965) Geomagnetic secular variation
revealed in baked earths from western Japan. Journal
of geomagnetism and geoelectricity 17:413-416.

0925 Schwarz, E. J. and Christie, K. W. (1967) Original
remanent magnetization of Ontario potsherds. Journal
of geophysical research 72:3263-3269.

0926 Smith, P. J. (1967) Ancient geomagnetic field inten-
sities--1. Historic and archaeological data: sets
H1-H9. Geophysical journal of the Royal Astronomical
Society 13:417.

0927 Smith, P. J. (1967) Ancient geomagnetic field inten-
sities--2. Geophysical journal of the Royal
Astronomical Society 13:483-486.

0928 Smith, P. J. (1967) Intensity of the Earth's magnetic
field in the geological past. Nature 216:989-990.

0929 Smith, P. J. (1967) The intensity of the ancient geomagnetic field: a review and analysis. Geophysical
journal of the Royal Astronomical Society
12:321-362.

0930 Smith, P. J. (1968) Ancient geomagnetic field inten-
sities--3. Historic and archaeological data: sets
H13X and H14-15. Geological data: sets G22-29.
Geophysical journal of the Royal Astronomical
Society 16:457-460.

0931 Tanguy, J. C. (1970) An archaeomagnetic study of
Mount Etna: the magnetic direction recorded in
lava flows subsequent to the twelfth century.
Archaeometry 12(2):115-128.

0932 Tarling, D. H. (1971) Principles and applications of
palaeomagnetism. London: Chapman & Hall.

0933 Tarling, D. H. (1975) Archaeomagnetism: the dating of
archaeological materials by their magnetic properties. World archaeology 7(2):185-197.

0934 Thellier, E. (1936) Détermination de la direction de l'aimantation permanente des roches. Comptes rendus des séances de l'académie des sciences 203:743-744.

0935 Thellier, E. (1966) Le champ magnétique terrestre fossile. Nucleus 7(1-3):1-35.

0936 Thellier, E. (1976) Méthode archéomagnétique de datation. Colloque 1. IX Congrès, Union internationale des sciences préhistoriques et protohistoriques. Nice, 133-159.

0937 Thellier, E. and Thellier, O. (1946) Sur l'intensité du champ magnétique terrestre en France, à l'époque gallo-romaine. Compte rendue mensuels de séances de l'académie des sciences d'outre-mer. Paris, 222.

0938 Thellier, E. and Thellier, O. (1951) Sur la direction du champ magnétique terrestre, retrouvée dur des parois des fours des époques Punique et Romaine, à Carthage. Compte rendus des séances de l'académie des sciences 223:1476-1478.

0939 Thellier, E. and Thellier, O. (1959) Sur l'intensité du champ magnétique terrestre dans le passé historique et géologique. Annales de géophysique 15(3):285-376.

0940 Thellier, E. and Thellier, O. (1962) Sur la possibilité de contrôles precis en archéomagnétisme. Journal of geomagnetism and geoelectricity 13:120-126.

0941 Thompson, R. et al. (1974) Palaeomagnetic study of Hoxnian lacustrine sediments. Archaeometry 16(2):233-237.

0942 Walton, D. (1977) Archaeomagnetic intensity measurements using a SQUID magnetometer. Archaeometry 19(2):192-200.

0943 Walton, D. (1979) Geomagnetic intensity in Athens between 2000 B.C. and A.D. 400. Nature 277(5698):643-644.

0944 Watanabe, N. (1958) Secular variation in the direction of geomagnetism as the standard scale for geomagnetochronology in Japan. Nature 182:383-384.

0945 Watanabe, N. (1959) The direction of remanent mag-
netism of baked earth and its applications to
chronology for anthropology and archaeology in
Japan: an introduction to geomagnetochronology.
Journal of the faculty of science, University of
Tokyo, section 5, 2:1-188.

0946 Watanabe, N. and DuBois, R. L. (1965) Some results of
an archaeomagnetic study of the secular variation in
the Southwest of North America. Journal of geomagnetism and geoelectricity 17:395-397.

0947 Weaver, G. H. (1962) Archaeomagnetic measurements on
the second Boston experimental kiln. Archaeometry
5:93-107.

0948 Weaver, G. H. (1966) Measurement of the past intensity
of the Earth's magnetic field. Archaeometry
9:174-186.

0949 Weaver, G. H. (1970) Some temperature related errors
in palaeomagnetic intensity measurements.
Archaeometry 12(1):87-95.

0950 Weaver, K. F. (1970) Magnetic clues help date the past.
National geographic 131:696-701.

0951 Wolfman, D. (1977) Archaeomagnetic date from the Baca
Float sites. In: D. E. Doyel, Excavations in the
middle Santa Cruz River valley, southeastern
Arizona. Contribution to highway salvage archaeology
in Arizona 44:187.

0952 Wolfman, D. (1979) Archeomagnetic dating in Arkansas.
Archaeo-Physika 10:522-533.

0953 Wollin, G. et al. (1971) Magnetism of the Earth and
climatic changes. Earth and planetary science
letters 12:175-183.

0954 Yukutake, T. (1961) Archaeomagnetic study on volcanic
rocks in Japan. Bulletin of the earthquake research
institute 39:467-476.

0955 Yukutake, T. (1971) Spherical harmonic analysis of the
earth's magnetic field for the 17th and 18th centuries. Journal of geomagnetism and geoelectricity
23(1):11.

2. Dendrochronology

0956 Baillie, M. G. L. (1973) A recently developed Irish tree-ring chronology. Tree-ring bulletin 33:15-28.

0957 Baillie, M. G. L. (1974) A tree-ring chronology for the dating of Irish post-medieval timbers. Ulster folklife 20:1-23.

0958 Baillie, M. G. L. (1976) Dendrochronology as a tool for the dating of vernacular buildings in the north of Ireland. Vernacular architecture 7:3-10.

0959 Baillie, M. G. L. (1977) The Belfast oak chronology to A.D. 1001. Tree-ring bulletin 37:1-12.

0960 Baillie, M. G. L. (1977) Dublin medieval dendro-chronology. Tree-ring bulletin 37:13-20.

0961 Baillie, M. G. L. (1977) An oak chronology for central Scotland. Tree-ring bulletin 37:33-44.

0962 Baillie, M. G. L. (1978) Dendrochronology for the Irish Sea province. British archaeological reports, British series 54(1):25-37.

0963 Baillie, M. G. L. and Pilcher, J. R. (1973) A simple crossdating program for tree-ring research. Tree-ring bulletin 33:7-14.

0964 Baldwin, G. C. (1935) Dates from Kinishba Pueblo. Tree-ring bulletin 1(4):30.

0965 Baldwin, G. C. (1935) Ring record of the Great Drought (1276-1299) in eastern Arizona. Tree-ring bulletin 2(2):11-12.

0966 Baldwin, G. C. (1938) Excavations at Kinishba Pueblo, Arizona. American antiquity 4:11-21.

0967 Baldwin, G. C. (1939) Dates from King's ruin. Tree-ring bulletin 5(3):23-24.

0968 Bannister, B. (1951) Tree-ring dates for the Gallina area, New Mexico. Tree-ring bulletin 17(3):21-22.

0969 Bannister, B. (1960) Southwestern dated ruins, VII. Tree-ring bulletin 23(1-4):19-21.

0970   Bannister, B. (1962) The interpretation of tree-ring
        dates. American antiquity 27(4):508-514.

0971   Bannister, B. (1965) Tree-ring dating of the ar-
        cheological sites in the Chaco Canyon region, New
        Mexico. Southwestern monuments association, technical
        series 6, part 2.

0972   Bannister, R. (1970) Dendrochronology in the Near East:
        current research and future potentialities. Pro-
        ceedings of the VII international congress of anthro-
        pology and ethnology. Moskva, 5:336-340.

0973   Barefoot, A. C. (1975) A Winchester dendrochronology
        for 1635 to 1972 A.D.: its validity and possible
        extension. Journal of the institute of wood science
        7:25-32.

0974   Bartholin, T. S. (1975) Dendrochronology of oak in
        southern Sweden. Tree-ring bulletin 35:25-29.

0975   Bartholin, T. S. (1978) Dendrochronology, wood
        anatomy and landscape development in south Sweden.
        British archaeological reports, supplementary series
        51:125-130.

0976   Batley, R. A. L. (1956) Some practical aspects of
        dendrochronology in New Zealand. Journal of the
        Polynesian society 65(3):232-244.

0977   Bauch, J. (1968) Die Problematik der geographischen
        Reichweite von Jahrringdatierungen an Beispielen aus
        der norddeutschen Tiefebene. (The problem of the
        geographical range of annual ring dating based on the
        examples from the North German Plain). Kunstchronik
        21:144-145.

0978   Bauch, J. (1970) Aufbau regionaler Standardjahrring-
        kurven zur Datierung historischer Bauten und Bild-
        tafeln. (The construction of regional standard annual
        ring curves for the dating of historical buildings
        and paintings). Mitteilungen der Bundesforschungs-
        anstatt für Forst- und Holzwirtschaft 77:43-58.

0979   Bauch, J. (1978) Tree-ring chronologies for the
        Netherlands. British archaeological reports,
        supplementary series 51:133-137.

0980 Bauch, J., Liese, W. and Eckstein, D. (1967) Über die Altersbestimmung von Eichholz in Norddeutschland mit Hilfe der Dendrochronologie. (On the age determination of oak wood in north Germany with the aid of dendrochronology). Holz als Roh- und Werkstoff 25:285-291.

0981 Becker, B. (1972) Absolute Chronologie der Nacheiszeit (Holozän) mit Hilfe der Dendrochronologie. (The absolute chronology of the Holocene with the aid of dendrochronology). Jahrbuch der Akademie der Wissenschaften und Literature, 143-145.

0982 Becker, B. (1972) Möglichkeiten für den Aufbau einer absoluten Jahrringschronologie des Postglazials anhand subfossiler Eichen aus Donauschottern. (Possibilities for the construction of an absolute annual ring chronology of the post-glacial period with the aid of subfossil oaks from the Danube). Berichte der deutschen botanischen Gesellschaft 85(1-4):29-45.

0983 Becker, B. (1978) Dendroecological zones of central European forest communities. British archaeological reports, supplementary series 51:101-114.

0984 Becker, B. and Delorme, A. (1978) Oak chronologies for Central Europe and their extension from medieval to prehistoric times. British archaeological reports, supplementary series 51:59-64.

0985 Becker, B. and Giertz-Siebenlist, V. (1970) Eine über 1100 jährige mitteleuropäische Tannenchronologie. (A Central European fir chronology over 1100 years). Flora 159:310-346.

0986 Bell, V. and Bell, R. E. (1958) Dendrochronological studies in New Zealand. Tree-ring bulletin 22(1-4):7-11.

0987 Berger, R., Giertz-Siebenlist, V. and Horn, W. (1971) Can German tree-ring curves be applied to France and England? Vernacular architecture 2:3-6.

0988 Bräker, O. U. (1978) Applications of dendrochronology in Switzerland. British archaeological reports, supplementary series 51:203-210.

0989 Bräker, O. U. and Lambert, G. (1978) The new dendro-chronology laboratories at Neuchâtel and Zürich. British archaeological reports, supplementary series 51:315-316.

0990 Bramhall, A. E. (1977) An improved scribe for dendrochronological annotations. Tree-ring bulletin 37:45-46.

0991 Brubaker, L. B. (1978) Effects of defoliation by Douglas-fir tussock moth on ring sequences of Douglas-fir and Grand-fir. Tree-ring bulletin 38:49-60.

0992 Bryan, B. (1934) Reading history from the diary of the trees. American forests 40:10-14.

0993 Bryson, R. A. and Dutton, J. A. (1961) Some aspects of the variance spectra of tree-rings and varves. Annals of the New York academy of sciences 95(1):580-604.

0994 Burgh, R. F. (1950) A Fremont Basket Maker house in Dinosaur National Monument. Tree-ring bulletin 16(3):19-20.

0995 Caldwell, W. W. (1960) Tree-ring dating in the Missouri Basin chronology program. Tree-ring bulletin 23(1-4):14-17.

0996 Černykh, N. B. (1967) Dendrokhronologija postroek drevnego Smolenska. (Dendrochronology of buildings of ancient Smolensk). Kratkie soobščenija Instituta Arkheologii 110:129-135.

0997 Colton, H. S. (1939) The date of Three Turkey House. Tree-ring bulletin 5(4):26.

0998 Corona, E. (1971) Studi dendrocronologici su S. Antimo di Montalcino (Siena). L'Italia forestale e montana 26:208-210.

0999 De Geer, E. H. (1935) Prehistoric bulwark in Gotland biochronologically dated. Geografiska annaler 17:501-531.

1000 Delorme, A. (1973) Aufbau einer Eichenjahrring-
chronologie für das südliche Weser- und Lineberg-
land. (The construction of an oak annual ring
chronology for the southern Weser and Leine uplands).
Forstarchiv 44:205-209.

1001 Delorme, A. (1977) Möglichkeiten der Überbrückung
regionaler teilchronologien zu einer überregionalen
Postglazialchronologie der Eiche für Mitteleuropa.
(Possibilities of bridging regional partial
chronologies and establishing a cross-regional post-
glacial chronology of the oak for Central Europe).
In: Dendrochronologie und postglaziale Klimaschwankungen in Europa. Wiesbaden: F. Steiner, 62-67.

1002 Delorme, A. (1978) A mean curve for oaks of the
southern Weser and Leine uplands: its usefulness
and characteristics. British archaeological reports,
supplementary series 51:45-53.

1003 Douglass, A. E. (1919-1936) Climatic cycles and tree
growth. Carnegie institution of Washington,
publication no. 289, three volumes.

1004 Douglass, A. E. (1921) Dating our prehistoric ruins.
Natural history 21:27-30.

1005 Douglass, A. E. (1935) Dating Pueblo Bonito and other
ruins of the Southwest. National geographic society,
contributed technical papers, Pueblo Bonito series 1.

1006 Douglass, A. E. (1935-1938) Estimated tree-ring
chronology. Tree-ring bulletin 1(4):27; 2(1):6;
2(2):13-16; 2(3):24; 3(2):16; 4(3):8; 5(1):8;
5(3):18-20.

1007 Douglass, A. E. (1936) The central pueblo chronology.
Tree-ring bulletin 2(4):29-34.

1008 Douglass, A. E. (1937) Typical ring record from Chaco
Canyon, 700 to 850, CK-331. Tree-ring bulletin
3(3):20-21.

1009 Douglass, A. E. (1938) Southwestern dated ruins: V.
Tree-ring bulletin 5(2):10-13.

1010 Douglass, A. E. (1939) Notes on beam dating by sap-
heart contact. Tree-ring bulletin 6(1):3-6.

1011 Douglass, A. E. (1941) Age of Forestdale ruin ex-
     cavated in 1939. Tree-ring bulletin 8(1):7-8.

1012 Douglass, A. E. (1941) Crossdating in dendrochronology.
     Journal of forestry 39(10:825-831.

1013 Douglass, A. E. (1941) Notes on the technique of tree-
     ring analysis, II. Tree-ring bulletin 7(4):28-34.

1014 Douglass, A. E. (1942) Checking the date of Bluff
     Ruin, Forestdale: a study in technique. Tree-ring
     bulletin 9(2):2-7.

1015 Douglass, A. E. (1943) Advances in dendrochronology,
     1943. Tree-ring bulletin 9(3):18-24.

1016 Douglass, A. E. (1944) Tabulation of dates for Bluff
     Ruin, Forestdale, Arizona. Tree-ring bulletin
     11(2):10-16.

1017 Douglass, A. E. (1945) Survey of sequoia studies.
     Tree-ring bulletin 11(4):26-32.

1018 Douglass, A. E. (1945) Survey of sequoia studies, II.
     Tree-ring bulletin 12(2):10-16.

1019 Douglass, A. E. (1946) Researches in dendrochronology.
     University of Utah bulletin 37(2); Biological series
     10(1).

1020 Douglass, A. E. (1946) Sequoia survey--III; miscel-
     laneous notes. Tree-ring bulletin 13(1):5-8.

1021 Douglass, A. E. (1947) Photographic tree-ring
     chronologies and the Flagstaff sequence. Tree-ring
     bulletin 14(2):10-16.

1022 Drew, L. G., ed. (1972) Tree-ring chronologies of
     western America: vol. II, Arizona, New Mexico,
     Texas. Chronology series 1. Laboratory of Tree-Ring
     Research.

1023 Drew, L. G., ed. (1972) Tree-ring chronologies of
     western America: vol. III, California and Nevada.
     Chronology series 1. Laboratory of Tree-Ring
     Research.

98

1024   Eckstein, D. (1972) Tree-ring research in Europe.
        Tree-ring bulletin 32:1-18.

1025   Eckstein, D. (1978) Regional tree-ring chronologies
        along parts of the North Sea coast. British
        archaeological reports, supplementary series 51:117-
        124.

1026   Eckstein, D., Bauch, J. and Liese, W. (1970) Aufbau
        einer Jahrringchronologie von Eichenholz für die
        Datierung historischer Bauten in Norddeutschland.
        (Construction of an annual ring chronology from oak
        for the dating of historical buildings in north
        Germany). Holz Zentralblatt 96:674-676.

1027   Eckstein, D., Brongers, J. A. and Bauch, J. (1975)
        Tree-ring research in the Netherlands. Tree-ring
        bulletin 35:1-13.

1028   Eckstein, D. and Es, W. A. van (1972) Dendro-
        chronologische Untersuchungen von Daubenbrunnen aus
        der frühmittelalterlichen Siedlung Dorestad, Holland.
        (Dendrochronological investigations of staved wells
        from the early medieval settlement of Dorestad,
        Holland). Kunde 23:220-226.

1029   Eckstein, D. and Liese, W. (1971) Jahrring-
        chronologische Untersuchungen zur Altersbestimmungen
        von Holzbauten der Siedlung Haithabu. (Investigations
        of the annual ring chronology for age determinations
        of the wooden buildings at the settlement Haithabu).
        Germania 49:155-168.

1030   Eckstein, D., Mathieu, K. and Bauch, J. (1972) Jahr-
        ringanalyse und Baugeschichtsforschung--Aufbau einer
        Jahrringchronologie für die Vier- und Marschlande bei
        Hamburg. (Annual ring analysis and the investigation
        of architectural history--the construction of an
        annual ring chronology for the marshlands by
        Hamburg). Verhandlungen des naturwiss. Vereins
        Hamburg 16:73-100.

1031   Ferguson, C. W. (1949) Additional dates for Nine Mile
        Canyon, northeastern Utah. Tree-ring bulletin
        16(2):10-11.

1032   Ferguson, C. W. (1968) Bristlecone pine: science and
        esthetics. Science 159:839-846.

1033 Ferguson, C. W. (1969) A 7104-year annual tree-ring chronology for bristlecone pine, Pinus aristata, from the White Mountains, California. Tree-ring bulletin 29(3/4):3-29.

1034 Ferguson, C. W. (1970) Dendrochronology of bristlecone pine, Pinus aristata. Establishment of a 7484-year chronology in the White Mountains of eastern-central California, U.S.A. In: I. U. Olsson, ed., Radiocarbon variations and absolute chronology. Stockholm: Almqvist & Wiksell; New York: J. Wiley, 237-259.

1035 Ferguson, C. W. (1972) Dendrochronology of bristlecone pine prior to 4000 B.C. Proceedings of the eighth international conference on radiocarbon dating. Lower Hutt City, New Zealand, 1:A1-A10.

1036 Ferguson, C. W. and Black, D. M. (1952) Tree-ring chronologies on the north rim of the Grand Canyon. Tree-ring bulletin 19(2):12-18.

1037 Ferguson, C. W., Huber, B. and Suess, H. E. (1966) Determination of the age of Swiss lake dwellings as an example of dendrochronologically-calibrated radiocarbon dating. Zeitschrift für Naturforschung 21A(7):1173-1177.

1038 Fletcher, J. M. (1977) Tree-ring chronologies for the 6th. to 16th. centuries for oaks of southern and eastern England. Journal of archaeological science 4:335-352.

1039 Fletcher, J. M. (1978) Dating the geographical migration of Quercus petraea and Q. robur in holocene times. Tree-ring bulletin 38:45-47.

1040 Fletcher, J. M. (1978) Oak chronologies for eastern and southern England: principles for their construction and application: their comparison with others in North-West Europe. British archaeological reports, supplementary series 51:139-156.

1041 Fletcher, J. M. (1980) A list of tree-ring dates for building timber in southern England and Wales. Vernacular architecture 11:32-38.

1042 Fletcher, J. M. and Dabrowska, A. (1976) Tree-ring examination of timbers from the sixth-century well at Portchester Castle. Archaeometry 18(1):92-99.

1043 Fletcher, J. M. and Switsur, R. (1973) North Elmham; the dating. Current archaeology 4(1):25-28.

1044 Fletcher, J. M., Tapper, M. C. and Walker, F. S. (1974) Dendrochronology--a reference curve for slow grown oaks, A.D. 1230 to 1546. Archaeometry 16(1):31-40.

1045 Fletcher, J. M., Tapper, M. C. and Walker, F. S. (1978) Tree-ring studies. In: V. Fenwick, ed., The Graveney Boat: a 10th century find from Kent. British archaeological reports, British series 53:111-124.

1046 Franke, P. R. (1933) New dates for Mesa Verde ruins. Mesa Verde notes. Colorado: Mesa Verde National Park, 4:19-20.

1047 Freundlich, J. C. (1977) C-14 Datierung und Dendro- chronologie. (C-14 dating and dendrochronology). In: Dendrochronologie und postglaziale Klimaschwankungen in Europa. Wiesbaden: F. Steiner, 99-114.

1048 Fritts, H. C. (1966) Growth-rings of trees: their correlation with climate. Science 154(3752):973-979.

1049 Fritts, H. C. (1969) Bristlecone pine in the White Mountains of California: growth and ring-width characteristics. Papers of the laboratory of tree- ring research, 4. Tuscon: Univ. of Arizona Press.

1050 Fritts, H. C. et al. (1965) Tree-ring characteristics along a vegetation gradient in northern Arizona. Ecology 46(4):393-401.

1051 Fürst, O. (1978) Geographical and temporal differences in the fluctuations of ring widths in central Europe: climatic implications. British archaeological reports, supplementary series 51:65-76.

1052 Getty, H. T. (1935) New dates from Mesa Verde. Tree- ring bulletin 1(3):21-23.

1053 Getty, H. T. (1935) Dates from Spruce Tree House. Tree- ring bulletin 1(4):29.

1054 Giddings, J. L. (1938) Buried wood from Fairbanks,
      Alaska. Tree-ring bulletin 4(4):3-5.

1055 Giddings, J. L. (1938) Recent tree-ring work in Alaska.
      Tree-ring bulletin 5(2):16.

1056 Giddings, J. L. (1940) The application of tree-ring
      dates to Arctic sites. Tree-ring bulletin 7(2):10-14.

1057 Giddings, J. L. (1941) Dendrochronology in northern
      Alaska. University of Alaska publication 4. 107p.

1058 Giddings, J. L. (1942) Dated sites on the Kobuk River,
      Alaska. Tree-ring bulletin 9(1):2-8.

1059 Giddings, J. L. (1947) Mackenzie River delta
      chronology. Tree-ring bulletin 13(4).

1060 Giddings, J. L. (1948) Chronology of the Kobuk-
      Kotzebue sites. Tree-ring bulletin 14(4):26-32.

1061 Giddings, J. L. (1951) The forest edge at Norton Bay,
      Alaska. Tree-ring bulletin 18(1):2-6.

1062 Giddings, J. L. (1953) Yukon River spruce growth.
      Tree-ring bulletin 20(1):2-5.

1063 Giddings, J. L. (1954) Tree-ring dating in the
      American Arctic. Tree-ring bulletin 20(3/4):23-25.

1064 Gindel, J. (1944) Aleppo pine as a medium for tree-
      ring analysis. Tree-ring bulletin 11(1):6-8.

1065 Glock, W. S. (1937) Principles and methods of tree-
      ring analysis. Carnegie institution of Washington
      publication 486.

1066 Golson, J. (1955) Dating New Zealand's prehistory.
      Journal of the Polynesian society 64(1):113-136.

1067 Guyan, W. U. (1977) Archäologie und Dendrochronologie
      der jungsteinzeitlichen Moordörfer Thayngen-Weier.
      (Archaeology and dendrochronology of the Neolithic
      moor settlements at Thayngen-Weier). In: Dendro-
      chronologie und postglaziale Klimaschwankungen in
      Europa. Wiesbaden: F. Steiner, 126-142.

1068 Hall, E. T. (1951) Southwestern dated ruins. VI. Tree-ring bulletin 17(4):26-28.

1069 Hargrave, L. L. (1933) Pueblo II houses of the San Francisco Mts., Arizona. Museum of northern Arizona bulletin 4:15-75.

1070 Hargrave, L. L. (1936) The field collector of beam material. Tree-ring bulletin 2(3):22-24.

1071 Harlan, T. P. (1966) Tree-ring dates from the Navajo Reservoir district. In: F. W. Eddy, ed., Prehistory in the Navajo Reservoir district, northwestern New Mexico. Museum of New Mexico papers in anthropology 15:516-522.

1072 Haugen, R. K. (1967) Tree ring indices: a circumpolar comparison. Science 158:773-775.

1073 Haury, E. W. (1935) Dates from Gila Pueblo. Tree-ring bulletin 3(1):3-4.

1074 Haury, E. W. (1935) Tree-rings: the archaeologist's timepiece. American antiquity 1:98-108.

1075 Haury, E. W. (1938) Southwestern dated ruins: II. Tree-ring bulletin 4(3):3-4.

1076 Haury, E. W. (1940) New tree-ring dates from the Forestdale Valley, east-central Arizona. Tree-ring bulletin 7(2):14-16.

1077 Haury, E. W. (1942) Some implications of the Bluff Ruin dates. Tree-ring bulletin 9(2):7-8.

1078 Haury, E. W. and Flora, I. F. (1937) Basket-maker III dates from the vicinity of Durango, Colorado. Tree-ring bulletin 4(1):7-8.

1079 Haury, E. W. and Hargrave, L. L. (1931) Recently dated pueblo ruins in Arizona. Smithsonian miscellaneous coll. 82, no. 11.

1080 Hawley, F. (1934) The significance of the dated pre-history of Chetro Ketl, Chaco Canyon, New Mexico. Albuquerque: Univ. of New Mexico. 100p.

1081 Hawley, F. (1938) Dendrochronology: can we fix pre-
      historic dates in the Middle West by tree-rings?
      Indiana history bulletin 15:118-128.

1082 Hawley, F. (1938) Dendrochronology in two Mississippi
      drainage tree-ring areas. Tree-ring bulletin 5(1):
      3-6.

1083 Hawley, F. (1938) Southwestern dated ruins: IV. Tree-
      ring bulletin 5(1):6-7.

1084 Hayes, A. C. and Lancaster, J. A. (1962) Site 1060, a
      Basket Maker III pithouse of Chapin Mesa, Mesa
      Verde National Park. Tree-ring bulletin 24(1/2):
      14-16.

1085 Heyworth, A. (1978) Submerged forests around the
      British Isles: their dating and relevance as in-
      dicators of postglacial land and sea-level changes.
      British archaeological reports, supplementary series
      51:279-290.

1086 Hillam, J. and Ryder, P. (1980) Tree-ring dating of
      vernacular buildings from Yorkshire. Vernacular
      architecture 11:23-31.

1087 Høeg, O. A. (1956) Growth-ring research in Norway.
      Tree-ring bulletin 21(1-4):2-15.

1088 Hollstein, E. (1965) Jahrringchronologische Datierung
      von Eichenhölzern ohne Waldkante. (Annual ring
      dating of oak timbers without bark). Bonner
      Jahrbücher 165:12-27.

1089 Hollstein, E. (1966) Jahrringchronologien aus dem
      romanischen Haus in Münstereifel. (Annual ring
      chronologies from the romanesque house in
      Münstereifel). Jahrbuch der rheinischen
      Denkmalpflege 26:149-151.

1090 Hollstein, E. (1967) Jahrringchronologien aus vor-
      römischer und römischer Zeit. (Annual ring
      chronologies from the pre-Roman and Roman period).
      Germania 45:70-83.

104

1091   Hollstein, E. (1968) Dendrochronologische Unter-
        suchungen an den Domen von Trier und Speyer. (Dendro-
        chronological investigations on the domes at Trier
        and Speyer). Kunstchronik 21(6):168-181.

1092   Hollstein, E. (1970) Jahrringchronologie der 'Luxuria'.
        (Annual ring chronology of the 'Luxuria').
        Berliner Museen 20(1):16-23.

1093   Hollstein, E. (1978) Wood technology and the dating of
        oak: West German chronologies for oak and beech.
        British archaeological reports, supplementary series
        51:33-44.

1094   Hollstein, E. (1980) Mitteleuropäische Eichen-
        chronologie. (Central European oak chronology).
        Mainz am Rhein: Zabern.

1095   Huber, B. (1943) Über die Sicherheit jahrringchronolo-
        gischer Datierung. (On the certainty of ring
        chronology dating). Holz als Roh- und Werkstoff
        6:263-268.

1096   Huber, B. (1962) Jahrringchronologische Untersuchungen
        zur Baugeschichte der urnenfelderzeitlichen Siedlung
        Zug-Sumpf. (Annual ring chronology investigations
        for the building history of the Urnfield period
        settlement of Zug-Sumpf). Germania 40:44-56.

1097   Huber, B. (1967) Seeberg, Burgäschisee-Süd--
        Dendrochronologie. (Seeberg, Burgäschisee-Süd--
        dendrochronology). Acta bernensia 2:145-156.

1098   Huber, B. (1970) Dendrochronology of Central Europe.
        In: I. U. Olsson, ed., Radiocarbon variations and
        absolute chronology. Stockholm: Almqvist & Wiksell;
        New York: J. Wiley, 233-235.

1099   Huber, B. (1978) Annual tree-rings as an aid to
        climatology and chronology. British archaeological
        reports, supplementary series 51:11-14.

1100   Huber, B. (1978) Dendrochronology. British archaeolog-
        ical reports, supplementary series 51:15-26.

1101   Huber, B. and Giertz-Siebenlist, V. (1978) Our 1000-
        year-oak annual-ring chronology. British archaeolog-
        ical reports, supplementary series 51:27-32.

1102 Huber, B. and Holdheide, W. (1942) Jahrringchronologische Untersuchungen an Hölzern der bronze-
zeitlichen Wasserburg Buchau am Federsee. (Annual
ring chronology investigations on timbers of the
Bronze Age period Wasserburg Buchau on the Federsee).
Berichte der Deutschen botanischen Gesellschaft
60:261-283.

1103 Huber, B. and Jazewitsch, W. von (1956) Tree-ring
studies of the Forestry-Botany Institutes of
Tharandt and Munich. Tree-ring bulletin 21(1-4):
28-30.

1104 Huber, B. and Merz, W. (1963) Jahrringchronologische
Synchronisierungen der jungsteinzeitlichen Sied-
lungen Thayngen-Weier und Burgäschisee-Süd und
-Südwest. (Annual ring chronology synchronization of
the Neolithic settlements of Thayngen-Weier and
Burgäschisee-Süd and -Südwest). Germania 41:1-9.

1105 Hughes, J. F. (1978) Techniques for tree-ring dating.
British archaeological reports, supplementary series
51:325-328.

1106 Hughes, M. K. et al. (1978) Climatic signals in
British Isles tree-ring chronologies. Nature
272:605-606.

1107 Hughes, M. K. et al. (1978) Dendrochronology of oak in
north Wales. Tree-ring bulletin 38:15-23.

1108 Jährig, M. (1971) Dendrochronologische Untersuchungen
von Holzproben aus der jungslawischen Siedlung auf
der Fischerinsel bei Neubrandenburg. (Dendrochronological investigations of wood specimens from
the Early Slavic settlement on Fischerinsel by
Neubrandenburg). Zeitschrift für Archäologie
5:134-140.

1109 Jährig, M. (1972) Dendrochronologische Untersuchungen
an Deckenbalken des Güstrower Schlosses als Beitrag
zu einer Dendrochronologie des nördlichen Raumes der
Deutschen Demokratischen Republik. (Dendrochronological investigations on roof beams of the Güstrow
castle as a contribution to a dendrochronology of
the northern region of the German Democratic
Republic). Bodendenkmalpflege in Mecklenburg,
Jahrbuch 1971:333-341.

1110 Jährig, M. (1977) Die Ergebnisse der dendro-
     chronologischen Untersuchung der Holzproben vom
     slawischen Burgwall 'Grodisch' bei Wiesenau, Kr.
     Eisenhüttenstadt. (The results of dendrochronolog-
     ical investigation on wood specimens from the Slavic
     fortress wall 'Grodisch' by Wiesenau, district of
     Eisenhüttenstadt). Zeitschrift für Archäologie
     11:101-120.

1111 Jährig, M. (1978) Dating for archaeological research
     in the G.D.R. British archaeological reports,
     supplementary series 51:263-266.

1112 Jansen, H. S. (1962) Comparison between ring-dates
     and C14 dates in New Zealand kauri trees. New
     Zealand journal of science 5:74-84.

1113 Jones, F. W. and Parker, M. L. (1970) G.S.C. tree-ring
     scanning densitometer and data acquisition system.
     Tree-ring bulletin 30(1-4):23-31.

1114 Judd, N. M. (1930) Dating our prehistoric pueblo
     ruins. Smithsonian institution report for 1929,
     167-176.

1115 Kairiukstis, L. A. (1978) Dendroclimatic and dendro-
     chronological investigations in the USSR. British
     archaeological reports, supplementary series
     51:55-58.

1116 Kairiukstis, L. A. and Juodvalkis, A. (1978) Growth
     rings in the south Baltic area and their relation
     in climatic factors. British archaeological reports,
     supplementary series 51:173-178.

1117 Knipe, D. A. (1942) A date from Chaco Yuma West,
     southern Arizona. Tree-ring bulletin 8(3):24.

1118 Kolčin, B. A. (1963) Dendrokhronologija Novgoroda.
     (Dendrochronology of Novgorod). Materialy i
     issledovanija po arkheologii SSSR 117:5-103.

1119 Kolčin, B. A. (1963) Dendrokhronologija postroek
     Nerevskogo raskopa. (Dendrochronology of the buil-
     dings at the Nerevskij excavation). Materialy i
     issledovanija po arkheologii SSSR 123 166-227.

1120 Kolčin, B. A. (1964) K itogam rabot Novgorodskoj arkheologičeskoj ékspeditsii. (1951-1962 gg.). (On the results of the work of the Novgorod archaeological expedition, 1951-1962). Kratkie soobšćenija Instituta Arkheologii 99:3-20.

1121 Kolčin, B. A. (1965) Dendrokhronologija drevnego Polotska. (Dendrochronology of ancient Polotsok). Materialy i issledovanija po arkheologii SSSR 130:262-266.

1122 Kolčin, B. A. (1965) Dendrokhronologija Vostočnoj Evropy. (Dendrochronology of Eastern Europe). Materialy i issledovanija po arkheologii SSSR 129:62-85.

1123 LaMarche, V. C. (1970) Frost-damage rings in subalpine conifers and their application to tree-ring dating problems. In: J. H. G. Smith and J. Worrall, eds., Tree-ring analysis with special reference to Northwest America. The University of British Columbia faculty of forestry bulletin 7:99-100.

1124 LaMarche, V. C. and Fritts, H. C. (1971) Tree-rings, glacial advance, and climate in the Alps. Zeitschrift für Gletscherkunde und Glazialgeologie 7(1/2): 125-131.

1125 LaMarche, V. C. and Harlan, T. P. (1973) Accuracy of tree-ring dating of bristlecone pine for calibration of the radiocarbon time scale. Journal of geophysical research 78:8849-8858.

1126 LaMarche, V. C. and Stockton, C. W. (1974) Chronologies from temperature-sensitive bristlecone pines at upper treeline in western United States. Tree-ring bulletin 34:21-45.

1127 Lambert, G. E. and Orcel, C. (1977) L'état de la dendrochronologie en Europe occidentale et les rapports entre dendrochronologie et archéologie en Suisse. Archives suisses d'anthropologie générale 41(2):73-97.

1128 Leggett, P., Hughes, M. K. and Hibbert, F. A. (1978) A modern oak chronology from north Wales and its interpretation. British archaeological reports, supplementary series 51:187-194.

1129 Liese, W. (1978) Bruno Huber: the pioneer of European dendrochronology. British archaeological reports, supplementary series 51:1-10.

1130 Liese, W. and Bauch, J. (1965) Das Alter der Bremer Kogge. (The age of the Bremen 'Kogge'). Bremisches Jahrbuch 50:14-19.

1131 Lockerbie, L. (1950) Dating the Moa-hunter. Journal of the Polynesian society 59(1):78-82.

1132 Lyon, C. J. (1939) The first dating of preserved wood in New England. Science 90:419-420.

1133 Lyon, C. J. (1946) Hemlock chronology in New England. Tree-ring bulletin 13(1):2-4.

1134 McGinnies, W. G. (1963) Dendrochronology. Journal of forestry 61(1):5-11.

1135 McGrail, S. (1978) Dating ancient wooden boats. British archaeological reports, supplementary series 51:239-258.

1136 McGregor, J. C. (1930) Tree-ring dating. Museum notes. Museum of northern Arizona. Flagstaff, 3(4).

1137 McGregor, J. C. (1932) Additional prehistoric dates from Arizona. Museum notes. Museum of northern Arizona. Flagstaff, 5(3).

1138 McGregor, J. C. (1934) Dates from Tsegi. Tree-ring bulletin 1:6-8.

1139 McGregor, J. C. (1936) Dates from Tsegi and Nalakihu. Tree-ring bulletin 3:15-16.

1140 McGregor, J. C. (1936) Additional dates from Tsegi. Tree-ring bulletin 2:37.

1141 McGregor, J. C. (1936) Dating the eruption of Sunset Crater, Arizona. American antiquity 2:15-26.

1142 McGregor, J. C. (1936) Effects of a volcanic cinder fall on tree growth. Tree-ring bulletin 3(2):11-13.

1143 McGregor, J. C. (1938) Southwestern dated ruins: III. Tree-ring bulletin 4:6.

1144 McGregor, J. C. (1942) Dates from Kinnikinnick Pueblo.
Tree-ring bulletin 8(3):21-23.

1145 McGregor, J. C. (1942) Dates from Wupatki Pueblo.
Tree-ring bulletin 8(3):18-21.

1146 Mikola, P. (1956) Tree-ring research in Finland. Tree-
ring bulletin 21(1-4):16-20.

1147 Miller, C. F. (1934; 1935) Report of dates from the
Allantown, Arizona ruins. Tree-ring bulletin
1(2):15-16; 1(4):31.

1148 Miller, J. L. (1942) Dates from Fort Grant Pueblo,
southern Arizona. Tree-ring bulletin 8(3):24.

1149 Milsom, S. J. and Hughes, M. K. (1978) X-ray densitometry as a dendrochronological technique. British
archaeological reports, supplementary series
51:317-324.

1150 Molski, B. (1965) Preliminary dendrochronological investigation in archaeological stand on 'vegetable
market' in Szczecin (Poland). Archaeologia Polona
8:190-207.

1151 Morgan, R. A. (1975) The selection and sampling of
timber from archaeological sites for identification
and tree-ring analysis. Journal of archaeological
science 2(3):221-230.

1152 Morgan, R. A. (1977) Dendrochronological dating of a
Yorkshire timber building. Vernacular architecture
8:9-14.

1153 Morgan, R. A. (1977) Tree-ring dating of the London
waterfronts. London archaeologist 3:40-45.

1154 Morgan, R. A. (1977) Tree-ring studies in the Somerset
Levels: the hurdle tracks on Ashcott Heath
(Rowlands) and Walton Heath. Somerset levels papers
3:61-65.

1155 Morgan, R. A. (1978) Tree-ring studies in the Somerset
Levels: the Meare Heath Track. Somerset levels
papers 4:40-41.

1156 Morgan, R. A. (1978) Tree-ring studies in the Somerset
     Levels: Tinney's Ground. Somerset levels papers
     4:82-85.

1157 Morgan, R. A. (1978) Two tree-ring dated cruck
     buildings. Vernacular architecture 9:32-33.

1158 Morgan, R. A. (1979) Tree-ring studies in the Somerset
     Levels: the Drove site of the Sweet track. Somerset
     levels papers 5:65-75.

1159 Morgan, R. A. (1979) Tree-ring studies in the Somerset
     Levels: floating oak tree-ring chronologies from
     the trackways and their radiocarbon dating.
     Somerset levels papers 5:98-100.

1160 Morgan, R. A., Coles, J. M. and Orme, B. J. (1978)
     Tree-ring studies in the Somerset Levels. British
     archaeological reports, supplementary series
     51:211-222.

1161 Morris, E. H. (1936) Archaeological background of
     dates in early Arizona chronology. Tree-ring
     bulletin 2(4):34-36.

1162 Morris, E. H. (1949) Basketmaker II dwellings near
     Durango, Colorado. Tree-ring bulletin 15(4).

1163 Morris, E. H. (1952) Note on the Durango dates. Tree-
     ring bulletin 18(4):36.

1164 Munaut, A. V. (1966) Recherches dendrochronologiques
     sur Pinus silvestris, 1. Etude de 45 sylvestres
     récents originaires de Belgique. Agricultura
     14(2):193-232.

1165 Munaut, A. V. (1966) Recherches dendrochronologiques
     sur Pinus silvestris, 2. Premiere application des
     méthodes dendrochronologiques à l'étude de pins
     sylvestres subfossile (Terneuzen, Pays-Bas).
     Agricultura 14:361-389.

1166 Naylor, T. N. (1971) Dendrochronology in Oaxaca,
     Mexico: a preliminary study. Tree-ring bulletin
     31:25-29.

111

1167 Nichols, R. F. (1962) Dates from the Site 1060 pithouse, Mesa Verde National Park. Tree-ring bulletin 24(1-2):12-14.

1168 Nichols, R. F. and Harlan, T. P. (1967) Archaeological tree-ring dates from Wetherill Mesa. Tree-ring bulletin 28(1-4):13-40.

1169 Ogden, J. (1978) Investigations of the dendrochronology of the genus Athrotaxis D. Don (Taxodiaceae) in Tasmania. Tree-ring bulletin 38:1-13.

1170 Oliver, W. R. B. (1931) An ancient Maori oven on Mt. Egmont. Journal of the Polynesian society 40(2): 73-80.

1171 Oswalt, W. (1949) Dated houses at Squirrel River, Alaska. Tree-ring bulletin 16(1):7-8.

1172 Oswalt, W. (1950) Spruce borings from the lower Yukon River, Alaska. Tree-ring bulletin 16(4):26-30.

1173 Oswalt, W. (1951) The origin of driftwood at Hooper Bay, Alaska. Tree-ring bulletin 18(1):6-8.

1174 Oswalt, W. (1952) Spruce samples from the Copper River drainage, Alaska. Tree-ring bulletin 19(1):5-10.

1175 Oswalt, W. (1954) Regional chronologies in spruce of the Kuskokwim River, Alaska. Anthropological papers of the University of Alaska 2(2):203-214.

1176 Oswalt, W. (1958) Tree-ring chronologies in south-central Alaska. Tree-ring bulletin 22(1-4):16-22.

1177 Parker, M. L. (1976) Improving tree-ring dating in northern Canada by X-ray densitometry. Syesis 9:163-172.

1178 Parker, M. L., Barton, G. M. and Smith, J. H. G. (1976) Annual ring contrast enhancement without affecting X-ray densitometry studies. Tree-ring bulletin 36:29-31.

1179 Parker, M. L. and Meleskie, K. R. (1970) Preparation of X-ray negatives of tree-ring specimens for dendrochronological analysis. Tree-ring bulletin 30(1-4):11-22.

1180 Peterson, A. (1935-1939) Specimens from the Pueblo
area. Tree-ring bulletin 1(3):23-24; 3(3):23-24;
6(1):6-8.

1181 Pilcher, J. R. (1973) Tree-ring research in Ireland.
Tree-ring bulletin 33:1-5.

1182 Pilcher, J. R. (1976) A statistical oak chronology
from the north of Ireland. Tree-ring bulletin
36:21-27.

1183 Pilcher, J. R. et al. (1977) A long sub-fossil oak
tree-ring chronology from the north of Ireland. New
phytologist 79:713-729.

1184 Polge, H. (1970) The use of X-ray densitometric
methods in dendrochronology. Tree-ring bulletin
30(1-4):1-10.

1185 Polge, H. (1978) The contribution of wood density to
dendrochronology and dendroclimatology. British
archaeological reports, supplementary series
51:77-87.

1186 Robinson, W. J. (1976) Tree-ring dating and archaeology
in the American Southwest. Tree-ring bulletin
36:9-20.

1187 Rudakov, V. E. (1964) K voprosu o metodakh dendro-
khronologičeskogo analiza v arkheologii. (On the
question of methods of dendrochronological analysis
in archaeology). Sovetskaja arkheologija 2:79-86.

1188 Schmidt, B. (1973) Dendrochronologische Untersuchungen
an Eichen aus der Kölner Bucht und dem Werre-Weser-
Gebiet. (Dendrochronological investigations on oaks
from the Kölner Bucht and the Werre-Weser region).
Archäologisches Korrespondenzblatt 3(1):155-158.

1189 Schove, D. J. (1955) Droughts of the Dark Ages and
tree-rings. Weather 10(11):368-371.

1190 Schove, D. J. (1959) Cross-dating of Anglo-Saxon
timbers at Old Windsor and Southampton. Medieval
archaeology 3:288-290.

113

1191 Schove, D. J. (1964) Medieval dendrochronology in the
      U.S.S.R. Medieval archaeology 8:216-217.

1192 Schove, D. J. (1973) Dates for Hamwih and Old Windsor.
      Current archaeology 37:44.

1193 Schove, D. J. (1974) Dendrochronological dating of
      oak from Old Windsor, Berks. Medieval archaeology
      18:165-172.

1194 Schove, D. J. (1975) Tree-ring teleconnections in
      Europe. MASCA newsletter 11(1):9.

1195 Schove, D. J. and Lowther, A. W. G. (1957) Tree-rings
      and medieval archaeology. Medieval archaeology
      1:78-95.

1196 Schulman, E. (1939) Classification of false annual
      rings in west Texas pines. Tree-ring bulletin
      6(2):11-13.

1197 Schulman, E. (1940) A bibliography of tree-ring
      analysis. Tree-ring bulletin 6(4):27-39.

1198 Schulman, E. (1941) Douglass fir chronology in Santa
      Catalina Mountains, Arizona. Tree-ring bulletin
      7(3):18-19.

1199 Schulman, E. (1942) Dendrochronology in pines of
      Arkansas. Ecology 23:309-318.

1200 Schulman, E. (1944) Dendrochronology in Mexico. Tree-
      ring bulletin 10(3):18-24.

1201 Schulman, E. (1944) Tree-ring work in Scandinavia.
      Tree-ring bulletin 11(1):2-6.

1202 Schulman, E. (1946) Dendrochronology at Mesa Verde
      National Park. Tree-ring bulletin 12(3):18-24.

1203 Schulman, E. (1946/1947) Dendrochronologies in south-
      western Canada. Tree-ring bulletin 13(2/3):10-24.

1204 Schulman, E. (1948) Dendrochronology at Navajo
      National Monument. Tree-ring bulletin 14(3):18-24.

1205 Schulman, E. (1948) Dendrochronology in northeastern
      Utah. Tree-ring bulletin 15(1/2).

1206 Schulman, E. (1949) Chronology characters at ruins in the Gila Basin. Tree-ring bulletin 15(3):21-22.

1207 Schulman, E. (1949) Early chronologies in the San Juan basin. Tree-ring bulletin 15(4):24-32.

1208 Schulman, E. (1949) An extension of the Durango chronology. Tree-ring bulletin 16(2):12-16.

1209 Schulman, E. (1950) Miscellaneous ring records. I. Tree-ring bulletin 16(3):21.

1210 Schulman, E. (1951) Miscellaneous ring records. III. Tree-ring bulletin 17(4):28-29.

1211 Schulman, E. (1951/1952) Dendrochronology in Big Bend National Park, Texas. Tree-ring bulletin 18(2/3): 18-27.

1212 Schulman, E. (1952) Extension of the San Juan chronology to B.C. times. Tree-ring bulletin 18(4):30-35.

1213 Schulman, E. (1953) Rio Grande chronologies. Tree-ring bulletin 19(3/4):20-33.

1214 Schwabedissen, H. (1977) Archäologische Chronologie des 2. vorchristlichen Jahrtausends und Jahrring-Korrektur der C14-Daten. (Archaeological chronology of the second millennium B.C. and tree-ring correction of C-14 dates). In: Dendrochronologie und postglaziale Klimaschwankungen in Europa. Wiesbaden: F. Steiner, 119-125.

1215 Schweingruber, F. H., Bräker, O. U. and Schär, E. (1978) X-ray densitometric results for subalpine conifers and their relationship to climate. British archaeological reports, supplementary series 51:89-100.

1216 Scott, S. D. (1966) Dendrochronology in Mexico. Papers of the laboratory of tree-ring research 2. Tucson: Univ. of Arizona Press.

1217 Senter, D. (1937) The application of tree-ring analysis to deposition problems in Chaco Canyon, New Mexico. Tree-ring bulletin 3(3):19-20.

1218 Serre, F. (1977) A factor analysis of correspondences applied to ring widths. Tree-ring bulletin 37:21-31.

1219 Siebenlist-Kerner, V. (1978) The chronology, 1341-1636, for certain hillside oaks from western England and Wales. British archaeological reports, supplementary series 51:157-161.

1220 Smiley, T. L. (1947) Dates from a surface pueblo at Mesa Verde. Tree-ring bulletin 13(4).

1221 Smiley, T. L. (1949) Tree-ring dates from Point of Pines. Tree-ring bulletin 15(3):20-21.

1222 Smiley, T. L. (1950) Miscellaneous ring records, II. Tree-ring bulletin 16(3):22-23.

1223 Smiley, T. L. (1951) A summary of tree-ring dates from some Southwestern archaeological sites. Laboratory of tree-ring research bulletin 5; University of Arizona bulletin vol. 22, no. 4.

1224 Smiley, T. L., Stubbs, S. A. and Bannister, B. (1953) A foundation for dating of some late archaeological sites in the Rio Grande area, New Mexico: based on studies in tree-ring methods and pottery analyses. Laboratory of tree-ring research bulletin 6; University of Arizona bulletin vol. 24, no. 3.

1225 Stallings, W. S. (1936) Dates from Gallo Canyon, east-central New Mexico. Tree-ring bulletin 3(1):6-8.

1226 Stallings, W. S. (1936) Dates from Five Kiva House, Utah. Tree-ring bulletin 3(2):13-14.

1227 Stallings, W. S. (1937) The tree-ring material from the Riana ruin. Univ. of New Mexico bulletin, anthropological series 2:51-60.

1228 Stallings, W. S. (1937) Southwestern dated ruins: I. Tree-ring bulletin 4(2):3-5.

1229 Stallings, W. S. (1941) A Basketmaker II date from Cave du Pont, Utah. Tree-ring bulletin 8(1):3-6.

1230 Stein, W. T. (1964) Comparison and analysis of modern and prehistoric tree specimens in the Flagstaff area, Arizona. Tree-ring bulletin 26(1-4):6-12.

116

1231 Stokes, M. A., Drew, L. G. and Stockton, C. W., eds.
(1973) Tree-ring chronologies of western North
America. I. Selected tree-ring stations. Laboratory
of tree-ring research, chronology series 1. Tucson:
Univ. of Arizona Press.

1232 Stokes, M. A. and Smiley, T. L. (1963) Tree-ring dates
from the Navajo Land Claim. I: the northern sector.
Tree-ring bulletin 25(3/4):8-18.

1233 Stokes, M. A. and Smiley, T. L. (1964) Tree-ring dates
from the Navajo Land Claim. II: the western sector.
Tree-ring bulletin 26(1-4):13-27.

1234 Stokes, M. A. and Smiley, T. L. (1966) Tree-ring dates
from the Navajo Land Claim. III: the southern
sector. Tree-ring bulletin 27(3/4):2-11.

1235 Stokes, M. A. and Smiley, T. L. (1968) An introduction
to tree-ring dating. Chicago: Univ. of Chicago
Press.

1236 Stokes, M. A. and Smiley, T. L. (1969) Tree-ring dates
from the Navajo Land Claim. IV: the eastern sector.
Tree-ring bulletin 29(1/2):2-15.

1237 Studhalter, R. A. (1956) Early history of crossdating.
Tree-ring bulletin 21(1-4):31-35.

1238 Stuiver, M. (1970) Tree-ring, varve and carbon-14
chronologies. Nature 228:454-455.

1239 Tapper, M. C., Fletcher, J. and Walker, F. S. (1978)
Abnormal small earlywood vessels in oak as
chronological indicators: their relation to
arrested heartwood formation (included sapwood)
after cold winters. British archaeological reports,
supplementary series 51:339-342.

1240 Tout, R. and Gilboy, W. (1978) Trace element concentrations in tree rings. British archaeological
reports, supplementary series 51:343-348.

1241 Van Stone, J. W. (1953) Notes on Kotzebue dating.
Tree-ring bulletin 20(1):6-8.

1242 Van Stone, J. W. (1958) The origin of driftwood on
     Nunivak Island, Alaska. Tree-ring bulletin
     22(1-4):12-15.

1243 Varley, G. (1978) The effects of insect defoliation on
     the growth of oaks in England. British archaeological
     reports, supplementary series 51:179-184.

1244 Vikhrov, V. E. (1965) Dendrokhronologija Novgoroda i
     eë značenie dlja dendroklimatologii. (Dendro-
     chronology of Novgorod and its significance for
     dendroclimatology). Voprosy lesovedenija i
     lesovodstva 1:155-159.

1245 Vikhrov, V. E. and Kolčin, B. A. (1962) Osnovy i metod
     dendrokhronologii. (The principles and method of
     dendrochronology). Sovetskaja arkheologija 1:95-112.

1246 Walker, F. S. (1978) Pendenculate and sessile oaks:
     species determination from differences between their
     wood. British archaeological reports, supplementary
     series 51:329-338.

1247 Watson, D. (1947) Note on the dating of Pipe Shrine
     House. Tree-ring bulletin 13(4).

1248 Weakly, H. E. (1950) Dendrochronology and its climatic
     implications in the Central Plains. Univ. of Utah
     anthropological papers 11:90-94.

1249 Wendland, W. M. (1975) An objective method to identify
     missing or false rings. Tree-ring bulletin 35:41-47.

1250 Will, G. F. (1948) Additional notes on dendrochronology
     in the Dakotas. Plains archaeological conference
     news letter 1(4):68-70.

1251 Willey, G. (1937) Notes on central Georgia dendro-
     chronology. Tree-ring bulletin 4(2):6-8.

1252 Wissler, C. (1921) Dating our prehistoric ruins.
     Natural history 21:13-26.

1253 Worrall, J. (1970) Growth-ring analysis and dendro-
     chronology. In: J. H. G. Smith and J. Worrall, eds.,
     Tree-ring analysis with special reference to north-
     west America. Univ. of British Columbia faculty of
     forestry bulletin 7:31-32.

118

1254 Zakharieva, E. I. (1976) Dendrokhronologičeskoe
      issledovanie kurgana Aržan. (Dendrochronological
      study of the Aržan kurgan). Sovetskaja arkheologija
      1:100-107.

1255 Zamotorin, I. M. (1963) O vozmožnosti ustanovlenija
      otnositel'nykh datirovok territorial'no udalennykh
      sooruženij metodom analiza drevesnykh stvolov v
      uslovijakh Gornogo Altaja. (On the possibilities of
      the establishment of relative dates for construc-
      tions that are isolated by the method of dendro-
      chronological analysis in the Altai Mountains).
      Sovetskaja arkheologija 2:131-138.

3. Hydration dating of obsidian, glass, and stone

1256 Ackerman, R. E. (1964) Lichens and the patination of
      chert in Alaska. American antiquity 29(3):386-387.

1257 Alciati, G. (1978) Datazione di manufatti pre- e
      protostorici della Sardegna e dell'isola di Lipari
      mediante il metodo dell'ossidiana. Rivista di
      scienze preistoriche 33(1):271-281.

1258 Barrera, W. M. and Kirch, P. V. (1973) Basaltic glass
      artefacts from Hawaii. Journal of the Polynesian
      society 82(2):176-187.

1259 Bell, R. E. (1977) Obsidian hydration studies in
      highland Ecuador. American antiquity 42(1):68-78.

1260 Berger, R. and Ericson, J. E. (1974) Natural solid
      solution: obsidians and tektites. In: Recent
      advances in science and technology of materials.
      New York: Plenum Press, 3:187-189.

1261 Brill, R. H. and Hood, H. P. (1961) A new method for
      dating ancient glass. Nature 189:12-14.

1262 Brill, R. H. (1961) The record of time in weathered
      glass. Archaeology 14:18-22.

1263 Clark, D. E. and Purdy, B. A. (1979) Surface charac-
      terization of weathered Florida cherts. Archaeo-
      Physika 10:428-439.

1264 Clarke, D. L. (1961) The obsidian dating method.
Current anthropology 2:111-114.

1265 Clarke, D. L. (1964) Archaeological chronology in
California and the obsidian-hydration method. Annual
report of the archaeological survey, department of
anthropology, University of California, Los Angeles
6:143-211.

1266 Davis, L. B. (1966) Cooperative obsidian dating
research in the northwestern Plains: a status
report. Montana archaeological society 7(2):3-5.

1267 Davis, L. B. (1977) Preliminary hydration rate
determinations and associated hydration rate alter-
natives: the Alyeska archaeology project. Pipeline
archeology. University of Alaska, institute of Arctic
biology 10-65.

1268 De Atley, S. P. and Findlow, F. J. (1979/1980) A new
obsidian hydration rate in the greater Southwest.
North American archaeologist 1(2):139-144.

1269 Dixon, K. A. (1966) Obsidian dates from Temesco, Valley
of Mexico. American antiquity 31(5):640-643.

1270 Dixon, L. E. (1969) Catalog of obsidian hydration
measurement data for Mexico. Washington, D.C.:
Smithsonian Institution.

1271 Ericson, J. E. (1975) New results in obsidian hydration
dating. World archaeology 7(2):151-159.

1272 Ericson, J. E. (1978) Obsidian hydration dating in
California. Occasional papers in method and theory
in California archaeology 2:43-52.

1273 Ericson, J. E. and Berger, R. (1976) Physics and
chemistry of the hydration process in obsidians II:
experiments and measurements. In: R. E. Taylor, ed.,
Advances in obsidian glass studies. Park Ridge, New
Jersey: Noyes Press, 46-62.

1274 Ericson, J. E., MacKenzie, J. D. and Berger, R. (1976)
Physics and chemistry of the hydration process in
obsidians, I: theoretical implications. In: R. E.
Taylor, ed., Advances in obsidian glass studies. Park
Ridge, New Jersey: Noyes Press, 25-45.

120

1275 Evans, C. (1965) The dating of Easter Island
archaeological obsidian specimens. Reports of the
Norwegian archaeological expedition to Easter Island
and the east Pacific 2(18):469-495.

1276 Evans, C. and Meggers, B. J. (1960) A new dating
method using obsidian: part II, an archaeological
evaluation of the method. American antiquity
25(4):523-537.

1277 Findlow, F. J. et al. (1975) A new obsidian hydration
rate for certain obsidians in the American
Southwest. American antiquity 40(3):344-348.

1278 Friedman, I. (1968) Hydration rind dates rhyolite
flows. Science 159:878-880.

1279 Friedman, I. (1978) Obsidian: the dating stone.
American scientist 66(1):44-51.

1280 Friedman, I. et al. (1973) Obsidian hydration dates
glacial loading? Science 180(4087):733-734.

1281 Friedman, I. and Long, W. D. (1976) Hydration rate of
obsidian. Science 191(4225):347-352.

1282 Friedman, I. and Smith, R. L. (1960) A new dating
method using obsidian, part 1. The development of
the technique. American antiquity 25(4):476-522.

1283 García-Bárcena González, J. (1972) Obsidian hydration
dating in Central Mexico: preliminary results.
Atti del XL congresso internazionale degli
Americanisti. Genova, 2:91-98.

1284 García-Bárcena González, J. (1974) Fechas por
hidratación de obsidiana: posible incremento en su
exactitud a través de la determinación directa de la
temperatura efectiva de hidratación. Notas
antropológicas 1(15):113-119.

1285 García-Bárcena González, J. (1975) Estudios sobre
fechamiento por hidratación de la obsidian. Boletin,
Instituto nacional de antropologia e historia,
Mexico. Epoca II. 12:27-38.

1286 García-Bárcena González, J. (1976) Paleotemperaturas
      e hidratación de la obsidiana. Boletín, Instituto
      nacional de antropologia e historia, Mexico. Epoca
      II. 17:19-24.

1287 Green, R. C. (1964) Sources, ages and exploitation of
      New Zealand obsidian. New Zealand archaeological
      association newsletter 7(3):134-143.

1288 Johnson, L. (1969) Obsidian hydration rate for the
      Klamath basin of California and Oregon. Science
      165:1354-1356.

1289 Katsui, Y. and Kondo, Y. (1965) Dating of stone im-
      plements by using hydration layer of obsidian.
      Japanese journal of geology and geography
      46(2-4):45-60.

1290 Kimberlin, J. (1976) Obsidian hydration rate deter-
      minations on chemically characterized samples. In:
      R. E. Taylor, ed., Advances in obsidian glass
      studies. Park Ridge, New Jersey: Noyes Press,
      63-80.

1291 Lanford, W. A. (1977) Glass hydration: a method of
      dating glass objects. Science 196(4293):975-976.

1292 Laursen, T. and Lanford, W. A. (1978) Hydration of
      obsidian. Nature 276(5684):153-156.

1293 Layton, T. N. (1973) Temporal ordering of surface-
      collected obsidian artifacts by hydration
      measurement. Archaeometry 15(1):129-132.

1294 Lee, R. R., Leich, D. A. and Tombrello, T. A. (1974)
      Obsidian hydration profile measurements using a
      nuclear reaction technique. Nature 250:44.

1295 Meighan, C. W. (1978) Application of obsidian dating
      to west Mexican archaeological problems. In: Across
      the Chichimec Sea. Carbondale, Illinois: Southern
      Illinois Univ. Press, 127-133.

1296 Meighan, C. W., Findlow, F. J., and De Atley, S. P.,
      eds. (1974) Obsidian dates I: a compendium of the
      obsidian determinations made at the UCLA Obsidian
      Hydration Laboratory. Univ. of California, Los

Angeles, archaeological survey monograph, no. 3.

1297 Meighan, C. W., Foote, L. J. and Aiello, P. V. (1968)
Obsidian dating in west Mexican archaeology. Science
160(3832):1069-1075.

1298 Michels, J. W. (1967) Archaeology and dating by
hydration of obsidian. Science 158(3798):211-214.

1299 Michels, J. W. (1969) Testing stratigraphy and artifact re-use through obsidian hydration dating.
American antiquity 34:15-22.

1300 Michels, J. W. (1973) Radiocarbon and obsidian dating:
a chronometric framework for Kaminaljuyu.
Pennsylvania State Univ., Department of anthropology.
Occasional papers 9:21-66.

1301 Morgenstein, M. and Riley, T. J. (1975) Hydration-rind
dating of basaltic glass: a new method for
archaeological chronologies. Asian perspectives
17(2):145-159.

1302 Morland, R. E. (1967) Chronometric dating in Japan.
Arctic anthropology 4(2):180-211.

1303 Newton, R. G. (1966) Some problems in the dating of
ancient glass by counting the layers in the
weathering crust. Glass technology 7:22-25.

1304 Newton, R. G. (1969) Some further observations on the
weathering crusts of ancient glass. Glass technology
10:40-42.

1305 Purdy, B. A. and Clark, D. E. (1979) Weathering
studies of chert: a potential solution to the
chronology problem in Florida. Archaeo-Physika
10:440-450.

1306 Singleton, W. L. (1973) The mechanisms of obsidian
hydration and their application to determining a
general hydration rate. California anthropologist
3:41-46.

1307 Taylor, R. E., ed. (1976) Advances in obsidian glass
studies: archaeological and geochemical perspectives. Park Ridge, New Jersey: Noyes Press.

1308 Tsong, I. S. T. et al. (1978) Obsidian hydration profiles measured by sputter-induced optical emission. Science 201:339.

4. Amino acid racemization

1309 Abelson, P. H. (1954) Amino acids in fossils. Science 119:576.

1310 Amino acid dating. (1973) MASCA newsletter 9(2):6-8.

1311 Bada, J. L. (1972) The dating of fossil bones using the racemization of isoleucine. Earth and planetary science letters 15:223-231.

1312 Bada, J. L. et al. (1974) Concordance of collagen-based radiocarbon and aspartic-acid racemization ages. Proceedings of the national academy of sciences, U.S. 71:914-917.

1313 Bada, J. L. and Deems, L. (1975) Accuracy of dates beyond the C-14 dating limit using the aspartic acid recemization technique. Nature 255:218-219.

1314 Bada, J. L., Kvenvolden, K. A. and Peterson, E. (1973) Racemization of amino acids in bones. Nature 245:308-310.

1315 Bada, J. L., Luyendyk, B. P. and Maynard, J. B. (1970) Marine sediments: dating by the racemization of amino acids. Science 170:730-732.

1316 Bada, J. L. and Masters, P. M. (1978) The antiquity of human beings in the Americas: evidence derived from amino acid racemization dating of Paleoindian skeletons. Occasional papers in method and theory in California archaeology 2:15-24.

1317 Bada, J. L. and Masters-Helfman, P. (1976) Application of amino acid racemization dating in paleoanthropology and archaeology. Colloque 1. IX Congrès, Union internationale des sciences préhistoriques et protohistoriques. Nice, 39-62.

1318 Bada, J. L. and Protsch, R. (1973) Racemization
reaction of aspartic acid and its use in dating
fossil bones. Proceedings of the national academy
of sciences, U.S. 70:1331-1334.

1319 Bada, J. L., Protsch, R. and Schroeder, R. A. (1973)
The racemization reaction of isoleucine used as a
palaeotemperature indicator. Nature 241:394-395.

1320 Bada, J. L. and Schroeder, R. A. (1972) Racemization
of isoleucine in calcareous marine sediments:
kinetics and mechanism. Earth and planetary science
letters 15:1:11.

1321 Bada, J. L. and Schroeder, R. A. (1976) A review of
the geochemical applications of the amino acid
racemization method. Earth science reviews 12:
347-390.

1322 Bada, J. L., Schroeder, R. A. and Carter, G. F. (1974)
New evidence for the antiquity of man in North
America deduced from aspartic acid racemization.
Science 184:791-793.

1323 Bender, M. L. (1974) Reliability of amino acid
racemisation dating and paleotemperature analysis on
bones. Nature 252(5482):378-379.

1324 Dennison, K. J. (1980) Amino acids in archaeological
bone. Journal of archaeological science 7(1):81-86.

1325 Endt, D. W. von (1979) Techniques of amino acid
dating. Pre-Llano cultures of the Americas.
Washington, D.C.: Anthropological Society of
Washington, 71-100.

1326 Ezra, H. C. and Cook, S. F. (1957) Amino acids in
fossil human bone. Science 126:84.

1327 Glowatzki, G. and Protsch, R. (1973) Das absolute
Alte der Kopfbestattungen in der grossen Offnet-Höhle
bei Nördlingen in Bayern. (The absolute age of the
head interment in the large rock shelter by
Nördlingen in Bavaria). Homo 24(1):1-6.

1328 Hare, P. E. (1974) Amino acid dating--a history and an
evaluation. MASCA newsletter 10(1):4-7.

1329 Hare, P. E. (1975) Amino acid dating of bone: the influence of water. Carnegie institution of Washington year book 73:576-581.

1330 Hare, P. E. and Abelson, P. H. (1968) Racemization of amino acids in fossil shells. Carnegie institution of Washington year book 66:516-528.

1331 Hare, P. E. and Mitterer, R. M. (1969) Laboratory simulation of amino-acid diagenesis in fossils. Carnegie institution of Washington year book 67:205-208.

1332 Hare, P. E., Turnbull, H. F. and Taylor, R. E. (1978) Amino acid dating of Pleistocene fossil materials: Olduvai Gorge, Tanzania. In: L. G. Freemen, ed., Views of the past. The Hague: Mouton, 7-12.

1333 Ike, D. et al. (1979) Aspartic acid racemization and radiocarbon dating of an early milling stone horizon burial in California. American antiquity 44(3): 524-530.

1334 King, K. (1978) Gamma-carboxyglutamic acid in fossil bones and its significance for amino acid dating. Nature 273:41-43.

1335 King, K. and Bada, J. L. (1979) Effect of in situ leaching on amino acid racemisation rates in fossil bone. Nature 281:135-137.

1336 King, K. and Neville, C. (1977) Isoleucine epimerization for dating marine sediments: importance of analyzing monospecific foraminiferal samples. Science 195:1333.

1337 Kriausakul, N. and Mitterer, R. M. (1978) Isoleucine epimerization in peptides and proteins: kinetic factors and application to fossil proteins. Science 201:1011.

1338 Masters, P. M. and Bada, J. L. (1979) Amino acid racimization dating of fossil shell from southern California. In: Radiocarbon dating. Berkeley, Calif.: Univ. of California Press, 757-773.

126

1339 Masters, P. M. and Zimmerman, M. R. (1978) Age
      determination of an Alaskan mummy: morphological
      and biochemical correlation. Science 201(4359):
      811-812.

1340 Montgomery, J. L. (1976) Aspartic acid racemization as
      a dating technique. Transactions of the eleventh
      regional archeological symposium for southeastern
      New Mexico and western Texas, 98-102.

1341 Protsch, R. (1974) Florisbad: its palaeoanthropology,
      chronology and archaeology. Homo 25(2):68-78.

1342 Protsch, R. (1975) The absolute dating of Upper
      Pleistocene SubSaharan fossil hominids and their
      place in human evolution. Journal of human evolution
      4:297-322.

1343 Protsch, R. (1976) Comparison of absolute bone dates
      by radiocarbon and amino-acid dating on Upper
      Pleistocene hominids. Colloque 1. IX Congrès, Union
      internationale des sciences préhistoriques et proto-
      historiques. Nice, 180-211.

1344 Protsch, R. and Glowatzki, G. (1974) Das absolute Alte
      des paläolithischen Skeletts aus der Mittleren
      Klause bei Neuessing, Kreis Kelheim in Bayern.
      (The absolute age of the Palaeolithic skeleton from
      the middle Klause by Neuessing, district of Kelheim
      in Bavaria). Anthropologischer Anzeiger 34(2):
      140-144.

1345 Schroeder, R. A. and Bada, J. L. (1973) Glacial-
      Postglacial temperature difference deduced from
      aspartic acid racemization in fossil bones. Science
      182:479-481.

1346 Wehmiller, J. and Hare, P. E. (1971) Racemization of
      amino acids in marine sediments. Science 173:907-911.

5. Fluorine-uranium-nitrogen dating

1347 Baden-Powell, D. F. W. and Oakley, K. P. (1953) Report
      on the re-investigations of the Westley (Bury St.
      Edmonds) skull site. Proceeding of the prehistoric
      society 18:1-20.

1348 Bleck, R.-D. and Böhml, M. (1977) Zur Anwendbarkeit
      der "Flurotests" für die relative Alterbestimmung
      von Knochen. (The applicability of the fluorine
      test for the relative dating of bones). Ausgrabungen
      und Funde 22(4):152-162.

1349 Buczko, C. M., Nemeskéri, J. and Sas, L. (1978) Age
      dating of bones from Vlasac based on their nitrogen
      and fluorine contents. In: Vlasac. Mesolitsko
      naselje u Djerdapu, vol. 2. Kniha--Odeljenje
      istorijskih nauka. Beograd, 62:75-76.

1350 Cook, S. F. and Ezra-Cohn, H. C. (1959) An evaluation
      of the fluorine dating method. Southwestern journal
      of anthropology 15:276-290.

1351 Ezra-Cohn, H. C., Cook, S. F. and Leon, H. A. (1958)
      Current status of the fluorine method of age
      determination. Kroeber anthropological society,
      papers 19:17-19.

1352 Glover, M. J. and Phillips, G. F. (1965) Chemical
      methods for dating of fossils. Journal of applied
      chemistry 15(2):570-576.

1353 Häusler, A. (1974) Der Fluortest und andere Methoden
      zur Datierung von Knochen. (The fluorine test and
      other methods for the dating of bones). Wissen-
      schaftliche Beiträge der Martin-Luther-Universität
      Halle-Wittenberg 4:110-114.

1354 Hamaguchi, H. and Tatsumoto, M. (1958) Fluorine content
      of human bone. Kroeber anthropological society,
      papers 19:41-45.

1355 Hoskins, C. R. and Fryd, C. F. M. (1955) The deter-
      mination of fluorine in Piltdown and related fossils.
      Journal of applied chemistry 5:85-87.

1356 Knight, B. and Lauder, I. (1969) Methods of dating
      skeletal remains. Human biology 41:323-341.

1357 McConnell, D. (1962) Dating of fossil bones by the
      fluorine method. Science 136:241-244.

1358 Oakley, K. P. (1949) Some applications of the fluorine
      test. Archaeological news letter 2(7):101-103.

1359 Oakley, K. P. (1950) The fluorine dating method. Yearbook of physical anthropology, 1949, 5:44-52.

1360 Oakley, K. P. (1950) The fluorine content of some Miocene horse bones. Science 112:620-621.

1361 Oakley, K. P. and Hoskins, C. R. (1950) New evidence on the antiquity of Piltdown man. Nature 165:379.

1362 Oakley, K. P. and Hoskins, C. R. (1951) Application du test de la fluorine aux crânes de Fontéchevade. L'Anthropologie 55:239-247.

1363 Oakley, K. P. and Howells, W. W. (1961) Age of skeleton from the Lagow sand pit, Texas. American antiquity 26(4):543-545.

1364 Ortner, D. J., Endt, D. W. von and Robinson, M. S. (1972) The effect of temperature on protein decay in bone: its significance in nitrogen dating of archaeological specimens. American antiquity 37(4):514-520.

1365 Parker, R. B., Murphy, J. W. and Toots, H. (1974) Fluorine in fossilized bone and tooth: distribution among skeletal tissues. Archaeometry 16(1):98-102.

1366 Seitz, M. G. (1972) Uranium variations in bovid teeth of the Olduvai Gorge. Carnegie institution of Washington yearbook 71:557.

1367 Seitz, M. G. and Taylor, R. E. (1974) Uranium variations in a dated fossil bone series from Olduvai Gorge, Tanzania. Archaeometry 16(2):129-135.

1368 Stewart, T. D. (1952) The fluorine content of associated human and extinct animal bones from the Conkling Cavern, New Mexico. Science 166:457-458.

1369 Turekian, K. K. et al. (1970) Uranium-helium ratios for fossil bone. Earth and planetary science letters 7:420-424.

D. Other dating methods

1370 Antevs, E. (1955) Varve and radiocarbon chronology appraised by pollen data. Journal of geology 63:495-499.

1371 Fraser, H. J. (1929) An experimental study of varve deposition. Transactions of the royal society of Canada 23(4):49-60.

1372 Fromm, E. (1970) An estimation of errors in the Swedish varve chronology. In: I. U. Olsson, ed., Radiocarbon variations and absolute chronology. Stockholm: Almqvist & Wiksell; New York: J. Wiley, 163-172.

1373 Hwang, F. S. W. and Fremlin, J. H. (1970) A new dating technique using thermally stimulated current. Archaeometry 12(1):67-71.

1374 Ikeya, M. (1978) Electron spin resonance as a method of dating. Archaeometry 20(2):147-158.

1375 Ikeya, M. and Miki, T. (1980) Electron spin resonance dating of animal and human bones. Science 207(4434):977-979.

1376 Robins, G. V. et al. (1978) Identification of ancient heat treatment in flint artefacts by ESR spectroscopy. Nature 276(5689):703-704.

1377 Schove, D. J. 91971) Varve-teleconnection across the Baltic. Geografiska annaler 53A:214-234.

1378 Schove, D. J. (1975) Transatlantic varve-teleconnections. MASCA newsletter 11(1):10.

1379 Tauber, H. (1970) The Scandinavian varve chronology and C14 dating. In: I. U. Olsson, ed., Radiocarbon variations and absolute chronology. Stockholm: Almqvist & Wiksell; New York: J. Wiley, 173-196.

1380 Vitaliano, D. B. and Vitaliano, C. J. (1978) Tephrochronological evidence for the time of the Bronze Age eruption of Thera. In: Thera and the Aegean world. London: Thera and the Aegean World, 217-219.

1381 Wenner, C.-G. (1968) Comparison of varve chronology, pollen analysis and radiocarbon dating. Stockholm contributions in geology 18(3):75-97.

IV. ENVIRONMENTAL RECONSTRUCTION

A. General studies

1382   Brunnacker, K. (1977) Archäologie und Naturwissen-
       schaften: zum Beispiel Gönnersdorf. (Archaeology
       and natural sciences: for example Gönnersdorf).
       Archäologie und Naturwissenschaften 1:85-92.

1383   Butzer, K. W. (1971) Environment and archeology: an
       ecological approach to prehistory. Chicago: Aldine;
       London: Methuen.

1384   Butzer, K. W. (1977) Environment, culture, and human
       evolution. American scientist 65:572-584.

1385   Butzer, K. W. (1980) Context in archaeology: an
       alternative perspective. Journal of field archaeolo-
       gy 7(4):417-422.

1386   Evans, J. G. (1978) An introduction to environmental
       archaeology. Ithaca: Cornell University. 154p.

1387   Evans, J. G., Limbrey, S. and Cleere, H., eds. (1975)
       The effect of man on the landscape: the highland
       zone. Council for British archaeology research
       report no. 11. London. 129p.

1388   Higgs, E. S., ed. (1972-1975) Palaeoeconomy. Papers in
       economic prehistory. Two volumes. Cambridge:
       Cambridge University Press.

131

1389 Kudarskie peščernye paleolitičeskie stojanki v jugo-Osetii. (The Kudaro Palaeolithic cave sites in southern Osetia). (1980) Moskva: Geologičeskij Institut, Akademija Nauk SSSR.

1390 Price Williams, D. (1973) Environmental archaeology in the western Negev. Nature 242:501-503.

1391 Smith, C., ed. (1979) Fisherwick: the reconstruction of an Iron Age landscape. British archaeological reports, British series no. 61. Oxford.

1392 Ucko, P. J. and Dimbleby, G. W., eds. (1969) The domestication and exploitation of plants and animals. London: Duckworth.

1393 Wood, W. R. and McMillan, R. B., eds. (1976) Prehistoric man and his environment. A case study in the Ozark highland. New York: Academic Press. 271p.

B. Lithosphere/atmosphere

1. Soil, sediment and phosphate analysis

1394 Ahler, S. A. (1973) Chemical analysis of deposits at Rodgers Shelter, Missouri. Plains anthropologist 18:116-131.

1395 Almy, M. M. (1978) The archaeological potential of soil survey reports. Florida anthropologist 31(3):75-91.

1396 Arrhenius, O. (1931) Bodenuntersuchung im Dienste der Archäologie. (Soil investigation in the service of archaeology). Pflanzenernährung, Düngung und Bodenkunde 10B:427-439.

1397 Bandi, H. (1945) Archäologische Erforschung des zukünftigen Stauseegebietes Rossens-Broc. (Archaeological research of the future lake dam area Rossens-Broc). Jahrbuch der schweizerischen Gesellschaft für Urgeschichte 36:100-106.

1398 Bellmann, W. (1954) Die Phosphatmethode im Dienste der Vorgeschichtsforschung. (The phosphate method in the service of prehistoric research). Jahresschrift mitteldeutsche Vorgeschichte 38:265-275.

1399 Buehrer, T. F. (1950) Chemical study of the material from several horizons of the Ventana Cave profile. In: E. Haury et al., The stratigraphy and archaeology of Ventana Cave, Arizona. Tucson: Univ. of Arizona Press, 549-563.

1400 Burleigh, E. (1980) Appendix E--chemical analysis of sediments. Bulletin of the Texas archeological society 51:162-163.

1401 Butzer, K. W., Beaumont, P. B. and Vogel, J. C. (1978) Lithostratigraphy of Border Cave, Kwazulu, South Africa: a Middle Stone Age sequence beginning c. 195,000 B.P. Journal of archaeological science 5:317-341.

1402 Cook, S. F. and Heizer, R. F. (1965) Studies on the chemical analysis of archaeological sites. Univ. of California publications in anthropology, no. 2. Los Angeles.

1403 Cornwall, I. W. (1953) Soil science and archaeology. Proceedings of the prehistoric society 19:129-147.

1404 Cornwall, I. W. (1954) Archaeology and soil studies. Archaeological newsletter (London) 5:21-23; 69-73.

1405 Cornwall, I. W. (1958) Soils for the archaeologist. London: Phoenix.

1406 Coughlin, E. A. and Ericson, J. E. (1980) Biogeochemical residues as ethnobotanical indicators. Botanical Museum, Harvard University. Botanical Museum leaflets 28(1):71-80.

1407 Cruxent, J. M. (1962) Phosphorus content of the Texas Street 'hearths'. American antiquity 28:90-91.

1408 Dalrymple, J. B. (1958) The application of soil micromorphology to fossil soils and other deposits from archaeological sites. Journal of soil science 9:199-209.

134

1409 Davidson, D. A. (1973) Particle size and phosphate analysis: evidence for the evolution of a tell. Archaeometry 15(1):143-152.

1410 Davidson, D. A. (1978) Aegean soils during the second millennium B.C. with reference to Thera. In: Thera and the Aegean world. London: Thera and the Aegean World, 725-739.

1411 Deetz, J. and Dethlefsen, E. (1963) Soil pH as a tool in archaeological site interpretation. American antiquity 29:242-243.

1412 Dietz, E. F. (1957) Phosphorus accumulation in soil of an Indian habitation site. American antiquity 22:405-409.

1413 Dekker, L. W. and Weerd, M. D. de (1973) The value of soil survey for archaeology. Geoderma 10:169-178.

1414 Eddy, F. W. and Dregne, H. E. (1964) Soil tests on alluvial and archaeological deposits, Navajo Reservoir district. El palacio 71:5-21.

1415 Eidt, R. C. (1973) A rapid chemical field test for archaeological site surveying. American antiquity 38:206-210.

1416 Eidt, R. C. (1977) Detection and examination of anthrosols by phosphate analysis. Science 197(4311):1327-1333.

1417 Eidt, R. C. and Woods, W. I. (1974) Abandoned settlement analysis: theory and practice. Milwaukee, Wisconsin: Field Test Associates.

1418 Evans, J. G. and Valentine, K. W. G. (1974) Ecological changes induced by prehistoric man at Pitstone, Buckinghamshire. Journal of archaeological science 1(4):343-351.

1419 Evans, R. and Jones, R. J. A. (1977) Crop marks and soils at two archaeological sites in Britain. Journal of archaeological science 4(1):63-76.

1420 Farrand, W. R. (1975) Sediment analysis of a prehistoric rockshelter: the Abri Pataud. Quaternary research 5:1-26.

1421 Frauendorf, E. (1953/1954) Neue siedlungs-
      archäologische Erkenntnisse mit der Phosphatmethode.
      (New settlement archaeological knowledge with the
      phosphate method). Alt-Thüringen 1:84-98.

1422 Frauendorf, E. and Lorch, W. (1940) Einfache Boden-
      untersuchungen im Dienste der Vorzeitforschung.
      (Simple soil investigations in the service of
      prehistoric research). Nachrichtenblatt für deutsche
      Vorzeit 16:265.

1423 Gardner, R. A. M. (1977) Evidence concerning the
      existence of loess deposits at Tell Fara, northern
      Negev, Israel. Journal of archaeological science
      4:377-386.

1424 Geiger, H. (1936) Bodenuntersuchung und Archäologie.
      Naturwissenschaften 24:608.

1425 Goldberg, P. and Nathan, Y. (1975) The phosphate
      mineralogy from et-Tabun Cave, Mt. Carmel, Israel.
      Mineralogical magazine 40:253-258.

1426 Griffith, M. A. and Frazer, M. (1978) The use of soil
      analysis in archeological research. Man in the
      northeast 15/16:118-124.

1427 Grimm, P. (1962) Phosphatuntersuchungen zur Besiedlung
      der Pfalz Tilleda. (Phosphate investigations on the
      settlement of the Pfalz Tilleda). Ausgrabungen und
      Funde 7:8-12.

1428 Grubb, T. C. (1979) Experience with the phosphate test
      to locate ancient habitation sites. Ohio
      archaeologist 29(2):52-55.

1429 Grundlach, H. (1961) Tüpfelmethode auf Phosphat,
      angewand in prähistorischer Forschung (als Feld-
      methode). (Spot method for phosphate, applied in
      prehistoric research as a field method). Mikro-
      chimica acta 5:735-737.

1430 Helgren, D. M. and Butzer, K. W. (1977) Paleosols of
      the southern Cape coast, South Africa: implications
      for laterite definition, genesis and age. Geo-
      graphical review 67:430-445.

136

1431 Hughes, P. J. and Lampert, R. J. (1977) Occupational disturbance and types of archaeological deposit. Journal of archaeological science 4:135-140.

1432 Hunt, C. B. and Hunt, A. P. (1957) Stratigraphy and archeology of some Florida soils. Bulletin of the geological society of America 68:797-806.

1433 Jacob, H. (1955) Die Bedeutung der Phosphatmethode für die Urgeschichte und Bodenforschung. (The significance of the phosphate method for prehistory and soil research). Beiträge zur Frühgeschichte der Landwirtschaft 2:67-85.

1434 Keeley, H. C. M., Hudson, G. E. and Evans, J. (1977) Trace element contents of human bones in various states of preservation, 1. The soil silhouette. Journal of archaeological science 4(1):19-24.

1435 Kiefman, H.-M. (1980) Geographische Untersuchungen in der Siedlungskammer Haereid in Norwegen unter besonderer Verwendung der Phosphatmethode. (Geographical investigations of the Haereid settlement in Norway with special application of phosphate methods). Offa 37:394-407.

1436 Lal, B. B. (1965) Soil as an environmental and chronological tool. Indian prehistory: 1964, no. 32:237-257.

1437 Law, J. (1977) The fate of particle size analysis in sedimentology. Science and archaeology 19:30-34.

1438 Leaf, A. G. (1972) Experiments in soil chemistry. Proceedings of the 28th southeastern archaeological conference, bulletin no. 15:67-77.

1439 Limbrey, S. (1975) Soil science in archaeology. London: Seminar Press; New York: Academic Press.

1440 Linke, B. (1979) Die Reichsbodenschatzung als Hilfsmittel der Prähistorie. (Soil evaluation as an aid to prehistory). Prähistorische Zeitschrift 54:177-186.

1441 Lisitsyna, G. N. and Kostjučenko, V. P. (1976) Počva kak istočnik informatsii pri izučenii drevnego zemledelija. (Soil, a source of information for the study of ancient agriculture). Sovetskaja arkheologija 1:23-41.

1442 Lorch, W. (1940) Die siedlungsgeographische Phosphat-methode. (The phosphate method of settlement geo-graphy). Naturwissenschaften 28:635-640.

1443 Lorch, W. (1954) Die anthropogenen Bodenphosphate des Hohenstaufen-Gipfels. (The anthropogenic soil phosphate of the Hohenstaufen-Gipfels). Jahrbücher für Statistik und Landeskunde von Baden-Württemberg 1:367-375.

1444 Lord, A. C. (1961) An introduction to soils. Massachusetts archaeological society bulletin 23(1):14-18.

1445 Lutz, H. J. (1951) The concentration of certain chemical elements in the soils of Alaskan archaeo-logical sites. American journal of science 249:925-928.

1446 McCawley, J. C. and McKerrell, H. (1971/1972) Soil phosphorus levels at archaeological sites. Pro-ceedings of the society of antiquaries of Scotland 104:301-315.

1447 Mahula, R. (1977) The geosphere: physiography, stratigraphy and soil analysis. Hop Hill: culture and climatic change in central Texas. Center for archaeological research, Univ. of Texas at San Antonio special report 5:121-136.

1448 Mattingly, S. E. G. and Williams, R. J. B. (1962) A note on the chemical analysis of a soil buried since Roman times. Journal of soil science 13(2):254-257.

1449 Modderman, P. J. R. (1971) Neolithische und früh-bronzezeitliche Siedlungsspuren aus Hienheim, Ldkr. Kelheim. (Neolithic and Early Bronze Age settlement traces from Hienheim, vicinity of Kelheim). Analecta praehistorica leidensia 4:1-25.

138

1450 Mulvaney, D. J. and Joyce, E. B. (1965) Archaeological
      and geomorphological investigations on Mt. Moffatt
      Station, Queensland, Australia. Proceedings of the
      prehistoric society 31:147-212.

1451 Olson, G. W. (1978) Field report on sampling of buried
      Maya soils around San Salvador and in the Zapotitan
      Basin, El Salvador: an evaluation of soil properties
      and potentials in different volcanic deposits.
      Research of the protoclassic project in the Zapotitan
      Basin, El Salvador. Boulder, Colorado: Dept. of
      Anthropology, Univ. of Colorado, 22-30.

1452 Palmieri, A. M. (1976/1977) Sedimentological study of
      the upper Paleolithic site of Palidoro. Quaternaria
      (Roma) 19:163-179.

1453 Pearsall, D. M. (1978) Phytolith analysis of archaeo-
      logical soils: evidence for maize cultivation in
      Formative Ecuador. Science 199(4325):177-178.

1454 Piperno, M. (1976/1977) Analyse du sol Moustérien de la
      Grotte Guattari au Mont Circé. Quaternaria (Roma)
      19:71-92.

1455 Pollock, G. E., Cheng, C.-N. and Cronin, S. E. (1977)
      Determination of the D and L isomers of some protein
      amino acids present in soils. Analytical chemistry
      49(1):2-7.

1456 Poupet, P. and Trichet, J. (1977) Contribution à
      l'étude du site de Djaffarabad (Susiane, Iran);
      apport des observations pédologiques et géochimiques.
      Cahiers de la délégation archéologique française en
      Iran, Paris 7:55-60.

1457 Provan, D. M. J. (1971) Soil phosphate analysis as a
      tool in archaeology. Norwegian archaeological review
      4:37-50.

1458 Provan, D. M. J. (1973) The soils of an Iron Age farm
      site--Bjellandsøynae, SW Norway. Norwegian
      archaeological review 6(1):30-42

1459 Rosenfeld, A. (1966) Analysis of residual deposits as-
      sociated with interments. In: I. F. Smith and D. D.
      A. Simpson, Excavations of a round barrow on Overton
      Hill, North Wiltshire. Proc. Prehistoric Soc. 32:142.

1460 Salim, M. (1979) Soil analysis from the Middle Stone Age sites in northern Pakistan. Man and environment (Ahmedabad) 3:1-6.

1461 Saucier, R. (1966) Soil-survey reports and archaeological investigations. American antiquity 31:419-422.

1462 Sauter, F. (1967) Phosphatanalytische Untersuchungen von Erdproben aus einem awarischen Grab. (Phosphate analysis investigations of soil samples from an Avar grave). Archaeologia austriaca 41:41-43.

1463 Schmid, E. (1958) Höhlenforschung und Sedimentanalyse, Basel. (Cave research and sediment analysis, Basel). Schriften des Institutes für Ur- und Frühgeschichte der Schweiz 13:21-36.

1464 Schraps, W. G. (1975) Pedologisch-geologische Untersuchungen bei archäologischen Ausgrabungen. (Pedological-geological investigations at archaeological excavations). Decheniana 128:37-40.

1465 Schwarz, G. T. (1967) A simplified chemical test for archaeological field work. Archaeometry 10:57-63.

1466 Shackley, M. L. (1975) Archaeological sediments. A survey of analytical methods. London and Boston: Butterworths.

1467 Sieveking, G. de G. et al. (1973) A new survey of Grime's Graves, Norfolk. Proceedings of the prehistoric society 39:182-218.

1468 Sjöberg, A. (1976) Phosphate analysis of anthropic soils. Journal of field archaeology 3(4):447-454.

1469 Slager, S. and Wetering, H. T. J. van de (1977) Soil formation in archaeological pits and adjacent loess soils in southern Germany. Journal of archaeological science 4:259-267.

1470 So, C. L. (1979) Sham Wan archaeological site: further observations on soil samples. Journal of the Hong Kong archaeological society 7:118-124.

1471 Solecki, R. S. (1951) Notes on soil analysis and archaeology. American antiquity 16:254-256.

140

1472 Stoye, K. (1950) Die Anwendung der Phosphatmethode auf
einem mittelalterlichen Friedhof. (The application
of the phosphate method on a medieval cemetery).
Jahresschrift für mitteldeutsche Vorgeschichte
34:180-184.

1473 Strunk-Lichtenberg, G. (1980) Versuch einer Charak-
terisierung von anthropogenen Boden durch Korn-
klassierung und Messung von Farbquotienten. (An
experiment in characterizing anthropogenic soil by
grain size and measurement of color quotients).
Archaeo-Physika 7:1-6.

1474 Taylor, T. P. (1979) Soil mark studies near Winchester,
Hampshire. Journal of archaeological science
6(9):93-100.

1475 Trinkley, M. B. and Ward, H. T. (1978) The use of soil
science at a South Carolina Thom's Creek culture
shell ring. Florida anthropologist 31(2):64-73.

1476 Villa, P. (1976/1977) Sols et niveaux d'habitat du
paléolithique inférieur en Europe et au Proche
Orient. Quaternaria (Roma) 19:107-134.

1477 Weide, D. L. (1966) Soil pH as a guide to archaeological investigation. Archaeological Survey, Univ.
of California, Los Angeles. Annual report, 155-163.

1478 White, L. P. (1977) Aerial photography and remote
sensing for soil survey. Oxford: Clarendon Press.

1479 Woods, W. I. (1975) The analysis of abandoned settlements by a new phosphate field test method. The
Chesopiean 13:1-45.

1480 Woods, W. I. (1977) The quantitative analysis of soil
phosphate. American antiquity 42(2):248-252.

2. Paleoclimatology and paleotemperature determination

1481 Addyman, P. V. et al. (1976) Palaeoclimate in urban
environmental archaeology at York, England:
problems and potential. World archaeology 8:220-233.

1482 Brehme, K. (1951) Jahrringchronologische und klima-
     tologische Untersuchungen an Hochgebirgslärchen des
     Berchtesgadener Landes. (Annual ring chronological
     and climatological investigations on high altitude
     larches of the Berchtesgarden region). Zeitschrift
     für Weltforstwirtschaft 14:65-80.

1483 Brett, D. W. (1978) Dendroclimatology of elm in London.
     Tree-ring bulletin 38:35-44.

1484 Buckland, P. C. and Kenward, H. K. (1973) Thorne Moor,
     the palaeoclimatological implications of a late
     Bronze Age site. Nature 241:405-406.

1485 Butzer, K. W. (1976) Pleistocene climates. Geoscience
     and man 13:27-44.

1486 Dansgaard, W. et al. (1969) One thousand centuries of
     climatic record from Camp Century on the Greenland
     ice sheet. Science 166:377-381.

1487 Dansgaard, W. et al. (1970) Ice cores and paleo-
     climatology. In: I. U. Olsson, ed., Radiocarbon
     cariations and absolute chronology. Stockholm:
     Almqvist & Wiksell; New York: J. Wiley, 338-348.

1488 Dennell, R. W. (1977) On the problems of studying
     prehistoric climate and crop agriculture.
     Proceedings of the prehistoric society 43:361-369.

1489 Drew, L. G., ed. (1976) Tree-ring chronologies for
     dendroclimatic analysis: an expanded western North
     American grid. Laboratory for tree-ring research,
     chronology series 2. Tucson: Univ. of Arizona.

1490 Emiliani, C. (1955) Pleistocene temperatures. Journal
     of geology 63:538-578.

1491 Emiliani, C. (1958) Paleotemperature analysis of core
     280 and Pleistocene correlations. Journal of geology
     66:264-275.

1492 Emiliani, C. (1966) Isotopic paleotemperatures. Science
     154:851-857.

1493 Ericson, D. B., Ewing, M. and Wollin, G. (1964) The
     Pleistocene epoch in deep-sea sediments. Science
     146:723-732.

1494   Ericson, D. B. et al. (1961) Atlantic deep-sea
       sediment cores. Bulletin of the geological society
       of America 75:193-286.

1495   Flint, R. F. (1959) Pleistocene climates in eastern
       and southern Africa. Geological survey of America
       bulletin 70:343-374.

1496   Fritts, H. C. (1962) An approach to dendroclimatology:
       screening by means of multiple regression techniques.
       Journal of geophysical research 67:1413-1420.

1497   Fritts, H. C. (1963) Recent advances in dendrochronol-
       ogy in America with reference to the significance of
       climatic change. In: Arid zone research X, changes
       of climate. Paris: UNESCO, 255-263.

1498   Fritts, H. C. (1965) Tree-ring evidence for climatic
       changes in western North America. Monthly weather
       review 93(7):421-443.

1499   Fritts, H. C. (1966) Growth-rings of trees: their
       correlation with climate. Science 154:973-979.

1500   Fritts, H. C. (1971) Dendroclimatology and dendro-
       ecology. Quaternary research 1(4):419-449.

1501   Fritts, H. C. (1977) Tree rings and climate. London/
       New York: Academic Press. 567p.

1502   Fritts, H. C. et al. (1965) The variability of ring
       characteristics within trees as shown by a re-
       analysis of four Ponderosa pine. Tree-ring bulletin
       27(1/2):3-18.

1503   Fritts, H. C. et al. (1971) Multivariate techniques
       for specifying tree-growth and climate relationships
       and for reconstructing anomalies in paleoclimate.
       Journal of applied meteorology 10(5):845-864.

1504   Fritts, H. C. and Shatz, D. J. (1975) Selecting and
       characterizing tree-ring chronologies for dendro-
       climatic analysis. Tree-ring bulletin 35:31-40.

1505   Fritts, H. C., Smith, D. G. and Stokes, M. A. (1965)
       The biological model for paleoclimatic interpreta-
       tion of Mesa Verde tree-ring series. American
       antiquity 31(2):101-121.

1506 Goldberg, P. (1979) Micromorphology of Pech-de-l'Aze II sediments. Journal of archaeological science 6(1):17-47.

1507 Graham, R. W. (1979) Paleoclimates and late Pleistocene faunal provinces in North America. In: Pre-Llano cultures of the Americas. Washington, D.C.: Anthropological Society of Washington, 49-69.

1508 Hafsten, U. (1977) Paleoecological studies in southeastern Norway, with special reference to the post-Weichselian climatic optimum. In: Dendrochronologie und postglaziale Klimaschwankungen in Europa. Wiesbaden: F. Steiner, 282-296.

1509 Haury, E. W. (1934) Climate and human history. Tree-ring bulletin 1(2):13-15.

1510 Hubbard, R. N. L. B. (1976) Crops and climate in prehistoric Europe. World archaeology 8:159-168.

1511 Julian, P. R. and Fritts, H. C. (1968) On the possibility of quantitatively extending climatic records by means of dendroclimatological analysis. Proceedings of the first statistical meteorological conference, American meteorological society, 76-82.

1512 LaMarche, V. C. (1969) Environment in relation to age of bristlecone pines. Ecology 50:53-59.

1513 LaMarche, V. C. (1974) Frequency-dependent relationships between tree-ring series along an ecological gradient and some dendroclimatic implications. Tree-ring bulletin 34:1-20.

1514 LaMarche, V. C. (1974) Paleoclimatic inferences from long tree-ring records. Science 183(4129):1043-1048.

1515 LaMarche, V. C. and Fritts, H. C. (1971) Anomaly patterns of climate over the United States, 1700-1930, derived from principal component analysis of tree-ring data. Monthly weather review 99:138-142.

1516 Lamb, H. H. (1974) Reconstructing the climatic patterns of the historical past. Endeavour 33:40-47.

144

1517   Lamb, H. H. (1974) University of East Anglia Climatic
        Research Unit School of Environmental Sciences:
        second annual report. Science and archaeology
        12:13-20.

1518   Paquerau, M. M. (1970) Flores et climats paléolithiques
        dans le Sud-Ouest de la France. Revue de géographie
        physique et géologie dynamique 12(2):109-116.

1519   Raikes, R. (1967) Water, weather and prehistory.
        London: John Baker. 208p.

1520   Salisbury, E. J. and Jane, F. W. (1940) Charcoals from
        Maiden Castle and their significance in relation to
        the vegetation and climatic conditions in prehistoric
        times. Journal of ecology 28:310-325.

1521   Schove, D. J. (1971) Biennial oscillations and solar
        cycles, A.D. 1490-1970. Weather 26:201-209.

1522   Schulman, E. (1950) Dendroclimatic histories in the
        Bryce Canyon area, Utah. Tree-ring bulletin
        17(1/2):2-16.

1523   Schulman, E. (1954) Dendroclimatic changes in semiarid
        regions. Tree-ring bulletin 20(3/4):26-30.

1524   Schulman, E. (1956) Dendroclimatic changes in semiarid
        America. Tucson: Univ. of Arizona Press.

1525   Schweingruber, F. H. et al. (1978) The X-ray technique
        as applied to dendroclimatology. Tree-ring bulletin
        38:61-91.

1526   Serre, F. (1978) The dendroclimatological value of the
        European larch (Larix decidua Mill.) in the French
        maritime Alps. Tree-ring bulletin 38:25-34.

1527   Shackleton, N. J. (1967) Oxygen isotope analyses and
        Pleistocene temperatures reassessed. Nature 215:
        15-17.

1528   Shackleton, N. J. (1973) Oxygen isotope analysis as a
        means of determining season of occupation of pre-
        historic midden sites. Archaeometry 15(1):133-141.

1529 Shackleton, N. J. and Turner, C. (1967) Correlation of marine and terrestrial Pleistocene successions. Nature 216:1079-1082.

1530 Smith, D. G. and Nichols, R. F. (1967) A tree-ring chronology for climatic analysis. Tree-ring bulletin 28(1-4):7-12.

1531 Stockton, C. W. and Fritts, H. C. (1971) Conditional probability of occurrence for variations in climate based on width of annual tree-rings in Arizona. Tree-ring bulletin 31:3-24.

1532 Wilson, A. T. and Grinsted, M. J. (1975) Palaeotemperatures from tree rings and the D/H ratio of cellulose as a biochemical thermometer. Nature 257:387-388.

C. Biosphere

1. Biological data retrieval

1533 Aschenbrenner, S. E. and Cooke, S. R. B. (1978) Screening and gravity concentration: recovery of small scale remains. In: G. Rapp and S. E. Aschenbrenner, eds., Excavations at Nichoria in southwest Greece. Minneapolis: Univ. of Minnesota Press, 156-165.

1534 Barker, G. (1975) To sieve or not to sieve. Antiquity 49:61-63.

1535 Bodner, C. C. and Rowlett, R. M. (1980) Separation of bone, charcoal, and seeds by chemical flotation. American antiquity 45(1):110-116.

1536 Cavallo, J. A. (1980) Subsistence retrieval techniques at 28MonC1: utility for archaeology in the northeast. Bulletin of the archaeological society of New Jersey 36:30-33.

1537 Cherry, J. F. (1975) Efficient soil searching: some comments. Antiquity 49:217-219.

1538 Coyler, M. and Osborne, D. (1965) Screening soil and
      fecal samples for recovery of small specimens.
      Memoirs of the society of American archaeology
      19:186-192.

1539 Davis, E. and Wesolowsky, A. (1975) The Izum: a
      simple water separation device. Journal of field
      archaeology 2:271-273.

1540 Diamint, S. (1979) A short history of sieving at
      Franchthi Cave, Greece. Journal of field archaeology
      6(2):203-217.

1541 Dye, D. H. and Moore, K. H. (1978) Recovery systems
      for subsistence data: water screening and water
      flotation. Tennessee anthropologist 3(1):59-69.

1542 French, D. (1971) An experiment in water-sieving.
      Anatolian studies 31:59-64.

1543 Guillet, B. and Planchais, N. (1969) Note sur une
      technique d'extraction des pollens des sols par une
      solution dense. Pollen et spores 11:141-145.

1544 Jarman, H. N. (1976) The retrieval and sampling of
      plant remains from archaeological sites. Folia
      quaternaria 47:41-45.

1545 Jarman, H. N., Legge, A. J. and Charles, J. A. (1972)
      Retrieval of plant remains from archaeological sites
      by froth flotation. In: E. S. Higgs, ed., Papers in
      economic prehistory. Cambridge: Cambridge Univ.
      Press, 39-48.

1546 Keeley, H. C. M. (1978) The cost-effectiveness of
      certain methods of recovering macroscopic organic
      remains from archaeological deposits. Journal of
      archaeological science 5:179-183.

1547 Keepax, C. (1977) Contamination of archaeological
      deposits by seeds of modern origin with particular
      reference to the use of flotation machines. Journal
      of archaeological science 4(3):221-229.

1548 Lange, F. and Carty, F. (1975) Salt water application
      of the flotation technique. Journal of field
      archaeology 2:119-123.

1549 Lees, P. M. (1964) A flotation method of obtaining mammal teeth from Mesozoic bonebeds. Curator 7(4):300-306.

1550 Limp, W. F. (1974) Water separation and flotation processes. Journal of field archaeology 1:337-342.

1551 Pendleton, M. W. (1979) A flotation apparatus for archaeological sites. Kiva (Tucson) 44(2/3):89-93.

1552 Streuver, S. (1968) Flotation techniques for the recovery of small-scale archaeological remains. American antiquity 33:353-362.

1553 Watson, P. J. (1976) In pursuit of economic subsistence: a comparative account of some contemporary flotation techniques. Mid-continental journal of archaeology 1:77-100.

1554 Weaver, M. E. (1971) a new water separation process for soil from archaeological excavations. Anatolian studies 31:65-68.

1555 Williams, D. (1973) Flotation at Siraf. Antiquity 47:288-292.

1556 Williams, D. (1976) Preliminary observations on the use of flotation apparatus in Sussex. Part XII of rescue archaeology in Sussex, 1975. Bulletin of the Institute of Archaeology, no. 13:51-58.

2. Faunal

a) Methodological, theoretical and general studies

1557 Armitage, P. L. (1978) A system for the recording and processing of data relating to animal remains from archaeological sites. Research problems in zoo-archaeology. Institute of Archaeology, occasional publication 3:39-45.

1558 Bahn, P. G. (1977) Seasonal migration in south west France during the late glacial period. Journal of archaeological science 4:245-257.

148

1559 Barber, M. (1978) On the preparation of a faunal type
      collection. Quarterly bulletin of the archaeological
      society of Virginia 32(3):49-55.

1560 Berry, R. J. (1978) Microevolutionary studies in
      animals: their relevance to archaeology. Institute
      of Archaeology, occasional publication 3:1-8.

1561 Boessneck, J. and Driesch, A. von den (1978) The sig-
      nificance of measuring animal bones from archaeo-
      logical sites. In: Approaches to faunal analysis in
      the Middle East. Peabody Museum bulletin 2:25-39.

1562 Bökönyi, S. (1970) A new method for the determination
      of the number of individuals in animal bone material.
      American journal of archaeology 74:291-292.

1563 Bökönyi, S. (1972) Zoological evidence for seasonal
      or permanent occupation of prehistoric settlements.
      Reading, Massachusetts: Warner Modular Publications.

1564 Bonnichsen, R. and Sanger, D. (1977) Integrating
      faunal analysis. Canadian journal of archaeology
      1:109-133.

1565 Brothwell, D. R., Thomas, K. D. and Clutton-Brock, J.
      (1979) Research problems in zooarchaeology.
      Occasional publications no. 3. London: Institute of
      Archaeology.

1566 Buckland, P. C. (1974) Archaeology and environment in
      York. Journal of archaeological science 1(4):303-316.

1567 Byers, D. S. (1951) On the interpretation of faunal
      remains. American antiquity 16:262-263.

1568 Casteel, R. W. (1965) The role of faunal remains in
      archaeological investigations. Sacramento archaeo-
      logical society papers 3:47-75.

1569 Casteel, R. W. (1970) Core and column sampling.
      American antiquity 35:465-466.

1570 Casteel, R. W. (1971) Differential bone destruction:
      some comments. American antiquity 36:466-468.

1571 Casteel, R. W. (1972) Some biases in the recovery of archaeological faunal remains. Proceedings of the prehistoric society 38:382-388.

1572 Casteel, R. W. (1974) On the number and sizes of animals in archaeological faunal assemblages. Archaeometry 16(2):238-243.

1573 Casteel, R. W. (1976/1977) A consideration of the behaviour of the minimum number of individuals index: a problem in faunal characterization. Ossa 3/4: 141-151.

1574 Casteel, R. W. (1977) Characterization of faunal assemblages and the minimum number of individuals determined from paired elements: continuing problems in archaeology. Journal of archaeological science 4(2):125-134.

1575 Casteel, R. W. and Grayson, D. K. (1977) Terminological problems in quantitative faunal analysis. World archaeology 9:235-242.

1576 Chaplin, R. E. (1965) Animals in archaeology. Antiquity 39:204-211.

1577 Chaplin, R. E. (1971) The study of animal bones from archaeological sites. New York: Academic Press.

1578 Clark, J. G. D. (1954) Excavations at Star Carr. Cambridge: Cambridge Univ. Press.

1579 Clark, J. G. D. (1972) Star Carr: a case study in bioarchaeology. Reading, Massachusetts: Addison-Wesley Modular Publications. No. 10. 42p.

1580 Clason, A. T. (1972) Some remarks on the use and presentation of archaeozoological data. Helinium 12:139-153.

1581 Clason, A. T., ed. (1975) Archaeozoological studies. New York: Am. Elsevier; Amsterdam: North Holland.

1582 Clason, A. T. and Brinkhuizen, D. C. (1978) Swifterbant mammals, birds, fishes. A preliminary report. Swifterbant contribution 8. Helinium 18(1):69-82.

1583 Clason, A. T. and Prummel, W. (1977) Collecting, sieving and archaeozoological research. Journal of archaeological science 4(2):171-175.

1584 Cleland, C. E. (1966) The prehistoric animal ecology and ethnozoology of the Upper Great Lakes region. Museum of Anthropology, University of Michigan. Anthropological papers, no. 29. 294p.

1585 Clutton-Brock, J. (1978) Bones for the zoologist. In: Approaches to faunal analysis in the Middle East. Peabody Museum bulletin 2:49-51.

1586 Cornwall, I. W. (1956) Bones for the archaeologist. London: Phoenix House.

1587 Coy, J. P. (1978) Comparative collections for zooarchaeology. Institute of Archaeology, occasional publication 3:143-145.

1588 Crabtree, P. J. (1979) Archaeological faunal analysis: some recent references. MASCA journal 1(3):87-89.

1589 Daly, P. (1969) Approaches to faunal analysis in archaeology. American antiquity 34(2):146-153.

1590 Driesch, A. von den (1976) A guide to the measurement of animal bones from archaeological sites. Harvard University. Peabody Museum bulletin 1. 136p.

1591 Ducos, P. (1978) Domestication defined and methodological approaches to its recognition in faunal assemblages. In: Approaches to faunal analysis in the Middle East. Peabody Museum bulletin 2:53-56.

1592 Friedman, E. (1973) Preparation of faunal specimens. American antiquity 38:113-114.

1593 Gamble, C. (1978) Optimizing information from studies of faunal remains. British archaeological reports, British series 50:321-353.

1594 Grayson, D. K. (1973) On the methodology of faunal analysis. American antiquity 38(4):432-438.

1595 Grayson, D. K. (1974) The Riverhaven no. 2 vertebrate fauna: comments on methods in faunal analysis and on aspects of the subsistence potential of prehistoric New York. Man in the northeast 8:23-40.

1596 Grayson, D. K. (1978) Minimum numbers and sample size in vertebrate faunal analysis. American antiquity 43(1):53-65.

1597 Grigson, C. (1978) Toward a blueprint for animal bone reports in archaeology. Institute of Archaeology, occasional publication 3:121-128.

1598 Harcourt, R. A. (1971) The palaeopathology of animal skeletal remains. Veterinary record 89:267-272.

1599 Hercus, B. H. (1960) Plant cuticle as an aid to determining the diet of grazing animals. Proceedings of the eighth international grasslands congress, 443-447.

1600 Higham, C. F. W. (1968) Faunal sampling and economic prehistory. Zeitschrift für Säugetierkunde 33: 297-305.

1601 Hill, A. (1979) Butchery and natural disarticulation: an investigatory technique. American antiquity 44(4):739-744.

1602 Hill, F. C. (1975) Techniques for skeletonizing vertebrates. American antiquity 40:215-219.

1603 Kubasiewicz, M. (1973) Spezifische Elemente der polnischen archäozoologischen Forschungen des letzten Vierteljahrhunderts. (Specific elements of Polish archaeozoological research of the last quarter century). In: J. Matolcsi, ed., Domestikations-forschung und Geschichte der Haustiere. Budapest: Akadémiai Kiadó, 371-376.

1604 Kubasiewicz, M. (1975) Zur Interpretation von zoo-archäologischen Materialien aus grossen frühmittel-alterlichen Siedlungen. (On the interpretation of zooarchaeological materials from large early medieval settlements). In: A. T. Clason, ed., Archaeozoolog-ical studies. New York: American Elsevier; Amsterdam: North Holland, 240-247.

1605 La Bianca, Ø. S. (1978) The logistic and strategic aspects of faunal analysis in Palestine. In: Approaches to faunal analysis in the Middle East. Peabody Museum bulletin 2:3-9.

1606 Lasota-Moskalewska, A. and Sulgostowska, Z. (1976/1977) The application of contingency table for comparison of archaeozoological materials. Ossa 3/4:153-168.

1607 Lawrence, B. (1973) Problems in the inter-site comparison of faunal remains. In: J. Matolcsi, ed., Domestikationsforschung und Geschichte der Haustiere. Budapest: Akadémiai Kiadó, 397-402.

1608 Leeds, A. and Vayda, A. P., eds. (1965) Man, culture and animals. Washington, D.C.: American Association for the Advancement of Science.

1609 Legge, A. J. (1978) Archaeozoology--or zooarchaeology? Institute of Archaeology, occasional publication 3:129-132.

1610 Lie, R. W. (1980) Minimum number of individuals from osteological samples. Norwegian archaeological review 13(1):24-30.

1611 Lyman, R. L. (1979) Available meat from faunal remains: a consideration of techniques. American antiquity 44(3):536-546.

1612 Lyman, R. L. (1979) Faunal analysis: an outline of method and theory with some suggestions. Northwest anthropological research notes 13(1):22-35.

1613 Lyon, P. J. (1970) Differential bone destruction: an ethnographic example. American antiquity 35:213-215.

1614 Meadow, R. H. (1978) Effects of context on the interpretation of faunal remains: a case study. In: Approaches to faunal analysis in the Middle East. Peabody Museum bulletin 2:15-21.

1615 Meadow, R. H. and Zeder, M. A., eds. (1978) Approaches to faunal analysis in the Middle East. Harvard University. Peabody Museum bulletin 2.

1616 Mori, J. L. (1970) Procedures for establishing a faunal collection to aid in archaeological analysis. American antiquity 35:387-388.

1617 Noddle, B. (1971) Estimation of body weight from measurements on bones. III Congres international des Musees d'Agriculture. Budapest, 232.

1618 Noe-Nygaard, N. (1977) Butchering and marrow fracturing as a taphonomic factor in archaeological deposits. Paleobiology 3:218-237.

1619 Olsen, S. J. (1971) Zooarchaeology: animal bones in archaeology and their interpretation. Reading, Massachusetts: Addison-Wesley Modular Publications. No. 2. 30p.

1620 Olsen, S. J. (1979) Archaeologically, what constitutes an early domestic animal? Advances in archaeological method and theory 2:175-197.

1621 Payne, S. (1975) Partial recovery and sample bias. In: A. T. Clason, ed., Archaeozoological studies. New York: American Elsevier; Amsterdam: North Holland, 7-17.

1622 Perkins, D. (1971) A new method of quantifying faunal remains. III Congrès international des Musées d'Agriculture. Budapest, 228-229.

1623 Perkins, D. (1973) A critique on the methods of quantifying faunal remains from archaeological sites. In: J. Matolcsi, ed., Domestikationsforschung und Geschichte der Haustiere. Budapest: Akadémiai Kiadó, 367-370.

1624 Perkins, D. and Daly, P. (1968) The potential of faunal analysis. An investigation of the faunal remains from Suberde, Turkey. Scientific American 219:96-106.

1625 Ryder, M. L. (1963) Animal bones in archaeology. Oxford: Blackwell Scientific.

1626 Sadek-Kooros, H. (1972) Primitive bone fracturing: a method of research. American antiquity 37:369-382.

1627 Shipman, P. (1975) Implications of drought for vertebrate fossil assemblages. Nature 257:667-668.

154

1628   Siegel, J. (1976) Animal palaeopathology: possibilities and problems. Journal of archaeological science 3:349-384.

1629   Stewart, F. L. and Stahl, P. W. (1977) A cautionary note on edible meat poundage figures. American antiquity 42:267-269

1630   Tappen, N. C. and Peske, G. R. (1970) Weathering cracks and split-line orientation in archaeological bone. American antiquity 35:383-386.

1631   Technique for determining animal domestication based on study of thin sections of bone under polarized light. (1973) MASCA newsletter 9(2):1-2.

1632   Thomas, D. H. (1969) Great Basin hunting patterns: a quantitative method for treating faunal remains. American antiquity 34:392-401.

1633   Thomas, D. H. (1971) On distinguishing natural from cultural bone in archaeological sites. American antiquity 36:366-370.

1634   Uerpmann, H.-P. (1971) Ein Beitrag zur Methodik der wirtschaftshistorischen Auswertung von Tierknochenfunden aus Siedlungen. (A contribution to the method of economic-historical utilization of animal bones from settlements). III Congrès international des Musées d'Agriculture. Budapest, 230-232.

1635   Uerpmann, H. P. (1973) Animal bone finds and economic archaeology: a critical study of "osteo-archaeological" method. World archaeology 4(3):307-322.

1636   Vehik, S. C. (1977) Bone fragments and bone grease manufacturing: a review of their archaeological use and potential. Plains anthropologist 23:169-182.

1637   Watson, J. P. N. (1972) Fragmentation analysis of animal bone samples from archaeological sites. Archaeometry 14(2):221-228.

1638   Watson, J. P. N. (1978) The interpretation of epiphyseal fusion data. Institute of Archaeology, occasional publication 3:97-101.

1639 White, T. E. (1952-1955) Observations on the butchering technique of some aboriginal peoples. American antiquity 17:337-338; 19:160-164; 19:254-264; 21:170-178.

1640 White, T. E. (1953) A method of calculating the dietary percentage of various food animals utilized by aboriginal peoples. American antiquity 18:396-398.

1641 White, T. E. (1953) Studying osteological material. Plains archaeological conference newsletter 6:8-15.

1642 White, T. E. (1956) The study of osteological materials in the Plains. American antiquity 21:401-404.

1643 Wilkinson, P. F. (1976) "Random" hunting and the composition of faunal samples from archaeological excavations: a modern example from New Zealand. Journal of archaeological science 3:321-328.

1644 Yesner, D. R. and Aigner, J. S. (1976) Comparative biomass estimates and prehistoric cultural ecology of the southwest Umnak region, Aleutian Islands. Arctic anthropology 13:91-112.

1645 Ziegler, A. C. (1965) The role of faunal remains in archaeological investigations. Sacramento anthropological society, papers 3:47-75.

1646 Ziegler, A. C. (1973) Inference from prehistoric faunal remains. Reading, Massachusetts: Addison-Wesley.

1647 Zeuner, F. E. (1963) A history of domesticated animals. London: Hutchinson Press.

b) Mammalia

1648 Aleksašina, K. C. (1950) Ostatki fauny iz nekotorykh gorodišč Verkhnego Povolž'ja. (The remains of fauna from some towns on the upper Volga River). Materialy i issledovanija po arkheologii SSSR 13:148-151.

1649 Allen, G. M. (1920) Dogs of the American aborigines. Bulletin of the Museum of Comparative Zoology, Harvard University 63(9):431-517.

156

1650 Allen, G. M. (1954) Canid remains from Pueblo Bonito and Pueblo del Arroyo. Smithsonian miscellaneous collections 124:385-389.

1651 Ambros, C. (1969) Bemerkungen zur Auswertung der Tierknochen aus Siedlungsgrabungen. (Remarks on the use of animal bones from settlement excavations). Deutsche Forschungsgemeinschaft, Forschungsberichte (Wiesbaden) 15:76-87.

1652 Andrews, A. H. and Noddle, B. A. (1975) Absence of premolar teeth from ruminant mandibles found at archaeological sites. Journal of archaeological science 2(2):137-144.

1653 Angress, S. and Reed, C. A. (1962) An annotated bibliography on the origin and descent of domestic animals. Fieldiana anthropology, Chicago Natural History Museum 54(1). 143p.

1654 Armitage, P. L. and Clutton-Brock, J. (1980) An investigation of the mummified cats held by the British Museum (Natural History). MASCA journal 1(6):185-188.

1655 Arnold, C. D. (1979) Possible evidence of domestic dog in a Paleoeskimo context. Arctic 32(3):263-265.

1656 Barber, M. B. (1978) The vertebrate faunal analysis of Jc 27 (James City County, Virginia): an exercise in plow zone archeology. Bulletin of the archeological society of Virginia 32(4):94-100.

1657 Barnes, B. et al. (1971) Skeleton of a late glacial elk associated with barbed points from Poulton-le-Fylde, Lancashire. Nature 232:488-489.

1658 Bate, D. M. A. (1940) The fossil antelopes of Palestine in Natufian times. Geological magazine 77:418-443.

1659 Bedford, J. N. (1978) Technique for sex determination of mature bison metapodials. Plains anthropologist 23(82), part 2, 40-43.

1660 Berwick, D. E. (1979) Faunal analysis of the Rehbein I site (47-Ri-81), Richland County, Wisconsin. Wisconsin archaeologist 60(2):215-219.

1661 Bibikova, V. I. (1950) Fauna Pekunovskogo gorodišča.
(Fauna of the town of Pekunovo). Materialy i
issledovanija po arkheologii SSSR 13:133-147.

1662 Bibikova, V. I. (1963) Iz istorii golotsenovoj fauny
pozvonočnykh v Vostočnoj Evrope. (History of the
Holocene vertebrate fauna in Eastern Europe).
Prirodnaja obstanovka i fauny prošlogo 1:119-146.

1663 Bibikova, V. I. (1978) Fauna iz mezolitičeskikh
poselenii Beloles'e i Girževo (Nižnee Podnestrov'e).
(Fauna from the Mesolithic settlements of Beloles'e
and Girževo, lower Dnestr River). In: Arkheologičeskie issledovanija severo-zapadnogo
Pričernomor'ja. Kiev: Akademija Nauk URSR, Odesskij
Arkheologičeskij Muzej, 17-29.

1664 Blumbergs, Z., Gejvall, N.-G. and Varenius, C. (1974)
Subboreal faunal remains from a peat-bog in Sandåkra
village, in the parish of Skurup, Scania, S. Sweden.
Ossa 1:24-37.

1665 Boessneck, J. (1957) Funde des Ures (Bos primigenius)
aus alluvialen Schichten Bayerns. (Aurochs finds, Bos
primigenius, from the alluvial layers of Bavaria).
Säugetierkundliche Mitteilungen Stuttgart 5:55-59.

1666 Boessneck, J. (1960) Zu den Tierknochen funden aus der
präkeramischen Schicht der Argissa-Magula. (On the
animal bone finds from the pre-ceramic level of
Argissa-Magula). Germania 38(3/4):336-340.

1667 Boessneck, J. (1962) Die Tierreste aus der Argissa-
Magula vom präkeramische Neolithikum bis zur
mittleren Bronzezeit. (The animal remains from
Argissa-Magula from the pre-ceramic Neolithic up to
the Middle Bronze Age). In: V. Milojčic,
J. Boessneck and M. Hopf, Argissa-Magula I. Beiträge
zur ur- und frühgeschichtlichen Archäologie des
Mittelmeer-Kulturraumes. Bonn, 2:27-99.

1668 Boessneck, J. (1970) Ein altägyptisches Pferdeskelett.
(An ancient Egyptian horse skeleton). Mitteilungen
der Deutschen Archäologischen Instituts Abteilung
Kairo 26:43-47.

158

1669 Boessneck, J. (1980) Steinzeitliche Tierknochenfunde
       aus der Bettelküche bei Sulzbach-Rosenberg
       (Oberpfalz). (Stone age animal bone finds from the
       Bettelküche near Sulzbach-Rosenberg, Upper
       Palatinate). Tübingen Monographien zur Urgeschichte
       5(2):119-122.

1670 Boessneck, J. (1980) Die Tierknochenfunde aus der
       mesolithischen Kulturschicht der Falkensteinhöhle,
       Markung Thiergarten, im oberen Donautal. (The animal
       bone finds from the Mesolithic cultural level of the
       Falkenstein Cave, Thiergarten, in the upper Danube
       valley). Tübinger Monographien zur Urgeschichte
       5(2):87-99.

1671 Boessneck, J. (1980) Die Tierknochenfunde aus den
       mesolithischen Kulturschichten der Jägerhaus-Höhle,
       Markung Bronnen, im oberen Donautal. (The animal bone
       finds from the Mesolithic cultural levels of the
       Jägerhaus Cave, Bronnen, in the upper Danube valley).
       Tübinger Monographien zur Urgeschichte 5(2):77-86.

1672 Boessneck, J. (1980) Tierknochenfunde aus der meso-
       lithischen Kulturschicht unter dem Felsdach
       Inzigkofen im oberen Donautal. (Animal bone finds
       from the Mesolithic cultural level under the
       Inzigkofen rock shelter in the upper Danube valley).
       Tübinger Monographien zur Urgeschichte 5(2):101-116.

1673 Boessneck, J. (1980) Die Tierknochenfunde von einer
       steinzeitlichen Fundstelle auf der Kleinen Kalmit bei
       Arzheim, Stadt Landau (Pfalz). (The animal bone finds
       from a stone age site on the Kleine Kalmit near
       Arzheim, city of Landau, the Palatinate). Tübinger
       Monographien zur Urgeschichte 5(2):123-126.

1674 Boessneck, J. et al. (1963) Seeberg, Burgäschisee-Süd.
       Teil III: Die Tierreste. (Seeberg, Burgäschisee-
       Süd. Part III: the animal remains). Acta bernensia
       vol. 2.

1675 Boessneck, J. et al. (1971) Die Tierknochenfunde aus
       dem Oppidum von Manching. (The animal bone finds
       from the Oppidum of Manching). In: Die Ausgrabungen
       in Manching, vol. 6. Wiesbaden: Franz Steiner
       Verlag.

159

1676 Boessneck, J. and Driesch, A. von den (1975) Tierknochenfunde vom Korucutepe bei Erâziğ in Ost-
anatolien. (Animal bone finds from Korucutepe near
Erâziğ in eastern Anatolia). In: M. N. van Loon,
ed., Korucutepe. Amsterdam: North-Holland
Publishing Company, 1:1-220.

1677 Boessneck, J., Müller, H. H. and Teichert, M. (1963)
Osteologische Unterscheidungsmerkmale zwischen Schaf
(Ovis aries Linné) and Ziege (Capra hircus Linné).
(Osteological differentiation criteria between sheep,
Ovis aries Linné, and goat, Capra hircus Linné).
Kühn-Archiv 78:1-129.

1678 Boessneck, J. and Wiedemann, U. (1977) Tierknochen aus
Yarikkaya bei Boğasköy, Anatolien. (Animal bones from
Yarikkaya near Boğasköy, Anatolia). Archäologie und
Naturwissenschaften 1:106-128.

1679 Bogucki, P. I. (1979) Animal remains from hut B at the
Eneolithic settlement of Homolka (Bohemia).
Archaeologické rozhledy 31(1)83-92.

1680 Bökönyi, S. (1962) Zur Naturgeschichte des Ures in
Ungarn und das Problem der Domestication des
Hausrindes. (On the natural history of the aurochs
in Hungary and the problem of the domestication of
cattle). Acta archaeologica hungarica 14:175-214.

1681 Bökönyi, S. (1968) Data on Iron Age horses of central
and eastern Europe. Peabody Museum, Harvard University. Bulletin of the American School of Prehistoric
Research 25:3-71.

1682 Bökönyi, S. (1973) Some problems of animal domestica-
tion in the Middle East. In: J. Matolcsi, ed.,
Domestikationsforschung und Geschichte der Haustiere.
Budapest: Akadémiai Kiadó, 69-75.

1683 Bökönyi, S. (1974) The Przevalsky horse. London:
Souvenir Press.

1684 Bökönyi, S. (1978) Environmental and cultural
differences as reflected in the animal bone samples
from five early Neolithic sites in Southwest Asia.
In: Approaches to faunal analysis in the Middle
East. Peabody Museum bulletin 2:57-62.

1685 Bökönyi, S. (1978) The vertebrate fauna of Vlasac.
Kniha--Odeljenje istorijskih nauka. Beograd: Srpska
Akadenija Nauka i Umetnosti, 62:35-65.

1686 Bolomey, A. (1973) The present state of knowledge of
mammal exploitation during the Epipalaeolithic and
the earliest Neolithic on the territory of Romania.
In: J. Matolcsi, ed., Domestikationsforschung und
Geschichte der Haustiere. Budapest: Akadémiai Kiadó,
197-203.

1687 Bouchud, J. (1954) Dents de rennes, bois de rennes et
migrations. Bulletin de la société préhistorique
française 51:340-345.

1688 Bouchud, J. (1954) Le renne et le problème des
migrations. L'anthropologie 58:79-85.

1689 Bouchud, J. (1966) Essai sur le renne et la
climatologie du Paléolithique Moyen et Supérieur.
Périgueux: Imprimerie Magne.

1690 Bouchud, J. (1971) La structure cristalline des os dans
les espèces sauvages et les formes domestiques.
L'anthropologie 75:269-272.

1691 Bouchud, J. (1974) Étude préliminaire de la fauna
provenant de la grotte du Djebel Qafzeh près de
Nazareth (Israël). Paléorient 2:87-102.

1692 Bouchud, J. (1975) Étude de la faune de l'Abri Pataud.
In: H. L. Movius, Excavation of the Abri Pataud,
Les Eyzies (Dordogne), vol. 1. Peabody Museum,
Harvard University. Bulletin of the American School
of Prehistoric Research 30:69-153.

1693 Bouchud, J., Cheynier, A. and Guillien, Y. (1953)
Dents de renne et migrations. Bulletin de la société
préhistorique française 50:127-132.

1694 Bourque, B. J., Morris, K. and Spiess, A. (1978)
Determining the season of death of mammal teeth from
archaeological sites. Science 199:530-531.

1695 Bramwell, D. (1974) Animal remains from Rudston and
Boynton grooved ware sites. British archaeological
reports, British series 9:103-108.

1696 Bramwell, D. (1976) The vertebrate fauna at Wetton Mill Rock Shelter. In: The excavation at Wetton Mill Rock Shelter, Manifold valley, Staffs. Sk. 096563. Stoke-upon-Trent, England. Report of the museum archaeological society (Hanley) 9:40-51.

1697 Brentjes, B. (1974) Die Rassen des taurinen Hausrindes und ihre Haltung im alten Orient. (The races of taurus domestic cattle and its position in the ancient East). Säugetierkundliche Mitteilungen 22:65-83.

1698 Brothwell, D. R. (1978) Growth and demography: neglected aspects of mammal studies in relation to archaeology. Institute of Archaeology, occasional publication 3:91-96.

1699 Brothwell, D. R. and Jones, R. (1978) The relevance of small mammal studies to archaeology. Institute of Archaeology, occasional publication 3:47-57.

1700 Brothwell, D. R., Malaga, A. and Burleigh, R. (1979) Studies on Amerindian dogs, 2: variation in early Peruvian dogs. Journal of archaeological science 6(2):139-161.

1701 Brumley, J. H. (1973) Quantitative methods for the analysis of butchered faunal remains. Archaeology in Montana 14:1-40.

1702 Burčak-Abramovič, N. I. (1963) Proiskhoždenie domašnikh košek Kavkaza. (The origin of domestic cats of the Caucasus). Priroda 7:101-102.

1703 Burch, E. (1972) The caribou/wild reindeer as a human resource. American antiquity 37:339-368.

1704 Burleigh, R. et al. (1977) A further consideration of Neolithic dogs with special reference to a skeleton from Grime's Graves (Norfolk), England. Journal of archaeological science 4:353-366.

1705 Caloi, L. (1978) The bone remains of small wild carnivores from Shahr-i Sokhta. In: Approaches to faunal analysis in the Middle East. Peabody Museum bulletin 2:129-132.

1706 Caloi, L., Compagnoni, B. and Tosi, M. (1978) Pre-
liminary remarks on the faunal remains from Shahr-i
Sokhta. In: Approaches to faunal analysis in the
Middle East. Peabody Museum bulletin 2:87-90.

1707 Carter, H. H. (1975) A guide to rates of tooth wear in
English lowland sheep. Journal of archaeological
science 2(3):231-233.

1708 Carter, H. H. (1976/1977) Vertebrae of the larger
mammals of Western Europe. Ossa 3/4:109-127.

1709 Cassoli, P. F. (1976/1977) Upper Palaeolithic fauna at
Palidoro (Rome): 1955 excavations. Quaternaria
29:187-196.

1710 Casteel, R. W. (1976) Incremental growth zones in
mammals and their archaeological value. Kroeber
anthropological society papers 46:1-27.

1711 Cheynier, A., Bouchud, J. and Guillien, Y. (1952) Les
bois de renne de Badegoule. Bulletin de la société
préhistorique française 49:53-56.

1712 Churcher, C. S. (1972) Late Pleistocene vertebrates
from archaeological sites in the plain of Kom Ombo,
upper Egypt. Life science contributions of the Royal
Ontario Museum of Geology 82.

1713 Cione, A. L. and Tonni, E. P. (1978) Paleoethno-
zoological context of a site of Las Lechiguanas Islands, Parana delta, Argentina. El Dorado 3(1):76-86.

1714 Clark, J. G. D. (1946) Seal hunting in the stone age of
NW Europe. Proceedings of the prehistoric society
12:12-48.

1715 Clason, A. T. (1971) Some problems concerning stock-
breeding and hunting after the Bandkeramik north of
the Alps. III Congrès international des Musées
d'Agriculture. Budapest, 252-254.

1716 Clason, A. T. (1978) Late Bronze Age--Iron Age zebu
cattle in Jordan? Journal of archaeological science
5:91-93.

1717   Clason, A. T. and Buitenhuis, H. (1978) A preliminary
       report on the faunal remains of Nahr el Homr, Hadidi
       and Ta'as in the Tabqa Dam region in Syria. Journal
       of archaeological science 5:75-83.

1718   Clutton-Brock, J. (1962) Near Eastern canids and the
       affinities of the Natufian dogs. Zeitschrift für
       Tierzüchtung und Züchtungsbiologie 76:326-333.

1719   Clutton-Brock, J. (1969) Carnivore remains from the
       excavations of the Jericho Tell. In: P. J. Ucko and
       G. W. Dimbleby, eds., The domestication and exploi-
       tation of plants and animals. London: Duckworth,
       337-345.

1720   Clutton-Brock, J. (1970) The fossil fauna from an upper
       Pleistocene site in Jordan. Journal of zoology
       162:19-29.

1721   Clutton-Brock, J. (1971) The primary food animals of
       the Jericho Tell from the proto-Neolithic to the
       Byzantine period. Levant 3:41-55.

1722   Clutton-Brock, J. (1974) The Buhen horse. Journal of
       archaeological science 1(1):89-100.

1723   Clutton-Brock, J. (1977) Man-made dogs. Science
       197:1340-1342.

1724   Clutton-Brock, J. (1979) The mammalian remains from the
       Jericho Tell. Proceedings of the prehistoric society
       45:135-157.

1725   Clutton-Brock, J. (1979) Report of the mammalian
       remains other than rodents from Quanterness. In:
       Investigations in Orkney. Reports of the research
       committee of the society of antiquaries of London
       38:112-149.

1726   Clutton-Brock, J. and Burleigh, R. (1978) The animal
       remains from Abu Salabikh: preliminary report. Iraq
       40(2):89-100.

1727   Clutton-Brock, J., Corbet, G. B. and Hills, M. (1976) A
       review of the family Canidae, with a classification
       by numerical methods. Zoology; Bulletin of the
       British Museum, Natural History 29(3):117-199.

164

1728   Clutton-Brock, J. and Uerpmann, H.-P. (1974) The sheep
of early Jericho. Journal of archaeological science
1(3):261-274.

1729   Compagnoni, B. (1978) The bone remains of Gazella
subgutturosa from Shahr-i Sokhta. In: Approaches to
faunal analysis in the Middle East. Peabody Museum
bulletin 2:119-128.

1730   Compagnoni, B. (1978) The bone remains of Equus
hemionus from Shahr-i Sokhta. In: Approaches to
faunal analysis in the Middle East. Peabody Museum
bulletin 2:105-118.

1731   Compagnoni, B. and Tosi, M. (1978) The camel: its
distribution and state of domestication in the
Middle East during the third millennium B.C. in
light of finds from Shahr-i Sokhta. In: Approaches
to faunal analysis in the Middle East. Peabody
Museum bulletin 2:91-103.

1732   Cooke, H. B. S. (1949) Fossil mammals of the Vaal
River deposits. Geological survey of South Africa,
Memoir 35(3):1-109.

1733   Coryndon, S. C. et al. (1972) Mammalian remains from
the Isimila prehistoric site, Tanzania. Nature
237(5353):292.

1734   Daly, P., Perkins, D. and Drew, I. M. (1973) The
effects of domestication on the structure of animal
bone. In: J. Matolcsi, ed., Domestikationsforschung
und Geschichte der Haustiere. Budapest: Akadémiai
Kiadó, 157-161.

1735   Davis, S. J. M. (1978) Étude de la faune. Mémoires et
travaux du Centre de recherches préhistoriques
français de Jerusalem 2:195-197.

1736   Davis, S. J. M. and Valla, F. R. (1978) Evidence for
domestication of the dog 12,000 years ago in the
Natufian of Israel. Nature 276(5688):608-610.

1737   Degerbøl, M. (1961) On a find of a preboreal domestic
dog (Canis familiaris L.) from Star Carr, Yorkshire,
with remarks on other Mesolithic dogs. Proceedings
of the prehistoric society 27:35-55.

1738 Degerbøl, M. (1962) Ur und Hausrind. (Aurochs and domestic cattle). Zeitschrift fur Tierzüchtung und Züchtungsbiologie 76:243-251.

1739 Degerbøl, M. (1963) Prehistoric cattle in Denmark and adjacent areas. In: A. E. Mourant and F. E. Zeuner, ed., Man and cattle. London: Royal Anthropological Institute, Occasional paper 18:69-79.

1740 Degerbøl, M. (1970) The Urus (Bos primigenius Bojanus) and Neolithic domesticated cattle (Bos taurus domesticus Linné) in Denmark. Det Kongelige Danske videnskabernes selskabs biologiske skrifter 17:1-177.

1741 Desse, J. (1979) Analyse ostéométrique de fragments osseux de bovides du gisement de Jean Cros. In: L'Abri Jean Cros. Toulouse: Centre d'Anthropologie des Sociétés Rurales, 307-310.

1742 Drew, I. M., Perkins, D. and Daly, P. (1971) Prehistoric domestication of animals: effects on bone structure. Science 171:280-282.

1743 Driesch, A. von den (1972) Osteoarchäologische Untersuchungen auf der Iberischen Halbinsel. (Osteoarchaeological investigations on the Iberian Peninsula). Studien über frühe Tierknochenfunde von der Iberischen Halbinsel 3:1-267.

1744 Driesch, A. von den (1974) Informe preliminar acerca de los huesos de animales del corte 3 del "Cerro de la Encina" (Monachil, Granada). In: A. Arribas Palau et al., Excavaciones en el poblado de la edad del "Cerro de la Encina". Excavaciones arqueológicas en España 81:151-157.

1745 Driesch, A. von den (1979) Tierknochenfunde aus Karlstein Ldkr. Berchtesgadener Land. (Animal bone finds from Karlstein, Berchtesgadener Land district). Bayerische Vorgeschichtsblätter (München) 44:149-170.

1746 Driesch, A. von den and Boessneck, J. (1969) Die Fauna des 'Cabezo Redondo' bei Villena (Prov. Alicante). (The fauna of 'Cabezo Redondo' near Villena, Alicante province). Studien über frühe Tierknochenfunde von der Iberischen Halbinsel 1:43-95, 101-106.

166

1747 Driesch, A. von den and Kokabi, M. (1977) Tierknochenfunde aus der Siedlung "Cerro de los Castellones" bei
Laborcillas/Granada. (Animal bone finds from the
settlement "Cerro de los Castellones" near
Laborcillas/Granada). Archäologie und Naturwissenschaften 1:129-143.

1748 Ducos, P. (1968) L'origine des animaux domestiques en
Palestine. Bordeaux: Delmas.

1749 Ducos, P. (1970) The Oriental Institute excavations at
Mureybit, Syria: preliminary report on the 1965
campaign. Part IV: Les restes d'equidés. Journal of
Near Eastern studies 29:273-289.

1750 Ducos, P. (1971) Sur quelques problèmes poses par
l'étude des premiers élevages en Asie du Sud-Ouest.
In: J. Matolcsi, ed., Domestikationsforschung und
Geschichte der Haustiere. Budapest: Akadémiai Kiadó,
77-85.

1751 Ducos, P. (1972) The Oriental Institute excavations at
Mureybit, Syria: preliminary report on the 1965
campaign. Part V: Les restes de bovidés. Journal of
Near Eastern studies 31:295-301.

1752 Ducos, P. (1975) A new find of an equid metatarsal bone
from Tell Mureibet in Syria and its relevance to the
identification of equids from the early Holocene of
the Levant. Journal of archaeological science 2(1):
71-73.

1753 Ducos, P. (1978) La faune d'Abou Gosh: proto-élevage
de la chèvre au néolithique pré-céramique. Mémoires
et travaux du Centre de recherches préhistoriques
français de Jerusalem 2:107-120.

1754 Ducos, P. (1978) La faune de Beisamoun dans les collections du Musée Préhistorique de la Vallée du
Houleh. Mémoires et travaux du Centre de recherches
préhistorique français de Jerusalem 2:257-268.

1755 Ekman, J. (1973) Early medieval Lund--the fauna and the
landscape. Archaeologica lundensia 5.

167

1756 Emerson, T. E. (1978) A new method for calculating the live weight of the northern white-tailed deer from osteoarchaeological material. Midcontinental journal of archaeology 3(1):35-44.

1757 Ewbank, J. M. et al. (1964) Sheep in the Iron Age: a method of study. Proceedings of the prehistoric society 30:423-426.

1758 Flannery, K. V. (1967) The vertebrate fauna and hunting patterns. In: D. S. Byers, ed., The prehistory of the Tehuacan Valley, vol. I. environment and subsistence. Austin: Univ. of Texas Press, 132-177.

1759 Flerov, K. K. (1965) Paleozoogeografija. Raspredelenie mlekopitajuščikh i landšafty prošlogo. (Paleozoogeography. The distribution of mammals and the landscapes of the past). Priroda 3:59-64.

1760 Fradkin, A. (1979) Faunal remains from the Alderman site, Volusia County, Florida. Florida anthropologist 32(2):75-83.

1761 Fraser, F. C. and King, J. E. (1954) Faunal remains. In: J. G. D. Clark, ed., Excavations at Star Carr. Cambridge: Cambridge University Press, 70-94.

1762 Freeman, L. G. (1973) The significance of mammalian faunas from Palaeolithic occupations in Cantabrian Spain. American antiquity 38:3-44.

1763 Gamble, C. (1978) The Bronze Age animal economy from Akrotiri: a preliminary analysis. In: Thera and the Aegean world I. London: Thera and the Aegean World, 745-753.

1764 Garrad, L. S. (1978) Evidence for the history of the vertebrate fauna of the Isle of Man. British archaeological reports, British series 54(1):61-75.

1765 Gautier, A. (1980) Contributions to the archaeozoology of Egypt. In: Prehistory of the eastern Sahara. New York: Academic Press, 317-344.

1766 Gejvall, N.-G. (1969) Lerna, a pre-Classical site in the Argolid. Vol. I: the fauna. Princeton: American School of Classical Studies at Athens.

1767 Gilbert, B. M. (1973) Mammalian osteo-archaeology:
     North America. Columbia, Missouri: Missouri
     Archaeological Society. 337p.

1768 Gilmore, R. M. (1946) To facilitate cooperation in the
     identification of mammal bones from archaeological
     sites. American antiquity 12:49-50.

1769 Gilmore, R. M. (1949) The identification and value of
     mammal bones from archaeological excavations. Journal
     of mammalogy 30:163-169.

1770 Grant, A. (1971) The animal bones. In: B. W. Cunliffe,
     ed., Excavations at Fishbourne, 1961-1969. London:
     Society of Antiquaries, 377-388.

1771 Grant, A. (1975) The animal bones. In: B. W. Cunliffe,
     ed., Excavations at Portchester Castle. Vol. I:
     Roman. London: Society of Antiquaries, 378-408.

1772 Grant, A. (1976) The animal bones. In: B. W. Cunliffe,
     ed., Excavations at Portchester Castle. Vol. II:
     Saxon. London: Society of Antiquaries, 262-287.

1773 Grigson, C. (1965) Faunal remains: measurements of
     bones, horncores, antlers and teeth. In: I. Smith,
     ed., Windmill Hill and Avebury: excavations by
     Alexander Keiller 1925-1939. Oxford: Clarendon
     Press, 145-167.

1774 Grigson, C. (1969) The uses and limitations of dif-
     ferences in absolute size in the distinction between
     the bones of aurochs (Bos primigenius) and domestic
     cattle (Bos taurus). In: P. J. Ucko and G. W.
     Dimbleby, eds., The domestication and exploitation
     of plants and animals. London: Duckworth, 277-294.

1775 Grigson, C. (1974) The craniology and relationships of
     four species of Bos. I. Basic craniology: Bos
     taurus L. and its absolute size. Journal of
     archaeological science 1(4):353-379.

1776 Grigson, C. (1975) The craniology and relationships of
     four species of Bos. II. Basic craniology: Bos
     taurus L. proportions and angles. Journal of
     archaeological science 2(2):109-128.

1777   Grigson, C. (1978) The craniology and relationships of
       four species of Bos. 4. The relationship between Bos
       primigenius Boj. and B. taurus L. and its implica-
       tions for the phylogeny of the domestic breeds.
       Journal of archaeological science 5:123-152.

1778   Grigson, C. (1978) The late glacial and early Flandrian
       ungulates of England and Wales. Council for British
       Archaeology research report 21:46-56.

1779   Grigson, C. (1980) The craniology and relationships of
       four species of Bos. 5. Bos indicus L. Journal of
       archaeological science 7(1):3-32.

1780   Gromova, V. I. (1948) Ostatki mlekopitajuščikh iz
       ranneslavjanskikh gorodišč vblizi g. Voroneža.
       (Remains of mammals from the Early Slavic town near
       Voronež). Materialy i issledovanija po arkheologii
       SSSR 8:113-123.

1781   Gromova, V. I. (1965) Kratkij obzor četvertičnykh
       mlekopitajuščikh Evropy. (A short survey of the
       Quaternary mammals of Europe). Moskva: Akademija
       Nauk SSSR. 144p.

1782   Guilday, J. (1970) Animal remains from archaeological
       excavations at Fort Ligonier. Annals of the Carnegie
       Museum 42:177-186.

1783   Guillien, Y. (1953) L'habitat saisonnier du renne
       paléolithique. Comptes rendus de l'académie des
       sciences 236:1188-1189.

1784   Guillien, Y. (1964) De quelques maxillaires de jeunes
       rennes trouvés au Petit-Puymoyen (Charente).
       Bulletins et mémoires de la société archéologique et
       historique de la Charente, 1962-1963.

1785   Guillien, Y. and Henri-Martin, G. (1968) Dentures de
       rennes et saisons de chasse: l'Abri Aurignacien de
       la Quina. L'anthropologie 72:337-348.

1786   Guillien, Y. and Henri-Martin, G. (1974) Croissance du
       renne et saison de chasse: le Moustérien à denti-
       cules et le Moustérien de tradition acheuléenne de la
       Quina. Inter-Nord 13/14:119-127.

1787   Haag, W. G. (1948) An osteometric analysis of some
       aboriginal dogs. University of Kentucky reports in
       anthropology 7(3):107-264.

1788   Haag, W. G. (1954) A mummified dog from the Lighthouse
       site, Supe. In: G. R. Willey and J. M. Corbett,
       eds., Early Ancon and early Supe culture. New York:
       Columbia University Press, 138-140.

1789   Haag, W. G. and Heizer, R. F. (1953) A dog burial from
       the Sacramento Valley. American antiquity 18:263-265.

1790   Hall, S. M. (1978) Restos alimenticios. Museo del
       Hombre Dominicano, Santo Domingo. Boletín 7(10):95-8.

1791   Hall, S. M. (1978) Sanate Abajo: Monticulo E, Pozo H.
       Estudios de los restos biologicos y materiales
       asociados. Museo del Hombre Dominicano, Santo
       Domingo. Boletín 7(10):99-124.

1792   Harcourt, R. A. (1967) Osteoarthritis in a Romano-
       British dog. Journal of small animal practice
       8:521-522.

1793   Harcourt, R. A. (1974) The dog in prehistoric and
       early historic Britain. Journal of archaeological
       science 1(2):151-175.

1794   Harcourt, R. A. (1974) Animal bones. In: D. S. Neal,
       The excavations of the Roman villa, Gadebridge Park,
       Hemel Hempstead 1963-1968. Society of Antiquaries of
       London. Reports of the research committee 31:256-262.

1795   Harris, S. (1977) Spinal arthritis (Spondylosis
       Deformans) in the red fox, Vulpes vulpes, with some
       methodology of relevance to zooarchaeology. Journal
       of archaeological science 4(2):183-195.

1796   Hatting, T. (1967) Ban Kao: the faunal remains. In:
       P. Sørensen, ed., Ban Kao: Neolithic settlements
       with cemeteries in Kanchanaburi province. Copenhagen.

1797   Hatting, T. (1978) Lidso. Zoological remains from a
       Neolithic settlement. Arkaeologiske studier 5:193-207.

1798 Heinrich, W.-D. (1980) Kleinsäugerfunde aus dem
      Travertinkomplex von Bilzingsleben. Vorläufige
      Mitteilung. (Small mammal remains from the travertine
      complex from Bilzingsleben. Preliminary report).
      Ethnographisch-archäologische Zeitschrift 21(1):
      36-41.

1799 Herre, W. (1949) Zur Abstammung und Entwicklung des
      Haustiere 1. Über das bisher älteste primigene
      Hausrind Nordeuropas. (On the origin and development
      of domestic animals 1. The hitherto oldest primal
      domestic cattle of northern Europe). Verhandlungen
      deutschen Zoologen (Kiel), 1948/1949, 312-324.

1800 Herre, W. and Röhrs, M. (1958) Die Tierreste an den
      Hethitiergräbern von Osmankayasi. (The animal remains
      on the Hittite animal graves from Osmankayasi). In:
      K. Bittel et al., Die Hethitischer Grabfunde von
      Osmankayasi. Berlin, 60-79.

1801 Hescheler, K. and Kuhn, E. (1949) Die Tierwelt der
      prähistorischen Siedlungen der Schweiz. (The animal
      world of prehistoric settlements of Switzerland). In:
      O. Tschuni, ed., Urgeschichte der Schweiz. Zürich.

1802 Higgs, E. S. (1961) Some Pleistocene faunas of the
      Mediterranean coastal areas. Proceedings of the
      prehistoric society 27:144-154.

1803 Higgs, E. S. (1967) Environment and chronology--the
      evidence from mammalian fauna. In: C. B. M.
      McBurney, The Haua Fteah (Cyrenaika) and the stone
      age of the south-east Mediterranean. Cambridge,
      16-44.

1804 Higham, C. F. W. (1975) Aspects of economy and ritual
      in prehistoric northeast Thailand. Journal of
      archaeological science 2(4):245-288.

1805 Higham, C. F. W. (1975) Non Nok Tha, the faunal
      remains. Studies in prehistoric anthropology 7.
      Dunedin, New Zealand: University of Otago.

1806 Higham, C. F. W. and Kijngam, A. (1979) Ban Chiang and
      northeast Thailand; the palaeoenvironment and econo-
      my. Journal of archaeological science 6(3):211-233.

1807 Higham, C. F. W., Kijngam, A. and Manly, B. F. J.
(1980) An analysis of prehistoric canid remains from
Thailand. Journal of archaeological science 7(2):
149-165.

1808 House, K. D. (1978) Faunal analysis in Texas archaeological site. Institute for the study of earth and
man, Reports of investigations (Dallas) 3:93-131.

1809 Jackson, J. W. (1925) Report on the animal remains
from the ancient village site at Swallowcliffe Down,
Wilts., of La Tene I date. In: R. C. C. Clay, An
inhabited site of La Tene I date on Swallowcliffe
Down. Wiltshire archaeological magazine 43:90-93.

1810 Jackson, J. W. (1933) Animal remains. In: G. Bersu,
The Roman villa, Hucclecote. Transactions of the
Bristol and Gloucestershire archaeological society
55:370-375.

1811 Janetsky, J. C. (1980) Analysis of dietary remains
from Potusa and Talemoa. Archaeological excavations
in Western Samoa. Bernice P. Bishop Museum of
Polynesian Ethnology and Natural History, Honolulu.
Pacific anthropological records 32:117-122.

1812 Jarman, M. R. (1969) The prehistory of upper Pleistocene and recent cattle. Part I. Proceedings of the
prehistoric society 35:236-266.

1813 Jewell, P. A. (1962) Changes in size and type of
cattle from prehistoric to medieval times in Britain.
Zeitschrift fur Tierzüchtung und Züchtungsbiologie
77:159-167.

1814 Jewell, P. A. (1963) Cattle from British archaeological sites. In: A. E. Mourant and F. E. Zeuner,
eds., Man and cattle. Royal Anthropological Institute occasional paper 18:80-100.

1815 Jourdan, L. (1979) Biometrie des ossements de suidés
de l'Abri Jean-Cros. In: L'Abri Jean-Cros.
Toulouse: Centre d'Anthropologie des Sociétés
Rurales, 311-314.

1816 Julien, M. (1978) L'ostéo-archéologie animale.
Recherches Amérindiennes au Québec 8(1):28-40.

1817 Kirikov, S. V. (1966) Promyslovye životnye,
     prirodnaja sreda i čelovek. (Traded animals, the
     natural environment, and man). Moskva: Akademija
     Nauk SSSR, Institut geografii. 348p.

1818 Klein, R. G. (1972) The late Quaternary mammalian
     fauna of Nelson Bay Cave (Cape Province, South
     Africa): its implications for megafaunal extinctions
     and for cultural and environmental change. Quaternary
     research 2:135-142.

1819 Klein, R. G. (1976) The mammalian fauna of the Klasies
     River mouth sites, southern Cape Province, South
     Africa. South African archaeological bulletin
     31:75-98.

1820 Klein, R. G. (1977) The mammalian fauna from the
     Middle and Later Stone Age (upper Pleistocene) levels
     of Border Cave, Natal Province, South Africa. South
     African archaeological bulletin 32:14-27.

1821 Klein, R. G. (1978) The fauna and overall interpreta-
     tion of the "Cutting 10" Acheulean site at
     Elandsfontein (Hopefield), southwestern Cape
     Province, South Africa. Quaternary research 10(1):
     69-83.

1822 Klein, R. G. (1978) A preliminary report on the larger
     mammals from the Boomplaas stone age cave site,
     Cango valley, Oudtshoorn district, South Africa.
     South African archaeological bulletin 33:66-75.

1823 Klein, R. G. (1978) Stone age predation on large
     African bovids. Journal of archaeological science
     5:195-217.

1824 Klein, R. G. (1979) Paleoenvironmental and cultural
     implications of late Holocene archaeological faunas
     from the Orange Free State and north-central Cape
     Province, South African archaeological bulletin
     34:34-49.

1825 Krantz, G. S. (1968) A new method of counting mammal
     bones. American journal of archaeology 72(3):
     286-288.

1826 Kretzoi, M. (1977) The fauna of small vertebrates of the Middle Pleistocene at Petralona. Anthropos (Athens) 4:131-143.

1827 Kuhn, E. (1938) Zur quantitativen Analyse der Haustierwelt der Pfahlbauten in der Schweiz. (On the quantitative analysis of the domestic animal world of the pile dwellings in Switzerland). Vierteljahresschrift der Naturforschende Gesellschaft 83:253-262.

1828 Kurtén, B. and Poulianos, A. N. (1977) New stratigraphic and faunal material from Petralona Cave, with special reference to the Carnivora. Anthropos (Athens) 4:47-130.

1829 Lachowicz, S. and Wyrost, P. (1977) Beobachtungen über Knochenveränderungen an Schädeln von früheisenzeitlichen und frühmittelalterlichen Hunden Osteuropas. (Observations on bone alterations on skulls from early Iron Age and early medieval dogs of Eastern Europe). Zoologica poloniae 26(1):25-37.

1830 Lacorre, F. (1951) Les migrations des rennes dans la province préhistorique des Eyzies. Comptes rendus de l'académie des sciences 232:1702-1704.

1831 Lacorre, F. (1953) Sur les bois et les dents de renne de Badegoule. Bulletin de la société préhistorique française 50:547-555.

1832 Lacorre, F. (1956) Les migrations des rennes dans la province préhistorique des Eyzies. Bulletin de la société préhistorique française 53:302-310.

1833 Lawrence, B. (1966) Early domestic dogs. Zeitschrift für Säugetierkunde 32(1):44-59.

1834 Laws, R. M. (1952) A new method of age determination for mammals. Nature 169:972-973.

1835 Legge, A. J. (1975) The fauna of Tell Abu Hureyra: preliminary analysis. Proceedings of the prehistoric society 41:74-75.

1836 Lernan, H. (1972) Animal remains from the early Bronze Age settlement at Arad. In: A. Ben Tor, Early Arad, the Chalcolithic and early Bronze Age City.

Jerusalem: Massada.

1837 Lownie, H. (1978) Research problems regarding the domestication of South American mammals. Institute of Archaeology, occasional publications 3:113-120.

1838 Lyman, R. L. (1977) Analysis of historic faunal remains. Historical archaeology (Detroit) 11:67-73.

1839 McConnell, D. and Foreman, D. W. (1971) Texture and composition of bone. Science 172:971-972.

1840 Maglio, V. J. (1970) Early Elephantidae of Africa and a tentative correlation of African Plio-Pleistocene deposits. Nature 225:328-332.

1841 Maltby, M. (1979) Faunal studies on urban sites. The animal bones from Exeter 1971-75. Department of Prehistory and Archaeology, University of Sheffield. Exeter archaeological reports 2.

1842 Mateer, N. J. (1974) Two examples of mammalian palaeopathology. Ossa 1:96-98.

1843 Matolcsi, J., ed. (1973) Domestikationsforschung und Geschichte der Haustiere. Budapest: Akadémiai Kiadó.

1844 Meadow, R. H. (1975) Mammal remains from Hajji Firuz: a study in methodology. In: A. T. Clason, ed., Archaeozoological studies. Amersterdam: North Holland Publishing Co., 265-283.

1845 Miller, H. M. and Lewis, L. G. (1977) Zoocultural resource utilization at a low country South Carolina plantation. Papers of the 18th conference on historic site archaeology 12:250-265.

1846 Müller, H.-H. (1971) Widerspiegelung gesellschaftlicher Verhältnisse im archäologischen Tierknochenmaterial. (Reflection of social conditions in archaeological animal bone material). III Congrès international des Musées d'Agriculture. Budapest, 264.

1847 Müller, H.-H. (1977) Die Tierreste aus dem slawischen Burgwall von Berlin-Blankenburg. (The animal remains from the Slavic city wall of Berlin-Blankenburg). In: Archäologie als Geschichtswissenschaft, 527-544.

176

1848 Müller, H.-H. (1978) Die Tierreste aus der Wiprechtsburg bei Groitzsch, Kr. Borna. (The animal remains
from the Wiprechtsburg near Groitzsch, Borna district). Arbeits- und Forschungsberichte zur
sächsischen Bodendenkmalpflege, 1977, 22:101-170.

1849 Müller, H.-H. (1978) Tierreste aus einer Siedlung der
Bernburger Gruppe bei Halle (Saale). (Animal remains
from a settlement of the Bernburg group near Halle,
Saale). Jahresschrift für Mitteldeutsche Vorgeschichte 62:203-220.

1850 Naik, S. N. (1978) Origin and domestication of Zebu
cattle (Bos indicus). Journal of human evolution
7(1):23-30.

1851 Nikiforova, K. V., ed. (1965) Stratigrafičeskoe
značenie antropogenovoj fauny melkikh mlekopitajuščikh. (The stratigraphical significance of
small mammals). Moskva: Akademija Nauk SSSR,
Geologičeskij Institut. 172p.

1852 Noddle, B. (1974) Ages of epiphyseal closure in feral
and domestic goats and ages of dental eruption.
Journal of archaeological science 1(2):195-204.

1853 Noddle, B. (1978) Some minor skeletal differences in
sheep. Institute of Archaeology, occasional
publication 3:133-141.

1854 Noddle, B. and Ryder, M. L. (1974) Primitive sheep in
the Aran Islands. Journal of archaeological science
1(1):109-112.

1855 Noe-Nygaard, N. (1974) Mesolithic hunting in Denmark
illustrated by bone injuries caused by human
weapons. Journal of archaeological science 1(3):
217-248.

1856 Noyes, M. J. S. and Hill, F. C. (1974) Faunal remains
from a Lewis focus stone fort in southern Illinois.
Transactions of the Illinois state academy of
sciences 67:336-340.

1857 Olsen, S. J. (1960) Post-cranial skeletal characters
of Bison and Bos. Harvard University. Papers of the
Peabody Museum 35(4). 62p.

1858 Olsen, S. J. (1961) The relative value of fragmentary mammalian remains. American antiquity 26:538-540.

1859 Olsen, S. J. (1964) Mammal remains from archaeological sites, part I, southeastern and southwestern United States. Harvard University. Papers of the Peabody Museum 61(1). 161p.

1860 Olsen, S. J. (1974) Early domestic dogs in North America and their origins. Journal of field archaeology 1:343-345.

1861 Olsen, S. J. and Olsen, J. W. (1977) The Chinese wolf, ancestor of New World dogs. Science 197:533-535.

1862 Paaver, K. L. (1958) K metodike opredelenija otnositel'nogo značenija vidov i grupp mlekopitajuščikh v osteologičeskom materiale iz raskopok arkheologičeskikh pamjatnikov. (On the method of determination of relative significance of species and groups of mammals in osteological material from archaeological excavations). Izvestija Akademija Nauk Éstonskoj SSR, serija biologičeskaja 7(4):277-290.

1863 Paaver, K. L. (1965) Formirovanie teriofauny i izmenčivost' mlekopitajuščikh Pribaltiki v golotsene. (The formation of avifauna and the change of mammals of the Baltic region in the Holocene). Tartu-Tallin: Akademija Nauk Éstonskoj SSR, Institut Zoologii i Botaniki. 498p.

1864 Painter, F. (1978) Bison remains from the Currituck site. The Chesopiean (Norfolk, Virginia) 16(1-3): 28-31.

1865 Payne, S. (1973) Animal bones. In: T. W. Jacobsen, ed., Excavations in the Franchthi Cave, 1969-1971, part I. Hesperia 42:59-66.

1866 Payne, S. (1975) Faunal change at Franchthi Cave from 20,000 B.C. to 3000 B.C. In: A. T. Clason, ed., Archaeozoological studies. Amsterdam: North Holland Publishing Co., 120-131.

1867 Perkins, D. (1964) Prehistoric fauna from Shanidar, Iraq. Science 144:1565-1566.

1868 Pidopličko, I. G. (1963) Sovremennye problemy i zadači izučenija istorii faun i sredy ikh obitanija. (Contemporary problems and objectives of the study of the history of fauna and their environment). Prirodnaja obstanovka i fauny prošlogo 1:9-30.

1869 Pires-Ferreira, J. C. W. (1975-1977) Tepe Tula'i: faunal remains from an early camp site in Khuzistan: Iran. Paléorient 3:275-280.

1870 Plug, I. (1979) Namakala and Nanga: faunal report on two early Iron Age sites, Zambia. South African archaeological bulletin 34:123-126.

1871 Redding, R. W. (1978) Rodents and the archaeological paleoenvironment: considerations, problems, and the future. In: Approaches to faunal analysis in the Middle East. Peabody Museum bulletin 2:63-68.

1872 Redding, R. W. (1979) The faunal remains from Tappeh Zabarjad. Museum of Anthropology, University of Michigan (Ann Arbor). Technical reports 10:91-93.

1873 Reed, C. A. (1961) Osteological evidences for prehistoric domestication in South-Western Asia. Zeitschrift für Tierzüchtung und Züchtungsbiologie 76:31-38.

1874 Reichstein, H. (1978) Bemerkungen zu einigen Tierknochen aus frühneolithischen Siedlungsgruben von Rosdorf, Kr. Göttingen. (Remarks on a few animal bones from early Neolithic settlement ditches from Rosdorf, Göttingen district). Nachrichten aus Niedersachsens Urgeschichte 46:1-26.

1875 Requate, H. von (1957) Zur Naturgeschichte des Ures, Bos primigenius, nach Schädel- und Skelettfunden in Schleswig-Holstein. (On the natural history of the aurochs, Bos primigenius, based on skull and skeleton finds in Schleswig-Holstein). Zeitschrift für Tierzüchtung und Züchtungsbiologie 70(4):297-338.

1876 Rímoli, R. O. (1980) Restos de fauna en el sitio arqueológico de Escalera Abajo. Museo de Hombre Dominicano, Santo Domingo. Boletín 9(13):171-192.

1877 Rudenko, S. I. (1966) O vozraste sibirskikh mamontov.
      (On the age of Siberian mammoths). Doklady po
      étnografii 3:51-55.

1878 Rutschkowsky, M. (1979) Les mammoths de l'U.R.S.S.
      Archéologia (Paris) 128:8-17.

1879 Ryder, M. L. (1970) The animal remains from Petergate,
      York, 1957-1958. Yorkshire archaeological journal
      42(168):126.

1880 Saxon, E. C. (1974) The mobile herding economy of
      Kebarah Cave, Mt. Carmel: an economic analysis of
      the faunal remains. Journal of archaeological
      science 1(1):27-45.

1881 Schmid, E. (1964) Die Tierknochen: Birsmatten-
      Basisgrotte. (The animal bones: Birsmatten grotto).
      Acta bernensia 1:93-100.

1882 Shawcross, F. W. and Higgs, E. S. (1961) The excava-
      tion of a Bos primigenius at Lowe's Farm, Littleport.
      Proceedings of the Cambridge antiquarian society
      54:3-16.

1883 Shotwell, J. A. (1955) An approach to the paleoecology
      of mammals. Ecology 36:327-337.

1884 Sloan, R. E. and Duncan, M. A. (1978) Zooarchaeology
      of Nichoria. In: Excavations at Nichoria in
      southwest Greece. Minneapolis: Univ. of Minnesota
      Press, 1:60-77.

1885 Soergel, E. (1969) Stratigraphische Untersuchungen am
      Tierknochenmaterial von Thayngen Weier: Archäologie
      und Biologie. Deutsche Forschungsgemeinschaft,
      Forschungsberichte 15:157-171.

1886 Sorrentino, C. (1978) La fauna delle grotte n. 2 e n.
      3 di Latronico. (Nota preliminare). Atti della XX
      riunione scientifica in Basilicata. Firenze:
      Instituto Italiano di Preistoria e Protostoria,
      219-226.

1887 Speer, R. D. (1978) Bison remains from the Rex Rodgers
      site. Plains anthropologist 23(2):113-127.

1888 Spiess, A. E. (1976) Determining season of death of
      archaeological fauna by analysis of teeth. Arctic
      29(1)53-55.

1889 Spiess, A. E. (1978) Zooarchaeological evidence
      bearing on the Nain area middle Dorset subsistence-
      settlement cycle. Arctic anthropology 15(2):48-60.

1890 Stampfli, H. R. (1966) Die Tierreste aus der römischen
      Villa 'Ersingen-Murain' in Gegenüberstellung zu
      anderen zeitgleichen Funden aus der Schweiz und dem
      Ausland. (The animal remains from the Roman villa
      'Ersingen-Murain' in contrast to other contem-
      poraneous finds from Switzerland and foreign
      countries). Jahrbuch des Bernischen Historischen
      Museum 45/46:449-469.

1891 Storch, G. (1980) Paläolithische und mesolithische
      Kleinsäugerfunde (Mammalia) von den Fohlenhaus-
      Höhlen im Lonetal (Schwäbische Alb). (Palaeolithic
      and Mesolithic small mammal finds from the
      Fohlenhaus Caves in the Lone valley, Swabian Alps).
      Tübinger Monographien zur Urgeschichte 5(2):133-137.

1892 Teichert, L. (1977) Zu den Tierknochenfunden von
      Fichtenberg, Kr. Bad Liebenwerda. (On the animal bone
      finds from Fichtenberg, Bad Liebenwerda district).
      Ausgrabungen und Funde 22:86-88.

1893 Teichert, M. (1974) Tierreste aus dem germanischen
      Opfermoor bei Oberdorla. (Animal remains from the
      Germanic sacrifice bog near Oberdorla). Weimar.

1894 Teichert, M. (1977) Fundnachweise von Wild- und Haus-
      katzenknochen aus ur- und frühgeschichtlichen Zeit.
      (Identification of finds of wild and domestic cat
      bones from the prehistoric and early historic
      period). Hercynia (Leipzig) 14:212-216.

1895 Teichert, M. (1979) Tierreste aus einer germanischen
      Kultgrube bei Grossfahner, Kr. Erfurt. (Animal
      remains from a Germanic cult pit near Grossfahner,
      Erfurt district). Ausgrabungen und Funde 24(5):
      229-242.

1896 Teichert, M. and Teichert, L. (1977) Tierknochenfunde
aus dem spätmesolithisch/frühneolithischen Rötelgrab
bei Bad Dürrenberg, Kr. Merseburg. (Animal bone
finds from the late Mesolithic/early Neolithic red
ochre grave near Bad Dürrenberg, Merseburg district).
Archäologie als Geschichtswissenschaft (Berlin),
521-525.

1897 Thackeray, J. F. (1979) An analysis of faunal remains
from archaeological sites in southern South West
Africa (Namibia). South African archaeological
bulletin 34:18-33.

1898 Tsalkin, V. I. (1956) Materialy dlja istorii skoto-
vodstva i okhoty v drevnej Rusi. (Materials for the
history of cattle-breeding and hunting in ancient
Russia). Materialy i issledovanija po arkheologii
SSSR, 51.

1899 Turnbull, P. F. and Reed, C. A. (1974) The fauna from
the terminal Pleistocene of Palegawra Cave, a Zarzian
occupation site in northeastern Iraq. Fieldiana
anthropology 63(3):81-146.

1900 Uerpmann, H.-P. (1971) Die Tierknochenfunde aus der
Talayot-Siedlung von S'Illot (San Lorenzo/Mallorca).
(The animal bone finds from the Talayot settlement
of S'Illot, San Lorenzo/Mallorca). Studien über
frühe Tierknochenfunde von der Iberischen Halbinsel,
2. München.

1901 Uerpmann, H.-P. (1978) Metrical analyses of faunal
remains from the Middle East. In: Approaches to
faunal analysis in the Middle East. Peabody Museum
bulletin 2:41-45.

1902 Uerpmann, H.-P. and Uerpmann, M. (1973) Tierknochenfunde aus der phönizischen Faktorei von Toscanos und
anderen phönizisch beeinflussten Fundorten der
Provinz Málaga in Südspanien. (Animal bone finds from
the Phoenician factory of Toscanos and other
Phoenician-influenced sites of the province of
Málaga in south Spain). Studien über frühe Tierknochenfunde von der Iberischen Halbinsel 4:35-100.

1903 Vereščagin, N. K. and Kolbutov, A. D. (1957) Ostatki životnykh na mustĕrskoj stojanke pod Stalingradom i stratigrafičeskoe položenie paleolitičeskogo sloja. (Remains of animals at the Mousterian site near Stalingrad and the stratigraphical position of the Palaeolithic level). Trudy Zoologičeskogo Instituta Akademii Nauk SSSR 22:75-89.

1904 Vrba, E. S. (1980) The significance of bovid remains as indicators of environment and predation patterns. In: Fossils in the making. Chicago: Univ. of Chicago Press, 247-271.

1905 Walker, A., Hoeck, H. N. and Perez, L. (1978) Microwear of mammalian teeth as an indicator of diet. Science 201:908-910.

1906 Walker, E. G. (1979) Vertebrate faunal remains from the Tschetter site (FbNr-1). Na'pao; a Saskatchewan anthropology journal 9(1/2):51-60.

1907 Watson, J. P. N. (1975) Domestication and bone structure in sheep and goats. Journal of archaeological science 2(4):375-383.

1908 Watson, J. P. N. (1979) The estimation of the relative frequencies of mammalian species: Khirokitia 1972. Journal of archaeological science 6(2):127-137.

1909 Wijngaarden-Bakker, L. H. van (1974) The animal remains from the Beaker settlement at Newgrange, Co. Meath--first report. Proceedings of the Royal Irish Academy 74(Section C):313-383.

1910 Wijngaarden-Bakker, L. H. van and Krauwer, M. (1979) Animal palaeopathology: some examples from the Netherlands. Helinium 19(1):37-53.

1911 Wing, E. S. (1980) Faunal remains. In: Guitarrero Cave. New York: Academic Press, 149-172.

1912 Wolff, R. G. (1973) Hydrodynamic sorting and ecology of a Pleistocene mammalian assemblage from California. Palaeogeography, palaeoclimatology, palaeoecology 13:19-101.

1913 Zeder, M. A. (1978) Differentiation between the bones
of caprines from different ecosystems in Iran by the
analysis of osteological microstructure and chemical
composition. In: Approaches to faunal analysis in
the Middle East. Peabody Museum bulletin 2:69-84.

1914 Zeuner, F. E. (1958) Animal remains from a late Bronze
Age sanctuary on Cyprus and the problem of the
domestication of fallow deer. Journal of the
palaeontological society of India 3:131-135.

c) Non-mammalia

1915 Amsden, A. F. and Boon, G. C. (1975) C. O. Waterhouse's
list of insects from Silchester. (With a note on
early identifications of insects in archaeological
contexts). Journal of archaeological science
2(2):129-136.

1916 Artz, J. A. (1980) Inferring season of occupation from
fish scales: an archaeological approach. Plains
anthropologist 25(87):47-61.

1917 Bailey, G. N. (1975) The role of molluscs in coastal
economies: the results of midden analysis in
Australia. Journal of archaeological science
2(1):45-62.

1918 Barthel, H.-J. and Cott, J. (1977) Eine Sumpfschild-
kröte aus der neolithischen Station Erfurt-
Gispersleben. (A pond turtle from the Neolithic
site Erfurt-Gispersleben). Ausgrabungen und Funde
22:170-173.

1919 Bate, D. M. A. (1934) On the domestic fowl in pre-
Roman Britain. Ibis (series 13) 3:390-395.

1920 Boessneck, J. (1973) Vogelknochen aus der phönizischen
und römischen Niederlassung von Toscanos. (Bird
bones from the Phoenician and Roman establishment at
Toscanos). Studien über frühe Tierknochenfunde von
der Iberischen Halbinsel 4:101-108.

1921 Borgogno, I. and Linares, O. F. (1980) Molluskan fauna
from both sides of the Isthmus. In: Adaptive
radiations in prehistoric Panama. Peabody Museum,
Harvard University. Monographs 5:216-222.

1922 Brendel, S. J. (1980) Wild turkey remains in Ozark Bluff shelters. Missouri archaeologist 41:94-106.

1923 Brunnacker, K. and Brunnacker, M. (1980) Die Sedimente und die Mollusken in spät- und postglazialen Höhlen-Profilen Süddeutschlands. (The sediments and the molluscs in late and postglacial cave profiles of southern Germany). Tübinger Monographien zur Urgeschichte 5(2):47-76.

1924 Burleigh, R. and Southgate, B. J. (1975) Insect infestation of stored Egyptian lentils in antiquity. Journal of archaeological science 2(4):391-392.

1925 Caloi, L. and Palombo, M. R. (1978) Anfibi, rettili e mammiferi di Torre del Pagliaccetto (Torre in Pietra, Roma). Quaternaria 20:315-428.

1926 Cameron, R. A. D. (1978) Interpreting buried landsnail assemblages from archaeological sites: problems and progress. Institute of Archaeology, occasional publication 3:19-23.

1927 Cassoli, P. (1978) L'avifauna pre-würmiana di Torre in Pietra. Quaternaria 20:429-440.

1928 Casteel, R. W. (1974) A method for estimation of live weight of fish from the size of skeletal elements. American antiquity 39(1):94-98

1929 Casteel, R. W. (1976) Comparison of column and whole unit samples for recovering fish remains. World archaeology 8:192-196.

1930 Casteel, R. W. (1976) Fish remains in archaeology and paleoenvironmental studies. New York: Academic Press. 175p.

1931 Casteel, R. W. (1976/1977) A comparison of methods for back-calculation of fish size from the size of scales found in archaeological sites. Ossa 3/4:129-139.

1932 Casteel, R. W., Adam, D. P. and Sims, J. D. (1977) Late-Pleistocene and Holocene remains of Hysterocarpus traski (Tule perch) from Clear Lake, California, and inferred Holocene temperature fluctuations. Quaternary research 7:133-143.

1933 Celoria, F. (1970) Insects and archaeology. Science and archaeology 1:15-19.

1934 Chan, W. (1978) Identification and analysis of excavated fish remains. Sham Wan, Lamna Island. Journal monograph--Hong Kong archaeological society 3:248-257.

1935 Clark, J. G. D. (1948) The development of fishing in prehistoric Europe. Antiquaries journal 28:45-85.

1936 Constantin, L., Tosi, M. and Vigna-Taglianti, A. (1975-1977) Typology and socio-economic implications of entomological finds from some ancient Near Eastern sites. Paléorient 3:247-258.

1937 Coope, G. R. and Osborne, P. J. (1967) Report on the coleopterous fauna of the Roman well at Barnsley Park, Glos. Transactions of the Bristol and Gloucester archaeological society 86:84-87.

1938 Coutts, P. J. F. (1970) Bivalve-growth patterning as a method for seasonal dating in archaeology. Nature 226:874.

1939 Coutts, P. J. F. (1971) Recent techniques of midden analysis and studies of modern shellfish populations in New Zealand. Transactions of the Royal Society of New Zealand, General 2:143-156.

1940 Dance, S. P. (1975) The molluscan fauna. In: H. L. Movius, Excavations of the Abri Pataud, Les Eyzies (Dorgogne). Peabody Museum, Harvard University. Bulletin of the American School of Prehistoric Research 30:154-159.

1941 Denford, S. (1978) Mites and their potential use in archaeology. Institute of Archaeology, occasional publication 3:77-83.

1942 Durante, S. and Settepassi, F. (1976/1977) Malacofauna e livelli marini tirreniani a Grotta Guattari, Monte Circeo (Latina). Quaternaria 19:35-69.

1943 Durante, S. and Settepassi, F. (1978) Nota sulla malacofauna di Torre in Pietra. Quaternaria 20:301-314.

1944 Evans, J. G. (1972) Land snails in archaeology with special reference to the British Isles. London: Seminar Press; New York: Academic Press.

1945 Feldman, L. H. (1978) Invertebrados arqueologicos. Boletín de la Escuela de Ciencias Antropologicas de la Universidad de Yucatan (Merida) 6(33):2-23.

1946 Fitch, J. E. (1969) Appendix A: fish remains, primarily otoliths, from a Ventura, California, Chumash village site (Ven-3). Memoirs of the Southern California Academy of Sciences 8:56-71.

1947 Follett, H. W. I. (1963) Preliminary report on fish remains from the Falcon Hill site, Washoe County, Nevada. Nevada State Museum anthropology papers 9:33-34.

1948 Fradkin, A. (1978) Archeological evidence of snake consumption among the aborigines of Florida. Florida anthropologist 31(1):36-43.

1949 Friedman, E. (1980) Avian faunal remains from archaeological middens, Makah territory, Washington. Northwest anthropological research notes (Moscow, Idaho) 14(1):91-106.

1950 Girling, M. A. (1977) Fossil insect assemblages from Rowland's Trackway. Somerset Levels papers 3:51-60.

1951 Girling, M. A. (1978) The application of fossil insect studies to the Somerset Levels. Institute of Archaeology, occasional publication 3:85-90.

1952 Girling, M. A. (1978) Fossil insect assemblages from Difford's I site. Somerset Levels papers 4:107-113.

1953 Girling, M. A. (1979) The fossil insect assemblages from the Meare Lake village. Somerset Levels papers 5:25-32.

1954 Girling, M. A. (1979) Fossil insects from the Sweet Track. Somerset Levels papers 5:84-97.

1955 Grayson, D. K. (1975) The Nightfire Island avifauna and the Altithermal. Nevada archaeological survey research papers 6.

1956 Greenwood, R. (1961) Quantitative analysis of shells
      from a site in Goleta, California. American antiquity
      26:416-420.

1957 Hamblin, N. L. and Rea, A. M. (1979) La avifauna ar-
      queológica de Cosumel. Boletin de la Escuela de
      Ciencias Antropologicas de la Universidad de Yucatan
      (Merida) 7(37):21-49.

1958 Hargrave, L. L. and Emslie, S. D. (1979) Osteological
      identification of sandhill crane versus turkey.
      American antiquity 44(2):295-299.

1959 Harrison, C. J. O. (1978) A new jungle-fowl from the
      Pleistocene of Europe. Journal of archaeological
      science 5:373-376.

1960 Harrison, C. J. O. (1980) A re-examination of British
      Devensian and earlier Holocene bird bones in the
      British Museum (Natural History). Journal of
      archaeological science 7(1):53-68.

1961 Harrison, C. J. O. and Cowles, G. S. (1977) The extinct
      large cranes of the north-west Palaearctic. Journal
      of archaeological science 4(1):25-27.

1962 Jiménez Lambertus, A. and Olmos Cordones, H. (1979)
      Estudio de los restos biológicos de las excavaciones
      arqueológicas realizadas en el antiguo colegio de
      Gorjon. Museo de Hombre Dominicano, Santo Domingo.
      Boletín 7(12):225-256.

1963 Kenward, H. K. (1974) Methods for palaeo-entomology on
      site and in the laboratory. Science and archaeology
      13:16-24.

1964 Kenward, H. K. (1975) The biological and archaeological
      implications of the beetle Aglenus brunneus
      (Gyllenhal) in ancient faunas. Journal of archaeolog-
      ical science 2(1):63-69.

1965 Kenward, H. K. (1975) Pitfalls in the environmental in-
      terpretation of insect death assemblages. Journal of
      archaeological science 2(2):85-94.

188

1966 Kenward, H. K. (1976) Reconstructing ancient ecological conditions from insect remains: some problems and an experimental approach. Ecological entomology 1:7-17.

1967 Kenward, H. K. (1978) The analysis of archaeological insect assemblages: a new approach. The archaeology of York. London: Council for British Archaeology, 19(1):1-68.

1968 Kenward, H. K. (1978) The value of insect remains as evidence of ecological conditions on archaeological sites. Institute of Archaeology, occasional publications 3:25-38.

1969 Koch, K. (1971) Zur Untersuchung subfossiler Käferreste aus römerzeitlichen und mittelalterlichen Ausgrabungen im Rheinland. (On the investigation of subfossil beetle remains from Roman period and medieval excavations in the Rhineland). In: Beiträge zur Archäologie des römischen Rheinlands. Düsseldorf: Rheinland Verlag, 2:373-448.

1970 Koike, H. (1975) The use of daily and annual growth lines of the clam Meretrix lusoria in estimating seasons of Jomon period shell gathering. Quaternary studies 13:189-193.

1971 Koike, H. (1979) Seasonal dating and the valve-pairing technique in shell-midden analysis. Journal of archaeological science 6(1):63-74.

1972 Koloseike, A. (1970) Costs of shell analysis. American antiquity 35:475-480.

1973 Leach, B. F. (1979) Fish and crayfish from the Washpool midden site, New Zealand: their use in determining season of occupation and prehistoric fishing methods. Journal of archaeological science 6(2):109-126.

1974 Leach, B. F. and Anderson, A. J. (1979) The role of labrid fish in prehistoric economies in New Zealand. Journal of archaeological science 6(1):1-15.

1975 Lepiksaar, J. (1980) Fischreste aus den mesolithischen Kulturschichten der Falkensteinhöhle bei Thiergarten und des Felsdaches Inzigkofen im oberen Donautal.

(Fish remains from the Mesolithic cultural levels of the Falkenstein Cave near Thiergarten and the Inzigkofen rock shelter in the upper Danube valley). Tübinger Monographien zur Urgeschichte 5(2):153-157.

1976 Lepiksaar, J. (1980) Vogelknochenfunde aus spät-paläolithischen und mesolithischen Kulturschichten der Bettelküche bei Sulzbach-Rosenberg (Oberpfalz) und der Fohlenhaus-Höhlen im Lonetal (Schwäbische Alb). (Bird bone finds from the late Palaeolithic and Mesolithic cultural levels of the Bettelküche near Sulzbach-Rosenberg (Upper Palatinate) and the Fohlenhaus Caves in the Lone valley, Swabian Alps). Tübinger Monographien zur Urgeschichte 5(2):141-150.

1977 Mahula, R. (1977) Environmental implications from molluscan analysis. Hop Hill: culture and climatic change in central Texas. Center for Archaeological Research, University of Texas, San Antonio. Special report 5:104-106.

1978 Mania, D. (1980) Die Molluskenfauna aus dem Travertin-komplex von Bilzingsleben. (Mollusca from the traver-tine complex of Bilzingsleben). Ethnographisch-archäologische Zeitschrift 21(1):20-25.

1979 Mienis, H. K. (1978) Molluscs from Abou Gosh and Beisamoun. Mémoires et travaux du Centre de recherches préhistorique français de Jerusalem 2:269-272.

1980 Morton, B. (1978) Molluscan evidence of environmental changes at Sham Wan. Journal monograph--Hong Kong archaeological society 3:45-51.

1981 Müller, H.-H. (1977) Subfossile Pelikanfunde aus dem Gebiet der DDR. (Subfossil pelican finds from the region of the GDR). Hercynia (Leipzig) 14(3):352-354.

1982 Müller, H.-H. and Stephan, B. (1977) Zur Geschichte der Avifauna auf Grund subfossiler Nachweise. (On the history of avifauna on the basis of subfossil information). In: G. Klafs and J. Stübs, eds., Die Vogelwelt Mecklenburgs. Avifauna der Deutschen Demo-kratischen Republik. Jena, 1:25-29.

1983 Northcote, E. M. (1980) Some Cambridgeshire Neolithic to Bronze Age birds and their presence or absence in England in the late-glacial and early Flandrian. Journal of archaeological science 7(4):379-383.

1984 Olsen, S. J. (1968) Fish, amphibian and reptile remains from archaeological sites. Part I, Southeastern and southwestern United States, Appendix: The osteology of the wild turkey. Harvard University. Papers of the Peabody Museum 61(2). 137p.

1985 Osborne, P. J. (1969) An insect fauna of late Bronze Age date from Wilsford, Wiltshire. Journal of animal ecology 38:555-566.

1986 Osborne, P. J. (1971) An insect fauna from the Roman site at Alcester, Warwickshire. Britannia 2:156-165.

1987 Osborne, P. J. (1973) Insects in archaeological deposits. Science and archaeology 10:4-6.

1988 Preece, R. C. (1980) The biostratigraphy and dating of a postglacial slope deposit at Gore Cliff, near Blackgang, Isle of Wight. Journal of archaeological science 7(3):255-265.

1989 Preece, R. C. (1980) The biostratigraphy and dating of the tufa deposit at the Mesolithic site at Blashenwell, Dorset, England. Journal of archaeological science 7(4):345-362.

1990 Robinson, M. A. (1980) Archaeological finds of wasp galls. Journal of archaeological science 7(1):93-95.

1991 Scott, D. H. (1979) Analysis of avifauna from five sites in northwestern Iowa. Journal of the Iowa archeological society (Iowa City) 26:43-79.

1992 Soergel, E. (1955) Über einige Vogelreste (Seeadler, Kraniche) aus dem Neolithikum von Ehrenstein bei Ulm. (On a few bird remains (eagle, crane) from the Neolithic at Ehrenstein near Ulm). Jahresheft des Vereins für Vaterländische Naturkunde in Württemburg, Stuttgart 110:121-124.

1993 Solomon, M. E. (1965) Archaeological records of stored
      pests: Sitophilus granarius L. (Coleoptera:
      Curculionidae) from an Egyptian pyramid tomb.
      Journal of stored products research 1:105-107.

1994 Speight, M. C. D. (1974) Potential contributions to
      archaeology from animal remains with special
      reference to insects. In: B. G. Scott, ed., Per-
      spectives in Irish archaeology. Belfast: Associa-
      tion of Young Irish Archaeologists, 24-34.

1995 Stafford, F. (1971) Insects of a medieval burial.
      Science and archaeology 7:6-10.

1996 Svetovidov, A. N. (1948) K istorij ikhtiofauny r.
      Dona. (On the history of ichthyo-fauna of the Don
      River). Materialy i issledovanija po arkheologii
      SSSR 8:124-127.

1997 Teichert, M. and Lepiksaar, J. (1977) Die Vogelknochen
      aus den urgeschichtlichen Kulthöhlen des
      Kyffhäusergebirges. (The bird bones from the pre-
      historic cult caves of the Kyffhäusergebirge). Alt-
      Thüringen 14:108-144.

1998 Thomas, K. D. (1978) Population studies on molluscs in
      relation to environmental archaeology. Instutite of
      Archaeology, occasional publication 3:9-18.

1999 Ulrich, W. G. (1972) Untersuchungen über die Käfer-
      fauna eines frühgeschichtlichen Bohlweges aus dem
      Wittmoor bei Duvenstedt. (Investigations on the
      beetle fauna of an early historic boll weevil from
      the Wittmoor near Duvenstedt). Faunistisch-
      Ökologische Mitteilungen 4:119-126.

2000 Voigt, E. (1975) Studies of marine mollusca from
      archaeological sites, dietary preferences, environ-
      mental reconstructions and ethnological parallels.
      In: A. T. Clason, ed., Archaeozoological studies.
      Amsterdam: North-Holland Publishing Co., 87-98.

2001 Wheeler, A. (1978) Problems of identification and in-
      terpretation of archaeological fish remains.
      Institute of Archaeology, occasional publication
      3:69-75.

2002 Wheeler, A. (1978) Why were there no fish remains at Star Carr? Journal of archaeological science 5:85-89.

2003 Wilmsen, E. N. and Myers, J. T. (1972) The mercury content of prehistoric fish. Ecology of food and nutrition 1:179-186.

2004 Wing, E. S. (1980) Aquatic fauna and reptile from the Atlantic and Pacific sites. In: Adaptive radiations in prehistoric Panama. Harvard University. Peabody Museum monographs 5:194-215.

2005 Yesner, D. R. (1977) Avian exploitation, occupational seasonality, and paleoecology of the Chugachik Island site. Anthropological papers of the University of Alaska 18:23-30.

2006 Žiteneva, L. D. (1969) Ryby poselenija Majaki (konets III tysjačeletija do n. e.). (Fish of the site of Majaki at the end of the third millennium B.C.). Zoologičeskij žurnal 48(1):93-98.

d) Animal by-products

2007 Cruise, A. J. (1970) Leathers, skins and parchments in archaeology. Science and archaeology 2/3:25-27.

2008 Hargrave, L. L. (1965) Identification of feather fragments by microstudies. American antiquity 31:202-205.

2009 Messinger, N. G. (1965) Methods used for the identification of feather remains from Wetherill Mesa. American antiquity 31:206-215.

2010 Reed, R. (1973) Ancient skins, parchments and leathers. London: Seminar Press; New York: Academic Press. 332p.

2011 Ryder, M. L. (1964) Report on the skin from Pyotdykes. Proceedings of the prehistoric society 30:193-197.

2012 Ryder, M. L. (1966) Report on hair and skin remains from Ashgrove Farm, Methik, Fife, and other Bronze Age sites. Proceedings of the society of antiquaries of Scotland 97:175-176.

2013 Ryder, M. L. (1968) Fleece structure in some native
      and unimproved breeds of sheep. Zeitschrift für
      Tierzüchtung und Züchtungsbiologie 85:143-170.

2014 Ryder, M. L. (1969) Changes in the fleece of sheep
      following domestication. In: P. J. Ucko and G. W.
      Dimbleby, eds., The domestication and exploitation
      of plants and animals. London: Duckworth, 495-521.

2015 Ryder, M. L. (1972) Wool of the 14th century B.C. from
      Tell el-Amarna, Egypt. Nature 240(5380):355-356.

2016 Ryder, M. L. (1974) Wools from antiquity. Textile
      history 5:100-110.

2017 Ryder, M. L. (1977) Some miscellaneous ancient fleece
      remains. Journal of archaeological science
      4(2):177-181.

2018 Ryder, M. L. (1980) Hair remains throw light on early
      British prehistoric cattle. Journal of archaeological
      science 7(4):389-392.

3. Floral

   a) Palynology

2019 Averdieck, F.-R. (1980) Zum Stand der palynologischen
      Untersuchungen an Erdbauten in Schleswig-Holstein.
      (On the status of palynological investigations of
      earthworks in Schleswig-Holstein). Offa 37:384-393.

2020 Barber, K. E. (1975) Pollen analysis. In: C. Platt
      and R. Coleman-Smith, eds., Excavations in medieval
      Southampton, vol. 1: the excavations. 348-349.

2021 Behre, K.-E. (1976) Pollenanalytische Untersuchungen
      zur Vegetations- und Siedlungsgeschichte bei Flögeln
      und im Ahlenmoor (Elb-Weser-Winkel). (Pollen inves-
      tigations for vegetation and settlement history near
      Flögeln and in the Ahlenmoor, Elb-Weser-Winkel).
      Probleme der Küstenforschung im südlichen Nordsee-
      gebiet 11:101.

2022 Bortenschlager, S. (1978) Das Pollendiagram von Kol-e
Ptukh (3272 m) im östlichen Wakhan. (The pollen
diagram of Kol-e Ptukh (3272 m) in eastern Wakhan).
In: Expoloration Pamir '75. Grosser Pamir. Graz:
Akademische Druck- und Verlagsanstalt, 193-200.

2023 Bottema, S. (1975-1977) A pollen diagram from the
Syrian anti-Lebanon. Paléorient 3:259-268.

2024 Boyer-Klein, A. (1980) Nouveaux résultats palynolo-
giques de sites solutréens et magdaléniens canta-
briques. Société préhistorique française. Bulletin,
Compte rendus de séances mensuelles 77(4):103-107.

2025 Bradley, R. and Keith-Lucas, M. (1975) Excavation and
pollen analysis on a bell barrow at Ascot, Berkshire.
Journal of archaeological science 2(2):95-108.

2026 Bryant, V. M. (1975) Pollen as an indicator of prehistoric diets in Coahuila, Mexico. Bulletin of the
Texas archaeological society 46:87-106.

2027 Campo, M. van (1975) Pollen analyses in the Sahara.
In: Problems in prehistory: North Africa and the
Levant. Southern Methodist University contributions
in anthropology 13:45-64.

2028 Cârciumaru, M. (1978) L'analyse pollinique des copro-
lithes de la station archéologique de Vlasac. Kniha--
Odeljenje istorijskih nauka. Beograd: Srpska
Akademija Nauka i Umetnosti, 62:31-34.

2029 Cârciumaru, M. (1979) Analyse pollinique des couches
néolithiques de Padea et de Leu (dép. de Dolj).
Dacia 23:65-68.

2030 Cârciumaru, M. (1979) Paysage paléophytogéographique,
variations du climat et géochronologie du paléolithique moyen et supérieur de Roumanie. (Etude
palynologique). Dacia 23:21-29.

2031 Clary, K. H. (1980) The identification of selected
pollen grains from a core at Isla Palenque. In:
Adaptive radiations in prehistoric Panama. Peabody
Museum, Harvard University. Monographs 5:488-491.

2032 Couteaux, M. (1977) A propos de l'interprétation des analyses polliniques de sédiments minéraux, principalement archéologiques. In: Approche écologique de l'homme fossile. Paris: Université Pierre et Marie Curie 47:259-276.

2033 Dimbleby, G. W. (1954) Pollen analysis as an aid to the dating of prehistoric monuments. Proceedings of the prehistoric society 20:231-236.

2034 Dimbleby, G. W. (1957) The pollen analysis of terrestrial soils. New phytologist 56:12-28.

2035 Dimbleby, G. W. (1976) A review of pollen analysis of archaeological sites. In: Geoarchaeology. Boulder, Colorado: Westview, 347-354.

2036 Dimbleby, G. W. and Bradley, R. J. (1975) Evidence of pedogenesis from a Neolithic site at Rackham, Sussex. Journal of archaeological science 2(3): 179-186.

2037 Dimbleby, G. W. and Evans, J. G. (1974) Pollen and land-snail analysis of calcareous soils. Journal of archaeological science 1(2):117-133.

2038 Elhaï, H. (1962) Les analyses polliniques en France de 1956 à 1961. L'anthropologie 66(3/4):416-423.

2039 Fedorova, R. V. (1965) Primenenie sporovo-pyl'tsevogo analyza v izučenii arkheologičeskikh ob"ektov lesostepnoj i stepnoj zon. (The use of spore-pollen analysis in the study of archaeological objects of the forest-steppe and steppe zones). Sovetskaja arkheologija 2:121-131.

2040 Filzer, P. (1965) Beiträge zur Problematik der Pollenanalyse kulturführender Lehme. (Contributions to the problems of pollen analyses of cultivated loams). Fundberichte aus Schwaben 17:214-223.

2041 Filzer, P. (1980) Pollenanalytische Untersuchungen in den mesolithischen Kulturschichten der Jägerhaus-Höhle an der oberen Donau. (Palynological investigations of the Mesolithic cultural levels of the Jägerhaus cave on the upper Danube). Tübinger Monographien zur Urgeschichte 5(2):21-32.

2042 Fortuna, L. (1978) Analisis polinico. Museo del Hombre Dominicano, Santo Domingo. Boletín 7(10):125-130.

2043 Frenzel, B. (1960) Über zwei bemerkenswerte russische pollenanalytische Arbeiten. (On two noteworthy Russian palynological works). Eiszeitalter und Gegenwart 11:211-218.

2044 Girard, M. (1973) Pollens et paléoethnologie. In: L'homme, hier et aujourd'hui. Paris: Editions Cujas, 317-332.

2045 Gish, J. W. (1979) Palynological research at Pueblo Grande ruin. Kiva (Tucson) 44(2/3):159-172.

2046 Godwin, H. (1940) Pollen analysis and forest history of England and Wales. New phytologist 39:370-400.

2047 Gonzalez Quintero, L. (1978) Aplicacion de tecnicas palinologicas en dos estudios arqueologicos. Coleccion cientifica (Mexico) 63:43-50.

2048 Gray, J. and Smith, W. (1962) Fossil pollen and archaeology. Archaeology 15(1):16-26.

2049 Greig, J. R. A. and Turner, J. (1974) Some pollen diagrams from Greece and their archaeological significance. Journal of archaeological science 1(2): 177-194.

2050 Grimm, P. (1957) Pollenanalyse und Frühgeschichte. (Pollen analysis and early history). Ausgrabungen und Funde 2:4-7.

2051 Gringmuth-Dallmer, E. (1973) Zur Kulturlandschaftsentwicklung in frühgeschichtlicher Zeit. (On the cultural landscape development in early historic times). Zeitschrift für Archäologie 6(1):64-90.

2052 Groenman-van Waateringe, W. (1979) Palynological investigations of five German burial mounds. Archaeo-Physika 8:69-84.

2053 Grüss, J. (1935) Ein Fund von Honig in einem alamannischen Totenbaum von Oberflacht. (A find of honey in an Alemanni sacrificial tree from Oberflacht). Mannus 27:239-241.

2054 Hebda, R. J. and Rouse, G. E. (1979) Palynology of two
Holocene cores from the Hesquiat Peninsula,
Vancouver Island. Syesis (Victoria, B.C.) 12:121-130.

2055 Heim, J.-L. (1969) Intérêt et l'étude des relations
entre les spectres polliniques récents et la végétation actuelle. Congrès international du
quaternaire. Paris, 1:225-232.

2056 Hicks, S. P. (1971) Pollen analytical evidence for the
effect of prehistoric agriculture on the vegetation
of north Derbyshire. New phytologist 70:647-667.

2057 Holland, S. M. (1975) Pollen analytical investigations
at Crosby Warren, Lincolnshire, in the vicinity of
the Iron Age and Romano-British settlement of
Dragonby. Journal of archaeological science 2(4):
353-363.

2058 Horowitz, A. (1971) Climate and vegetational developments in northeastern Israel during upper
Pleistocene-Holocene times. Pollen et spores
13:255-278.

2059 Irwin, H. T. J. and Barghoorn, E. S. (1965) Identification of the pollen of maize, teosinte and
tripsacum by phase contrast microscopy. Botanical
Museum, Harvard University. Botanical Museum
leaflets 21(2):37-64.

2060 Iversen, J. (1941) Land occupation in Denmark's stone
age. A pollen-analytical study of the influence of
farmer culture on the vegetational development.
Danmarks geologiske undersøgelse, series 2, no. 66.
Copenhagen.

2061 Jacob, H. (1963) Pollenanalytische Untersuchung einer
Torfschicht im Travertin von Weimar. (Palynological
investigations of a peat layer in the travertine
from Weimar). Ausgrabungen und Funde 8(5):233-236.

2062 Jalut, G. (1979) Étude palynologique de l'abri Jean-
Cros. In: L'Abri Jean Cros. Toulouse: Centre
d'Anthropologie des Sociétés Rurales, 233-237.

2063 Kautz, R. R. (1980) Pollen analysis and paleoethnobotany. In: Guitarrero Cave. New York: Acacemic
Press, 45-63.

2064 Khotinskij, N. A. et al. (1978) Palinologičeskie i radiouglerodnye datirovki jazykovskikh stojanok v Kalininskoj Oblasti. (Palynological and radiocarbon dating of sites in Jazykov in the district of Kalinin). Kratkie soobščenija Instituta Arkheologii 153:62-67.

2065 Kubitzki, K. (1961) Zur Synchronisierung der nordwesteuropäischen Pollendiagramme (mit Beiträgen zur Waldgeschichte Nordwestdeutschlands). (On the synchronization of the northwest European pollen diagrams, with contributions on the forest history of northwest Germany). Flora 150:43.

2066 Kurtz, E. B., Tucker, H. and Liverman, J. L. (1960) Reliability of identification of fossil pollen as corn. American antiquity 25:605-606.

2067 Lange, E. (1969) Pollenanalyse und Siedlungsgeschichte. (Pollen analysis and settlement history). Zeitschrift für Archäologie 3(2):211-222.

2068 Lange, E. (1973) Pollenanalytische Untersuchung in Ragow, Kr. Calau. (Palynological investigation in Ragow, district of Calau). Zeitschrift für Archäologie 7(1):86-93.

2069 Lange, E. (1975) Die Pollenanalyse. (Pollen analysis). In: Wege zur Datierung und Chronologie der Urgeschichte. Wissenschaftliche Beiträge der Martin-Luther-Universität Halle-Wittenberg. 4:73-81.

2070 Lange, E. (1977) Das Pollendiagramm von Berlin-Blankenburg. Ein Beitrag zur frühgeschichtlichen Landwirtschaft und Vegetation. (The pollen diagram from Berlin-Blankenburg. A contribution to protohistoric agriculture and vegetation). In: Archäologie als Geschichtswissenschaft. Berlin, 545-549.

2071 Leroi-Gourhan, A. (1956) Analyse pollinique et carbone 14. Bulletin de société préhistorique française 53:291-301.

2072 Leroi-Gourhan, A. (1958) Résultats de l'analyse pollinique du gisement d'El Guettar (Tunisie). Bulletin de société préhistorique française 55:546-551.

2073 Leroi-Gourhan, A. (1959) Résultats de l'analyse pol-
      linique de la grotte d'Isturitz. Bulletin de société
      préhistorique française 56:619-624.

2074 Leroi-Gourhan, A. (1973) Les possibilités de l'analyse
      pollinique en Syrie et au Liban. Paléorient 1:39-47.

2075 Leroi-Gourhan, A. and Girard, M. (1971) L'Abri de la
      Cure à Baulmes (Suisse). Analyse pollinique. Jahrbuch
      der schweizerishe Gesellschaft für Ur- und Früh-
      geschichte 56:7-15.

2076 Leroi-Gourhan, A. and Renault-Miskovsky, J. (1977) Le
      palynologie appliquée à l'archéologie: méthodes et
      limites. In: Approche écologique de l'homme fossile.
      Paris: Université Pierre et Marie Curie, 47:35-49.

2077 Liese-Kleiber, H. (1977) Pollenanalytische Unter-
      suchungen der spätneolithischen Ufersiedlung Avenu
      des Sports in Yverden am Neuenbergersee, Schweiz.
      (Palynological investigations of the late Neolithic
      shore-line settlement Avenu des Sports in Yverden on
      the Neuenbergersee, Switzerland). Jahrbuch der
      schweizerische Gesellschaft für Ur- und Früh-
      geschichte 60:7-41.

2078 Lopez García, P. (1978) Resultados polínicos del
      holoceno en la Península Iberica. Trabajos de pre-
      historia, neuva serie (Madrid) 35:9-44.

2079 Maloney, B. K. (1980) Pollen analytical evidence for
      early forest clearance in north Sumatra. Nature
      287(5780):324-326.

2080 Mangelsdorf, P. C., Borghoon, E. S. and Banerjee, U. C.
      (1978) Fossil pollen and the origin of corn: ancient
      pollen from deep cores in Mexico shows the ancestor
      of corn to be corn and not its relative, teosinte.
      Botanical Museum, Harvard University. Botanical
      Museum leaflets 26(7):237-255.

2081 Martin, P. S. (1963) Early man in Arizona: the pollen
      evidence. American antiquity 29(1):67-73.

2082 Martin, P. S. and Sharrock, T. W. (1964) Pollen
      analysis of prehistoric human feces: a new approach
      to ethnobotany. American antiquity 30:168-180.

2083 Mehringer, P. J., Petersen, K. L. and Hassan, F. A.
      (1979) A pollen record from Birket Qarun and the
      recent history of the Fayum, Egypt. Quaternary
      research 11(2):238-256.

2084 Menendez Amor, J. (1961) Resultado del análisis
      polínico de una serie de muestras de turba recogidas
      en la Ereta del Pedregal (Navarrés, Valencia).
      Archivo de prehistoria levantina (Valencia) 9:97-99.

2085 Mildenberger, G. (1972) Pollenanalyse und Siedlungs-
      geschichte im Vogtland. (Pollen analysis and
      settlement history in Vogtland). Prähistorische
      Zeitschrift 47(1):110-115.

2086 Moore, P. D. (1980) Resolution limits of pollen
      analysis as applied to archaeology. MASCA journal
      1(4):118-120.

2087 Morzadec-Kerfourn, M. T. (1977) Remarques concernant la
      corrosion des grains de pollen dans les sédiments
      soumis à l'altération. In: Approche écologique de
      l'homme fossile. Paris: Université Pierre et Marie
      Curie, 47:51-52.

2088 Paquerau, M. M. (1974/1975) Le Würm ancien en
      Périgord. Étude palynologique. Première partie.
      Quaternaria 18:1-49.

2089 Paquerau, M. M. (1974/1975) Le Würm ancien en
      Périgord--étude palynologique--Première partie: les
      diagrammes palynologiques--la zonation climatique.
      Part II: L'évolution des climats et des flores.
      Quaternaria 18:67-159.

2090 Pennington, W. (1975) The effect of Neolithic man on
      the environment in northwest England: the use of
      absolute pollen diagrams. In: J. G. Evans, S.
      Limbrey and H. Cleere, eds., The effect of man on
      the landscape: the highland zone. Council for
      British Archaeology research report 11:74-86.

2091 Pilcher, J. R. (1968) Some applications of scanning
      electron microscopy to the study of modern and fossil
      pollen. Ulster journal of archaeology 31:87-91.

2092   Pilcher, J. R. et al. (1971) Land clearance in the
       Irish Neolithic: new evidence and interpretation.
       Science 172:560-562.

2093   Robinson, M. and Hubbard, R. N. L. B. (1977) The trans-
       port of pollen in the bracts of hulled cereals.
       Journal of archaeological science 4(2):197-199.

2094   Schoenwetter, J. (1974) Pollen records of Guila
       Naquitz Cave. American antiquity 39(2)L292-303.

2095   Schoenwetter, J. (1979) Initial assessments of the
       palynological record: Gila Butte--Santan region.
       Anthropological research paper. Tempe, Arizona:
       Arizona State University, 18:164-177.

2096   Shutler, R. (1961) Applications of palynology to
       archaeological and environmental problems in the
       Pacific. Asian perspectives 5(2):188-192.

2097   Short, S. K. (1978) Palynology: a Holocene environ-
       mental perspective for archaeology in Labrador-
       Ungava. Arctic anthropology 15(2):9-35.

2098   Sørensen, I. (1976) Pollen analytical dating of bone
       material from the Svaedborg I excavation in 1943-44.
       Arkaeologiske studier (Copenhagen) 3:149-160.

2099   Staines, S. (1979) Environmental change on Dartmoor.
       Prehistoric Dartmoor in its context. Proceedings of
       the Devon archaeological society 37:21-47.

2100   Steckhan, H. U. (1961) Pollenanalytisch-vegetations-
       geschichtliche Untersuchungen zur frühen Siedlungs-
       geschichte im Vogelsberg, Knüll und Solling.
       (Palynological-paleobotanical investigations on
       early settlement history in Vogelsberg, Knüll and
       Solling). Flora 150:514-551.

2101   Tolonen, M. (1978) The history of agriculture in
       Sääksmäki traced by pollen analysis. Annales
       botanici fennici 15(1):47-54.

2102   Troels-Smith, J. (1955) Pollenanalytische Untersuchung-
       en zu einigen Schweizerischen Pfahlbauproblemen.
       (Palynological investigations on a few Swiss pile-
       dwelling problems). In: W. U. Guyan, ed., Das Pfahl-

bauproblem. Monographien zur Ur- und Frühgeschichte der Schweiz 11:9-58.

2103   Tsukada, M. (1967) Chenopod and amaranth pollen: electron-microscopic identification. Science 157(3784):80-82.

2104   Turner, J. (1975) The evidence for land use by prehistoric farming communities: the use of three-dimensional pollen diagrams. In: J. G. Evans, S. Limbrey and H. Cleere, eds., The effect of man on the landscape: the highland zone. Council for British Archaeology research report 11:86-95.

2105   Turner, J. (1978) The vegetation of Greece during prehistoric times: the palynological evidence. In: Thera and the Aegean world. London: Thera and the Aegean World, 765-773.

2106   Waterbolk, H. T. (1956) Pollen spectra from Neolithic grave monuments in the northern Netherlands. Palaeohistoria 5:39-51.

2107   Welten, M. (1955) Pollenanalytische Untersuchungen über die neolithischen Siedlungsverhältnisse. (Palynological investigations on the Neolithic settlement circumstances). Monographien zur Ur- und Frühgeschichte der Schweiz 11:59-88.

2108   West, G. J. (1980) Sediment analysis of a core from Isla Palenque. In: Adaptive radiations in prehistoric Panama. Peabody Museum, Harvard University. Monographs 5:484-488.

2109   Wijmstra, T. A. (1975) Palynology and palaeoclimatology of the last 100,000 years. In: Proceedings of the WMO IAMAP symposium on long-term climatic fluctuations. Norwich, 5-20.

2110   Wilkinson, P. F. (1971) Pollen, archaeology and man. Archaeology and physical anthropology in Oceania 6(1):1-20.

2111   Woosley, A. I. (1978) Pollen extraction for arid-land sediments. Journal of field archaeology 5(3):349-355.

2112 Woosley, A. I. and Hole, F. (1978) Pollen evidence of subsistence and environment in ancient Iran. Paleorient 4:59-70.

2113 Zeist, W. van (1956) Die palynologische Bearbeitung des Münzfundes von Bargercompascuum. (The palynological work on the mint find from Bargercompascuum). Palaeohistoria 5:93-99.

2114 Zeist, W. van (1967) Archaeology and palynology in the Netherlands. Review palaeobotany and palynology 4:45-65.

2115 Zeist, W. van and Bottema, S. (1977) Palynological investigations in western Iran. Palaeohistoria 19:19-85.

2116 Zeist, W. van, Polhaupessy, N. A. and Stuijts, I. M. (1979) Two pollen diagrams from West Java, a preliminary report. Modern Quaternary research in Southeast Asia 5:43-56.

2117 Zeist, W. van, Woldring, H. and Stapert, D. (1975) Late Quaternary vegetation and climate of southwestern Turkey. Palaeohistoria 17:44-143.

b) Paleoethnobotany

2118 Armitage, P. L. (1975) The extraction and identification of opal phytoliths from the teeth of ungulates. Journal of archaeological science 2(3):187-197.

2119 Asch, D. L. and Asch, N. B. (1977) Chenopod as cultigen: a re-evaluation of some prehistoric collections from eastern North America. Mid-Continental journal of archaeology 2(1):3-45.

2120 Bakels, C. (1979) Linearbandkeramische Früchte und Samen aus den Niederlanden. (Linear Pottery Culture fruit and seeds from the Netherlands). Archaeo-Physika 8:1-10.

2121 Bakhteev, F. Kh. (1958) Materialy k proiskhoždeniju i filogenii jačmenja--Hordeum sativum s. 1. (Materials on the origin and phylogeny of barley--Hordeum sativum s. 1.). Problemy botaniki 3:308-316.

2122 Bakhteev, F. Kh. (1962) Vpervye najdennyj dikij
     šestirjadnyj jačmen'. (The first finds of wild 6-row
     barley). Akademija Nauk Turkmenskoj SSR. Izvestija,
     serija biologičeskaja 5:86-89.

2123 Bakhteev, F. Kh. (1964) Sovremennoe sostojanie pro-
     blemy proiskhoždenija jačmenja. (Current status of
     the problem of the origin of barley). Akademija Nauk
     SSSR. Izvestija, serija biologičeskaja 5:655-667.

2124 Bakhteev, F. Kh. (1975) Present problems on the origin
     of barley. Folia quaternaria 46:73-81.

2125 Bakhteyev, F. Kh. and Yanushevich, Z. V. (1980) Dis-
     coveries of cultivated plants in the early farming
     settlements of Yarym-Tepe I and Yarym-Tepe II in
     northern Iraq. Journal of archaeological science
     7(2):167-178.

2126 Bartley, D. D. (1976) Palaeobotanical evidence. In:
     Medieval settlement. London: Edward Arnold, 226-235.

2127 Beckett, S. C. (1978) Paleobotanical investigations at
     the Difford's I site. Somerset Levels papers
     4:101-106.

2128 Beckett, S. C. (1979) The paleobotanical background to
     the Meare Lake Village sites. Somerset Levels papers
     5:18-24.

2129 Behre, K.-E. (1969) Untersuchungen des botanischen
     Materials der frühmittelalterlichen Siedlung
     Haithabu (Ausgrabung 1963-1964). (Investigations of
     the botanical materials of the early medieval
     settlement Haithabu, 1963-1964 seasons). Berichte
     über die Ausgrabungen in Haithabu 2:7-55.

2130 Behre, K.-E. (1969) Die Werte von Holzartenbestimmungen
     aus vorgeschichtlichen Sielungen (dargestellt an
     Beispielen aus Norddeutschland). (The value of wood
     species determinations from prehistoric settlements,
     based upon examples from north Germany). Neue
     Ausgrabungen und Forschungen in Niedersachsen
     4:348.

2131 Behre, K.-E. (1970) Die Entwicklungsgeschichte der natürlichen Vegetation im Gebiet der unteren Ems und ihre Abhängigkeit von den Bewegungen des Meeresspiegels. (The developmental history of the natural vegetation in the region of the lower Ems River and its relationship to the fluctuation in sea level). Probleme der Küstenforschung im südlichen Nordseegebiet 9:13.

2132 Behre, K.-E. (1972) Kultur- und Wildpflanzenreste aus der Marschgrabung Jemgumkloster/Ems (um Christi Geburt). (Domestic and wild plant remains from the marsh grave Jemgumkloster/Ems River, B.C.). Neue Ausgrabungen und Forschungen in Niedersachsen 7:164-184.

2133 Behre, K.-E. (1973) Mittelalterliche Kulturpflanzen funde aus der Kirche von Middels (Stadt Aurich/Ostfriesland). (Medieval domestic plant finds from the church at Middels, city of Aurich/East Friesland). Probleme der Küstenforschung im südlichen Nordseegebiet 10:39-47.

2134 Behre, K.-E. (1975) Wikingerzeitlicher Ackerbau in der Seemarsch bei Elisenhof/Schleswig-Holstein (deutsche Nordseeküste). (Viking period agriculture in the sea marsh near Elisenhof/Schleswig-Holstein, German North Sea coast). Folia quaternaria 46:49-62.

2135 Behre, K.-E. (1976) Die Pflanzenreste aus der frühgeschichtlichen Wurt Elisenhof. (The plant remains from the early historic Wurt Elisenhof). In: Studien zur Küstenarchäologie Schleswig-Holsteins, Ser. A: Elisenhof. Die Ergebnisse der Ausgrabung der frühgeschichtlichen Marschensiedlung beim Elisenhof in Eiderstedt 1957-1958 und 1961-1964. Vol. 2. 144p.

2136 Behre, K.-E. (1977) Acker, Grünland und natürliche Vegetation während der römischen Kaiserzeit im Gebiet der Marschensiedlung Bentumersiel/Unterems. (Field, fen and natural vegetation during the Roman Imperial period in the area of the marsh settlement Bentumersiel/lower Ems River). Probleme der Küstenforschung im südlichen Nordseegebiet 12:67.

206

2137 Behre, K.-E. (1979) Ein jungbronzezeitlicher Getreidefund aus Ostfriesland. (An early Bronze Age grain
find from east Friesland). Archaeo-Physika 8:11-20.

2138 Benn, D. W. (1974) Seed analysis and its implications
for an initial middle Missouri site in South
Dakota. Plains anthropologist 19(63):55-72.

2139 Bohrer, V. L. (1970) Ethnobotanical aspects of
Snaketown, a Hohokam village in southern Arizona.
American antiquity 35:413-430.

2140 Bohrer, V. L. and Adams, K. R. (1977) Ethnobotanical
techniques and approaches at Salmon Ruin, New
Mexico. San Juan Valley archaeological project
technical series no. 2. Eastern New Mexico University
contributions in anthropology 8, no. 1.

2141 Brooks, R. H. et al. (1962) Plant material from a cave
on the Rio Zape, Durango, Mexico. American antiquity
27:356-369.

2142 Brunken, J., Wet, J. M. J. de and Harlan, J. R. (1977)
The morphology and domestication of pearl millet.
Economic botany 31:163-174.

2143 Buurman, J. (1979) Cereals in circles--crop processing
activities in Bronze Age Bovenkarspel (the
Netherlands). Archaeo-Physika 8:21-37.

2144 Casparie, W. A. et al. (1977) The palaeobotany of
Swifterbant. Helinium 17:28-55.

2145 Castelletti, L. (1978) I carboni della grotta
"Latronico 3" (Latronico, provincia di Potenza).
Atti della XX riunione scientifica in Basilicata.
Firenze: Instituto Italiano di Preistoria e
Protostoria, 227-239.

2146 Cohen, M. N. (1975) Some problems in the quantitative
analysis of vegetable refuse illustrated by a Late
Horizon site on the Peruvian coast. Nawpa Pacha
10-12:49-60.

2147 Conolly, A. (1971) Plant remains. In: E. Greenfield,
The Roman villa at Denton, Lincolnshire pt. II. The
bathhouse and well. Lincolnshire history and
archaeology 1(6):29-57.

2148 Coughlin, E. A. (1979) Chemical test for silica
      determinations as an archaeological feature in ethno-
      botany. Botanical Museum, Harvard University.
      Botanical Museum leaflets 27(5/6):161-165.

2149 Crabtree, P. J. (1979) Paleoethnobotany: some recent
      references. MASCA journal 1(3):85-86.

2150 Crites, G. D. (1978) Plant food utilization patterns
      during the Middle Woodland Owl Hollow phase in
      Tennessee: a preliminary report. Tennessee
      anthropologist 3(1):79-92.

2151 Cutler, H. C. (1960) Cultivated plant remains from
      Waterfall Cave, Chihuahua. American antiquity
      26:277-279.

2152 Davies, O. and Gordon-Gray, K. (1977) Tropical African
      cultigens from Shongweni excavations, Natal. Journal
      of archaeological science 4(2):153-162.

2153 Davies, O. (1968) Origins of agriculture in West
      Africa. Current anthropology 7:479-483.

2154 Davies, O. (1975) Excavations at Shongweni South Cave:
      the oldest evidence to date for cultigens in southern
      Africa. Natal Museum annals 22:627-662.

2155 Dembinska, M. (1976) Wild corn plants gathered in the
      9th-13th centuries in the light of paleobotanical
      materials. Folia quaternaria 47:97-103.

2156 Dennell, R. W. (1970) Seeds from a medieval sewer in
      Woolster Street, Plymouth. Economic botany 24:151.

2157 Dennell, R. W. (1974) Botanical evidence for prehis-
      toric crop processing activities. Journal of
      archaeological science 1(3):275-284.

2158 Dennell, R. W. (1978) Archaeobotany and early farming
      in Europe. Archaeology 31(1):8-13.

2159 Derbyshire, E. et al. (1977) The extraction, com-
      position and intra-cellular distribution of protein
      in early maize grains from an archaeological site in
      northeast Arizona. New phytologist 78(2):499-504.

2160   Dieck, A. (1976) Weinvorkommen an der Mittelweser in
       der Spätbronzezeit, Frühlatènezeit und Spätlatène-
       zeit. (Wine occurrence on the middle Weser River in
       the late Bronze Age, early La Tène and late La Tène).
       Die Kunde 26/27:89-91.

2161   Dieck, A. (1979) Malva silvestris, Capsella bursa
       pastoralis und Juniperus communis in vor- und früh-
       geschichtlichen Funden. (Malva silvestris, Capsella
       bursa pastoralis and Juniperus communis in pre- and
       protohistoric finds). Curare (Braunschweig)
       2(2):117-124.

2162   Dimbleby, G. W. (1967) Plants and archaeology. London:
       John Baker. 190p.

2163   Ellison, R., et al. (1978) Some food offerings from Ur,
       excavated by Sir Leonard Woolley, and previously
       unpublished. Journal of archaeological science
       5:167-177.

2164   Endtmann, K.-J. (1976) Zur Determination und Ver-
       breitung der "Hirse"-Arten (Panicum s. 1.) im Norden
       der DDR. (On the identification and distribution of
       the millet species, Panicum s. 1., in the northern
       GDR). Gleditschia 4:75-81.

2165   Fasham, P. J. and Monk, M. A. (1978) Sampling for plant
       remains from Iron Age pits: some results and im-
       plications. British archaeological reports, British
       series 50:363-371.

2166   Feinbrun, N. (1938) New data on some cultivated plants
       and weeds of the early Bronze Age in Palestine.
       Palestine journal of botany, J. ser. 1(2):238-240.

2167   Feindt, F. (1975) Vorläufiger Bericht über einen Fund
       von verkohltem Getreide aus einem kaiserzeitlichen
       Haus auf der nordfriesischen Insel Amrum. (Pre-
       liminary report on a find of charred grain from an
       Imperial period house on the north Frisian Island of
       Amrum). Folia quaternaria 46:41-48.

2168   Fietz, A. (1926) Prähistorische Holzkohlen aus der
       Umgebung Brunns. I. Theil. (Prehistoric charred wood
       from the vicinity of Brunns. Part I). Planta
       2:414-423.

2169 Fitting, J. E. (1978) Archaeological interpretation
based on ethnobotanical inferences in the upper
Giola region. Museum of Anthropology, Univ. of
Michigan, Ann Arbor. Anthropological papers
67:367-388.

2170 Fljaksberger, K. A. (1940) Arkheologičeskie nakhodki
khlebnykh rastenij v oblastjakh, prilegajuščikh k
Černomu morju. (Archaeological discovery of bread
plants in the district bordering the Black Sea).
Kratkie soobščenija Instituta Istorii Material'noj
Kul'tury, no. 8. Leningrad, 117-119.

2171 Ford, R. I. (1979) Paleoethnobotany in American
archaeology. Advances in archaeological method and
theory 2:285-336.

2172 Friedrich, W. L. (1978) Fossil plants from Weichselian
interstadials, Santorini. In: Thera and the Aegean
world. London: Thera and the Aegean World, 741-744.

2173 Galinat, W. C. (1961) Corn's evolution and its significance for breeding. Economic botany
15:320-325.

2174 Galinat, W. C. (1980) The archaeological maize remains
from Volcan Panama--a comparative perspective. In:
Adaptive radiations in prehistoric Panama. Peabody
Museum, Harvard University. Monographs 5:175-180.

2175 Gall, W. (1980) Neue pflanzliche Grossreste aus
Thüringen. (New plant remains from Thuringia).
Ausgrabungen und Funde 25(5):240-241.

2176 Gasser, R. E. (1980) Exchange and the Hohokam
archaeobotanical record. In: Current issues in
Hohokam prehistory. Anthropological research paper.
Tempe, Arizona: Arizona State University, 23:72-77.

2177 Godwin, H. (1967) The ancient cultivation of hemp.
Antiquity 45:42, 137.

2178 Godwin, H. and Tansley, A. G. (1941) Prehistoric
charcoals as evidence of former vegetation, soil and
climate. Journal of ecology 29:117-126.

2179 Gott, B. (1978) Sham Wan flora. Sham Wan, Lamma
      Island. Journal monograph--Hong Kong archaeological
      society 3:25-30.

2180 Green, F. J. (1979) Collection and interpretation of
      botanical information from medieval urban excavations
      in southern England. Archaeo-Physika 8:39-55.

2181 Greig, J. R. A. (1976) The plant remains. In: P. C.
      Buckland, The environmental evidence from the Church
      Street Roman sewer system. Council for British
      Archaeology. The archaeology of York 1:23.

2182 Griffin, K. O. (1975) Macrofossils from Gamlebyen, an
      archaeological site in Oslo, Norway: a preliminary
      report. Folia quaternaria 46:63-67.

2183 Griffin, K. O. (1979) Fossil records of fig, grape and
      walnut in Norway from medieval time. Archaeo-Physika
      8:57-67.

2184 Grobman, A., Bonavia, D. and Kelley, D. H. (1977) Study
      of Pre-Ceramic maize from Huarmey, north central
      coast of Peru. Botanical Museum, Harvard University.
      Botanical Museum leaflets 25(8):221-242.

2185 Hajnalová, E. (1975) Some aspects of plant growing in
      the La Tène and early Roman periods in north-west
      Slovakia. Folia quaternaria 46:35-40.

2186 Hajnalová, E. (1979) Archäobotanische Funde aus
      Krivina, Bez. Ruse (Bulgarien). (Archaeobotanical
      finds from Krivina, vicinity of Ruse, Bulgaria).
      Archaeo-Physika 8:85-96.

2187 Hall, A. R. and Kenward, H. K. (1980) An interpre-
      tation of biological remains from Highgate,
      Beverley. Journal of archaeological science 7(1):
      33-51.

2188 Hansen, J. M. (1978) The earliest seed remains from
      Greece: Paleolithic through Neolithic at Franchthi
      Cave. Berichte der Deutschen Botanischen
      Gesellschaft 91(1):39-46.

2189 Harlan, J. R. and Zohary, D. (1966) Distribution of
      wild wheats and barley. Science 153:1074-1080.

2190 Hartyányi, B. P. and Máthé, M. S. (1979) Pflanzliche
      Überreste einer Wohnsiedlung aus dem Neolithikum im
      Karpaten-Becken. (Plant residues of a settlement
      from the Neolithic in the Carpathians). Archaeo-
      Physika 8:97-114.

2191 Hartyányi, B. P. and Nováki, G. (1975) Samen- und
      Fruchtfunde in Ungarn von der Neusteinzeit bis zum
      18. Jahrhundert. (Seed and fruit finds in Hungary of
      the Neolithic until the 18th century). Agrártörténeti
      Szemle (Historia Rerum Rusticarum) 17, supplementum
      1, 1-65.

2192 Heim, J.-L. (1979) Recherches paléobotaniques au site
      néolithique (Roessen) de la "Bosse de l'Tombe" à
      Givry. Société Royale Belge d'Anthropologie et de
      Préhistoire. Bulletin 90:65-78.

2193 Helbaek, H. (1952) Early crops in southern England.
      Proceedings of the prehistoric society 18:194-233.

2194 Helbaek, H. (1952) Preserved apples and Panicum on the
      prehistoric site at Nørre Sandegaad in Bornholm.
      Acta archaeologica 23:108-115.

2195 Helbaek, H. (1952) Spelt (Triticum spelta L.) in Bronze
      Age Denmark. Acta archaeologica 23:97-107.

2196 Helbaek, H. (1954) Prehistoric food plants and weeds in
      Denmark. A survey of archaeobotanical research 1923-
      1954. Danmarks geologiske undersøgelse 2, raekke nr.
      80:250.

2197 Helbaek, H. (1955) The botany of the Vallhagar Iron Age
      field. In: M. Steenberger, Vallhagar. A migration
      period settlement on Gotland/Sweden. Part 2:653.

2198 Helbaek, H. (1958) Plant economy in ancient Lachish.
      In: O. Tufnell, ed., Lachish IV--the Bronze Age.
      London: Oxford Univ. Press, 309-317.

2199 Helbaek, H. (1960) Comment on Chenopodium album as a
      food plant in prehistory. Berichte über das Geo-
      botanische Forschungsinstitut Rübel in Zürich 31:16.

2200 Helbaek, H. (1960) The palaeoethnobotany of the Near
      East and Europe. In: R. B. Braidwood and B. Howe,
      eds., Prehistoric investigations in Iraqi Kurdistan.
      Chicago: Univ. of Chicago Press, 99-118.

2201 Helbaek, H. (1961) Late Bronze Age and Byzantine crops
      at Beycesultan in Anatolia. Anatolian studies 11:
      77-97.

2202 Helbaek, H. (1964) The Isca grain, a Roman plant intro-
      duction in Britain. New phytologist 63:158-164.

2203 Helbaek, H. (1965) Isin Larsan and Horian food remains
      at Tell Bazmosian in the Dokan valley. Sumer 19:
      27-35.

2204 Helbaek, H. (1966) Early Hassunan vegetable at Tell
      es-Sawwan near Samarra. Sumer 20:45-48.

2205 Helbaek, H. (1966) The plant remains. In: M. E. L.
      Mallowan, ed., Nimrud and its remains. London:
      Collins, 613-620.

2206 Helbaek, H. (1969) Plant collecting, dry-farming and
      irrigation agriculture in prehistoric Deh Luran. In:
      F. Hole, K. V. Flannery and J. A. Neely, eds.,
      Prehistory and human ecology of the Deh Luran Plain.
      Memoirs of the Museum of Anthropology, Univ. of
      Michigan 1:383-426.

2207 Hilu, K. H., Wet, J. M. J. de and Harlan, J. R. (1979)
      Archaeobotanical studies of Eleusine coracana ssp.
      coracana (finger millet). American journal of botany
      66(3):330-333.

2208 Hinz, H. (1955) Kaiserzeitliche Samen aus Westerohr-
      stedt, Kreis Husum (Nachtrag). (Imperial period
      seeds from Westerohrstedt, vicinity of Husum,
      supplement). Offa 13:87.

2209 Hopf, M. (1954) Anatomische Untersuchungen an Weizens-
pelzen und -körnern verschiedener Polyploidiestufen
als Vorarbeit für die Bestimmung prähistorische
Funde. (Anatomical investigations on wheat, outer
sheaths and kernels, of varying polyploidy as a preliminary work for the identification of prehistoric
finds). Der Züchter 24(6):174-180.

2210 Hopf, M. (1955) Getreidebau vor 4000 Jahren. (Corn
farming before 4000 years). Jahrbuch des Ems-
ländischen Heimatvereins 3:5-11.

2211 Hopf, M. (1955) Formveränderungen von Getreidekörnern
beim Verkohlen. (Changes in the form of grain kernels
through charring). Berichte der Deutschen Botanischen
Gesellschaft 68:191-193.

2212 Hopf, M. (1957) Botanik und Vorgeschichte. (Botany and
prehistory). In: Die Bernburger Getreidefunde vom
Lietfeld bei Burgdorf, Kr. Goslar. Jahrbuch des
Römisch-Germanischen Zentralmuseums Mainz 4:1-22.

2213 Hopf, M. (1958) Neolithische Getreidefunde aus Bosnien
und der Hercegovina. (Neolithic grain finds from
Bosnia and Hercegovina). Glasnik Zemaljskog Muzeja u
Sarajevu. Arheologija 13:97-103.

2214 Hopf, M. (1959) Gutachten über pflanzliche Reste aus
den aufgelösten Salzhandstücken der Gewebe Nr. 6 und
18-20. (Opinions on the plant remains from the hand-
size salt pieces from textiles nos. 6 and 18-20). In:
H.-J. Hundt, Vorgeschichtliche Gewebe aus dem
Hallstätter Salzberg. Jahrbuch des Römisch-
Germanischen Zentralmuseums Mainz 6:94-96.

2215 Hopf, M. (1960) Die Getreideuntersuchung. (The grain
investigation). In: E. Reinbacher, Beiträge zur
Frühgeschichte Spandaus. Prähistorische Zeitschrift
38:301-303.

2216 Hopf, M. (1960) Untersuchung des Hüttenlehms des bandkeramischen Hauses von Rödingen. (Investigation of
the hut clay of the Linear Pottery house of
Rödingen). In: W. Piepers, Bandkeramische Siedlungsreste bei Rödingen, Ldkr. Jülich. Bonner Jahrbücher
160:281-284.

2217   Hopf, M. (1961) Pflanzenfunde aus Lerna/Argolis.
       (Plant finds from Lerna/Argolis). Der Züchter
       5:239-247.

2218   Hopf, M. (1962) Bericht über die Untersuchung von
       Samen und Holzkohlenresten von der Argissa-Magula
       aus den präkeramischen bis mittlebronzezeitlichen
       Schichten. (Report on the investigation of seeds and
       charred wood remains from the Argissa-Magula of the
       preceramic up to the middle Bronze Age layers). Die
       deutschen Ausgrabungen auf der Argissa-Magula in
       Thessalien 1:101-110.

2219   Hopf, M. (1962) Nutzpflanzen vom Lernaischen Golf.
       (Nut plants from the Lerna Gulf). Jahrbuch des
       Römisch-Germanischen Zentralmuseums Mainz 9:1-19.

2220   Hopf, M. (1963) Untersuchungen am Inhalt des römischen
       Doliums aus Alzey. (Investigations on the content of
       a Roman wine-cask from Alzey). Jahrbuch des Römisch-
       Germanischen Zentralmuseums Mainz 10:68-75.

2221   Hopf, M. (1963) Walnüsse und Esskastanien in Holz-
       schalen als Beigaben im frankischen Grab von Gellep
       (Krefeld). (Walnuts and chestnuts in wooden bowls as
       gifts in a Frankish grave at Gellep, Krefeld).
       Jahrbuch des Römisch-Germanischen Zentralmuseums
       Mainz 10:200-203.

2222   Hopf, M. (1963) Die Untersuchung von Getreideresten
       und anderen Feldfrüchten aus Altkalkar, Kr. Kleve,
       und Xanten, Kr. Moers. (The investigation of grain
       remains and other farm products from Altkalkar,
       Kleve district, and Xanten, Moers district). Bonner
       Jahrbücher 163:416-423.

2223   Hopf, M. (1964) Getreidefunde von El Cigarralejo bei
       Mula (Prov. Murcia). (Grain finds from El Cigarralejo
       near Mula, Murcia province). Madrider Mitteilungen
       5:157-166.

2224   Hopf, M. (1964) Neolithische Getreidekörner aus der
       Lüneburger Heide. (Neolithic grain kernels from the
       Lüneburger Heide). Die Kunde 15:109-112.

2225 Hopf, M. (1966) Ein neuer Fund von Dinkel in
      Württemberg. (A new find from Dinkel in Württemberg).
      Jahrbuch des Römisch-Germanischen Zentralmuseums
      Mainz 13:287-291.

2226 Hopf, M. (1966) Triticum monococcum L. y Triticum
      dicoccum Schübl. en el neolitico antiguo español.
      Archivo de prehistoria levantina 11:53-73.

2227 Hopf, M. (1966) Identifications. In: G. Kohl and H.
      Quitta, Berlin--radiocarbon measurements II.
      Radiocarbon 8:27-45.

2228 Hopf, M. (1966/1967) Untersuchungsbericht über die
      botanischen Reste aus der neolithischen Ansiedlung
      in Gornja Tuzla. (Investigation report on the
      botanical remains from the Neolithic settlement in
      Gornja Tuzla). Glasnik Zemaljskog Muzeja Bosne i
      Hercegovine u Sarajevu. Arheologija 21/22:169-171.

2229 Hopf, M. (1967) Analyse de céréales du niveau III
      (Chasséen). In: A. Galan, La station néolithique de
      la Perte du Cros à Saillac (Lot). Gallia préhistoire
      10:70-73.

2230 Hopf, M. (1967) Einige Bemerkungen zu römerzeitlichen
      Fassern. (Some comments on Roman period casks).
      Jahrbuch des Römisch-Germanischen Zentralmuseums
      Mainz 14:212-216.

2231 Hopf, M. (1968) Früchte und Samen. (Fruits and seeds).
      In: H. Zürn, Das jungsteinzeitliche Dorf Ehrenstein
      (Kreis Ulm) Ausgrabung 1960. Veröffentlichungen des
      Staatlichen Amtes für Denkmalpflege Stuttgart, Reihe
      A, 10(2):7-77.

2232 Hopf, M. (1968) Reste von pflanzlichen Funden aus Grab
      200 von El Cigarralejo. (Remains of plants from
      Grave 200 of El Cigarralejo). Madrider Mitteilungen
      9:206-212.

2233 Hopf, M. (1969) Zur Frage der Ausbreitung unserer
      Kulturpflanzen und ihrer Beziehungen zu vorgeschicht-
      lichen Kulturgruppen. (The question of the diffusion
      of our cultivated plants and their connection to pre-
      historic cultural groups). In: Archäologie und Biolo-
      gie. Forschungsberichte 15 der Deutsche Forschungs-
      gemeinschaft, 39-47.

2234 Hopf, M. (1969) Beobachtungen an Getreidekörnen in
Töpferton. (Observations on grain kernels in pottery
clay). Jahrbuch des Römisch-Germanischen Zentralmuseums Mainz 16:169-173.

2235 Hopf, M. (1969) Carbonized plant remains from Chassemy
(Aisne). In: R. M. Rowlett, E. Rowlett and M.
Boureux, A rectangular early La Tène Marnian house at
Chassemy (Aisne). World archaeology 1:130-133.

2236 Hopf, M. (1970) Zur Geschichte der Ackerbohne (Vicia
faba L.). (On the history of the field bean, Vicia
faba L.). Jahrbuch des Römisch-Germanischen Zentralmuseums Mainz 17:306-322.

2237 Hopf, M. (1971) Vorgeschichtliche Pflanzenreste aus
Ostspanien. (Prehistoric plant remains from eastern
Spain). Madrider Mitteilungen 12:101-114.

2238 Hopf, M. (1972) Über einen Roggen aus dem Dreissig-
jährigen Kriege. (On rye from the Thirty Years' War).
Die Kunde 23:232-244.

2239 Hopf, M. (1973) Getreideabdrücke in Gefässscherben.
(Grain impressions in vessel sherds). In: W.
Wegewitz, Der Urnenfriedhof der älteren und jüngeren
vorrömischen Eisenzeit von Putensen, Kr. Harburg.
Urnenfriedhöfe in Niedersachsen 11:152-155.

2240 Hopf, M. (1973) Frühe Kulturpflanzen aus Bulgarien.
(Early cultivated plants from Bulgaria). Jahrbuch
des Römisch-Germanischen Zentralmuseums Mainz
20:1-55.

2241 Hopf, M. (1973) Pflanzenfunde aus Nordspanien. (Plant
finds from northern Spain). Cortes de Navarra--El
Soto de Medinilla. Madrider Mitteilungen 14:133-142.

2242 Hopf, M. (1973) Domestication of pulses in the Old
World. Legumes were companions of wheat and barley
when agriculture began in the Near East. Science
182(4115):887-894.

2243 Hopf, M. (1974) Verkohlte Pflanzenreste aus Grab 48 von
Schwyz-St. Martin. (Charred plant remains from Grave
48 from Schwyz-St. Martin). In: M. Martin, Das
Frauengrab 48 in der Pfarrkirche St. Martin von

Schwyz. Mitteilungen des historischen Vereins des
Kantons Schwyz 66:153-156.

2244 Hopf, M. (1974) Pflanzenreste aus Siedlungen der Vinča-
Kultur in Jugoslawien. (Plant remains from settlements of the Vinča Culture in Jugoslavia). Jahrbuch
des Römisch-Germanischen Zentralmuseums Mainz 21:
1-11.

2245 Hopf, M. (1975) Beobachtungen und Überlegungen bei der
Bestimmung von verkohlten Hordeum-Früchten. (Observations and reflections on the determination of
charred Hordeum grains). Folia quaternaria 46:83-92.

2246 Hopf, M. (1975) Palaeo-Ethnobotanik. (Paleoethnobotany). Ausgrabungen in Deutschland. Gefördert von
der Deutschen Forschungsgemeinschaft 1950-1975,
3:166-173.

2247 Hopf, M. (1977) Sämereien und Holzkohlefunde. (Seeds
and charred wood finds). In: J. Lüning and H. Zürn,
Die Schussenrieder Siedlung im "Schlösslesfeld",
Markung Ludwigsburg. Forschungen und Berichte zur
Vor- und Frühgeschichte in Baden-Württemberg 8:91-96.

2248 Hopf, M. (1978) Plant remains. In: R. Amiran, Early
Arad I. The Chalcolithic settlement and early Bronze
city. Israel exploration journal 28:64-77.

2249 Hopf, M. (1978) Frühe Kulturpflanzen in Südeuropa.
(Early domestic plants in southern Europe). Berichte
der Deutschen Botanischen Gesellschaft 91:31-38.

2250 Hopf, M. and Catalán, M. P. (1970) Neolithische
Getreidefunde in der Höhle von Nerja (Prov. Málaga).
(Neolithic grain finds in the cave at Nerja, Málaga
province). Madrider Mitteilungen 11:18-34.

2251 Hopf, M. and Frías, T. O. y (1974) Ein eisenzeitlicher
Getreidefund von Castilviejo de Yuba, Prov. Soria.
(An Iron Age grain find at Castilviejo de Yuba, Soria
province). Madrider Mitteilungen 15:136-144.

2252 Hopf, M. and Muñoz, A. M. (1974) Neolithische Planzen-
reste aus der Höhle Los Murciélagos bei Zuheros
(Prov. Córdoba). (Neolithic plant remains from the
Los Murciélagos cave near Zuheros, Córdoba province).
Madrider Mitteilungen 15:9-27.

2253 Hopf, M. and Schubart, H. (1965) Getreidefunde aus der
Coveta de L'Or (Prov. Alicante). (Grain finds from
the Coveta de L'Or, Alicante province). Madrider
Mitteilungen 6:20-38.

2254 Hopf, M. and Zachariae, G. (1971) Determination of
botanical and zoological remains from Ramat Matred
and Arad. Israel exploration journal 21:60-64.

2255 Jacob, H. (1977) Zur Pflanzenumwelt der Seen im
Niedermoor von Oberdorla. (On the plant environment
of the lakes in the Niedermoor of Oberdorla). Alt-
Thüringen 14:145-147.

2256 Janusevic, Z. V. (1975) Fossil remains of cultivated
plants in the southwest of the Soviet Union. Folia
quaternaria 46:23-30.

2257 Janusevic, Z. V. (1976) Kul'turnye rastenija jugo-
zapada SSSR po paleobotaniceskim issledovanijam.
(Cultivated plants of the southwestern USSR
according to paleobotanical investigations). Kisinev:
Ştiinţa. 214p.

2258 Janushevich, Z. V. and Nikolaenko, G. M. (1979) Fossil
remains of cultivated plants in the ancient Tauric
Chersonesos. Archaeo-Physika 8:115-134.

2259 Jensen, H. A. (1979) Seeds and other diaspores in
medieval layers from Svendborg. In: The archaeology
of Svendborg, Denmark Vol. 2. Odense: University
Press.

2260 Jones, V. H. (1936) The vegetal remains of Newt Kash
Hollow shelter. Univ. of Kentucky reports in
archaeology and anthropology 3:147-165.

2261 Jørgensen, G. (1975) Triticum aestivum s.l. from the
Neolithic site of Weier in Switzerland. Folia
quaternaria 46:7-21.

2262 Jørgensen, G. (1979) A new contribution concerning the cultivation of spelt, Triticum spelta L., in pre-historic Denmark. Archaeo-Physika 8:135-145.

2263 Jørgensen, G. and Fredskild, B. (1978) Plant remains from TRB culture, period MNV. Arkaeologiske studier 5:189-192.

2264 Kade, C. (1921/1922) Vorgeschichtliche Getreidefunde von der Steinsburg. (Prehistoric grain finds from Steinsburg). Prähistorische Zeitschrift 13/14:83-94.

2265 Kaplan, L. (1980) The paleoethnobotany of Green Hill. Bulletin of the Massachusetts archaeological society (Attleboro) 41(1):15-19.

2266 King, F. B. and Hofman, J. L. (1979) Plant remains from Twenhafel, a multi-component site on the Mississippi River in southern Illinois. Wisconsin archaeologist 60(3):249-259.

2267 Kline, G. W. and Crites, G. D. (1979) Paleoethnobotany of the Ducks Nest site: early Mississippi plant utilization in the eastern highland rim. Tennessee anthropologist (Knoxville) 4(1):82-100.

2268 Knörzer, K.-H. (1966) Über Funde römische Importfrüchte in Novaesium (Neuss/Rh.). (On the finds of Roman imported fruits in Novaesium, Neuss/Rh.). Bonner Jahrbücher 166:424-443.

2269 Knörzer, K.-H. (1967) Subfossile Pflanzenreste von bandkeramischen Fundstellen im Rheinland. (Sub-fossil plant remains from Linear Pottery sites in the Rhineland). Archaeo-Physika 2:3-29.

2270 Knörzer, K.-H. (1968) 6000 jährige Geschichte der Getreidenahrung im Rheinland. (6000-year history of cereal food in the Rhineland). Decheniana 119: 113-124.

2271 Knörzer, K.-H. (1968) Ein Teilergebnis der Untersuchung pflanzlicher Grossreste bei der Ausgrabung an der Niederungsburg bei Haus Meer, Gemeinde Büderich. (A partial result of the investigation of plant remains at the excavation on the Niederungsburg near Haus Meer, vicinity of Büderich). Rheinische Ausgrabungen 1:97.

2272 Knörzer, K.-H. (1971) Eisenzeitliche Pflanzenfunde im
Rheinland. (Iron Age plant finds in the Rhineland).
Bonner Jahrbücher 171:40.

2273 Knörzer, K.-H. (1971) Pflanzliche Grossreste aus der
rössenerzeitlichen Siedlung bei Langweiler, Kreis
Jülich. (Plant remains from the Rössen period settlement near Langweiler, Jülich district). Bonner
Jahrbücher 171:9-33.

2274 Knörzer, K.-H. (1971) Römerzeitliche Getreideunkräuter
von kalkreichen Böden. (Roman period cereal weeds
from calcium-rich soils). Rheinische Ausgrabungen
10:467.

2275 Knörzer, K.-H. (1971) Urgeschichtliche Unkräuter im
Rheinland. Ein Beitrag zur Entstehungsgeschichte der
Segetalgesellschaften. (Prehistoric weeds in the
Rhineland. A contribution to the history of the
origin of sedge colonies). Vegetatio 23:89.

2276 Knörzer, K.-H. (1972) Subfossile Pflanzenreste aus der
bandkeramischen Siedlung Langweiler 3 und 6, Kreis
Jülich, und ein urnenfelderzeitlicher Getreidefund
innerhalb dieser Siedlung. (Subfossil plant remains
from the Linear Pottery settlement Langweiler 3 and
6, Jülich district, and an Urnfield period grain find
within this settlement). Bonner Jahrbücher 172:395.

2277 Knörzer, K.-H. (1973) Der bandkeramische Siedlungs-
platz Langweiler 2, Gemeinde Aldenhoven, Kreis Düren.
Pflanzliche Grossreste. (The Linear Pottery settlement Langweiler 2, Aldenhoven municipality, Düren
district. Plant remains). Rheinische Ausgrabungen
13:139.

2278 Knörzer, K.-H. (1974) Bandkeramische Pflanzenfunde von
Bedburg-Garsdorf, Kreis Bergheim/Erft. (Linear
Pottery plant finds from Bedburg-Garsdorf, district
of Bergheim/Erft). Rheinische Ausgrabungen 15:173.

2279 Knörzer, K.-H. (1974) Eisenzeitliche Pflanzenfunde aus
Frixheim-Anstel, Kreis Grevenboich. (Iron Age plant
finds from Frixheim-Anstel, Grevenboich district).
Rheinische Ausgrabungen 15:405.

2280 Knörzer, K.-H. (1976) Späthallstattzeitliche Pflanzen-
     funde bei Bergheim, Erftkreis. (Late Hallstatt
     period plant finds near Bergheim, Erft district).
     Rheinische Ausgrabungen 17:151.

2281 Knörzer, K.-H. (1977) Pflanzliche Grossreste des band-
     keramischen Siedlungsplatzes Langweiler 9. (Plant
     remains of the Linear Pottery settlement Langweiler
     9). Rheinische Ausgrabungen 18:279.

2282 Knörzer, K.-H. (1979) Über den Wandel der angebauten
     Körnerfrüchte und ihrer Unkrautvegetation auf einer
     niederrheinischen Lössfläche seit dem Frühneolithi-
     kum. (On the alteration of cultivated grain crops
     and their weeds on a lower Rhine loess plain since
     the early Neolithic). Archaeo-Physika 8:147-163.

2283 Knörzer, K.-H. (1980) Bandkeramische Pflanzenfunde aus
     Bergheim-Zieverich. (Linear Pottery plant finds from
     Bergheim-Zieverich). Archaeo-Physika 7:21-23.

2284 Knörzer, K.-H. (1980) Neue metallzeitliche Pflanzen-
     funde im Rheinland. (New metal age plant finds in
     the Rhineland). Archaeo-Physika 7:25-34.

2285 Knörzer, K.-H. (1980) Pflanzliche Grossreste des band-
     keramischen Siedlungsplatzes Wanlo (Stadt Mönchen-
     gladbach). (Plant remains of the Linear Pottery
     settlement Wanlo, city of Mönchengladbach). Archaeo-
     Physika 7:35-60.

2286 Knörzer, K.-H. (1980) Römerzeitliche Pflanzenfunde aus
     Aachen-Burgscheid. (Roman period plant finds from
     Aschen-Burgscheid). Archaeo-Physika 7:35-60.

2287 Knörzer, K.-H. and Müller, G. (1968) Mittelalterliche
     Fäkalien-Fassgrube mit Pflanzenresten aus Neuss.
     (A medieval cesspit barrel with plant remains from
     Neuss). Rheinische Ausgrabungen 1:137.

2288 Körber-Grohne, U. (1977) Botanische Untersuchungen des
     Tauwerks der frühmittelalterlichen Siedlung Haithabu
     und Hinweise zur Unterscheidung einheimischer
     Gehölzbaste. (Botanical investigations of the
     cordage of the medieval settlement Haithabu and
     hints for distinguishing indigenous wood bast).
     Berichte über die Ausgrabungen in Haithabu 11:64.

2289 Körber-Grohne, U. (1978) Möglichkeiten botanischer
     Untersuchungen alter Bodenoberflächen in ur- und
     frühgeschichtlichen Grabungen. (Possibilities of
     botanical investigations of ancient ground surfaces
     in pre- and protohistoric excavations). Archäolo-
     gische Informationen 4:118-119.

2290 Körber-Grohne, U. (1979) Zwei römerzeitliche Seilfunde
     aus den römischen Provinzen in Germanien. (Two cord
     finds from the Roman provinces in Germania).
     Archaeo-Physika 8:165-171.

2291 Körber-Grohne, U. and Piening, U. (1979) Verkohlte
     Nutz- und Wildpflanzenreste aus Bad Bondorf, Kreis
     Böblingen. (Charred domesticated and wild plant
     remains from Bondorf, Böblingen district). Fund-
     berichte aus Baden-Württemberg 4:152-169.

2292 Kofahl, K. (1936) Ein langobardischer Getreidesilo von
     Küsten, Kr. Dannenberg-Lüchow. (A Langobard grain
     silo from Küsten, Dannenberg-Lüchow district). Die
     Kunde 4:128.

2293 Kommert, R. (1977) Holzfunde bei archäologischen Aus-
     grabungen. (Wood finds from archaeological excava-
     tions). Arbeits- und Forschungsberichte zur
     sächsischen Bodendenkmalpflege 22:171-186.

2294 Kommert, R. (1977) Zu Stand und Ergebnissen von Unter-
     suchungen an Holz aus Ausgrabungen--Veränderungen im
     anatomischen Aufbau und in der chemischen Zusammen-
     setzung sowie der physikalischen und Festigkeits-
     eigenschaften des Holzes. (On the status and results
     of investigations on wood from excavations--changes
     in the anatomical structure and in the chemical
     composition as well as the physical and tensile
     properties of wood). Zeitschrift für Archäologie
     11:73-83.

2295 Kroll, H. (1975) Pflanzliche Reste aus subfossilen
     Ackerböden der bronze- bis wikingerzeitlichen
     Siedlungen in Archsum auf Sylt (Schleswig-Holstein).
     (Plant remains from subfossil arable soil of
     Bronze Age to Viking period settlements in Archsum
     on Sylt, Schleswig-Holstein). Folia quaternaria
     46:31-34.

2296 Kroll, H. (1975) Ur- und frühgeschichtlicher Ackerbau
      in Archsum auf Sylt--eine botanische Grossrest-
      analyse. (Pre- and protohistoric agriculture in
      Archsum on Sylt--a botanical analysis). Kiel. 190p.

2297 Kroll, H. (1979) Kulturpflanzen aus Dimini. (Cultivated
      plants from Dimini). Archaeo-Physika 8:173-189.

2298 Lange, E. (1972) Ein Getreidefund von Hetzdorf aus der
      jüngeren vorrömischen Eisenzeit. (A grain find from
      Hetzdorf of the late pre-Roman Iron Age). Zeitschrift
      für Archäologie 6:258-266.

2299 Lange, E. (1975) Kultur- und Wildpflanzenfunde aus
      germanischen und slawischen Objekten. (Cultivated and
      wild plant finds from Germanic and Slavic objects).
      Zeitschrift für Archäologie 9:301-306.

2300 Lange, E. (1976) Grundlagen und Entwicklungstendenzen
      der frühgeschichtlichen Agrarproduction aus
      botanischer Sicht. (Foundations and developmental
      tendencies of early historic agricultural products
      from a botanical point of view). Zeitschrift für
      Archäologie 10:75-120.

2301 Lange, E. (1976) Probleme und Möglichkeiten der Aus-
      wertung von Unkrautfunden in frühgeschichtlichem
      Siedlungsmaterial. (Problems and possibilities of
      utilization of weed finds in early historic settle-
      ment material). Folia quaternaria 47:63-65.

2302 Lange, E. (1978) Unkräuter in Leinfunden von der Spät-
      latènezeit bis zum 12. Jahrhundert--ein Beitrag zur
      Entwicklung der Unkrautvegetation des Leins. (Weeds
      in flax finds from the late La Tène period until the
      12th century--a contribution on the development of
      weeds of flax). Berichte der Deutschen Botanischen
      Gesellschaft 91:197.

2303 Lange, E. (1979) Verkohlte Pflanzenreste aus den
      slawischen Siedlungsplätzen Brandenburg und Zirzow
      (Kr. Neubrandenburg). (Charred plant remains from
      the Slavic settlement sites Brandenburg and Zirzow,
      Neubrandenburg district). Archaeo-Physika 8:191-207.

224

2304 Leney, L. and Casteel, R. W. (1975) Simplified procedure for examining charcoal specimens for identification. Journal of archaeological science 2(2):
153-159.

2305 Lisitsyna, G. N. and Priščepenko, L. V. (1976) The
significance of palaeoethnobotanical remains for the
reconstruction of early farming in the arid regions
of the USSR. Folia quaternaria 47:83-88.

2306 Lisitsyna, G. N. and Priščepenko, L. V. (1977) Paleo-
ètnobotaniČeskie nakhodki Kavkaza i Bliževo Vostoka.
(Paleoethnobotanical finds of the Caucasus and the
Near East). Moskva: Akademija Nauk SSSR. 127p.

2307 McBride, K. A. (1978) Archaic subsistence in the lower
Connecticut River valley: evidence from Woodchuck
Knoll. Man in the northeast 15/16:124-132.

2308 McClung de Tapia, E. (1977) Recientes estudios paleo-
etnobotanicos en Teotihuacan. Anales de antropologia
14:49-61.

2309 MacNeish, R. S., Nelken-Terner, A. and Garcia Cook, A.
(1970) Second annual report of the Ayacucho
archaeological-botanical project. Andover, Mass.:
R. S. Peabody Foundation.

2310 Mai, D. H. (1980) Pflanzenreste des mittelpleistozänen
Travertins von Bilzingsleben. (Plant remains from the
middle Pleistocene travertine of Bilzingsleben).
Ethnographisch-archäologische Zeitschrift 21(1):4-15.

2311 Marcello, A. (1976) Archaeological experiences and the
ancient traditions of Venice. Folia quaternaria
47:19-24.

2312 Matthias, W. and Schultze-Motel, J. (1969) Kultur-
pflanzenabdrücke an schnurkeramischen Gefässen aus
Mitteldeutschland. Teil II. (Cultivated plant
remains on Corded Ware vessels from central Germany.
Part II). Jahresschrift mitteldeutsche Vorgeschichte
53:309-344.

2313 Miller, N. (1977) Plant remains from Tepe Djaffarabad.
Cahiers de la délégation archéologique française en
Iran, Paris 7:49-53.

2314 Minnis, P. E. (1978) Paleoethnobotanical indicators of prehistoric environmental disturbance: a case study. Anthropological papers of the Museum of Anthropology, Univ. of Michigan 67:347-366.

2315 Müller-Stoll, W. R. (1936) Untersuchsungen urgeschichtlicher Holzreste nebst Anleitung zu ihrer Bestimmung. (Investigations of prehistoric wood remains, including an introduction to its identification). Prähistorische Zeitschrift 27:3-57.

2316 Nickel, R. K. (1977) The study of archaeologically recovered plant materials from the middle Missouri subarea. Plains anthropologist 22:53-58.

2317 Opravil, E. (1976) Die Kornelkirsche (Cornus mas L.) aus archäologischen Funden des ČSSR-Gebietes. (The cornelian cherry (Cornus mas L.) from archaeological finds in Czechoslovakia). Folia quaternaria 47:25-27.

2318 Opravil, E. (1979) Efeu, Hedera helix L., aus der mittelalterlichen Stadt Most (Tschechoslowakei). (Ivy, Hedera helix L., from the medieval city of Most in Czechoslovakia). Archaeo-Physika 8:209-215.

2319 Pals, J.-P. and Voorrips, A. (1979) Seeds, fruits and charcoals from two prehistoric sites in northern Italy. Archaeo-Physika 8:217-235.

2320 Pawlik, B. and Schweingruber, F. H. (1976) Die archäologisch-vegetationskundliche Bedeutung der Hölzer und Samen in den Sedimenten der Seeufersiedlung Horgen "Dampfschiffsteg". (The archaeological-vegetation significance of wood and seeds in the sediments of the coastal settlement Horgen "Dampfschiffsteg"). Jahrbuch der Schweizerische Gesellschaft für Ur- und Frühgeschichte 59:77-91.

2321 Pearsall, D. M. (1978) Paleoethnobotany in western South America: progress and problems. Anthropological papers of the Museum of Anthropology, Univ. of Michigan 67:389-416.

2322 Pinto da Silva, A. R. (1976) Carbonized grains and plant imprints in ceramics from the Castrum of Baiões (Beira Alta, Portugal). Folia quaternaria 47:3-9.

2323 Pinto da Silva, A. R. (1979) The carbonized fruits of
      myrtle found at Castelo do Giraldo, near Évora (S.
      Portugal). Archaeo-Physika 8:237-241.

2324 Priščepenko, L. V. (1973) Rastitel'nye ostatki s
      poselenija Ak-Tepe. (Plant remains from the settle-
      ment of Ak-Tepe). Sovetskaja arkheologija
      1:239-243.

2325 Pyrgała, J. (1980) Sources et méthodes des sciences
      naturelles, appliquées à l'étude sur l'habitat pré-
      historique. Archaeologia polona 19:229-233.

2326 Rackham, O. (1978) The flora and vegetation of Thera
      and Crete before and after the great eruption. In:
      Thera and the Aegean world. London: Thera and the
      Aegean World, 755-764.

2327 Renault-Miskovsky, J. (1980) L'environment végétal de
      l'homme préhistorique au paléolithique inférieur dans
      le Sud-est de la France. Anthropologie (Brno)
      18(2/3):305-313.

2328 Renfrew, J. M. (1966) A report on recent finds of
      carbonized cereal grains and seeds from prehistoric
      Thessaly. Thessalika 5E:21.

2329 Renfrew, J. M. (1971) Recent finds of Vitis from
      Neolithic contexts in S. E. Europe. Acta museorum
      agriculturae pragae 6(1/2).

2330 Renfrew, J. M. (1973) Palaeoethnobotany--the prehis-
      toric food plants of the Near East and Europe.
      New York: Columbia University Press. 248p.

2331 Renfrew, J. M. (1974) Report on the carbonized cereal
      grains and seeds from Obre 1, Kakanj and Obre 2.
      Wissenschaftliche Mitteilungen des Bosnisch-
      Herzegowinischen Landesmuseums 4:47.

2332 Renfrew, J. M. (1976) Carbonized seeds from Anza. In:
      M. Gimbutas, ed., Neolithic Macedonia. Institute of
      Archaeology, University of California, Los Angeles.
      Monumenta archaeologica 1:300-312.

2333 Renfrew, J. M. (1979) The first farmers in South East
      Europe. Archaeo-Physika 8:243-265.

2334 Root, M. J. (1979) The paleoethnobotany of the Nebo Hill site. Plains anthropologist 27(85):239-247.

2335 Rosengarten, F. (1977) An unusual spice from Oaxaca: the flowers of Quararibea funebris. Botanical Museum, Harvard University. Botanical Museum leaflets 25(7):183-202.

2336 Rothmaler, W. (1955) Die neolithischen Getreidefunde von Wahlitz aus den Jahren 1951-1952. (The Neolithic grain finds of Wahlitz from the years 1951-1952). Beiträge Frühgesch. Landwirtschaft 2:35.

2337 Sahni, M. R. (1956) A century of palaeontology, palaeobotany and prehistory in India and adjacent countries. Journal of the palaeontological society of India 1(1):7-51.

2338 Scamoni, A. (1975) Vegetationskundlicher Nachweis einer aufgelassenen Siedlung. (Botanical identification at an excavated settlement). Naturschutzarbeit in Berlin und Brandenburg 11:16-24.

2339 Schiemann, E. (1940) Die Getreidefunde der neolithischen Siedlung Trebus, Kr. Lebus/Mark. (The grain finds of the Neolithic settlement Trebus). Berichte der Deutschen Botanischen Gesellschaft 58:446.

2340 Schiemann, E. (1954) Einkorn im Alten Ägypten? Untersuchungen zum Unterschied von Einkorn und Emmer. (Einkorn in ancient Egypt? Investigations to differentiate einkorn and emmer). Der Züchter 24:139.

2341 Schlichtherle, H. (1977) Abdrücke in Hüttenlehm aus Michelsberger Gruben bei Ammerbuch-Reusten, Kreis Tübingen. (Impressions in hut clay from the Michelsberg excavations near Ammerbuch-Reusten, Tübingen district). Fundberichte aus Baden-Württemberg 3:107-114.

2342 Schlichtherle, H. (1977/1978) Vorläufiger Bericht über die archäobotanischen Untersuchungen am Demircihüyük (Nordwestanatolien). (Preliminary report on the archaeobotanical investigations at Demircihüyük, NW Anatolia). In: M. Korfmann, Demircihüyük. Eine vorgeschichtliche Siedlung an der phrygisch-bithynischen Grenze. Vorbericht über die Ergebnisse der Grabung von 1975. Instanbuler Mitteilungen 27/28:45.

2343 Schultes, R. E. (1972) Ilex guayusa from 500 A.D. to
the present. Etnologiska studier 32:115-138.

2344 Schultes, R. E. (1979) Discovery of an ancient
guayusa plantation in Colombia. Botanical Museum,
Harvard University. Botanical Museum leaflets
27(5/6):143-153.

2345 Schultze-Motel, J. (1968) Literatur über archäologische
Kulturpflanzenreste (1965-1967). (Literature on
archaeological cultivated plant remains, 1965-7). Die
Kulturpflanze 16:215-230.

2346 Schultze-Motel, J. (1971) Literatur über archäologische
Kulturpflanzenreste (1968). (Literature on archaeological cultivated plant remains, 1968). Jahresschrift für mitteldeutsche Vorgeschichte 55:55-62.

2347 Schultze-Motel, J. (1971) Literatur über archäologische
Kulturpflanzenreste (1969). (Literature on archaeo-
logical cultivated plant remains, 1969). Die
Kulturpflanze 19:265-282.

2348 Schultze-Motel, J. (1972) Die archäologischen Reste
der Ackerbohne, Vicia faba L., und die Genese der
Art. (The archaeological remains of the field bean,
Vicia faba L., and the genesis of the species).
Die Kulturpflanze 19:321-358.

2349 Schultze-Motel, J. (1972) Literatur über archäologische
Kulturpflanzenreste (1970/1971). (Literature on ar-
chaeological cultivated plant remains, 1970/1971).
Die Kulturpflanze 20:191-207.

2350 Schultze-Motel, J. (1973) Literatur über archäologische
Kulturpflanzenreste (1971/1972). (Literature on ar-
chaeological cultivated plant remains, 1971/1972).
Die Kulturpflanze 21:61-76.

2351 Schultze-Motel, J. (1974) Literatur über archäologische
Kulturpflanzenreste (1972/1973). (Literature on ar-
chaeological cultivated plant remains, 1972/1973).
Die Kulturpflanze 22:61-76.

2352 Schultze-Motel, J. (1976) Auswertung von Pflanzenab-
      drücken an Keramik. (Evaluation of plant impressions
      on ceramics). Folia quaternaria 47:47-51.

2353 Schultze-Motel, J. (1976) Probleme bei der Zusammen-
      stellung der paläoethnobotanischen Bibliographie.
      (Problems in the compilation of a palaeoethnobotany
      bibliography). Folia quaternaria 47:105-110.

2354 Schultze-Motel, J. (1979) Die Anbaugeschichte des
      Leindotters, Camelina sativa (L.) Crantz. (The
      cultivation history of the gold-of-pleasure,
      Camelina sativa (L.) Crantz). Archaeo-Physika
      8:267-281.

2355 Schultze-Motel, J. (1980) Neolithische Kulturpflanz-
      reste von Eilsleben, Kr. Wanzleben. (Neolithic
      domesticated plant remains from Eilsleben, district
      of Wanzleben). Zeitschrift für Archäologie 14(2):
      213-216.

2356 Schweingruber, F. (1975) Das Holz als Rohstoff in der
      Urgeschichte. (Wood as a raw material in prehistory).
      Helvetia archaeologica 21:2-15.

2357 Schweingruber, F. (1979) Wildäpfel und prähistorische
      Äpfel. (Wild apples and prehistoric apples). Archaeo-
      Physika 8:283-294.

2358 Schweingruber, F. (1980) Vegetationsgeschichtlich-
      archäologische Auswertung der Holzkohlenfunde
      mesolithischer Höhlensedimente Süddeutschlands.
      (Paleobotanical-archaeological evaluation of
      charcoal finds from Mesolithic cave sediments of
      southern Germany). Tübinger Monographien zur
      Urgeschichte 5(2):33-46.

2359 Shafer, H. J. and Holloway, R. G. (1979) Organic
      residue analysis in determining stone tool function.
      In: B. Hayden, ed., Lithic use-wear analysis. New
      York: Academic Press, 385-399.

2360 Shay, J. M. and Shay, C. T. (1978) Modern vegetation
      and fossil plant remains. In: Excavations at
      Nichoria in southwest Greece. Minneapolis: Univ. of
      Minnesota Press, 1:41-59.

2361 Simmons, I. G. and Dimbleby, G. W. (1974) The possible role of ivy (Hedera heliz L.) in the Mesolithic economy of Western Europe. Journal of archaeological science 1(3):291-296.

2362 Smith, A. G. (1970) The influence of Mesolithic and Neolithic man on British vegetation: a discussion. In: D. Walker and R. G. West, eds., Studies in the vegetational history of the British Isles. Cambridge: Cambridge Univ. Press, 81-96.

2363 Smith, C. E. (1980) Plant remains from Guitarrero Cave. In: Guitarrero Cave. New York: Academic Press, 87-119.

2364 Smith, F. H. and Gannon, B. L. (1973) Sectioning of charcoals and dry ancient woods. American antiquity 38:468-472.

2365 Smith, J. E. (1979) Carbonized botanical remains from Quachilco, Cuayucatepec, and La Coyotera: a preliminary report. Museum of Anthropology, Univ. of Michigan (Ann Arbor). Technical reports 11:217-250.

2366 Staudt, G. (1961) The origin of cultivated barleys: a discussion. Economic botany 15(3):205-212.

2367 Stemler, A. B. L. and Falk, R. (1980) A scanning electron microscope study of cereal grains from Nabta Playa. In: Prehistory of the eastern Sahara. New York: Academic Press, 393-399.

2368 Tallantire, P. A. (1976) Provisional key for the identification of sub-fossil seeds of Vaccinium spp. Folia quaternaria 47:39-40.

2369 Tallantire, P. A. (1979) Late Viking and early medieval plant material from Trondheim--a problem in interpretation. Archaeo-Physika 8:295-301.

2370 Tempír, Z. (1979) Kulturpflanzen im Neolithikum und Äneolithikum auf dem Gebiet von Böhmen und Mähren. (Cultivated plants in the Neolithic and Eneolithic in the region of Bohemia and Moravia). Archaeo-Physika 8:303-308.

2371 Tempír, Z. and Gall, W. (1972) Fruchtkornabdrücke an
     bandkeramischen Scherben aus Nerkewitz, Kr. Jena.
     (Grain seed impressions on Linear Pottery sherds
     from Nerkewitz, district of Jena). Ausgrabungen und
     Funde 17:226-229.

2372 Trzcińska-Tacik, H. and Wieserowa, A. (1976) Flora of
     Cracow in the early medieval and medieval periods.
     Folia quaternaria 47:67-81.

2373 Tuganaev, V. V. and Frolova, V. I. (1975) Botaničeskie
     materialy iz gorodišča Biljar (XI--načalo XIII vv.
     n. e.), Tatarskaja ASSR. (Botanical materials from
     the town of Biljar, 11th--beginning of the 13th
     centuries A.D., Tartar ASSR). Botaničeskij žurnal
     60:976.

2374 Tumanjan, M. G. (1944) Kul'turnye rastenija
     urartskogo perioda v Arm. SSR. (Cultivated plants of
     the Urartu period in the Armenian SSSR). Izvestija
     Akademii Nauk Armjanskoj SSR, Obščestvennye Nauki
     No. 1/2:73.

2375 Valkó, E. (1971) Botanische Angaben aus der Bronzezeit
     im Gebiet Ungarns. (Botanical data from the Bronze
     Age in Hungary). III Congrès international des
     Musées d'Agriculture. Budapest, 203-205.

2376 Vasari, Y. (1976) The state of palaeoethnobotanical
     research in northern Finland. Folia quaternaria
     47:89-95.

2377 Villaret-von Rochow, M. (1958) Die Pflanzenreste der
     bronzezeitlichen Pfahlbauten von Valeggio am Mincio.
     (The plant remains of the Bronze Age pile dwellings
     from Valeggio am Mincio). Bericht über das Geo-
     botanische Forschungsinstitut Rübel in Zürich,
     1957, 96.

2378 Villaret-von Rochow, M. (1967) Frucht- und Samenreste
     aus der neolithischen Station Seeberg, Burgäschisee-
     Süd. (Fruit and seed remains from the Neolithic site
     Seeberg, Burgäschisee-Süd. Acta bernensia 2(4):21-64.

2379 Villaret-von Rochow, M. (1971) Samenanalysen aus der
     spätneolithischen Grabung Auvernier (Neuenburger
     See). (Analyses of seeds from the late Neolithic

232

excavation Auvernier, Neuenburger See). III Congrès
international des Musées d'Agriculture. Budapest,
206.

2380 Waines, J. G. and Stanley Price, N. P. (1975-1977)
Plant remains from Khirokitia in Cyprus. Paléorient
3:281-284.

2381 Watson, P. J. and Yarnell, R. A. (1966) Archaeological
and paleoethnobotanical investigations in Salts
Cave, Mammoth Cave, National Park, Kentucky.
American antiquity 31:842-849.

2382 Wendorf, F. et al. (1979) Use of barley in the
Egyptian late Paleolithic. Science 205(4413):
1341-1347.

2383 Werneck, H. L. (1961) Ur- und frühgeschichtliche sowie
mittelalterliche Kulturpflanzen und Hölzer aus den
Ostalpen und dem südlichen Böhmerwald. (Pre- and
protohistoric as well as medieval domesticated plants
and wood from the eastern Alps and the south Bohemian
Forest). Archaeologia austriaca 30:68-117.

2384 Wet, J. M. J. de and Huckabay, J. L. (1967) The origin
of Sorghum bicolor II; distribution and domestication. Evolution 21:787-802.

2385 Wetterstrom, W. (1978) Cognitive systems, food patterns
and paleoethnobotany. Museum of Anthropology, Univ.
of Michigan (Ann Arbor). Anthropological papers
67:81-95.

2386 Wilke, P. J., DeDecker, M. and Dawson, L. E. (1979)
Dicoria canescens T. and G., an aboriginal food
plant in the arid west. Journal of California and
Great Basin anthropology (Banning, Calif.)
1:188-192.

2387 Willcox, G. H. (1977) Exotic plants from Roman
waterlogged sites in London. Journal of archaeological science 4(3):269-282.

2388 Willerding, U. (1960) Beiträge zur jüngeren Geschichte
der Flora und Vegetation der Flussauen (Untersuchungen aus dem Leinetal bei Göttingen). (Contributions to the early history of the flora and vegetation of the river islands--investigations from the

Leine River valley near Göttingen). Flora 149:435.

2389 Willerding, U. (1965) Die Pflanzenreste aus der band-
     keramischen Siedlung. (The plant remains from the
     Linear Pottery settlement). Neue Ausgrabungen und
     Forschungen in Niedersachsen 2:44.

2390 Willerding, U. (1966) Pflanzenreste aus einer eisen-
     zeitlichen Siedlung von Göttingen. (Plant remains
     from an Iron Age settlement at Göttingen).
     Göttinger Jahrbücher 14:19.

2391 Willerding, U. (1966) Urgeschichtliche Siedlungsreste
     in Rosdorf, Kreis Göttingen, 2: Pflanzenreste aus
     bronzezeitlichen und eisenzeitlichen Gruben. (Pre-
     historic settlement remains in Rosdorf, Göttingen
     district, 2: plant remains from Bronze and Iron Age
     excavations). Neue Ausgrabungen und Forschungen in
     Niedersachsen 3:49.

2392 Willerding, U. (1970) Vor- und frühgeschichtliche
     Kulturpflanzenfunde in Mitteleuropa. (Pre- and proto-
     historic domestic plant finds in central Europe).
     Neue Ausgrabungen und Forschungen in Niedersachsen
     5:288-375.

2393 Willerding, U. (1971) Methodische Probleme bei der
     Untersuchung und Auswertung von Pflanzenfunden in
     vor- und frühgeschichtlichen Siedlungen. (Methodo-
     logical problems with the investigation and evalua-
     tion of plant finds in pre- and protohistoric
     settlements). Nachrichten aus Niedersachsens
     Urgeschichte 40:180.

2394 Willerding, U. (1974) Latènezeitliche Pflanzenreste
     von der Pipinsburg, Kr. Osterode/Harz. (La Tene
     period plant remains from the Pipinsburg, district
     of Osterode/Harz). Nachrichten aus Niedersachsens
     Urgeschichte 43:134.

2395 Willerding, U. (1975) Untersuchungen in der Kleinen
     Jettenhöhle bei Düna, Gem. Hörden, Kr. Osterode am
     Harz, 4: Eisenzeitliche Pflanzenreste aus der
     Kleinen Jettenhöhle. (Investigations in the Kleinen
     Jettenhöhle near Düna, Hörden municipality, district
     of Osterode am Harz, 4: Iron Age plant remains from
     the Kleinen Jettenhöhle). Nachrichten aus Nieder-
     sachsens Urgeschichte 44:107.

2396 Willerding, U. (1979) Zum Ackerbau in der jüngeren vorrömischen Eisenzeit. (On agriculture in the early pre-Roman Iron Age). Archaeo-Physika 8:309-330.

2397 Williams, D. (1975) Identification of water-logged wood by the archaeologist. Science and archaeology 14:3-4.

2398 Williams, D. (1976) Bryophytes in archaeology. Science and archaeology 18:12-14.

2399 Williams, D. (1977) A consideration of the subfossil remains of Vitis vinifera L. as evidence for viticulture in Roman Britain. Britannia 8:327-334.

2400 Wilson, D. G. (1979) Horse dung from Roman Lancaster: a botanical report. Archaeo-Physika 8:331-350.

2401 Zeist, W. van (1970) The palaeobotanical investigation of Paddepoel. Palaeohistoria 14:282-283.

2402 Zeist, W. van (1970) Prehistoric and early historic food plants in the Netherlands. Palaeohistoria 14:41-173.

2403 Zeist, W. van (1972) Palaeobotanical results of the 1970 season at Çayönü, Turkey. Helinium 12:3-19.

2404 Zeist, W. van (1974) Palaeobotanical studies of settlement sites in the coastal area of the Netherlands. Palaeohistoria 16:223-369.

2405 Zeist, W. van (1975) Preliminary report on the botany of Gomolava. Journal of archaeological science 2(4):315-325.

2406 Zeist, W. van (1976) On macroscopic traces of food plants in southwestern Asia. Philosophical transactions of the Royal Society of London B275:27-41.

2407 Zeist, W. van and Bakker-Heeres, J. A. H. (1975) Evidence for linseed cultivation before 6000 bc. Journal of archaeological science 2(3):215-219.

2408 Zeist, W. van and Bottema, S. (1966) Palaeobotanical investigations at Ramad. Annales archéologiques Arabes Syriennes 16:179-180.

2409 Zinderen Bakker, E. M. van (1980) The origin of crop cultivation with special reference to Africa. South African archaeological bulletin 35(132):67-72.

2410 Zohary, D. (1959) Is Hordeum agriocrithon the ancestor of six-rowed cultivated barley? Evolution 13:279-280.

2411 Zohary, D. and Hopf, M. (1973) Domestication of pulses in the Old World. Legumes were companions of wheat and barley when agriculture began in the Near East. Science 182:887-894.

2412 Žukovskij, P. M. (1964) Kul'turnye rastenija i ikh sorodiči. (Domesticated plants and their weeds). Second edition. Leningrad: Kolos.

4. Human

a) Paleodietary research and coprolite analysis

2413 Ambro, R. D. (1967) Dietary, technological, ecological aspects of Lovelock Cave coprolites. University of California Archaeological Survey 70:37-48.

2414 Brothwell, D. R. (1969) Dietary variation and the siology of earlier human populations. In: P. J. Ucko and G. W. Dimbleby, eds., The domestication and exploitation of plants and animals. London: Duckworth, 531-545.

2415 Brothwell, D. R. and Brothwell, P. (1963) Food in antiquity. London: Thames & Hudson.

2416 Bryant, V. M. (1974) Prehistoric diet in southwest Texas: the coprolite evidence. American antiquity 39:407-420.

2417 Bryant, V. M. and Williams-Dean, G. (1975) The coprolites of man. Scientific American 232:100-109.

2418 Burleigh, R. and Brothwell, D. (1978) Studies on Amerindian dogs, I: carbon isotopes in relation to maize in the diet of domestic dogs from early Peru and Ecuador. Journal of archaeological science 5:355-362.

2419   Calder, A. M. (1977) Survival properties of organic
       residues through the human digestive tract. Journal
       of archaeological science 4:141-151.

2420   Callen, E. O. (1965) Food habits of some pre-Columbian
       Mexican Indians. Economic botany 19:335-343.

2421   Callen, E. O. (1967) Analysis of Tehuacan coprolites.
       In: D. S. Byers, ed., The prehistory of the
       Tehuacan Valley: vol. 1. Environment and subsis-
       tence. Austin: Univ. of Texas Press, 261-289.

2422   Callen, E. O. (1969) Les coprolithes de la cabane
       Acheuléene du Lazaret. In: H. de Lumley, ed., Une
       cabane Acheuléene dans la Grotte du Lazaret. Nice:
       Mémoires de la Société Préhistorique Française,
       7:123-124.

2423   Callen, E. O. and Cameron, T. M. W. (1960) A prehis-
       toric diet revealed in coprolites. New scientist
       8:35-40.

2424   Celoria, F. S. C. (1970) Food and archaeology in
       Britain, 1900-1970. Science and archaeology 4:8-14.

2425   Coughlin, E. A. (1977) Chemical test for identification
       of coprolites. Botanical Museum, Harvard University.
       Botanical Museum leaflets 25(7):217-220.

2426   Crawford, D. J. (1979) Food: tradition and change in
       Hellenistic Egypt. World archaeology 11(2):136-146.

2427   Dennell, R. W. (1979) Prehistoric diet and nutrition:
       some food for thought. World archaeology 11(2):
       121-135.

2428   Follett, H. W. I. (1967) Fish remains from coprolites
       and midden deposits at Lovelock Cave, Churchill
       County, Nevada. University of California Archaeolog-
       ical Survey 70:93-116.

2429   Fortuna, L. (1980) El maíz en la dieta indígena. Museo
       de Hombre Dominicano, Santo Domingo. Boletín
       9(13):159-164.

2430   Fuchs, A. (1978) Strontium/calcium ratios in bone: an
       assessment of their use in paleodietary research.
       MASCA journal 1:10-11.

2431 Gilbert, B. M. (1969) Some aspects of diet and butchering techniques among prehistoric Indians in South Dakota. Plains anthropologist 14:277-294.

2432 Grzyvinski, L. (1961) Analysis of feces from the Middle Age period. Zoologica poloniae 10:195-199.

2433 Heizer, R. F. (1967) Analysis of human coprolites from a dry cave. University of California Archaeological Survey 70:1-20.

2434 Heizer, R. F. and Napton, L. K. (1969) Biological and cultural evidence from prehistoric human coprolites. The diet of prehistoric Great Basin Indians can be reconstructed from desiccated fecal material. Science 165(3893):563-568.

2435 Helbaek, H. (1951) Seeds of weeds as food in the pre-Roman Iron Age. Kuml 65-74.

2436 Helbaek, H. (1958) The last meal of Grauballe Man. Kuml 83.

2437 Lambert, J. B., Szpunar, C. B. and Buikstra, J. E. (1979) Chemical analysis of excavated human bone from Middle and Late Woodland sites. Archaeometry 21(2):115-129.

2438 Merwe, N. J. van der and Vogel, J. C. (1978) C-13 content of human collagen as a measure of prehistoric diet in Woodland North America. Nature 276(5690): 815-816.

2439 Pozorski, S. G. (1979) Prehistoric diet and subsistence of the Moche Valley, Peru. World archaeology 11(2):163-184.

2440 Rouse, N. L. (1967) Preliminary examination of prehistoric human coprolites from four western Nevada caves. University of California Archaeological Survey 70:49-88.

2441 Santley, R. S. and Rose, E. K. (1979) Diet, nutrition and population dynamics in the Basin of Mexico. World archaeology 11(2):185-207.

2442 Schoeninger, M. J. (1979) Dietary reconstruction at
     Chalcatzingo, a Formative period site at Morelos,
     Mexico. Museum of Anthropology, Univ. of Michigan
     (Ann Arbor). Technical reports 9.

2443 Scott, L. J. (1979) Dietary inferences from Hay House
     coprolites: a palynological interpretation. Kiva
     44(2/3):257-281.

2444 Shawcross, W. (1967) An investigation of prehistoric
     diet and economy on a coastal site at Galatea Bay,
     New Zealand. Proceedings of the prehistoric society
     33:107-131.

2445 Trevor-Deutsch, B. and Bryant, V. M. (1978) Analysis
     of suspected human coprolites from Terra Amata, Nice,
     France. Journal of archaeological science 5:387-390.

2446 Wing, E. S. and Brown, A. B. (1979) Paleonutrition:
     method and theory in prehistoric foodways. New York
     and London: Academic Press.

     b) Paleopathology

2447 Abbot, K. H. and Courville, C. B. (1939) Historical
     notes on the meningiomas. I. A study of hyperostoses
     in prehistoric skulls. Bulletin of Los Angeles
     neurological societies 4:101.

2448 Abd-Elael, M. S. (1962) Diseases of mummies. Zentral-
     blatt für Arbeitsmedizin und Arbeitsschutz 12:133.

2449 Ackerknecht, E. H. (1953) Palaeopathology; a survey.
     In: Anthropology today. Chicago, 120-127.

2450 Adis-Castro, E. and Neumann, G. (1948) The incidence
     of ear exostosis in the Hopewell people of Illinois
     valley. Proceedings of the Indiana Academy of Science
     57:33-36.

2451 Alfred, C. and Sandison, A. T. (1962) The pharaoh
     Akhenaten. A problem in Egyptology and pathology.
     Bulletin of the history of medicine 36(4):293-316.

2452 Allison, J. M., Mendoza, D. and Pezzia, A. (1974) A
     radiographic approach to childhood illness in pre-
     Columbian inhabitants of southern Peru. American
     journal of physical anthropology 40:409-416.

2453 Alpagut, B. (1979) Some paleopathological cases of the ancient Anatolian mandibles. Journal of human evolution 8(6):571-574.

2454 Angel, J. L. (1946) Skeletal change in ancient Greece. Americna journal of physical anthropology 4:69-97.

2455 Angel, J. L. (1964) Osteoporosis: thalassemia? American journal of physical anthropology 22(3): 369-374.

2456 Angel, J. L. (1966) Ecology and health in early skeletons from Tranquility, California. Smithsonian contributions to anthropology 2(1):1-19.

2457 Angel, J. L. (1966) Porotic hyperostosis, anemias, malarias and marshes in the prehistoric eastern Mediterranean. Science 153:760-763.

2458 Antonutto, G., Melato, M. and Pezzoli, A. (1979) Histological and immuno-chemical investigations on the organic substance present in human bones of the Iron Age. Journal of human evolution 8(7):711-714.

2459 Armelagos, G. J. (1969) Diseases in ancient Nubia. Science 163:255-259.

2460 Armelagos, G. J., Mielke, J. H. and Winter, J. (1971) Bibliography of human paleopathology. Dept. of Anthropology, Univ. of Massachusetts (Amherst). Research reports 8. 159p.

2461 Arnaud, G. and Arnaud, S. (1980) Un cas d'ostéomiélite cronique d'époque medievale. Antropologia contemporanea (Torino) 3(1):115-119.

2462 Babant, H. (1966) Contribution to the knowledge of the pathology of the teeth and jaws among early populations of Belgium and the Nord region of France, the ossuary of Marville (Meuse, France). Bulletin de groupement international pour la recherche scientifique en stomatologie 9:224-241.

2463 Bach, A., Diez, C. and Klinger, G. (1980) Physikalisch-chemische Untersuchungen zur Struktur und Zusammensetzung des Zahnsteins ur- und frühgeschichtlicher Bevölkerungen. (Physical chemistry investigations of the structure and composition of tartar in prehistoric and early historic populations). Ausgrabungen und Funde 25(5):223-226.

2464 Bach, A., Juchert, C. and Kämpf, A. (1978) Degenerative Gelenk- und Wirbelsäulenveränderungen an Skeletten aus dem Neolithikum. (Degenerative skeletal changes in spine and joints in the Neolithic period). Alt-Thüringen 15:18-31.

2465 Banerjee, D. N. (1941) Paleopathology. Journal of the Indian Medical Association 10:263-267.

2466 Barraco, R. A. (1978) Preservation of proteins in mummified tissues. American journal of physical anthropology 48(4):487-491.

2467 Barraco, R. A., Reyman, T. A. and Cockburn, T. A. (1977) Paleobiochemical analysis of an Egyptian mummy. Journal of human evolution 6:533-546.

2468 Berg, E. (1972) Paleopathology: bone lesions in ancient peoples. Clinical orthopedics 82:263-267.

2469 Blake, I. M. and Weber, J. C. (1967) Radioactivity of Jericho bones. Archaeometry 10:127-128.

2470 Blakely, R. L. and Walker, P. L. (1968) Mortality profile of the Middle Mississippian population of Dickson Mound, Fulton County, Illinois. Proceedings of the Indiana Academy of Science 77:102-108.

2471 Borgognini-Tarli, S. M. (1979) Paleoserology--general bibliography. Journal of human evolution 8(7): 735-740.

2472 Bowers, W. F. (1966) Pathological and functional changes found in 864 pre-Captain Cook contact Polynesian burials from the sand dunes at Mokapu, Oahu, Hawaii. International surgery 45(2):206-217.

2473 Boyd, W. C. and Boyd, L. G. (1934) An attempt to determine the blood group of mummies. Proceedings of the society of experimental biology and medicine 31:671-672.

2474 Boyd, W. C. and Boyd, L. G. (1937) Blood grouping
       tests on 300 mummies. Journal of immunology 32:
       307-319.

2475 Bräuer, G. and Fricke, R. (1980) Zur Phänomenologie
       osteoporotischer Veränderungen bei Bestehen sys-
       temischer hämatologischer Affectionen. Palaopatholo-
       gische Analyse eines Skelettes der geometrischen
       Periode (900-700 v.u.Z.) aus Tiryns (Peloponnes).
       (On the phenomenology of osteoporotic alterations in
       conjunction with systemic hematologic affections.
       Paleopathological analysis of a Geometric period
       (900-700 B.C.) skeleton from Tiryns, Peleponnesus).
       Homo 31(3/4):198-211.

2476 Brothwell, D. R. (1958) Evidence of leprosy in British
       archaeological material. Medical history 2:287-291.

2477 Brothwell, D. R. (1959) Teeth in earlier human
       populations. Proceedings of the nutrition society
       18:59-65.

2478 Brothwell, D. R. (1961) The palaeopathology of early
       British man: an essay on the problems of diagnosis
       and analysis. Journal of the Royal Anthropological
       Insititute of Great Britain and Ireland 91(2):
       318-344.

2479 Brothwell, D. R. (1963) Dental anthropology. Oxford:
       Pergamon Press.

2480 Brothwell, D. R. (1965) Digging up bones. London:
       British Museum (Natural History).

2481 Brothwell, D. R. (1968) The skeletal biology of
       earlier human populations. Oxford: Pergamon Press.

2482 Brothwell, D. R. (1974) Osteological evidence of the
       use of a surgical modiolus in a Romano-British
       population: an aspect of primitive technology.
       Journal of archaeological science 1(2):209-211.

2483 Brothwell, D. R. and Burleigh, R. (1975) Radiocarbon
       dates and the history of treponematoses in man.
       Journal of archaeological science 2(4):393-396.

2484 Brothwell, D. R. and Carr, H. G. (1962) The dental
health of the Etruscans. British dental journal
113:207.

2485 Brothwell, D. R. and Sandison, A. T. (1967) Diseases
in antiquity. Springfield, Illinois: C. C. Thomas
Publ. 766p.

2486 Brothwell, D. R., Sandison, A. T. and Gray, P. H. K.
(1969) Human biological observations on a Guanche
mummy with anthracosis. American journal of physical
anthropology 30:333-347.

2487 Browne, S. G. (1970) How old is leprosy? British
medical journal 3:640-641.

2488 Campbell, T. D. (1944) The dental condition of a skull
from the Silyatki site, Arizona. Journal of the
Washington Academy of Sciences 34(10):321-322.

2489 Campillo Valero, D. (1978) Dos notas de paleopatológia.
Archivo de prehistoria levantina (Valencia) 15:
311-323.

2490 Candela, P. B. (1936) Blood group reactions in ancient
human skeletons. American journal of physical
anthropology 21:429-432.

2491 Candela, P. B. (1937) Blood group determinations upon
Minnesota and New York skeletal material. American
journal of physical anthropology 23:71-78.

2492 Candela, P. B. (1939) Blood group determinations upon
the bones of thirty Aleutian mummies. American
journal of physical anthropology 24:361-383.

2493 Candela, P. B. (1939) Blood group tests on stains,
mummified tissues and cancellous bone. American
journal of physical anthropology 25:187-214

2494 Candela, P. B. (1940) Reliability of blood tests on
bones. American journal of physical anthropology
27:367.

2495 Carbonell, V. M. (1964) The paleo-dental-pathology of
ancient Mesopotamians. Journal of dental research
43(5):798.

2496   Carr, H. G. (1960) Some dental characteristics of the
        Middle Minoans. Man 60:119-122.

2497   Cave, A. J. E. (1939) The evidence for the incidence
        of tuberculosis in ancient Egypt. British journal of
        tuberculosis 33:142.

2498   Chapman, F. H. (1962) Incidence of arthritis in a pre-
        historic Indian population. Proceedings of the
        Indiana Academy of Science 72:59-62.

2499   Chapman, F. H. (1964) Comparison of osteoarthritis in
        three aboriginal populations. Proceedings of the
        Indiana Academy of Science 74:84-85.

2500   Chapman, F. H. (1964) The incidence and age distri-
        butions of osteoarthritis in an archaic American
        Indian population. Proceedings of the Indiana
        Academy of Science 74:64-66.

2501   Chapman, F. H. (1976) Dental paleopathology at
        Florianopolis, Brazil. Yearbook of physical
        anthropology (New York) 20:347-348.

2502   Christophersen, K. M. and Pedersen, P. O. (1939) In-
        vestigations into dental conditions in the Neolithic
        period and in the Bronze Age in Denmark. Dental
        record 59:575-585.

2503   Clabeaux, M. S. (1976) Health and disease in the
        population of an Iroquois ossuary. Yearbook of
        physical anthropology (New York) 20:359-370.

2504   Clarke, J. M. (1921) Organic dependence and disease:
        their origin and significance. Yale Univ. Press 113p.

2505   Clement, A. J. (1956) Caries in the South African
        ape-man: some examples of undoubted pathological
        authenticity believed to be 800,000 years old.
        British dental journal 101:4-7.

2506   Clement, A. J. (1957) The bacteriology of the primi-
        tive mouth. Journal of the Dental Association of
        South Africa 12:281.

2507   Clement, A. J. (1958) The antiquity of caries. British
        dental journal 104:115-123.

244

2508   Cockburn, A. and Cockburn, E., eds. (1980) Mummies,
        disease and ancient cultures. Cambridge: Cambridge
        Univ. Press. 340p.

2509   Cockburn, T. A. (1971) Infectious disease in ancient
        populations. Current anthropology 12(1):45-62.

2510   Cockburn, T. A. et al. (1975) Autopsy of an Egyptian
        mummy. Science 187:1155-1160.

2511   Cole, H. N. et al. (1955) Pre-Columbian osseus
        syphilis. American Medical Association. Archives of
        dermatology and syphilology 71:231-238.

2512   Cook, S. F. (1946) The incidence and significance of
        disease among the Aztecs and related tribes.
        Hispanic American historical review 26:320-335.

2513   Cook, S. F., Brooks, S. T. and Ezra-Cohn, H. C. (1962)
        Histological studies on fossil bone. Journal of
        paleontology 36:483-494.

2514   Crosby, W. A. (1969) The early history of syphilis: a
        reappraisal. American anthropologist 71(2):218-227.

2515   Curzon, M. E. J. (1976/1977) Dental disease in Eskimo
        skulls in British museums. Ossa 3/4:83-95.

2516   Czarnetzki, A. (1980) Pathological changes in the
        morphology of the young Paleolithic skeletal remains
        from Stette (south-west Germany). Journal of human
        evolution 9(1):15-17.

2517   Dastugue, J. (1967) Pathologie des hommes fossiles de
        l'abri de Cro-Magnon. L'anthropologie 71:479-492.

2518   Dastugue, J. (1969) Les lesions pathologique du
        squelette de chancelade. L'anthropologie 73:247-252.

2519   Dastugue, J. (1975) Pathologie des hommes épipaléo-
        lithiques d'Afalou-Bou-Rhummel (Algérie).
        L'anthropologie 79:483-506.

2520   Dastugue, J. (1980) Possibilities, limits and prospects
        in paleopathology of the human skeleton. Journal of
        human evolution 9(1):3-8.

2521   Dastugue, J. and de Lumley, M.-A. (1976) Les maladies des hommes préhistoriques du Paléolithique et du Mésolithique. In: H. de Lumley, ed., La préhistoire française. Paris, 1:612-622.

2522   Dávalos, H. E. (1955) Un ejemplo de patologia oseo prehispanico de Mexico. Instituto Nacional Anthropologia e Historia, Mexico. Anales 7:147-155.

2523   Dávalos, H. E. (1970) Pre-hispanic osteopathology. In: T. D. Stewart, ed., Handbook of Middle American Indians: physical anthropology 9:68-81.

2524   Denninger, H. S. (1938) Syphilis of a Pueblo skull before 1350. Archives of pathology (Chicago) 26:724-727.

2525   Dĕrums, V. JA. (1963) Kostnye zabolevanija u drevnikh žitelej Pribaltiki po materialam arkheologičeskikh raskopok. (Bone diseases among ancient inhabitants of the Baltic based on materials from archaeological excavations). Iz istorii meditsiny 5:81-97.

2526   Dĕrums, V. JA. (1963) Tuberkuleznyj spondilit u drevnikh žitelej Pribaltiki po materialam arkheologičeskikh raskopok. (Tuberculosis spondylitis among ancient inhabitants of the Baltic based on materials from archaeological excavations). Problemy tuberkuleza 10:86.

2527   Dĕrums, V. JA. (1964) O paleopatologii. (On paleopathology). Iz istorii meditsiny 6:259-261.

2528   Dĕrums, V. JA. (1967) O sifilise v Pribaltike po dannym arkheologii. (On syphilis in the Baltic based on archaeological data). Iz istorii meditsiny 7:163-168.

2529   Dĕrums, V. JA. (1967) Rentgenologičeskij analiz kostnoj patologii žitelej Pribaltiki po materialam arkheologičeskikh raskopok. (Radiographic analysis of bone pathology of inhabitants of the Baltic region, based on data of archaeological excavations). Vestnik rentgenologii i radiologii 3:69-73.

2530   DeVasto, M. A. (1976) The percentage of calcium and phosphorus in human bone as diagnostic of severe hypothyroidism. Yearbook of physical anthropology 20: 338-346.

2531 Dickson, D. F. and Morse, D. (1956) Prehistoric
      pathology. Central states archaeological journal
      2(4):143-151.

2532 Dreyer, T. F. (1935) Dental caries in prehistoric
      South Africans. Nature 136:302-303.

2533 Dzierzykraj-Rogalsky, T. (1980) Paleopathology of the
      Ptolemaic inhabitants of Dakhleh Oasis (Egypt).
      Journal of human evolution 9(1):71-74.

2534 El-Najjar, M. Y. (1976) Maize, malaria and the anemias
      in the pre-Columbian New World. Yearbood of physical
      anthropology (New York) 20:329-337.

2535 Enlow, D. H. and Brown, S. O. (1958) A comparative
      histological study of fossil and recent bone tissues.
      Texas journal of science 10:187-235.

2536 Ewing, H. E. (1924) Lice from human mummies. Science
      60:389-390.

2537 Farkas, L. G. and Marsciki, A. B. (1979) Paläo-
      pathologische Fälle in der awarenzeitlichen Serie
      von Backa-Topolo, SFR Jugoslawien. (Paleopatholog-
      ical cases in the Avar period series from Backa-
      Topolo, Jugoslavia). Ethnographisch-archäologische
      Zeitschrift 20(1):15-33.

2538 Feigenbaum, A. (1957) Archaeological evidence of the
      occurrence of regular seasonal ophthalmias in
      ancient Egypt. Janus 46:165.

2539 Feigenbaum, A. (1958) History of ophthalmia in Egypt:
      evidence for its seasonal occurrence in antiquity.
      Acta medica orientalia 17:130.

2540 Feingold, B. (1933) Roentgenologic skull changes in
      anemias of childhood; report of case: a few notes
      on similar findings among skulls of Peruvian Indians.
      American journal of roentgenology 29:194-202.

2541 Ferembach, D. (1963) Frequency of spina bifida occulta
      in prehistoric human skeletons. Nature 199:100-101.

2542 Fichter, G. and Volk, P. (1980) The eastern orientation of Merovingian graves and the seasonal distribution of morbidity and mortality (using the Sasbach-Behans and Bischoffingen-Bigärlen cemeteries as examples). Journal of human evolution 9(1):49-59.

2543 Finnegan, M. and Marcsik, A. (1980) Anomaly of pathology: the stafne defect as seen in archaeological material and modern clinical practice. Journal of human evolution 9(1):19-31.

2544 Foote, J. A. (1927) Evidence of rickets prior to 1650. American journal of diseases of children 443-452.

2545 Fry, G. F. and Moore, J. G. (1969) Enterobius vermicularis: 10,000 year-old human infection. Science 166:1620.

2546 Gabriele, F. M. (1980) Morfologia dei mascellari e anomalie dentarie degli Egiziani dinastici. Antropologia contemporanea (Torino) 3(1):83-95.

2547 García-Frias, J. E. (1940) La tuberculosis en los antiguos Peruanos. Actualidad médica Peruana 5:274-291.

2548 García-Godoy, F. (1980) Caries dental en craneos primitivos de la isla Santo Domingo. Museo de Hombre Dominicano, Santo Domingo. Boletín 9(13):235-243.

2549 Gaspardy, G. (1961) Paläopathologische Untersuchungen an äneolithischen Skellettfunden in Ungarn. Ethnographisch-archäologische Zeitschrift 1:1-32.

2550 Gaspardy, G. and Nemeskéri, J. (1960) Palaeopathological studies on Copper Age skeletons found at Alsónémedi. Acta morphologica (Budapest) 9:203-219.

2551 Germanà, F. (1978) Dettagli di paleopatologia traumatica in un osso carpale proveniente dalla grotto "rifugio" di Oliena-Nuoro (neolitico medio). Società Italian di Antropologia e Etnologia. Archivio per l'antropologia e l'etnologia (Firenze) 108:323-331.

2552 Germanà, F. (1980) Esiti traumatici in un doliocranio preistorico sardo. Antropologia contemporanea (Torino) 3(1):45-56.

2553   Gilbey, B. E. and Lubran, M. (1952) Blood groups of
       South American Indian mummies. Man 52:115.

2554   Gilbey, B. E. and Lubran, M. (1953) The ABO and Rh
       blood antigens in predynastic Egyptian mummies.
       Man 53:23.

2555   Gilfillan, S. C. (1965) Lead poisoning and the fall of
       Rome. Journal of occupational medicine 7:53-60.

2556   Gładykowska-Rzeczycka, J. (1980) Some cases of
       diseases from prehistoric and medieval cemeteries in
       Poland. Antropologia contemporanea (Torino) 3(1):
       145-152.

2557   Glemser, M. S. (1960) Blood groups of the ancient
       dead. Science 131:699-702.

2558   Goff, C. W. (1953) New evidence of pre-Columbian bone
       syphilis in Guatemala. In: R. B. Woodbury and A. S.
       Trik, eds., The ruins of Zaculen, Guatemala.
       Richmond: Wm. Byrd Press, 312-319.

2559   Goldstein, M. S. (1957) Skeletal pathology of early
       Indians in Texas. American journal of physical
       anthropology 15:299-311.

2560   Goldstein, M. S. (1969) Human paleopathology and some
       diseases in living societies: a review of the
       recent literature. American journal of physical
       anthropology 31(3):285-294.

2561   Goodman, A. H., Armelagos, G. J. and Rose, J. C.
       (1980) Enamel hypoplasias as indicators of stress in
       three prehistoric populations from Illinois. Human
       biology 52(3):515-528.

2562   Graf, W. (1949) Presence of a spasmogenic substance,
       presumably histamine in extracts of mummy tissue.
       Nature 164(4173):701-702.

2563   Gray, P. H. K. (1968) Bone infarction in antiquity.
       Clinical radiology 19:436-437.

2564   Gray, P. H. K. (1969) A case of osteogenesis imper-
       fecta associated with dentinogenesis imperfecta
       dating from antiquity. Clinical radiology 20:106-108.

2565 Gregg, J. B. (1965) Human paleopathology in the Dakotas. Northwest Iowa archaeological society newsletter (Cherokee, Iowa) 15(1):3-7.

2566 Gregg, J. B. (1965) Ear disease in the Indian skulls at the Museum of the State Historical Society of North Dakota. North Dakota history 32:3-12.

2567 Gregg, J. B., Steele, J. P. and Clifford, S. (1965) Ear disease in skulls from the Sully site. Plains anthropologist 10(30):233-239.

2568 Grilletto, R. R. (1980) Un cas de pied équin dans une mummie Egyptienne. Antropologia contemporanea (Torino) 3(1):131-134.

2569 Grimm, H. (1976) Paläopathologische Befunde an Menschenresten aus dem Neolithikum in der DDR als Hinweise auf Lebensablauf und Bevölkerungsgeschichte. (Paleopathological finds on human remains from the Neolithic in the GDR as an indication of life expectancy and population history). Ausgrabungen und Funde 21(6):268-277.

2570 Grimm, H. (1978) Paläopathologische Befunde an Menschenresten der vorrömischen Eisenzeit in der DDR. (Paleopathological finds on human remains of the pre-Roman Iron Age in the GDR). Ausgrabungen und Funde 23(6):261-266.

2571 Grimm, H. (1979) Paläopathologische Befunde an Menschenresten der römischen Kaiserzeit und Völkerwanderungszeit in der DDR als Hinweise auf Lebensablauf und Bevölkerungsgeschichte. (Paleopathological finds on human remains of the Roman Empire and migration periods in the GDR as indications of life expectancy and population history). Ausgrabungen und Funde 24(6):267-274.

2572 Guarneti, G. (1968) Osteoporosis in prehistory and proto-history. Minerva medica (Torino) 59:547-554.

2573 Hackett, C. J. (1976) Diagnostic criteria of syphilis, yaws and treponarid (treponematoses) and of some other diseases in dry bones (for use in osteo-archaeology). Berlin: Springer Verlag. 134p.

2574   Hahn, R. and Czarnetzki, A. (1980) Premature
       senescence of the skeleton of a young woman from the
       Merowingian burial field of Neresheim. Antropologia
       contemporanea (Torino) 3(1):137-144.

2575   Haltom, W. L. and Shands, A. R. (1938) Evidence of
       syphilis in mound builders' bones. Archives of
       pathology (Chicago) 25:228-242.

2576   Hamperl, H. and Weiss, P. (1955) Über die Spongiose
       Hyperostose an Schadeln aus Alt-Peru. (On spongy
       hyperostoses on skulls from ancient Peru). Virchows
       Archiv für pathologische Anatomie und Physiologie
       und für klinische Medizin (Berlin) 327:629-642.

2577   Hare, R. (1954) Pomp and pestilence: infectious
       diseases, its origins and conquest. London:
       Gollancz. 224p.

2578   Harper, R. M. J. (1962) Evolution and illness.
       Baltimore: Williams and Wilskins Co.

2579   Harris, R. I. (1949) Osteological evidence of disease
       amongst the Huron Indians. University of Toronto
       medical journal 27:71-75.

2580   Hart, G. V. et al. (1980) Blood group testing of
       ancient material. MASCA journal 1(5):141-145.

2581   Hartweg, R. (1945) Remarques sur la denture et statis-
       tiques sur la carie en France aux époques préhis-
       torique. Bulletin mémoire de société anthropologie
       (series 9) 6:71-113.

2582   Hedges, R. E. M. and Wallace, C. J. A. (1978) The sur-
       vival of biochemical information in archaeological
       bone. Journal of archaeological science 5:377-386.

2583   Helmuth, H. Z. (1966) Die menschlichen Skelettfunde
       des mittelalterlichen Gertrudenfriedhofs in Kiel.
       (The human skeletal finds of the medieval Gertruden-
       friedhof in Kiel). Zeitschrift für Morphologie und
       Anthropologie (Stuttgart) 57(3):272.

2584   Hengen, O. P. (1968) Arthritis in Ohio Indians.
       Journal of the American Dental Association
       77:792-793.

2585 Hillson, S. W. (1979) Diet and dental disease. World archaeology 11(2):147-162.

2586 Hillson, S. W. (1980) Chronic anaemias in the Nile Valley. MASCA journal 1(6):172-174.

2587 Hodjimarkos, D. M. and Bonhorst, C. W. (1962) Fluoride and selenium levels in contemporary and ancient Greek teeth in relation to dental caries. Nature 192:177-178.

2588 Hohndorf-Hoferer, M. (1980) The importance of the measurements of the female pelvis for the diagnosis of pregnancy problems by pathological narrow pelves in ancient populations (examples from the Turin osteological collection). Antropologia contemporanea (Torino) 3(1):135-136.

2589 Houghton, P. (1975) A renal calculus from proto-historic New Zealand. Ossa 2(1):11-14.

2590 Hrdlicka, A. (1935) Ear exostoses. Smithsonian miscellaneous collections 93:1-100.

2591 Hsieh-Chuin, M. and Yin, Y. (1959) Dental condition of the Shang Dynasty skulls excavated from Anyang and Huu-Xian. Vertebrata palasiatica 3:185.

2592 Hudson, E. H. (1965) Treponematosis and man's social evolution. American anthropologist 67:885-901.

2593 Hudson, E. H. (1968) Christopher Columbus and the history of syphilis. Acta tropica 25:1-15.

2594 Hurtado, E. D. (1970) Pre-Hispanic osteopathology. In: R. Wauchop, ed., Handbook of Middle American Indians. Austin: Univ. of Texas Press, vol. 9.

2595 Janssens, P. A. (1970) Palaeopathology--diseases and injuries of prehistoric man. London: John Baker; New York: Humanities Press.

2596 Jarcho, S. (1964) Lead in the bones of prehistoric lead glaze potters. American antiquity 30:94-96.

2597 Jarcho, S. (1964) Some observations on disease in pre-historic North America. Bulletin of the history of medicine 38:1-19.

2598   Jarcho, S., ed. (1966) Human palaeopathology. New
        Haven: Yale University Press.

2599   Jaworowski, Z. (1968) Stable lead in fossil ice and
        bones. Nature 217:152-153.

2600   Jimenez Lambertus, A. (1978) Paleopatología osea
        columnar en esqueletos Indígenas pre-colombinos de
        la Isla de Santo Domingo. Museo de Hombre
        Dominicano, Santo Domingo. Boletín 7(9):111-124.

2601   Katzenberg, M. A. (1976) An investigation of spinal
        disease in a Midwest aboriginal population. Yearbook
        of physical anthropology (New York) 20:349-355.

2602   Kellermann, G. (1977) Paläoserologische Untersuchungen
        an Skelettfunden aus dem 17. und 14. Jahrhundert.
        (Paleoserological investigations on skeletal finds
        from the 17th and 14th centuries). In: W. Bernhard
        and A. Kandler, eds., Bevölkerungsbiologie. Beiträge
        zur Struktur und Dynamik menschlicher Populationen
        in anthropologischer Sicht. Stuttgart, 483-488.

2603   Kerley, E. R. and Bass, W. M. (1967) Paleopathology:
        meeting ground for many disciplines. Science
        157:638-644.

2604   Kidd, K. E. (1954) A note on the palaeopathology of
        Ontario. American journal of physical anthropology
        12:610-615.

2605   Klafstad, J. (1978) Odontopathology of a Norwegian
        medieval population--a pilot study. Ossa 5:43-55.

2606   Kramar, C. (1980) Méthodologie de la paléopathologie.
        Archives suisses d'anthropologie générale
        44(1):45-49.

2607   Krogman, W. M. (1940) The skeletal and dental pathol-
        ogy of an early Iranian site. Bulletin of the
        history of medicine 8(1):28-48.

2608   Krogman, W. M. (1949) The record of human illness.
        Scientific American 180:52-56.

2609   Krogman, W. M. (1951) The scars of human evolution.
        Scientific American 185:54-57.

2610 Lagiglia, H. A. (1976) Párvulo momificado del Atuel, (estudio bioantropológico y arqueológico). Revista del Museo de Historia Natural de San Rafael-Mendoza (San Rafael, Argentina) 3(1-4):159-181.

2611 Larocque, R. (1980) Les maladies chez les Iroquoiens préhistoriques. Recherches Amérindiennes au Québec 10(3):165-180.

2612 Lausarot, P. M. et al. (1972) Preservation and amino acid composition of Egyptian mummy structure proteins. Journal of human evolution 1:489-499.

2613 Lazier, R. and Baud, C. A. (1980) Some comments on paleopathology suggested by a case of myosites ossificans circumscripta observed on a medieval skeleton. Journal of human evolution 9(1):9-13.

2614 Lengyel, I. A. (1975) Paleoserology. Blood typing with the fluorescent antibody method. Budapest: Akadémiai Kiadó.

2615 Leigh, R. W. (1925) Dental pathology of Indian tribes of varied environmental and food conditions. American journal of physical anthropology 8:179-199.

2616 Leigh, R. W. (1934) Notes on the stomatology and pathology of ancient Egypt. Berkeley, Calif.: Univ. of California Press.

2617 Leigh, R. W. (1937) Dental morphology and pathology of pre-Spanish Peru. American journal of physical anthropology 22:267-296.

2618 Lichtor, J. and Lichtor, A. (1957) Paleopathological evidence suggesting pre-Columbian tuberculosis of the spine. Journal of bone and joint surgery 39A(6):1398-1399.

2619 Lippold, L. K. (1971) The mixed cell agglutination method for typing mummified human tissue. American journal of physical anthropology 34:377-383.

2620 Logan, M. H. and Hunt, E. E., eds. (1978) Health and the human condition. Perspectives on medical anthropology. Boston: Duxbury. 443p.

2621   Luna Calderón, F. (1980) Estudio antropológico del
       osario de Escalera Abajo. Museo de Hombre Dominicano,
       Santo Domingo. Boletín 9(13):193-211.

2622   Luna Calderón, F. (1980) Estudio de un caso de
       amputación de Isla Gonave, Haití. Museo de Hombre
       Dominicano, Santo Domingo. Boletín 9(13):213-227.

2623   MacArthur, W. (1953) Medieval 'leprosy' in the British
       Isles. Leprosy review 24:8-19.

2624   MacArthur, W. (1958) The plague of Athens. Bulletin of
       the history of medicine 32:242-246.

2625   McHenry, H. (1968) Transverse lines in long bones of
       prehistoric California Indians. American journal of
       physical anthropology 29:1-18.

2626   Mackie, A., Townshend, A. and Waldron, H. A. (1975)
       Lead concentrations in bones from Roman York. Journal
       of archaeological science 2(3):235-237.

2627   Manchester, K. (1978) Paleopathology of a Royalist
       Garrison. Ossa 5:25-33.

2628   Marcovitch, S. (1943) An early record of vitamin C
       deficiency. Bulletin of the history of medicine
       14:393-397.

2629   Møller-Christensen, V. and Hughes, D. R. (1962) Two
       early cases of leprosy in Great Britain. Man 62:
       177-179.

2630   Moodie, R. L. (1921) Recent advances in paleopathology.
       Science 54:664.

2631   Moodie, R. L. (1923) The antiquity of disease. Chicago:
       Univ. of Chicago Press. 148p.

2632   Moodie, R. L. (1923) Palaeopathology: an introduction
       to the study of ancient evidences of disease.
       Urbana, Illinois: Univ. of Illinois Press. 567p.

2633   Moodie, R. L. (1926) Recent advances in paleopathology.
       Annals of medical history 8:327-330.

2634   Moodie, R. L. (1928) The study of paleopathology in
        France. Annals of medical history 10:86-89.

2635   Moodie, R. L. (1928) The paleopathology of Patagonia.
        Annals of medical history 10:314.

2636   Moodie, R. L. (1929) Archaeological evidences of the
        antiquity of disease in South America. Scientific
        American 140:193-211.

2637   Moodie, R. L. (1930) Suggestion of rickets in the
        Pleistocene. American journal of surgery 10:162-163.

2638   Moore, J. G., Fry, G. F. and Englert, E. (1969) Thorny-
        headed worm infection in North American prehistoric
        man. Science 163:1324-1325.

2639   Moore, S. (1929) The bone change in sickle cell anemia
        with similar changes observed in the skull of ancient
        Maya Indians. Journal of the Missouri Medical
        Association 26(11):561-564.

2640   Morse, D. (1961) Prehistoric tuberculosis in America.
        American review of respiratory diseases 83:489-503.

2641   Morse, D. (1969) Ancient disease in the Midwest.
        Illinois State Museum, Springfield, Illinois. Report
        of investigations no. 15. 153p.

2642   Morse, D. (1980) Methods for the pathological examina-
        tion of human skeletons. Southeastern archaeological
        conference bulletin (Morgantown, W. Virginia)
        17:22-25.

2643   Morse, D., Brothwell, D. R. and Ucko, P. J. (1964)
        Tuberculosis in ancient Egypt. American review of
        respiratory diseases 90:524.

2644   Nemeskéri, J. and Harsányi, L. (1959) Die Bedeutung
        paläopathologischer Untersuchungen für die histori-
        sche Anthropologie. (The significance of paleo-
        pathological investigations for historical anthro-
        pology). Homo 10:203-226.

2645   Neumann, H. W. (1967) The paleopathology of the archaic
        Modoc Rock Shelter inhabitants. Illinois State
        Museum, Springfield, Illinois. Report of
        investigations no. 11.

256

2646 Nicola, M. (1979) Morphologische und pathologische
Befunde von Zähnen und Kiefern aus der mittleren
Bronzezeit (Pitten, Nieder-Österreich). (Morpholog-
ical and pathological results from teeth and jaws
of the middle Bronze Age, Pitten, Lower Austria).
Anthropologischer Anzeiger 37(3):182-203.

2647 O'Bannon, L. G. (1957) Evidence of tuberculosis of the
spine from a Mississippi stone box burial: a pre-
Columbian probability. Tennessee archaeologist
(Knoxville) 13(2):75-80.

2648 Ortner, D. J. (1979) Disease and mortality in the early
Bronze Age people of Bab edh-Dhra, Jordan. American
journal of physical anthropology 51(4):589-597.

2649 Otten, C. M. and Flory, L. L. (1964) Blood typing of
Chilean mummy tissue: a new approach. American
journal of physical anthropology 21:238-285.

2650 Pahl, W. M. (1980) Computed tomography: a new
radio-diagnostical technique applied to medico-
archaeological investigation of Egyptian mummies.
Antropologia contemporanea (Torino) 3(1):37-44.

2651 Pahl, W. M. (1980) Paleopathological findings on a
head of a mummy from dynastic Egypt: preliminary
study. Antropologia contemporanea (Torino) 3(1):
27-33.

2652 Palès, L. (1930) Paléopathologie et pathologie comparative. Paris: Masson et Cie. 352p.

2653 Palès, L. (1930) Paléopathologie tuberculose préhistorique. Paris: Masson et Cie.

2654 Parrish, H. M. (1962) Has mankind always had coronary
disease? Journal of the Indiana Medical Association
55:464-471.

2655 Pedersen, P. O. (1938) Investigations into dental conditions of about 3,000 ancient and modern
Greenlanders. Dental record 58(4):191-198.

2656 Peluso, A. (1980) Patologia orale in una antica
popolazione egiziana. Antropologia contemporanea
(Torino) 3(1):57-82.

2657 Perrot, R. (1980) Un cas medieval de pseudarthrose du col femorale (Saint Just, Lyon, France). Antropologia contemporanea (Torino) 3(1):121-125.

2658 Perrot, R., Gonon, G. P. and Morin, A. (1980) Aspects paléopathologiques de vestiges vertebraux d'époque medievale. Antropologia contemporanea (Torino) 3(1):97-104.

2659 Pike, A. W. (1968) Recovery of helminth eggs from archaeological excavations and their possible usefulness in providing evidence for the purpose of an occupation. Nature 219:303-304.

2660 Pike, A. W. and Biddle, M. (1966) Parasite eggs in mediaeval Winchester. Antiquity 11:293-296.

2661 Price, J. L. (1975) The radiology of excavated Saxon and medieval human remains from Winchester. Clinical radiology (London) 26:363-370.

2662 Promińska, E. (1980) Changements pathologiques des squelettes découverts dans les églises de Dongola. Antropologia contemporanea (Torino) 3(1):153-156.

2663 Rabkin, S. (1942) Dental conditions among prehistoric Indians of northern Alabama. Journal of dental research (Chicago) 21:211-222.

2664 Reader, R. (1974) New evidence for the antiquity of leprosy in early Britain. Journal of archaeological science 1(2):205-207.

2665 Requena, A. (1946) Evidencia de tuberculosis en la America precolombina. Acta venozolana 1:1-20.

2666 Reyman, T. A. (1976) Schistosomal cirrhosis in an Egyptian mummy (circa 1200 B.C.). Yearbook of physical anthropology (New York) 20:356-358.

2667 Reyman, T. A., Barraco, R. A. and Cockburn, T. A. (1976) Histopathological examination of an Egyptian mummy. Bulletin of the New York Academy of Medicine 52:506-516.

2668 Ritchie, W. A. (1952) Paleopathological evidence
      suggesting pre-Columbian tuberculosis in New York
      state. American journal of physical anthropology
      10(3):305-317.

2669 Ritchie, W. A. and Warren, S. L. (1932) The occurrence
      of multiple bony lesions suggesting myeloma in the
      skeleton of a pre-Columbian Indian. American journal
      of roentgenology, radium therapy and nuclear
      medicine (New York) 28:622-628

2670 Rohen, J. (1959) Histologische Untersuchungen an
      Augen altkanarischer Mumien. (Histological inves-
      tigations on the eyes of ancient mummies).
      Homo 10:35-39.

2671 Rokhlin, D. G. (1963) Patologičeskie izmenenija na
      kostjakh ljudej v X-XI i načale XII stoletij po
      materialam mogil'nika Sarkela--Beloj Veži. (Patho-
      logical alterations on human bones in the 10th-11th
      and the beginning of the 12th centuries based on
      materials from the Sarkel burial mound--Beloj Veži).
      Materialy i issledovanija po arkheologii SSSR
      109:451-461, 501-514.

2672 Rokhlin, D. G. (1965) Bolezni drevnikh ljudij. (Kosti
      ljudej različnykh ėpokh--normal'nye i patologičeskie
      izmenennye). (Diseases of ancient man. Human bones
      from different periods--normal and pathological
      alterations). Moskva--Leningrad: Akademija Nauk
      SSSR. 304p.

2673 Rokhlin, D. G. and Rubaševa, A. E. (1935) Materialy po
      rentgenopaleoantropologii i rentgenopaleopatologii.
      (Materials on roentgeno-paleoanthropology and
      roentgeno-paleopathology). Vestnik rentgenologii i
      radiologii 14:164-176.

2674 Roney, J. G. (1959) Palaeopathology of a Californian
      archaeological site. Bulletin of the history of
      medicine 33(2):97-109.

2675 Ruffer, M. A. (1920) Study of abnormalities and
      pathology of ancient Egyptian teeth. American
      journal of physical anthropology 3(3):335-382.

2676 Rusconi, C. (1946) La piorrea en las indigenos pre-
hispanicos de Mendoza. Revista de odontologia
34:118-121.

2677 St. Hoyme, L. E. (1969) On the origins of New World
paleopathology. American journal of physical
anthropology 31(3):295-302.

2678 Salama, N. and Hilmy, A. (1951) An ancient Egyptian
skull and a mandible showing cysts. British dental
journal (London) 90:17-18.

2679 Salib, P. (1962) Orthopaedic and traumatic skeletal
lesions in ancient Egyptians. Journal of bone and
joint surgery 44:944-947.

2680 Salomen, C. D. (1967) Histological and histochemical
observations on undecalcified sections of ancient
bones from excavations in Israel. Israel journal of
medical science 3:747-754.

2681 Samuels, R. (1965) Parasitological study of long-dried
fecal samples. Memoirs of the society of American
archeology 19:175-179.

2682 Sandison, A. T. (1955) The histological examination of
mummified material. Stain technology 30:277-283.

2683 Sandison, A. T. (1957) Preparation of large histological sections of mummified tissues. Nature 179:1309.

2684 Sandison, A. T. (1962) Degenerative vascular diseases
in the Egyptian mummy. Medican history (London)
6:77-81.

2685 Sandison, A. T. (1963) Staining of vascular elastic
fibres in mummified and human tissue. Nature
198:597.

2686 Sandison, A. T. (1967) Sir Marc Armand Ruffer (1859-
1917) pioneer of palaeopathology. Medical history
(London). 11:150-156.

2687 Sandison, A. T. (1969) Diseases in ancient Egypt.
Rivista di antropologia 56:225-228.

2688 Satinoff, M. J. (1968) Preliminary report on the
palaeopathology of a collection of ancient Egyptian
skeletons. Revista di antropologia 55:41-50.

2689 Schaefer, U. (1955) Demographische Beobachtungen an
der wikingerzeitlichen Bevölkerung von Haithabu, und
Mitteilung einiger pathologischer Befunde an den
Skeletten. (Demographic observations on the Viking
period population at Haithabu, and report of some
pathological conditions on the skeletons). Zeitschrift für Morphologie und Anthropologie (Stuttgart)
47:221-228.

2690 Scheidegger, S. (1963) Paläopathologische Befunde an
Knochen. (Paleopathological conditions on bones).
Verhandlungen der Deutschen Gesellschaft für
Pathologie 47:198-202.

2691 Schultz, M. (1978) Pathologische Veränderungen an den
Dürrnberger Skeletten: Material und Methode, Zahn-
und Kiefererkrankungen, pathologische Veränderungen
an Schädelknochen und postcranialem Skelett. (Pathological alterations on Dürrnberg skeletons:
material and methods, tooth and jaw diseases, pathological alterations on skull bones and postcranial
skeleton). Der Dürrnberg bei Hallein III. Münchner
Beiträge zur Vor- und Frügeschichte 18(2):583-600.

2692 Schultz, M. (1979) Diseases of the ear region in early
and prehistoric populations. Journal of human
evolution 8(6):575-580.

2693 Smith, M. (1960) The blood groups of the ancient dead.
Science 131:699-702.

2694 Smith, P. and Tau, S. (1978) Dental pathology in the
period of the Roman Empire--a comparison of two
populations. Ossa 5:35-41.

2695 Snorrason, E. S. (1942) Rheumatism, past and present,
in the light of palaeopathology and social prehistory. Canadian Medical Association journal
46:589-594.

2696 Sognnaes, R. F. (1956) Histological evidence of
developmental lesions in teeth originating from
Palaeolithic, pre-historic and ancient times.
American journal of pathology (Boston) 32:547-577.

2697 Springer, G. F. and Williamson, P. (1960) Blood group
      determinations of ancient tissue. Science 131:1858.

2698 Stastny, P. (1974) HL-A antigens in mummified pre-
      Columbian tissues. Science 183:864-866.

2699 Strouhal, E. and Jungwirth, J. (1977) Ein verkalktes
      Myoma uteri aus der späten Römerzeit in Ägyptisch-
      Nubien. (A calcified Myoma uteri from the late Roman
      period in Egyptian Nubia). Mitteilungen der
      anthropologischen Gesellschaft in Wien 107:215-221.

2700 Strouhal, E. and Jungwirth, J. (1980) Paleopathology of
      the late Roman-early Byzantine cemeteries at Sayala,
      Egyptian Nubia. Journal of human evolution 9(1):
      61-70.

2701 Swedborg, I. (1975) Studies of macerated human spine--
      a background for the clinical approach to the
      degenerative process. Ossa 2(1):15-21.

2702 Sweeney, E. A. (1965) Dental caries in Tehuacan
      skeletons. Science 149:1118.

2703 Tattersall, I. (1968) Dental paleopathology of medieval
      Britain. Journal of the history of medicine and
      allied sciences 23(4):380-385.

2704 Taylor, E. L. (1955) Parasitic helminths in medieval
      remains. Veterinary records 67:216-218.

2705 Thieme, F. P. (1956) A blood typing of human skull
      fragments from the Pleistocene. American journal of
      physical anthropology 14:437-443.

2706 Thieme, F. P. and Otten, C. M. (1957) The unreliability
      of blood typing aged bone. American journal of
      physical anthropology 15:387-397.

2707 Thillaud, P. L. (1980) La problématique d'une classifi-
      cation a l'usage de l'ostéo-archéologie pathologique.
      Antropologia contemporanea (Torino) 3(1):11-18.

2708 Torre, C., Giacobini, G. and Sicuro, A. (1980) The
      skull and vertebral column pathology of ancient
      Egyptians. A study of the Marro collection. Journal
      of human evolution 9(1):41-44.

2709 Tubbs, D. and Berger, R. (1967) The viability of
       pathogens in ancient human coprolites. University of
       California Archaeological Survey 70:89-92.

2710 Vallois, H. V. (1934) Les maladies de l'homme pré-
       historique. Revue scientifique 72:666-678.

2711 Wade, W. D., ed. (1967) Miscellaneous papers in paleo-
       pathology: I. Flagstaff: Museum of Northern
       Arizona. 60p.

2712 Waldron, H. A. (1973) Lead poisoning in the ancient
       world. Medical history 17:392-399.

2713 Wakefield, E. G. and Dellinger, S. C. (1940) Diseases
       of prehistoric Americans of south central United
       States. Ciba symposia 2(2):453-464.

2714 Watermann, R. von (1960) Paläopathologische Beobach-
       tungen an altägyptischen Skeletten und Mumien.
       (Paleopathological remarks on ancient Egyptian
       skeletons and mummies). Homo 11:167-179.

2715 Weidenreich, F. (1939) The duration of life in fossil
       man in China and the pathological lesions found in
       his skeleton. Chinese medical journal 55:34-44.

2716 Wells, C. (1962) Joint pathology in ancient Anglo-
       Saxons. Journal of bone and joint surgery 44:
       948-949.

2717 Wells, C. (1962) Three cases of aural pathology of
       Anglo-Saxon date. Journal of laryngology and otology
       (London) 76:931.

2718 Wells, C. (1963) Ancient Egyptian pathology. Journal of
       laryngology and otology (London) 77:261-265.

2719 Wells, C. (1964) Bones, bodies and disease. London:
       Thames & Hudson.

2720 Williams, H. U. (1929) Human paleopathology, with some
       original observations on symmetrical osteoporosis of
       the skull. Archives of pathology (Chicago) 7:839-902.

2721 Williams, H. U. (1932) The origin and antiquity of syphilis: the evidence from diseased bones, a review with some new material from America. Archives of pathology (Chicago) 13:779-814, 931-983.

2722 Williams, H. U. (1935) Pathology of yaws. Archives of pathology (Chicago) 20:596-630.

2723 Witenberg, G. (1961) Human parasites in archeological faeces. Bulletin of the Israel exploration society 25:86.

2724 Woodall, J. N. (1968) Growth arrest lines in long bones of the Casas Grandes population. Plains anthropologist 13(40):152-160.

2725 Wrozosek, A. (1960) Histologische Untersuchungen an Augen altkanarischer Mumien. (Histological investigations on eyes of ancient mummies from the Canary Islands). Homo 10:35-39.

2726 Zaino, E. (1968) Elemental bone iron in the Anasazi Indians. American journal of physical anthropology 29:433-436.

2727 Zimmerman, M. R. (1979) Paleopathologic diagnosis based on experimental mummification. American journal of physical anthropology 51(2):235-253.

2728 Zimmerman, M. R., Yeatman, G. W. and Sprinz, H. (1971) Examination of an Aleutian mummy. Bulletin of the New York Academy of Medicine 47(1):80-103.

V. MATERIALS ANALYSIS

A. General studies

2729 Beck, C. W., ed. (1974) Archaeological chemistry I. Washington, D. C.: American Chemical Society.

2730 Biek, L. (1963) Archaeology and the microscope. London: Butterworth Press.

2731 Bleck, R.-D. (1966) Archäologische Chemie--Chemie im Dienste der Urgeschichtsforschung. (Archaeological chemistry--chemistry in the service prehistoric research). Alt-Thüringen 8:7-19.

2732 Bleck, R.-D. (1967-1971) Bibliographie der archäologisch-chemischen Literatur. (Bibliography of the archaeological-chemical literature). Three volumes. Weimar: Museum für Ur- und Fruhgeschichte Thüringens.

2733 Brandt, A.-C. and Riederer, J. (1978) Die Anfänge der Archäometrie-Literatur im 18. und 19. Jahrhundert. (The beginning of the archaeometry literature in the 18th and 19th centuries). Berliner Beiträge zur Archäometrie 3:161-173.

2734 Carter, G. F., ed. (1978) Archaeological chemistry II. Washington, D. C.: American Chemical Society.

2735 Hall, E. T. and Metcalf, D. M., eds. (1972) Methods of chemical and metallurgical investigation of ancient coinage. Royal Numismatic Society, London. Special publication no. 8.

2736   Lazzarini, L. et al. (1980) Chemical, mineralogical
       and Mössbauer studies of Venetian and Paduan
       Renaissance sgraffito ceramics. Archaeometry
       22(1):57-68.

2737   Levey, M., ed. (1967) Archaeological chemistry: a
       symposium. Philadelphia: Univ. of Pennsylvania
       Press.

2738   Noll, W. (1978) Material and techniques of the Minoan
       ceramics of Thera and Crete. In: Thera and the
       Aegean world. London: Thera and the Aegean World,
       493-505.

2739   Pyddocke, E., ed. (1963) The scientist and
       archaeology. New York: Roy Publishers.

2740   Riederer, J. (1978) Bibliographie zu Material und
       Technologie kulturgeschichtlicher Goldobjekte.
       (Bibliography on the material and technology of
       cultural-historical gold objects). Berliner Beiträge
       zur Archäometrie 3:175-191.

2741   Riederer, J. (1977) Die Erkennung von Fälschungen
       kunst- und kulturgeschichtlicher Objekte aus
       Bronze und Messing durch naturwissenschaftliche
       Untersuchungen. (The detection of frauds of art and
       historical objects of bronze and brass through
       natural science investigations). Berliner Beiträge
       zur Archäometrie 2:85-95.

B. Microscopy

1. Petrography

2742   Bareis, C. J. and Porter, J. W. (1965) Megascopic and
       petrographic analyses of a foreign pottery vessel
       from the Cahokia site. American antiquity 31:95-101.

2743   Bautsch, H. J. and Kelch, H. (1960) Mineralogisch-
       petrographische Untersuchungen an einigen in der
       Antike als Baumaterial verwendeten Gesteinen.
       (Mineralogical-petrographic investigations on a few
       stones used as building material in antiquity).
       Geologie 9:691-700.

2744   Buttler, W. (1933) Dünnschliffuntersuchungen an vor-
       geschichtlicher Keramik. (Thin-section investigations
       on prehistoric ceramics). Nachrichtenblatt für
       Deutsche Vorzeit 9:186-188.

2745   Campling, N. R. (1980) Identification of Swan River
       chert. In: Directions in Manitoba prehistory.
       Winnipeg: Association of Manitoba Archaeologists,
       291-301.

2746   Castiglioni, O. C., Fussi, F. and D'Agnolo, G. (1963)
       Indagini sulla provenienza dell'ossidiana utilizzata
       nelle industrie preistoriche del Mediterraneo
       occidentale. Atti della Società italiana di scienze
       naturali, e del Museo civile di storia naturale
       102:310-322.

2747   Clough, T. H. McK. and Cummins, W. A., eds. (1979)
       Stone axe studies. Archaeological, petrological,
       experimental and ethnographic. CBA research report
       no. 23. London: Council for British Archaeology.

2748   Cogné, J. and Giot, P.-R. (1952) Étude pétrographique
       des haches polies de Bretagne. Bulletin de la société
       préhistorique française 49:388-395.

2749   Cogné, J. and Giot, P.-R. (1953) Étude pétrographique
       des haches polies de Bretagne. Bulletin de la société
       préhistorique française 50:37-39.

2750   Cogné, J. and Giot, P.-R. (1954) L'étude pétrographique
       des haches polies. Bulletin de la société préhis-
       torique françiase 51:28.

2751   Cogné, J. and Giot, P.-R. (1957) L'étude pétrographique
       des haches polies de Bretagne. Bulletin de la société
       préhistorique française 54:240-241.

2752   Cornwall, I. and Hodges, H. W. M. (1964) Thin sections
       of British Neolithic pottery: Windmill Hill--a test
       site. Institute of Archaeology, London. Bulletin
       4:29-33.

2753   Courtois, L. (1963) Examen minéralogique de quelques
       roches de monuments gréco-bouddhiques. Arts
       asiatiques 9:107-113.

2754   Courtois, L. (1976) Examen au microscope pétrographique
       des céramiques archéologiques. Centre de recherches
       archéologiques, Paris. Notes et monographies 8:1-49.

2755   Cowgill, U. M. and Hutchinson, G. E. (1969) A chemical
       and mineralogical examination of the ceramic
       sequence from Tikal, El Peten, Guatemala. American
       journal of science 267:465-477.

2756   Crusoe, D. L. (1971) A study of aboriginal trade: a
       petrographic analysis of certain ceramic types from
       Florida. Florida anthropologist 24(1):31-43.

2757   Curtis, G. H. (1959) The petrology of artifacts and
       architectural stone at La Venta. Bulletin of the
       Bureau of American Ethnology 170:284-289.

2758   Desmaisons, H. (1935) La minéralogie en préhistoire.
       Bulletin de la société préhistorique française
       32:87-96.

2759   De Natale, D. (1980) Petrography, X-ray diffractometer
       analysis and quarry sites. Bulletin of the
       Massachusetts archaeological society (Attleboro)
       41(1):11-14.

2760   Einfalt, H.-C. (1978) Chemical and mineralogical in-
       vestigations from the Akrotiri excavations. In:
       Thera and the Aegean world. London: Thera and the
       Aegean World, 459-469.

2761   Ellis, L. (1980) Analysis of Cucuteni-Tripolye and
       Kurgan pottery and the implications for ceramic
       technology. Journal of Indo-European studies
       8(1/2):211-230.

2762   Ellis, S. E. (1969) The petrography and provenance of
       Anglo-Saxon and medieval honestones, with notes on
       other hones. Bulletin of the British Museum
       (Natural History) Mineralogy 2(3):133-187.

2763   Evans, E. D. et al. (1962) Fourth report of the sub-
       committee of the SW group of museums and art
       galleries on the petrological examination of stone
       axes. Proceedings of the prehistoric society 28:
       209-266.

2764 Farnsworth, M. (1964) Greek pottery: a mineralogical study. American journal of archaeology 68:221-228.

2765 Felts, W. M. (1942) A petrographic examination of potsherds from ancient Troy. American journal of archaeology 46:237-244.

2766 Fitting, J. E. and Stone, L. M. (1969) Distance and utility in the distribution of raw materials in the Cedar Mountains of New Mexico. The Kiva 34:207-212.

2767 Frechen, J. (1965) Petrographische Untersuchung von Steingeräte bzw. Rohmaterial. (Petrographic investigation of stone tools with respect to raw material). In: K. Schietzel, Muddersheim, eine Ansiedlung der jüngeren Bandkeramik im Rheinland. Köln, 39-43.

2768 Gajduk, I. M. (1965) Vyjavlenie mikrorajonov neolitičeskikh plemen metodom petrografičeskogo i spektral'nogo analyzov. (The discovery of micro-regions of Neolithic tribes by the methods of petrographic and spectroscopic analysis). Materialy i issledovanija po arkheologii SSSR 129:185-192.

2769 Garrett, E. M. (1976) A petrographic analysis of thirty Pottery Mound polychrome, San Clemente polychrome, and Glaze C sherds from Pottery Mound, New Mexico. Pottery Southwest 3(1):4-8.

2770 Giot, P.-R. (1951) A petrological investigation of Breton stone axes. Proceedings of the prehistoric society 17:228.

2771 Giot, P.-R. (1964) Résultats de l'identification pétrographique des matériaux des haches polies en France septentrionale. Studien aus Alteuropa 1:123-133.

2772 Hays, T. R. and Hassan, F. A. (1974) Mineralogical analysis of Sudanese Neolithic ceramics. Archaeometry 16(1):71-79.

2773 Hegde, K. T. M. (1979) Analysis of ancient Indian deluxe wares. Archaeo-Physika 10:141-155.

2774 Herz, N. (1955) Geology of the building stones of
ancient Greece. Transactions of the New York Academy
of Sciences, series 2, 17(7):499-505.

2775 Herz, N. (1955) Petrofabrics and classical archaeology.
American journal of science 253:299-305.

2776 Herz, N. and Pritchett, W. K. (1953) Marble in Attic
epigraphy. American journal of archaeology 57:71-83.

2777 Hodges, H. W. M. (1962) Thin sections of prehistoric
pottery: an empirical study. Institute of Archaeology, London. Bulletin 3:58-68.

2778 Jope, E. M. (1948/1949) Abingdan Abbey craftsmen and
building stone supplies. Berkshire archaeological
journal 51:53-64.

2779 Jope, E. M. (1953) History, archaeology and
petrography. Advancement of science 9:432-435.

2780 Kamilli, D. C. and Lamberg-Karlovsky, C. C. (1979)
Petrographic and electron microprobe analysis of
ceramics from Tepe Yahya, Iran. Archaeometry 21(1):
47-59

2781 Kânčev, K., Mavrudčiev, B. and Čatalov, G. (1976)
Petrografičeskie issledovanija kamennykh orudij iz
mnogoslojnogo poselenija Kazanlyk. (Petrographic
analysis of stone tools from the multi-level
settlement of Kazanlûk). Sovetskaja arkheologija
2:94-105.

2782 Keen, L. and Radley, J. (1971) Report on the petrological identification of stone axes from Yorkshire.
Proceedings of the prehistoric society 37:16-37.

2783 Keiller, A. (1937) Petrological analysis. Antiquity
11:484-485.

2784 Keiller, A., Piggott, S. and Wallis, F. S. (1941) First
report of the sub-committee of the southwestern
group of museums and art galleries on the petrological identification of stone axes. Proceedings of
the prehistoric society 7:50-72.

2785 Köhler, A. (1928) Mikroskopische Untersuchungen an
     römischer und vorgeschichtlicher Keramik von
     Hallstatt. (Microscopic investigations on Roman and
     prehistoric ceramics from Hallstatt). Mikroskopie
     4:368.

2786 Köhler, A. and Morton, F. (1954) Mineralogische Unter-
     suchung prähistorischer Keramik aus Hallstatt im
     Zusammenhang mit der Frage nach ihrer Herkunft.
     (Mineralogical investigation of prehistoric ceramics
     from Hallstatt in connection with the question of
     their origin). Germania 32:66-72.

2787 Kolderup, N. H. (1925) Petrologische Untersuchungen
     über das Material für Werkzeuge im westlichen
     Norwegen. (Petrological investigations on the materi-
     al for tools in western Norway). Tschermaks
     mineralogische und petrographische Mitteilungen
     38:165-174.

2788 Krug, O. JU. (1960) Petrografičeskij analiz keramiki.
     (Petrographic analysis of ceramics). In: I. B.
     Zeest, ed., Keramičeskaja tara Bospora. Materialy i
     issledovanija po arkheologii SSSR 83:128-132.

2789 Krug, O. JU. (1961) Petrografičeskij analiz keramiki.
     (Petrographic analysis of ceramics). In: O. N.
     Bader, ed., Otčety kamskoj arkheologičeskoj
     ėkspeditsii. Moskva: Institut Arkheologii,
     Akademija Nauk SSSR, 2:262-263.

2790 Krug, O. JU. (1963) Petrografičeskoe issledovanie
     sostava tmutarakanskoj polivnoj keramiki. (Petro-
     graphic investigations of the composition of
     Tmutarakan polished ware). In: Keramika i steklo
     Drevnej Tmutarakani. Moskva, 96-97.

2791 Krug, O. JU. (1965) Primenenie petrografii v arkhe-
     ologii. Materialy i issledovanija po arkheologii
     SSSR 129:146-152.

2792 Krug, O. JU. (1967) Petrografičeskoe issledovanie
     sostava polivnoj keramiki. (Petrographic investiga-
     tions of the composition of polished ceramics). In:
     T. I. Makarova, Polivnaja posuda. Iz istorii
     keramičeskogo importa i proizvodstva Drevnej Rusi.
     Moskva: Institut Arkheologii, AN SSSR, 69-70.

272

2793 Krug, O. JU. and Četverikov, S. D. (1961) Opyt primenenija petrografičeskikh metodov k izučeniju
keramiki Bosporskogo tsarstva. (The application of
petrographic methods to the study of ceramics of the
Bosporus kingdom). Sovetskaja arkheologija 3:34-44.

2794 Küpfer, T. and Maggetti, M. (1978) Die Terra Sigillata
von La Péniche (Vidy/Lausanne). (The terra sigillata
from La Peniche, Vidy/Lausanne). Schweizerische
mineralogische und petrographische Mitteilungen
58:189-212.

2795 Leitmeier, H. (1932) Mineralogische Untersuchungen an
den Werkzeugen von Willendorf. (Mineralogical investigations on the tools from Willendorf).
Mitteilungen der anthropologischen Gesellschaft in
Wien 62:361-366.

2796 Malina, J. (1970) Archäologische und petrographische
Bemerkungen zur Funktion der neolithischen
geschliffenen Steinindustrie. (Archaeological and
petrographic observations on the function of
Neolithic polished stone industry). Mährische
heimatkündliche Mitteilungen 22(3).

2797 Malina, J. (1970) Die jungpaläolithische Steinindustrie
aus Mähren, ihre Rohstoffe und ihre Patina. (The
Upper Palaeolithic stone industry of Moravia, its
raw materials and its patina). Acta praehistorica et
archaeologica 1:157-173.

2798 Misik, M. (1966) Die petrographische Zugehörigkeit von
Siliziten aus paläolithischen und neolithischen
Artefakten der Slowakei. (The petrographic association of siliceous material from Palaeolithic and
Neolithic artifacts from Slovakia). Acta geologica
et geographica universitatis comenianae, geologica
18:117-135.

2799 Moore, D. T. (1978) The petrography and archaeology of
English honestones. Journal of archaeological science
5:61-73.

2800 Morey, J. E. (1950) Petrographical identification of
stone axes. Proceedings of the prehistoric society
16:191-193.

2801 Morey, J. E. and Dunham, K. C. (1953) A petrological study of medieval hones from Yorkshire. Proceedings of the Yorkshire geological society 29:141-148.

2802 Morey, J. E. and Sabine, P. A. (1953) A petrological review of the porcellanite axes of northeast Ireland. Ulster journal of archaeology 15(2):56-60.

2803 Negbi, O. (1964) A contribution of mineralogy and paleontology to an archaeological study of terracottas. Israel exploration quarterly 14:187-189.

2804 North, F. J. (1938) Geology for archaeologists. Archaeological journal 94:73-115.

2805 Otto, H. (1961) Mineralogische und petrographische Untersuchungen an vor- und frühgeschichtlichen Gegenständen. (Mineralogical and petrographic investigations on pre- and protohistoric objects). Ausgrabungen und Funde 6:314-316.

2806 Peacock, D. P. S. (1967) The heavy mineral analysis of pottery: a preliminary report. Archaeometry 10:97-100.

2807 Peacock, D. P. S. (1968) A petrological study of certain Iron Age pottery from western England. Proceedings of the prehistoric society 34:414-427.

2808 Petrun', V. F. (1966) O mineralogo-petrografičeskikh issledovanijakh v arkheologii. (Mineralogical-petrographic investigations in archaeology). Zapiski Vsesojuznogo mineralogičeskogo obščestva (Leningrad) 95(5):627-632.

2809 Petrun', V. F. (1967) O dostovernosti petrografo-mineralogičeskikh opredelenij v arkheologičeskoj praktike. (On the reliability of petrographic-mineralogical determinations in archaeological practice). Zapiski Odesskogo arkheologičeskogo obščestva 2(35):3-11.

2810 Plesters, J. (1954) The preparation and study of paint cross-sections. Museums journal 54(4).

274

2811 Porter, J. W. and Szuter, C. R. (1978) Thin-section analysis of Schlemmer site ceramics. Midcontinental journal of archaeology (Kent, Ohio) 3(1):3-14.

2812 Renfrew, C. and Peacy, J. (1968) Aegean marbles: a petrological study. Annual of the British School of Archaeology at Athens 63:45-66.

2813 Rogers, A. F. (1924) Mineralogy and petrology of fossil bone. Bulletin of the geological society of America 35:535-536.

2814 Roobol, M. J. and Lee, J. W. (1976) Petrography and source of some Arawak artifacts from Jamaica. Proc. of the sixth international congress for the study of pre-Columbian cultures of the Lesser Antilles, Guadeloupe, 1975. Gainesville, Florida: Bullen, 304-313.

2815 Sajko, Ė. V. (1965) Tekhnologija keramiki sredne-vekovykh masterov (Srednej Azii). (Technology of ceramics of medieval craftsmen, Central Asia). Materialy i issledovanija po arkheologii SSSR 129:161-166.

2816 Sajko, Ė. V. (1966) Istorija tekhnologii keramičeskogo remesla Srednej Azii VIII-XII vv. (History of technology of the ceramic craft of Central Asia in the 8th-12th centuries). Dušanbe: Akademija Nauk, Tadžik. SSR, Institut Istorii. 212p.

2817 Sanderson, H. A. H. (1970) A petrographic review of some thin sections of stone axes. Bulletin of the geological survey of Great Britain 33:85-100.

2818 Schmitt, F. R. (1938) Petrographische Untersuchungen in der Vorgeschichtsforschung. (Petrographic investigations in prehistoric research). Rheinische Vorzeit in Wort und Bild 1:130-133.

2819 Schmitt, F. R. (1939) Möglichkeiten und Grenzen des Einsatzes der Petrographie bei der Untersuchung von Vorzeitfunden. (Possibilities and limitations of the inclusion of petrography in the investigation of prehistoric finds). Nachrichtenblatt für deutsche Vorzeit 15:47-51.

2820 Schneider, W. (1975) Erläuterungen zu mineralogisch-
petrographischen Untersuchungen an Keramikscherben
aus dem 3. und 4. Jahrhundert n. Chr. von Seinstedt,
Gielde und Haverlah. (Interpretations of mineralogical-petrographic investigations on ceramic sherds
from the 3rd and 4th centuries A.D. from Seinstedt,
Gielde and Haverlah). Neue Ausgrabungen und
Forschungen in Niedersachsen 9:195-200.

2821 Schneider, W. (1976) Geologisch-petrographische Untersuchungen im Bereich der frühbandkeramischen
Siedlung bei Eitzum, Kr. Wolfenbüttel. (Geological-
petrographic investigations in the region of the
early Linear Pottery settlement near Eitzum,
Wolfenbüttel district). Nachrichten aus Niedersachsens Urgeschichte 45:331-339.

2822 Schneider, W. (1979) Geologischer Überblick über den
Westharz und sein nördliches Vorland im Hinblick auf
Materialfragen aus archäologischer Sicht. (Geological
overview of the western Harz and its northern fore-
land in regard to material questions from archaeology). Nachrichten aus Niedersachsens Urgeschichte
48:1-15.

2823 Sedgley, J. P. (1970) Some problems connected with the
petrographic examination of stone artefacts. Science
and archaeology 2/3:10-12.

2824 Shotton, F. W. (1959) New petrological groups based on
axes from the west Midlands. Proceedings of the
prehistoric society 25:135-143.

2825 Shotton, F. W. and Hendry, G. L. (1979) The developing
field of petrology in archaeology. Journal of
archaeological science 6(1):75-84.

2826 Slatkine, A. (1978) Étude microscopique de poteries
anciennes du Negev et du Sinaï. Paléorient 4:113-130.

2827 Stanley, J. W. (1976) A preliminary description of
thin sections of some Neolithic stone axes from the
London region. Science and archaeology 18:3-11.

2828 Stelcl, J., Kalousek, F. and Malina, J. (1970) A
petro-archaeological study of a deposit of Neolithic
stone tools at Stará Břeclav, Czechoslovakia.

Proceedings of the prehistoric society 36:233-240.

2829 Stelcl, J. and Malina, J. (1969) Petrographie in der Archäologie. (Petrography in archaeology). Wissenschaftliche Zeitschrift der philosophischen Fakultät der Universität Brno 14:223-227.

2830 Stone, J. F. S. (1952) Reconstitution des voies de commerce: l'identification pétrographique des instruments de pierre. In: A. Laming, ed., La découverte du passé. Paris: A. and J. Picard, 247-262.

2831 Stone, J. F. S. and Wallis, F. S. (1947) Second report of the sub-committee of the southwestern group of museums and art galleries on the petrological identification of stone axes. Proceedings of the prehistoric society 13:47-55.

2832 Stone, J. F. S. and Wallis, F. S. (1951) Third report or the sub-committee of the SW group of museums and art galleries on the petrological determination of stone axes. Proceedings of the prehistoric society 17L99-158.

2833 Ulrich, F. (1935) Mineralogische Untersuchung des Obsidians. (Mineralogical investigation of obsidian). In: S. Jansak, Prähistorische Siedlungen mit Obsidiankultur in der Ostslowakei. Bratislava, 11-16; 147-150.

2834 Végh, A. and Viczián, I. (1964) Petrographische Untersuchungen an den Silexwerkzeugen. (Petrographic investigations on silex tools). In: L. Vertes, Tata; eine mittelpaläolithische Travertin-Siedlung in Ungarn. Budapest, 129-131.

2835 Wallis, F. S. (1955) Petrology as an aid to prehistoric and medieval archaeology. Endeavour 14(55):146-151.

2836 Walston, S. and Dolanski, J. (1976) Two painted and engraved sandstone sites in Australia. Studies in conservation 21(1):1-17.

2837 Weide, D. L. (1969) A petrographic examination of basalt artifacts from the Panamint Valley, California. In: E. L. Davis, et al., The western lithic co-tradition. San Diego Museum papers 6.

2838   Weiss, L. E. (1954) Fabric analysis of some Greek
        marbles and its application to archaeology. American
        journal of science 252:641-662.

2839   Williams, D. F. (1978) A petrological examination of
        pottery from Thera. In: Thera and the Aegean world.
        London: Thera and the Aegean World, 507-514.

2840   Williams, D. F. (1979) Ceramic petrology and the
        archaeologist. Institute of Archaeology, London.
        Occasional publication 4:73-76.

2841   Williams, D. F. (1979) Petrological analysis of some
        mica-dusted and 'London ware' pottery. In: H.
        Sheldon, ed., Excavations in Southwark, 1972-74.

2842   Williams, H. (1956) Petrographic notes on tempers of
        pottery from Chupicuaro, Cerro del Tepelcate and
        Ticoman, Mexico. Transactions of the American
        philosophical society 45:576-580.

2843   Williams, H. and Heizer, R. F. (1965) Sources of rocks
        used in Olmec monuments. Contributions of the
        University of California archaeological research
        facility 1:1-40.

2844   Williams, J. Ll. W. (1973) A petrological examination
        of the prehistoric pottery from the excavations in
        the Castello and Diana Plain of Lipari: an interim
        report. In: L. Bernabo Brea and M. Cavalier,
        Meligunis Lipara, vol. 4. Palermo.

2845   Williams, J. Ll. W., Jenkins, D. A. and Livens, R. G.
        (1974) An analytical study of the composition of
        Roman coarse wares from the fort of Bryn y Gefeiliau
        (Caer Llugwy) in Snowdonia. Journal of archaeological
        science 1(1):47-67.

2846   Witthoft, J. and Wilkins, E. S. (1967) Petrographic
        studies: lateritic flints. MASCA newsletter 3:3-4.

2847   Wright, F. E. (1920) A petrographic description of the
        material of the Copan monuments. In: D. G. Morley,
        The inscriptions of Copan. Carnegie Institution of
        Washington publication 219, Appendix 1:463-464.

2848   Youngblood, E., et al. (1978) Celtic vitrified forts:
       implications of a chemical-petrological study of
       glasses and source rocks. Journal of archaeological
       science 5:99-121.

2. Metallography

2849   Andrews, J. and Celoria, F. (1976) A 19th-century
       smith's leg vice from Staffordshire, England, with
       a metallographic analysis of parts of its screw box.
       Science and archaeology 17:21-34.

2850   Barral, M. et al. (1979) Metallurgical study of
       Coriosolite coin. Archaeo-Physika 10:29-42.

2851   Betancourt, P. et al. (1978) Metallurgy at Gournia.
       MASCA journal 1:7-8.

2852   Birmingham, J., Kennon, N. F. and Malin, A. S. (1964)
       A "Luristan" dagger: an examination of ancient
       metallurgical techniques. Iraq 26(1):44-49.

2853   Boehne, C. (1964) Wie die alten Waffenschmiede die
       Bronzeschwerter härteten. (How the ancient weapon
       smith hardened the bronze sword). Metalloberfläche
       18:1313-1315.

2854   Brewer, C. W. (1976) Metallographic examination of six
       ancient steel weapons. Historical metallurgy 10:1-9.

2855   Brown, G. T. (1964) Roman bloom from Cranbrook, Kent.
       Journal of the iron and steel institute 202:502-504.

2856   Caneva, C. and Maurizio, M. (1973) Analisi chimiche e
       metallografiche sul Canopo da Dolciano. Studi
       etruschi 41:237-244.

2857   Carpenter, H. and Robinson, J. M. (1930) The metallog-
       raphy of some ancient Egyptian implements. Journal
       of the iron and steel institute 1:417-454.

2858   Condamin, J. and Picon, M. (1964) The influence of
       corrosion and diffusion on the percentage of silver
       in Roman denarii. Archaeometry 7:98-105.

2859 Cope, L. H. (1972) The metallurgical analysis of
      Roman Imperial silver and Aes coinage. Royal
      Numismatic Society special publication 8:3-47.

2860 Cope, L. H. (1973) The metallurgical examination of a
      debased silver coin of Maximus Daza issued by
      Constantine I. Archaeometry 15(2):221-228.

2861 Curtis, J. E. et al. (1979) Neo-Assyrian iron-working
      technology. Proceedings of the American philosophical
      society 123(6):369-390.

2862 Elam, C. F. (1931) An investigation of the microstruc-
      ture of fifteen silver Greek coins (500-300 B.C.) and
      some forgeries. Journal of the institute of metals
      45:57.

2863 Emmerling, J. (1967) Technologische Untersuchungen an
      dem Schwert von Horrweiler. (Technological inves-
      tigations on the sword from Horrweiler). Forschungen
      und Berichte der Staatlichen Museen zu Berlin
      8:120-123.

2864 Farnsworth, M., Smith, C. S. and Rodda, J. L. (1949)
      Metallographic examination of a sample of metallic
      zinc from ancient Athens. Hesperia, supplement 8:
      126-129.

2865 Fink, C. G. and Kopp, A. H. (1933) Ancient Egyptian
      antimony plating on copper objects. A rediscovered
      ancient Egyptian craft. Metropolitan Museum studies
      4:163-167.

2866 Fink, C. G. and Polushkin, E. P. (1936) Microscopic
      study of ancient bronze and copper. Transactions of
      the American institute of mining and metallurgical
      engineers 122:90-120.

2867 Fraikor, A. L., Hester, J. J. and Fraikor, F. J. (1971)
      Metallurgical analysis of a Hopewell copper earspool.
      American antiquity 36(3):358-361.

2868 France-Lanord, A. (1964) La fabrication des épées de
      fer gauloises. Revue d'histoire de la sidérurgie
      5:315-327.

2869   Frank, L. (1951) A metallographic study of certain pre-
       Columbian American implements. American antiquity
       17(1):57-60.

2870   Garland, H. and Bannister, C. O. (1927) Ancient
       Egyptian metallurgy. London: Ch. Griffin & Co.

2871   Gurin, M. F. (1980) Metallografičeskie issledovanija
       železnykh predmetov iz Abidni (Belorussija). (Metal-
       lographic investigations of iron objects from Abidni,
       Belorussian SSR). Sovetskaja arkheologija 4:251-259.

2872   Hanemann, H. (1921/1922) Metallographische Unter-
       suchung einiger altkeltischen Eisenfunde von der
       Steinburg. (Metallographic investigation of some
       Celtic iron finds from Steinburg). Prähistorische
       Zeitschrift 13/14:94-98.

2873   Hermelin, E., Tholander, E. and Blomgren, S. (1979) A
       prehistoric nickel-alloyed iron axe. Historical
       metallurgy 13(2):69-94.

2874   Klein, E. (1979) Chemical and mineralogical studies on
       Siphnos ores and slags. Archaeo-Physika 10:223-229.

2875   Knox, R. (1963) Detection of iron carbide structure in
       the oxide remains of ancient steel. Archaeometry
       6:43-45.

2876   Lang, J. and Williams, A. R. (1975) The hardening of
       iron swords. Journal of archaeological science
       2(3):199-207.

2877   Lefferts, K. C. (1964) Technical notes on another
       Luristan iron sword. American journal of archaeology
       68:59-62.

2878   Len'kov, V. D. (1979) K kharakteristike čugunnykh
       izdelyj čžurčžen'skikh remeslennikov XII-XIII vv.
       (The characteristics of cast iron artifacts of the
       Čžurčžen' artisans of the 12th-13th centuries A.D.).
       In: Drevnye kul'tury Sibiri i Tikhookeanskogo
       bassejna. Novosibirsk, 182-191.

2879   Leoni, M. (1955) Archeologia e metallografia. Sibrium
       2:25-42.

2880 McGrath, J. N. (1968) A preliminary report on the metallographic examination of four fragmentary early Iron Age sword blades from Llyn Cerrig Bach, Anglesey. Bulletin of the historical metallurgy group 2:78-80.

2881 Maddin, R., Wheeler, T. S. and Muhly, J. D. (1980) Distinguishing artifacts made of native copper. Journal of archaeological science 7(3):211-225.

2882 Maxwell-Hyslop, K. R. and Hodges, H. W. M. (1964) A note on the significance of the technique of casting-on as applied to a group of daggers from north-west Persia. Iraq 26(1):50-53.

2883 Maxwell-Hyslop, K. R. and Hodges, H. W. M. (1966) Three iron swords from Luristan. Iraq 28:164-176.

2884 Neumann, B. and Klemm, H. (1949) Metallographische Untersuchung von eisernen Dübeln und Klammern aus dem über 2000 J. Alten Artemis Tempel von Magnesia am Mäander. (Metallographic investigation of iron clamps and dowel pins from the over 2000 year-old Artemis temple at Magnesia on the Menderes River). Archiv für Metallkunde 3:333-335.

2885 Oddy, W. A. and Meeks, N. D. (1978) A Parthian bowl: study of the gilding technique. MASCA journal 1:5-6.

2886 Oddy, W. A., Padley, T. G. and Meeks, N. D. (1979) Some unusual techniques of gilding in antiquity. Archaeo-Physika 10:230-242.

2887 Panseri, C. (1953) Ricerche metallografiche sopra una spada da guerra del XII secola. Associazione Italiana di metallurgia, quaderno I. Milano.

2888 Panseri, C. (1957) Ricerche metallografiche sopra alcune lame Etrusche di accaio. Documenti e contributi per la storia della metallurgia 2:9-42.

2889 Panseri, C. and Leoni, M. (1957) Sulla tecnica di fabricazione degli specchi Etruschi. La metallurgia Italiana 4:233-241.

282

2890 Panseri, C. and Leoni, M. (1956/1957) Esame di specchi bronzei, ritrowati in sepolereti romani dell'alte Lombardia, del I e II secolo d. C. Sibrium (Varese) 3.

2891 Panseri, C. and Leoni, M. (1957) Sulla tecnica della fabbricazione degli specchi di bronzo etruschi. Studi etruschi 25:305-319.

2892 Picon, M., Boucher, S. and Condamin, J. (1966) Recherches techniques sur les bronzes de Gaule romaine. Gallia 24:189-215.

2893 Picon, M., Condamin, J. and Boucher, S. (1967) Recherches techniques sur les bronzes de Gaule romaine II. Gallia 25:153-168.

2894 Pobol', L. D. and Gurin, M. G. (1980) Metallo- grafičeskie issledovanija železnykh izdelyj iz Tajmanova Bykhovskogo rajona Belorusskoj SSR. (Metal- lographic investigations of iron objects from Tajmanovo, district of Bykhovo, Belorussian SSR). III Congrès international d'archéologie Slave. Bratislava, 2:340-358.

2895 Rapp, G. et al. (1978) Analyses of the metal artifacts. In: Excavations at Nichoria in southwest Greece. Minneapolis: Univ. of Minnesota Press, 1:166-181.

2896 Reggiori, A. and Garino, G. (1955) Esame tecnologico di un gruppo di spade galliche della Lombardia Nord- Occidentale. Sibrium (Varese) 2:43-55.

2897 Ryndina, N. V. (1962) Analizy metalličeskikh izdelyj iz Tripol'skogo sloja poselenija Nezvisko. (Analysis of metal objects from the Tripolye Culture level of the site Nezvisko). Materialy i issledovanija po arkheologii SSSR 102:86-88.

2898 Ryndina, N. V. (1963) Tekhnologija proizvodstva novgorodskikh juvelirov X-XV vv. (Technology of production of Novgorod jewelry of the 10th-15th centuries). Materialy i issledovanija po arkheologii SSSR 117:200-268.

2899 Ryndina, N. V. (1965) Metallografija v arkheologii. (Metallography in archaeology). Materialy i issledo- vanija po arkheologii SSSR 129:119-129.

2900 Schroeder, D. L. and Ruhl, K. C. (1968) Metallurgical characteristics of North American prehistoric copper work. American antiquity 33:162-169.

2901 Schweizer, F. and Meyers, P. (1978) Authenticity of ancient silver objects: a new approach. MASCA journal 1:9-10.

2902 Selimkhanov, I. R. and Torosjan, R. A. (1969) Metallografičeskij analiz drevnejšikh metallov v Zakavkaz'e. (Metallographic analysis of ancient metals in the Transcaucasus). Sovetskaja arkheologija 229-234.

2903 Smith, C. S. (1957) A metallographic examination of some Japanese sword blades. Symposium la tecnica di fabbricazione della lame di acciaio presso gli antichi. Milano, 43-68.

2904 Smith, C. S. (1960) A history of metallography. Chicago.

2905 Smith, C. S. (1965) The interpretation of micro-structures of metallic artifacts. In: W. J. Young, ed., The application of science in the examination of works of art. Boston: Museum of Fine Arts.

2906 Smith, C. S. (1966) Iron from the slitting mill at Saugus. Revue d'histoire de la sidérurgie 7:7-15.

2907 Smith, C. S. (1968) Metallographic study of early artifacts made from native copper. Actes du XIe congrès international d'histoire des sciences 4:237-252.

2908 Smith, C. S. (1973) Bronze technology in the east: a metallurgical study of early Thai bronzes. In: M. Teich and R. Young, Changing perspectives in the history of science. London, 21-32.

2909 Stanley, G. H. (1929) The composition of some pre-historic South African bronzes with notes on the methods of analysis. South African journal of science 26:44-49.

2910 Ternbach, J. (1964) Technical aspects of the Herzfeld bent iron dagger of Luristan. Studies in Iranian and Anatolian archaeology 18:46-51.

2911   Varoufakis, G. J. (1977) Chemical polishing of ancient
       bronzes. Archaeometry 19(2):219-221.

2912   Voznesenskaja, G. A. (1965) Stal'nye noži drevnego
       Ljubeča. (Metallogr. issledovanija). (Steel knives
       of ancient Ljubeč, metallographic investigations).
       Kratkie soobščenija Instituta arkheologii 104:
       145-149.

2913   Voznesenskaja, G. A. (1967) Metallografičeskoe
       issledovanie kuznečnykh izdelij iz ranneslavjanskikh
       pamjatnikov. (Metallographic investigations of
       black smiths' products from early Slavic sites).
       Kratkie soobščenija Instituta arkheologii 110:
       124-128.

2914   Voznesenskaja, G. A. (1970) Metallografičeskoe issle-
       dovanie kuznečnykh izdelij Troitskogo gorodišča.
       (Metallographic investigations of black smiths'
       products from the town of Troitskij). Materialy i
       issledovanija po arkheologii SSSR 156:192-199.

2915   Voznesenskaja, G. A. (1979) Tekhnika kuznetsnogo pro-
       izvodstva u vostočnykh Slavjan v VIII-X vv. (The
       technology of blacksmith production of the eastern
       Slavs in the 8th-10th centuries A.D.). Sovetskaja
       arkheologija 2:70-76.

2916   Williams, A. R. (1977) Roman arms and armour: a
       technical note. Journal of archaeological science.
       4(1):77-87.

2917   Williams, A. R. (1978) Seven swords of the
       Renaissance from an analytical point of view.
       Glaudius 14:97-127.

2918   Zinjakov, N. M. (1976) Tekhnologija proizvodstva
       železnykh predmetov Elikaevskoj kollektsij. (Tech-
       nology of iron objects of the Elikaev Collection).
       In: JUžnaja Sibir' v skifo-sarmatskuju épokhu.
       Kemerovo, 106-114.

3. Electron microscopy

2919   Anderson, P. C. (1980) A testimony of prehistoric
       tasks: diagnostic residues on stone tool working.
       World archaeology 12(2):181-194.

2920   Conolly, A. (1976) Use of the scanning electron micro-
        scope for the identification of seeds, with special
        reference to Saxifraga and Papaver. Folia quaternaria
        47:29-32.

2921   Dauvois, M. (1977) Stigmates d'usure présentés par des
        outils de silex ayant travaillé l'os: premiers
        résultats. In: Colloque internationaux du centre
        national de la recherche scientifique. Paris,
        568:275-292.

2922   Everhart, T. E. and Hayes, T. L. (1972) The scanning
        electron microscope. Scientific American 179:55-69.

2923   Fedje, D. (1979) Scanning electron microscopy analysis
        of use-striae. In: B. Hayden, ed., Lithic use-wear
        analysis. New York: Academic Press, 179-187.

2924   Flamini, A., Graziani, G. and Grubessi, O. (1975)
        Inorganic inclusions in amber. Archaeometry 17(1):
        110-112.

2925   Giovanoli, R. (1968) Roman wall painting studied by
        electron microscopy techniques. Fourth European
        regional conference on electron microscopy. Roma,
        327-328.

2926   Giovanoli, R. (1969) Provincial Roman wall painting in-
        vestigated by electron microscopy. Archaeometry 11:
        53-59.

2927   Gwinnett, A. J. (1979) Ancient lapidary. A study using
        scanning electron microscopy and functional analysis.
        Expedition 22(1):17-32.

2928   Hegde, K. T. M. (1966) Electron microscopic study on
        the Northern Black Polished Ware of India. Current
        science 95:623.

2929   Keepax, C. (1975) Scanning electron microscopy of wood
        replaced by iron corrosion products. Journal of
        archaeological science 2(2):145-150.

2930   Leeson, T. S. (1959) Electron microscopy and mummified
        material. Stain technology (Baltimore) 34:317-320.

2931   Lewin, P. (1967) Palaeo-electron microscopy of mummi-
        fied tissue. Nature 213:416-417.

286

2932 Macadam, R. F. (1969) The electron microscope in paleopathology. Medical history (London) 13:81-85.

2933 Maniatis, Y. and Tite, M. S. (1978) Ceramic technology in the Aegean world during the Bronze Age. In: Thera and the Aegean world. London: Thera and the Aegean World, 483-492.

2934 Maniatis, Y. and Tite, M. S. (1978/1979) Examination of Roman and medieval pottery using the scanning electron microscope. Acta praehistorica et archaeologica 9/10:125-130.

2935 Noll, W. (1977) Hallstattzeitliche Keramik der Heuneburg an der oberen Donau. (Hallstatt period ceramics of the Heuneburg on the upper Danube). Archäologie und Naturwissenschaften 1:1-19.

2936 Rottländer, R. (1975) The formation of patina on flint. Archaeometry 17(1):106-110.

2937 Sagne, S. (1978) The use of the scanning electron microscope with X-ray equipment for the analysis of elements in medieval bones. Ossa 5:85-91.

2938 Schweizer, F. and Meyers, P. (1979) A new approach to the authenticity of ancient silver objects: the discontinuous precipitation of copper from a silver-copper alloy. Archaeo-Physika 10:287-298.

2939 Tite, M. S. and Maniatis, Y. (1975) Examination of ancient pottery using the scanning electron microscope. Nature 257:122-123.

2940 Zwicker, U. and Goudarzloo, F. (1979) Investigation on the distribution of metallic elements in copper slag, copper matte and copper and comparison with samples from prehistoric smelting places. Archaeo-Physika 10:360-375.

C. Classical methods of analytical chemistry

2941 Barton-Wright, E. C., Booth, R. G. and Pringle, W. J. S. (1944) Analysis of barley from King Tutankhamen's tomb. Nature 153:288.

2942 Beeley, J. G. and Lunt, D. A. (1980) The nature of the biochemical changes in softened dentine from archaeological sites. Journal of archaeological science 7(4):371-377.

2943 Birstein, V. J. (1975) On the technology of Central Asian wall paintings: the problem of binding media. Studies in conservation 20(1):8-19.

2944 Bleck, R.-D. (1965) Zur Durchführung der Phospatmethode. (On the accomplishment of the phosphate method). Ausgrabungen und Funde 10(5):213-218.

2945 Bleck, R.-D. (1969) Phosphatanalytische Untersuchungen von der Hauptburg der Pfalz Tilleda. (Phosphate analysis of the Hauptburg of Pfalz Tilleda). Zeitschrift für Archäologie 3:118-121.

2946 Bleck, R.-D. (1976) Anwendungsmöglichkeiten phosphatanalytischer Untersuchungen im Bereich der Ur- und Frühgeschichte. (The possibilities of application of the phosphate method in the domain of prehistory and early history). Ausgrabungen und Funde 21(6):259-268.

2947 Broderick, M. (1979) Ascending paper chromatographic technique in archaeology. In: B. Hayden, ed., Lithic use-wear analysis. New York: Academic Press, 375-383.

2948 Brown, J. and Gould, R. A. (1964) Column chromatography and the possibility of carbon lens migration in archaeological sites. American antiquity 29(3):387-389.

2949 Caley, E. R. (1964) Analysis of ancient metals. New York: Macmillan.

2950 Condamin, J. et al. (1976) The application of gas chromatography to the tracing of oil in ancient amphorae. Archaeometry 18(2):195-201.

2951 Cook, S. F. (1964) The nature of charcoal excavated at archaeological sites. American antiquity 29(4):514-517.

288

2952 Danilevskij, V. V. (1935) O metodike issledovanija
      drevnikh bronz. (On the method of investigating
      ancient bronze). In: Metodika khimiko-analitičes-
      kogo issledovanija drevnikh bronz. Moskva-Leningrad:
      Gosudarstvennaja Akademija Istorii Material'noj
      Kul'tury, 11-21.

2953 Denninger, E. (1971) The use of paper chromatography
      to determine the age of albuminous binders and its
      application to rock paintings. Supplement to the
      South African journal of science, special issue no.
      2:81-84.

2954 Duma, G. (1968) Methode zum Feststellen der Bestimmung
      von urzeitlichen Gefässen. (Methods for establish-
      ment of determinations from prehistoric vessels).
      Acta archaeologica academiae scientiarum hungaricae
      20:359-372.

2955 Endt, D. W. von (1977) Amino-acid analysis of the
      contents of a vial excavated at Axum, Ethiopia.
      Journal of archaeological science 4:367-376.

2956 Farrington, J. W. and Quinn, J. G. (1971) Comparison
      of sampling and extraction techniques for fatty
      acids in recent sediments. Geochimica et cosmo-
      chimica acta 7:735-741.

2957 Gangl, J. (1939) Untersuchung der Fettreste an
      Gefässbruchstucken aus dem Bergbaugebiet Kelchalpe
      bei Kitzbühel, Tirol. (Investigation of the fat
      residue on vessel sherds from the mining area
      Kelchalpe near Kitzbuhel, Tirol). Mitteilungen der
      prähistorische Kommission (Wien) 3:154.

2958 Geilmann, W. (1956) Chemie und Vorgeschichtsforschung.
      (Chemistry and prehistoric research). Die
      Naturwissenschaften 37:97-102.

2959 Grüss, J. (1929) Das älteste Braugetreide. Teil I.
      (The oldest brewing grain. Part I). Allgemeine
      Brauer- und Hopfen-Zeitung 69:1615-1618.

2960 Grüss, J. (1930) Das älteste Braugetreide. Teil II.
      (The oldest brewing grain. Part II). Allgemeine
      Brauer- und Hopfen-Zeitung 70:113-115.

2961 Grüss, J. (1930) Inhaltsreste aus der vor- und
frühgeschichtlichen Zeit. (Content residues from
prehistoric and early historic periods). Der
Naturforscher 9:156.

2962 Grüss, J. (1932) Zucker aus der Urzeit. (Sugar from
prehistory). Deutsche Zuckerindustrie 57:1108-1110.

2963 Guščina, A. F. (1935) Metodika količestvennogo
opredelenija sur'my i olova v drevnikh bronzakh pri
minimal'nykh naveskakh. (Method of quantitative
determination of antimony and tin in ancient bronzes).
In: Metodika khimiko-analitičeskogo issledovanija
drevnikh bronz. Moskva-Leningrad: Gosudarstvennaja
Akademija Istorii Material'noj Kul'tury, 78-89.

2964 Havernick, E. (1967) Römischer Wein? (Roman wine?).
Acta archaeologica academiae scientiarum hungaricae
19:15-23.

2965 Heller, W. (1971) Ein Beitrag zur Untersuchung fossiler
Aminosäuren und Peptide aus Schwarzschiefern. (A
contribution to the investigation of fossil amino
acids and peptides from black shale). Angewandte
Chemie 83(22):906.

2966 Hofenk-de Graaff, J. H. (1974) A simple method for the
identification of indigo. Studies in conservation
19(1):54-55.

2967 Jakob, H. (1954) Zur Gebrauchsbestimmung von Grabhügel-
keramik mittels der Phosphatmethode. (Determining the
use of grave mound ceramics using the phosphate
method). Forschungen und Fortschritte 28:10-11.

2968 Jaky, M., Peredi, J. and Palos, L. (1964) Untersuchung
eines aus römischen Zeiten stammenden Fettprodukts.
(Investigation of fat products from the Roman period).
Fette, Seifen, Anstrichmittel 66:1012-1017.

2969 Kononov, V. N. (1935) Opyt instruktsii po khimičeskomu
kačestvennomu analizu metallov v drevnikh splavakh po
kapel'nomu metodu. (An instructional essay on
qualitative chemical analysis of metals in ancient
alloys by the capillary method). In: Metodika
khimiko-analitičeskogo issledovanija drevnikh bronz.
Moskva-Leningrad: Gosudarstvennaja Akademija Istorii
Material'noj Kul'tury, 22-64.

2970 Laptev, A. A. (1935) Mikroelektroanaliz drevnikh bronz (med' i svinets). (Microelectric analisis of ancient bronze; copper and lead). In: Metodika khimiko-analitičeskogo issledovanija drevnikh bronz. Moskva-Leningrad: Gosudarstvennaja Akademija Istorii Material'noj Kul'tury, 90-100.

2971 Leek, F. F. (1973) Further studies on ancient Egyptian bread. Journal of Egyptian archaeology 59:199-204.

2972 Lippmann, E. O. von (1938) Über vorgeschichtliche Zuckerfunde. (On prehistoric sugar finds). Deutsche Zuckerindustrie 63:511-513.

2973 Mills, J. S. (1966) The gas chromatographic examination of paint media. Part I. Fatty acid composition and identification of dried oil films. Studies in conservation 11:92-107.

2974 Mills, J. S. and White, R. (1975) The identification of paint media from the analysis of the sterol composition--a critical review. Studies in conservation 20(4):176-182.

2975 Morgan, E. D. et al. (1973) The transformation of fatty material buried in soil. Science and archaeology 10:9-10.

2976 Pätzold, W. (1957) Gedanken zur Zweckbestimmung von Kragenflaschen. (Thoughts on the use determination of collared jars). Germania 35:110-113.

2977 Paret, O. (1934) Wie steinzeitliche Speisereste untersucht werden. (How stone age food residues may be investigated). Kosmos 31:185.

2978 Petrenko, G. M. (1935) O metodike bystrogo analiza drevnikh bronz. (On the method of quick analysis of ancient bronzes). In: Metodika khimiko-analitičeskogo issledovanija drevnikh bronz. Moskva-Leningrad: Gosudarstvennaja Akademija Istorii Material'noj Kul'tury, 65-77.

2979 Rinuy, A. and Schweizer, F. (1979) Analysis of the white "ground" and ancient adhesives found on Canosa vases (south Italy) of the third century B.C. Archaeo-Physika 10:253-258.

2980 Ritchie, J. (1940/1941) A keg of 'bog-butter' from Skye and its contents. Proceedings of the society of antiquaries of Scotland 75:5-22.

2981 Rottländer, R. C. A. (1980) Zum Phosphatgehalt keramischer Scherben. (On the phosphate content of ceramic sherds). Archaeo-Physika 7:87-94.

2982 Rottländer, R. C. A. and Blume, M. (1980) Chemische Untersuchungen an Michelsberger Scherben. (Chemical investigations on Michelsberg sherds). Archaeo-Physika 7:71-86.

2983 Rottländer, R. C. A. and Schlichtherle, H. (1979) Food identification of samples from archaeological sites. Archaeo-Physika 10:260-267.

2984 Rottländer, R. C. A. and Schlichtherle, H. (1980) Gefässinhalte: eine kurz kommentierte Bibliographie. (Vessel contents: a briefly annotated bibliography). Archaeo-Physika 7:61-70.

2985 Salvi, C. (1950) Colophony from ancient amphoras. Pitture e vernici 6:104.

2986 Sauter, F. H. (1959) Lipoidanalysen für urgeschichtliche Zwecke. (Lipid analyses for the purposes of prehistory). Mitteilungen der österreichischen Arbeitsgemeinschaft für Ur- und Frühgeschichte 10:25-27.

2987 Sauter, F. H. and Rosmanith, K. (1965) Chemische Untersuchung des Inhalts eines awarischen Gefässes aus Traiskirchen, NÖ. (Chemical investigation of the contents of an Avar vessel from Traiskirchen, lower Austria). Archaeologia austriaca 37:1-6.

2988 Sauter, F. and Zak, J. (1963) Chemische Untersuchungen zur Frage der Schäftung eines Gravettien-Klingenkratzers. (Chemical investigations on the question of the handle of a Gravettian blade-scraper). Archaeologia austriaca 34:1-4.

2989 Schlede, J. (1972) Phosphatanalyse in der Gemarkung Bujendorf, Gemeinde Süsel, Kr. Ostholstein. (Phosphate analysis in the Bujendorf field, Süsel municipality, Ostholstein district). Offa 29:157.

292

2990 Seher, A. (1965) Untersuchung von Öl-Funden aus
      römischen Brandgräbern. (Investigation of oil finds
      from Roman burnt graves). Jahrbuch des Römisch-
      Germanischen Zentralmuseums Mainz 12:199-202.

2991 Stokar, W. von (1937) Mikroskop und Reagenzglas bei
      den Ausgrabungen. (Microscope and test tube with
      excavations). Nachrichtenblatt deutsche Vorzeit
      13:33-36.

2992 Stokar, W. von (1937) Über Fette, Fettsäuren und ihre
      Auswertung für die Vorgeschichte. (On fats, fatty
      acids and their utilization for prehistory). Mannus
      29:545-549.

2993 Stokar, W. von (1938) Prehistoric organic remains.
      Antiquity 12:82-86.

2994 Stokar, W. von (1939) Über die Untersuchung organischer
      Reste aus paläolithischen Kulturschichten. (On the
      investigation of organic residues from Palaeolithic
      cultural levels). Quartär 2:147-150.

2995 Stokar, W. von (1941) Von römischen Augenärzten II:
      eine römische gestempelte Augensalbe aus Köln 2. Die
      Bestandteile des Kollyriums. (From Roman eye
      doctors II: a Roman eye salve from Köln 2. The
      ingredients of the collyrium). Germania 25:26-30.

2996 Thornton, N. D., Morgan, E. D. and Celoria, F. S. C.
      (1970) The composition of bog butter. Science and
      archaeology 2/3:20-25.

2997 White, R. (1978) The application of gas-chromatography
      to the identification of waxes. Studies in
      conservation 23(2):57-68.

2998 Zeven, A. C., Doekes, G. J. and Kislev, M. (1975)
      Proteins in old grains of Triticum sp. Journal of
      archaeological science 2(3):209-313.

D. Physical methods of analytical chemistry

1. Structural analysis

   a) X-ray diffractometry (XRD)

2999 Arnold, D. E. (1972) Mineralogical analyses of ceramic materials from Quinua, Department of Ayacucho, Peru. Archaeometry 14(1):93-102.

3000 Barbieri, M. et al. (1974) Huntite, a mineral used in antiquity. Archaeometry 16(2):211-220.

3001 Bertet, G. A. (1973) Analisis por diffracion de rayos X de ceramicas ibericas valencianas. Servicio investigation prehistorica (Valencia) 45.

3002 Bimson, M. (1969) The examination of ceramics by X-ray powder diffraction. Studies in conservation 14:83-89.

3003 Francaviglia, V., Minardi, M. E. and Palmieri, A. (1975) Comparative study of various samples of Etruscan bucchero by X-ray diffraction, X-ray spectrometry, and thermoanalysis. Archaeometry 17(2): 223-231.

3004 Frondel, J. W. (1967) X-ray diffraction study of some fossil and modern resins. Science 155(3768):1411-3.

3005 Guinea, M. and Galván, J. (1979) Relaciones comerciales en Esmeraldas comos resultado del análisis de las cerámicas por difracción de rayos X y microscopía electrónica. 42nd International congress of Americanists (1976). Paris, 9A:259-272.

3006 Isphording, W. C. (1974) Combined thermal and X-ray diffraction technique for identification of ceramicware temper and paste minerals. American antiquity 39:477-483.

3007 Kohl, P. L., Harbottle, G. and Sayre, E. V. (1979) Physical and chemical analyses of soft stone vessels from southwest Asia. Archaeometry 21(2):131-159.

3008 Kojic-Prodic, B. (1976) X-ray identification of some pigments on the Istra (Yugoslavia) frescoes. Journal of applied crystallography 9(6):485-490.

3009 Lahanier, C. (1970) La radio-cristallographie et l'analyse par spectrometrie de fluorescence X appliquées à la connaissance des objets de musée. Laboratoire de Recherche de Musées de France. Annales (Paris) 47-66.

3010 Maggetti, M. and Küpfer, T. (1978) Composition of the Terra Sigillata from La Péniche (Vidy/Lausanne, Switzerland). Archaeometry 20(2):183-188.

3011 Ostergård, M. (1980) X-ray diffractometer investigations of bones from domestic and wild animals. American antiquity 45(1):59-63.

3012 Noll, W., Holm, R. and Born, L. (1975) Painting of ancient ceramics. Angewandte Chemie (international edition) 14(9):602-613.

3013 Perinet, G. (1960) Contribution de la diffraction des rayons X à l'évaluation de la température de cuisson d'une céramique. Transactions of the 7th international ceram. congress 371-376.

3014 Riederer, J. (1974) Recently identified Egyptian pigments. Archaeometry 16(1):102-109.

3015 Saleh, S. A., George, A. W. and Helmi, F. M. (1972) Study of glass and glass-making processes at Wadi el-Natrun, Egypt in the Roman period 30 B.C. to 359 A.D.; Part I: fritting crucibles, their technical features and temperature employed. Studies in conservation 17(4):143-172.

3016 Stos-Fertner, Z., Hedges, R. E. M. and Evely, R. D. G. (1979) The application of the XRF-XRD method to the analysis of the pigments of Minoan painted pottery. Archaeometry 21(2):187-194.

3017 Tanabe, G. and Watanabe, N. (1968) Dating fossil bones from Japan by means of X-ray diffraction pattern. Journal of the faculty of science, University of Tokyo 3:199-216.

3018   Valle, F. J., Moya, J. S. and Cendrero, A. (1979)
       Montmorillonite: a cause of deterioration of rock
       paintings at Altamiro Cave. MASCA journal 1(2):36-38.

3019   Weymouth, J. W. and Mandeville, M. (1975) An X-ray
       diffraction study of heat-treated chert and its
       archaeological implications. Archaeometry 17(1):
       61-67.

       b) Infrared spectrophotometry (IRS)

3020   Beck, C. W. (1964) Determination of the provenance of
       archaeological amber by chemical analysis. Yearbook
       of the American philosophical society 241-243.

3021   Beck, C. W. (1965) Origin of the amber found at Gough's
       Cave, Cheddar, Somerset. Proceedings of the Univer-
       sity of Bristol spelaeological society 10(3):272-276.

3022   Beck, C. W. (1966) Determination of the provenience of
       amber by infrared spectrophotometry. American journal
       of archaeology 70:183.

3023   Beck, C. W. (1966) Analysis and provenience of Minoan
       and Mycenaean amber I. Greek, Roman and Byzantine
       studies 7:191-211.

3024   Beck, C. W. et al. (1978) The chemical identification
       of Baltic amber at the Celtic oppidum Staré
       Hradisko in Moravia. Journal of archaeological
       science 5:343-354.

3025   Beck, C. W. et al. (1965) Infrared spectra of amber
       and the identification of Baltic amber. Archaeometry
       8:96-109.

3026   Beck, C. W. and Liu, T. (1973) Provenance analysis of
       Yugoslavian amber artifacts. Zbornik Narodnog
       Muzeja 7:132-142.

3027   Beck, C. W., Southard, G. C. and Adams, A. B. (1972)
       Analysis and provenience of Minoan and Mycenaean
       amber, IV. Mycenae. Greek, Roman and Byzantine
       studies 13:359-385.

3028 Beck, C. W., Wilbur, E. and Meret, S. (1964) Infra-red
      spectra and the origin of amber. Nature 201(4916):
      256-257.

3029 De Barras e Vasconcelos, M., Cailliez, A. and
      Toussaint, A. (1967) Application de la spectro-
      photométrie dans l'infra-rouge à l'analyse des
      pigments minéraux. Chimie des peintures 30:357-367.

3030 Kühn, H. (1960) Detection and identification of waxes,
      including Punic wax, by infra-red spectrography.
      Studies in conservation 5:71-81.

3031 Langenheim, J. and Beck, C. W. (1965) Infrared spectra
      as a means of determining botanical sources of
      amber. Science 149:52-55.

3032 Low, M. J. D. and Baer, N. S. (1977) Application of
      infra-red Fourier transform spectroscopy to problems
      in conservation. Studies in conservation 22(3):116-
      128.

3033 Reindell, I. and Riederer, J. (1978) Infrarotspektral-
      analytische Untersuchungen von Farberden aus
      persischen Ausgrabungen. (Infrared spectral analysis
      of dyes from Iranian excavations). Berliner Beiträge
      zur Archäometrie 3:123-134.

3034 Riederer, J. (1977) Die Bemalung des Aphaia-Tempels
      auf Ägina. (The painting of the Aphaia temple on
      Aegina). Berliner Beiträge zur Archäometrie 2:67-72.

3035 Rottländer, R. C. A. (1970) On the formation of amber
      from Pinus resin. Archaeometry 12(1):35-51.

3036 Sismayer, B. et al. (1975) Application of infrared
      spectroscopy to the examination of mineral pigments
      of historical works of art in comparison with recent
      European deposits. Fresenius' Zeitschrift für
      analytische Chemie 277:193.

3037 Stevenson, F. J. and Goh, K. M. (1971) Infrared spectra
      of humic acids and related substances. Geochimica et
      cosmochimica acta 35(5):471-483.

3038 Van't Hul-Ehrnreich, E. H. (1970) Infrared micro-
      spectroscopy for the analysis of old painting
      materials. Studies in conservation 15:175-182.

c) Mössbauer spectrometry

3039 Aburto, S. et al. (1979) Mössbauer studies of ancient Mexican pottery. Archaeo-Physika 10:1-7.

3040 Bajot-Stoabants, J. and Bodart, F. (1977) Ancient pottery analysis by proton bombardment and Mössbauer spectroscopy. Nuclear instrumental methods 142:293.

3041 Bakas, T., Gangas, N. H. J. and Sigalas, I. (1980) Mössbauer study of Glozel tablet 198 bl. Archaeometry 22(1):69-80.

3042 Bouchez, R. et al. (1974) Mössbauer study of firing conditions used in the manufacture of the grey and redware of Tureng-Tepe. Journal de physique (Paris), 35, colloque 6:541-546.

3043 Coey, J. M. D. and Bouchez, R. (1979) Characterisation of early Bronze Age potsherds from Iran and Pakistan by magnetic properties of the iron they contain. Archaeo-Physika 10:97.

3044 Cousins, D. R. and Dharmawardena, K. G. (1969) Use of Mössbauer spectroscopy in the study of ancient pottery. Nature 223:732-733.

3045 Danon, J. et al. (1976) Mössbauer study of aging effects in ancient pottery from the mouth of the Amazon River. Journal de physique, colloque 6:866.

3046 Eissa, N. A. and Sallam, H. A. (1973) Mössbauer effect study of ancient Egyptian pottery. Acta phys. acad. sci. (Hungary) 34:337.

3047 Gangas, N. H. J. et al. (1971) Mössbauer spectroscopy of ancient Greek pottery. Nature 229(5285):485-486.

3048 Gangas, N. H. J., Sigalas, I. and Moukarika, A. (1976) Is the history of ancient pottery ware correlated with its Mössbauer spectrum? Journal de physique (Paris) colloque 6:867.

3049 Hess, J. and Perlman, I. (1974) Mössbauer spectra of iron in ceramics and their relation to pottery colours. Archaeometry 16(2):137-152.

3050 Janot, C. and Delcroix, P. (1974) Caractérisation de
      matériaux archéologiques par spectrométrie Mössbauer.
      Centre de recherches archéologiques, Paris. Notes et
      monographies techniques, no. 4.

3051 Janot, C. and Delcroix, P. (1974) Mössbauer study of
      ancient French ceramics. Journal de physique (Paris)
      35, colloque 6:557-561.

3052 Keisch, B. (1973) Mössbauer effect studies in the fine
      arts. Archaeometry 15(1):79-104.

3053 Keisch, B. (1976) Analysis of works of art. In: R. L.
      Cohen, ed., Applications of Mössbauer spectroscopy.
      New York: Academic Press, 1:263.

3054 Kostikas, A., Simopoulos, A. and Gangas, N. H. J.
      (1976) Analysis of archaeological artifacts. In:
      R. L. Cohen, ed., Applications of Mössbauer spectros-
      copy. New York: Academic Press, 1:241.

3055 Longworth, G. and Tite, M. S. (1977) Mössbauer and
      magnetic susceptibility studies of iron oxides in
      soils from archaeological sites. Archaeometry
      19(1):3-14.

3056 Longworth, G. and Warren, S. E. (1979) The application
      of Mössbauer spectroscopy to the characterisation of
      western Mediterranean obsidian. Journal of
      archaeological science 6(2):179-193.

3057 Manning, P. G. (1975) On the origin of grey and black
      'colours' of ancient pottery: role of Fe and Ti^{4+}
      ions. Archaeometry 17(2):233-235.

3058 Takeda, M., Mabuchi, H. and Tominaga, T. (1977) A
      tin-119 Mössbauer study of Chinese bronze coins.
      Radiochem. Radioanal. Letters 29:191.

3059 Tominaga, T. et al. (1977) A Mössbauer study of ancient
      Japanese artifacts. Radiochem. Radioanal. Letters
      28:221.

3060 Tominaga, T. et al. (1978) Characterization of ancient
      Japanese roofing tiles by Fe-56 Mössbauer spectros-
      copy. Archaeometry 20(2):135-146.

2. Elemental analysis

a) Optical emission spectrometry (OES)

3061 Baistrocchi, R. (1952) Ricerche spettrochimiche orientative su bronzi antichi Italiani. Spectrochimica acta 5:24-29.

3062 Bartseva, T. B. (1980) O khimičeskom sostave uzdečnykh naborov, najdennykh v Posul'skikh kurganakh. (The chemical analysis of bridle trappings, found in the Sula River tumuli). Kratkie soobščenija Instituta Arkheologii 162:28-31.

3063 Bartseva, T. B. and Černykh, E. N. (1968) O spektroanalitičeskikh issledovanijakh tsvetnogo metalla černjakhovskoj kul'tury. (On the spectral analysis of non-ferrous metal of the Černjakhov culture). Sovetskaja arkheologija 2:93-102.

3064 Bezborodov, M. A. (1965) Tekhničeskie metody izučenija drevnikh stekol. (Technical methods for the study of ancient glass). Materialy i issledovanija po arkheologii SSSR 129:174-177.

3065 Boesterd, M. H. P. den and Hoekstra, E. (1965) Spectrochemical analysis of Roman bronze vessels. Oudheidkundige mededelingen (Leiden) 46:100-127.

3066 Boomert, A. (1975) A contribution to the classification of spectrographic analyses of prehistoric metal objects. Helinium 15:134-161.

3067 Brandenstein, M. and Schroll, E. (1958) Spektralanalytische Untersuchungen von Bleifunden aus Kärntner Ausgrabungen. (Spectral analytical investigations of lead finds from the Kärntner excavations). Archaeologia austriaca 3:116-120.

3068 Britton, D. (1961) A study of the composition of Wessex culture bronzes. Archaeometry 4:39-52.

3069 Brown, M. A. and Blin-Stoyle, A. E. (1959) A sample analysis of British middle and late Bronze Age material, using optical spectrometry. Proceedings of the prehistoric society 25:188-208.

3070 Butler, J. J. and Waals, J. D. van der (1964) Metal analysis, SAM I, and European prehistory. A review article. Helinium 4:1-39.

3071 Cann, J. R. and Renfrew, C. (1964) The characterization of obsidian and its application to the Mediterranean region. Proceedings of the prehistoric society 33:111-133.

3072 Catling, H. W. (1963) Minoan and Mycenaean pottery: composition and provenance. Archaeometry 6:1-9.

3073 Catling, H. W. and Millett, A. (1965) A study of the composition patterns of Mycenaean pictorial pottery from Cyprus. Annual of the British School at Athens 60:212-224.

3074 Catling, H. W. and Millett, A. (1965) A study of the inscribed stirrup jars from Thebes. Archaeometry 8:3-85.

3075 Catling, H. W. and Millett, A. (1966) Composition and provenance: a challenge. Archaeometry 9:92-97.

3076 Catling, H. W. and Millett, A. (1967) Composition patterns of Minoan and Mycenaean pottery: survey and prospects. Archaeometry 10:70-77.

3077 Catling, H. W. and Millett, A. (1969) Theban stirrup-jars: questions and answers. Archaeometry 11:3-20.

3078 Catling, H. W., Blin-Stoyle, A. E. and Richards, E. E. (1961) Spectrographic analysis of Mycenaean and Minoan pottery. Archaeometry 4:31-38.

3079 Catling, H. W., Richards, E. E. and Blin-Stoyle, A. E. (1963) Correlations between composition and provenance of Mycenaean and Minoan pottery. Annual of the British School at Athens 58:94-115.

3080 Černykh, E. N. (1963) Issledovanija sostava mednykh i bronzovykh izdelij metodom spektral'nogo analiza. (Investigations of the composition of copper and bronze objects by the method of spectroscopic analysis). Sovetskaja arkheologija 3:145-156.

3081 Černykh, E. N. (1963) Spektral'nye issledovanija
metalličeskikh izdelij iz mogil'nika Gatyn-Kale.
(Spectroscopic investigations of metal objects from
the Gatyn-Kale burial mound). In: Drevnosti
Čečeno-Inguŝetii. Moskva: Akademija Nauk, 136-137.

3082 Černykh, E. N. (1963) Spektral'nye issledovanija
mednykh izdelij iz mogil'nikov balanovskogo i
fat'janovskogo tipov. (Spectroscopic investigations
of copper objects from burial mounds of the
Balanovo and Fat'janovo types). In: O. N. Bader,
ed., Balanovskij mogil'nik. Moskva: Akademija Nauk,
363-369.

3083 Černykh, E. N. (1965) O nekotorykh metodakh ustanovlenija rudnykh istočnikov dlja drevnejŝego metalla.
(On some methods for establishing mining sources for
ancient metals). Izvestija Akademii Nauk Armjanskoj
SSR (Erevan) 18(3/4):111-126.

3084 Černykh, E. N. (1965) Rezul'taty izučenija khimičeskogo sostava metalla Bessarabskogo klada. (Results
of a study of chemical composition of metal from the
Bessarabian hoard). Sovetskaja arkheologija 1:270-
272.

3085 Černykh, E. N. (1965) Spektral'nyj analiz i izučenie
drevnejŝej metallurgii Vostočnoj Evropy. (Spectroscopic analyses and the study of ancient metallurgy
of Eastern Europe). Materialy i issledovanija po
arkheologii SSSR 129:96-110.

3086 Černykh, E. N. (1966) K khimičeskoj kharakteristike
metalla Ingul'skogo klada. (On the chemical characterization of metal from the Ingul' hoard).
Sovetskaja arkheologija 1:143-154.

3087 Černykh, E. N. (1966) Metody obrabotki dannykh
khimičeskogo sostava metalla. (Methods of processing
data of chemical composition of metal). Materialy i
issledovanija po arkheologii SSSR 132:8-26.

3088 Černykh, E. N. (1966) O khimičeskom sostave metalla
klada iz Sosnovoj Mazy. (On the chemical composition
of metal from the Sosnovaja Maza hoard). Kratkie
soobŝčenija Instituta Arkheologii 108:123-131.

3089 Černykh, E. N. (1966) Pervye spektral'nye issledovanija
medi dnepro-donetskoj kul'tury. (The first spectroscopic investigations of copper of the Dnepr-Donets
culture). Kratkie soobščenija Instituta Arkheologii
106:66-68.

3090 Černykh, E. N. (1978) Aibunar--a Balkan copper mine of
the fourth millennium B.C. Proceedings of the
prehistoric society 44:203-217.

3091 Černykh, E. N. (1978) Gornoe delo i metallurgija v
drevnejšej Bolgarii. (Mining and metallurgy in
ancient Bulgaria). Sofija: Akademija na Naukite.

3092 Černykh, E. N. (1980) O khimičeskom sostave metalla
Tamanskogo klada. (On the chemical composition of
metal from the Taman hoard). Sovetskaja arkheologija
2:152.

3093 Černykh, E. N. (1980) Klad iz Konstantsy i voprosy
Balkano-Kavkazskikh svjazej v epokhu pozdnej bronzy.
(The hoard from Constanţa and the questions of Balkan
and Caucasian connections in the late Bronze Age).
Sovetskaja arkheologija 4:19-26.

3094 Charil, P. and Michel, F. (1972) Analyse quantitative
de bronzes antiques par spectrométrie d'émission à
lecture directe. Laboratoire de Recherche de Musées
de France. Annales 23-33.

3095 Condamin, J. and Picon, M. (1965) Notes on diffusion in
ancient alloys. Archaeometry 8:110-114.

3096 Conforto, L. et al. (1975) A preliminary evaluation of
chemical data (trace element) from Classical marble
quarries in the Mediterranean. Archaeometry 17(2):
201-213.

3097 Cremascoli, R. (1955) Esami spettografici di monete
d'argento romane e degli argenti di Ornavasso.
Sibrium 2:31-34.

3098 Doorselaer, M. van (1951) Une microméthode pour
l'analyse quantitative de bronzes archéologiques par
voie spectrographique. Mikrochemie 36/37:513-521.

3099   Dougherty, R. C. and Caldwell, J. R. (1966) Evidence of
       early pyrometallurgy in the Kerman range in Iran.
       Science 153(3739):984-985.

3100   Drews, G. (1979) Chromium, nickel and vanadium in
       Neolithic sherds and related clays. Archaeo-Physika
       10:98-100.

3101   Farnsworth, M. and Ritchi, P. (1937) Spectrographic
       studies on ancient glass: Chinese glass from pre-Han
       to T'ang times. Technical studies in the field of the
       fine arts 5(4):209-220.

3102   Feustel, R. et al. (1966) Beiträge zur Kultur und
       Anthropologie der mitteldeutschen Schnurkeramiker.
       (Contributions to the culture and anthropology of
       the central German Corded Ware culture). Alt-
       Thüringen 8:20-170.

3103   Green, R. C., Brooks, R. R. and Reeves, R. D. (1967)
       Characterization of New Zealand obsidians by emission
       spectroscopy. New Zealand journal of science 10(3):
       675-682.

3104   Härke, H. (1978) Probleme der optischen Emissions-
       spektralanalyse in der Urgeschichtsforschung.
       Technische Möglichkeiten und methodische Frage-
       stellungen. (Problems with optical emission spectral
       analyses in prehistoric research. Technical
       possibilities and methodological questions).
       Prähistorische Zeitschrift 58(2):165-276.

3105   Hahn-Weinheimer, P. (1954) Über spektrochemische
       Untersuchungen an römischen Fenstergläsern. (On
       spectrographic investigations of Roman window glass).
       Glastechnik (Berlin) 12:459-466.

3106   Hartley, K. F. and Richards, E. E. (1965) Spectro-
       graphic analysis of some Romano-British mortaria.
       Bulletin of the Institute of Archaeology, 5.

3107   Hartmann, A. (1964) Spektralanalytische Untersuchungen
       der Goldschalen aus dem Kom. Bihar. (Spectrographic
       investigations on the gold bowl from the province of
       Bihar). Mitteilungen der anthropologischen Gesell-
       schaft in Wien 93/94:112-114.

304

3108 Hartmann, A. (1965) Einige Ergebnisse der spektro-
      chemischen Analyse von irischen Goldfunden. (A few
      results on the spectro-chemical analyses of Irish
      gold objects). Celticum (Supplément à Ogam-Tradition
      celtique 98) 12:27-44. Rennes.

3109 Hartmann, A. (1968) Über die spektralanalytische Unter-
      suchung einiger Goldfunde aus dem Donauraum. (On the
      spectral analytical investigation of a few gold
      finds from the Danube region). Berichte der Römisch-
      Germanischen Kommission 46/47:63-73.

3110 Hartmann, A. (1969) Spektralanalytische Untersuchungen
      bronzezeitlicher Goldfunde des Donauraumes. (Spectral
      analytical investigations of Bronze Age gold finds
      of the Danube region). Germania 46:19-27.

3111 Hartmann, A. (1970) Prähistorische Goldfunde aus
      Europa. (Prehistoric gold finds from Europe).
      Studien zu den Anfängen der Metallurgie, vol. 3.
      Berlin: Mann.

3112 Hartmann, A. (1970) Über die spektralanalytische
      Untersuchung bronzezeitlicher Goldfunde des Donau-
      raumes. (On the spectral analytical investigation of
      Bronze Age gold finds of the Danube region). Actes
      du VIIe congrès des sciences préhistoriques et proto-
      historiques. Prague, 1:64-66.

3113 Hartmann, A. (1976) Ergebnisse spektralanalytischer
      Untersuchungen an keltischen Goldmunzen aus Hessen
      und Süddeutschland. (Results of spectroscopic inves-
      tigations on Celtic gold coins from Hessen and
      southern Germany). Germania 54:102-134.

3114 Hartmann, A. (1978) Ergebnisse spektralanalytischer
      Untersuchungen an späthallstattzeitlichen und
      latènezeitlichen Goldfunde von Dürrnberg, aus Süd-
      westdeutschland, Frankreich und der Schweiz. (Results
      of spectroscopic analysis of late Hallstatt and La
      Tène gold objects from southwest Germany, France
      and Switzerland). In: Der Dürrnberg bei Hallein III.
      Münchner Beiträge zur Vor- und Frühgeschichte 18(2):
      601-617.

3115 Hartmann, A. (1978) Ergebnisse der spektralanalytischen Untersuchung äneolithischer Goldfunde aus Bulgarien. (Results of spectroscopic investigation of Eneolithic gold finds from Bulgaria). Studia praehistorica (Sofija) 1/2:27-45.

3116 Hartmann, A. (1978) Die Goldsorten des Äneolithikums und der Frühbronzezeit im Donauraum. (The gold types of the Eneolithic and the early Bronze Age in the Danube region). Studia praehistorica (Sofija) 1/2:182-191.

3117 Hartmann, A. and Sangmeister, E. (1972) Zur Erforschung urgeschichtlicher Metallurgie. Angewandte Chemie 84(14):668-678. (English version: The study of pre-historic metallurgy. Angewandte Chemie, international edition, 11(7):620-629.)

3118 Hawkes, C. F. C. (1962) Analysis by optical spec-trometry. Atti del VI congresso internazionale delle scienze preistoriche e protoistoriche. Firenze, 1:33-54.

3119 Hennessy, J. B. and Millett, A. (1963) Spectrographic analysis of the foreign pottery from the royal tombs of Abydos and early Bronze Age pottery of Palestine. Archaeometry 6:10-17.

3120 Hill, W. E. and Neumann, R. W. (1966) Copper artifacts from prehistoric archeological sites in the Dakotas. Science 154:1171-1173.

3121 Hülle, W. (1933) Spektralanalyse im Dienst der Vor-geschichtsforschung. (Spectral analyses in the service of prehistoric research). Nachrichtenblatt für deutsche Vorzeit 9(6):84-86.

3122 Jolowicz, R. V. (1959) Spectrographic analysis of bronzes by a solution method. Archaeometry, supplement, 2:18-24.

3123 Jones, R. E. and Rutter, J. B. (1977) Resident Minoan potters on the Greek mainland? Pottery composition analyses from Ayios Stephanos. Archaeometry 19(2): 211-219.

3124 Junghans, S. (1969) Stuttgarter Bericht über den Fortgang spektralanalytischer Untersuchungen an Kupfer-
und Goldgegenständen der frühen Metallzeit Europas.
(Stuttgart report on the progress of spectrographic
investigations on copper and gold objects of the
early metal period of Europe). Germania 46:1-4.

3125 Junghans, S. and Sangmeister, E. (1957) Bericht über
den Fortgang spektralanalytischer Untersuchungen an
kupferzeitlichen und frühbronzezeitlichen Bodenfunden
Europas. (Report on the progress of spectrographic
investigations on Copper Age and early Bronze Age
finds from Europe). Germania 35:11-18.

3126 Junghans, S., Sangmeister, E. and Schröder, M. (1960)
Metallanalysen kupferzeitlicher und frühbronzezeit-
licher Bodenfunde aus Europa. (Metal analyses of
Copper Age and early Bronze Age finds from Europe).
Studien zu den Anfängen der Metallurgie, vol. I.
Berlin.

3127 Junghans, S., Sangmeister, E. and Schröder, M. (1968)
Kupfer und Bronze in der frühen Metallzeit Europas.
(Copper and bronze in the early metal period of
Europe). Studien zu den Anfängen der Metallurgie,
vol. 2(1-3). Berlin.

3128 Junghans, S., Sangmeister, E. and Schröder, M. (1974)
Kupfer und Bronze in der frühen Metallzeit Europas.
Katalog der Analysen Nr. 10041-22000 (mit Nach-
untersuchungen der Analysen Nr. 1-10040). (Copper and
bronze in the early metal period of Europe. Catalogue
of analyses nos. 10041-22000, with subsequent investigations of analyses nos. 1-10040). Studien zu den
Anfängen der Metallurgie, vol. 2(4). Berlin.

3129 Junghans, S. and Scheufele, E. (1951) Zur Frage spektralanalytischer Untersuchungen an prähistorischen
Metallgegenständen. (On the question of spectrographic investigations on prehistoric metal objects).
Germania 29:184-186.

3130 Key, C. A. (1963) The trace-element content of the
artifacts of the Kfar Monash hoard. Israel
exploration journal 13(4):289-290.

3131 Leonard, A. G. G. and Whelan, P. F. (1929) Spectro-
       graphic analyses of Irish ring-money. Scientific
       proceedings of the Royal Dublin Society 19:55.

3132 Lins, P. A. and Oddy, W. A. (1975) The origins of
       mercury gilding. Journal of archaeological science
       2(4):365-373.

3133 Maréchal, J.-R. (1956) L'application de la spectro-
       graphie à l'étude des origines de la métallurgie.
       Revue des sociétés savantes de Haute-Normandie
       (Rouen) 2:31-39.

3134 Maréchal, J.-R. (1959) Etat actuel des analyses spec-
       trographiques des objets protohistoriques en cuivre
       et en bronze. Revue des sociétés savantes de Haute-
       Normandie (Rouen) 14:19-31.

3135 Maréchal, J.-R. (1954) Application des méthodes spec-
       trographiques à l'étude d'alliages anciens. XVIIe
       Congrès du groupement pour l'avancement des méthodes
       d'analyses spectrographiques des produits
       métallurgiques. Paris, 347-385.

3136 Maréchal, J.-R. (1968) Etat actuel des recherches sur
       la corrélation entre la paragenèse des gisements
       miniers et de la composition des objets préhis-
       toriques en métal par les méthodes chimiques et spec-
       trographiques. Actes du 91e congrès national des
       sociétés savantes. Rennes (1966), 293-324.

3137 Millett, A., Pritchard, J. B. and Ralph, E. K. (1964) A
       spectrographic investigation of jar handles bearing
       the 'royal' stamp of Judah. Archaeometry 7:67-71.

3138 Mitričev, V. S. (1965) Spektral'nyj analiz keramiki.
       (Spectral analysis of ceramics). Materialy i issledo-
       vanija po arkheologii SSSR 129:171-174.

3139 Moorey, P. R. S. (1964) An interim report on some
       analyses of 'Luristan bronzes'. Archaeometry 7:72-80.

3140 Musty, J. W. G. and Thomas, L. C. (1962) The spectro-
       graphic examination of English and Continental
       medieval glazed pottery. Archaeometry 5:38-52.

3141 Naumov, D. V. (1961) Metod količestvennogo spektral'nogo analiza splavov na mednoj osnove primenitel'no k issledovanniju arkheologičeskikh predmetov. (Method of quantitative spectrographic analysis of alloys of copper on the basis of the application to investigating archaeological objects). Sovetskaja arkheologija 3:113-121.

3142 Naumov, D. V. (1967) Khimičeskoe i strukturnoe issledovanie nekotorykh predmetov iz Polotska XII-XIII vv. (Chemical and structural investigations of some objects from Polotsok of the 12th-13th centuries A.D.). In: Belorusskie drevnosti. Minsk, 298-306.

3143 Neuninger, H. (1962) Zur Frage der Koordinierung verschiedener spektralanalytischer Untersuchungsmethoden in der Urgeschichtsforschung. (On the question of coordinating different spectrographic analytical methods in prehistoric research). Archaeologia austriaca 31:103-107.

3144 Neuninger, H. (1976) Spektralanalytische Untersuchung eines Tüllenmeissels aus Feistritz, Kärnten. (Spectrographic investigation of a socketed chisel from Feistritz, Kärnten). Archaeologia austriaca 59/60:441-443.

3145 Neuninger, H. and Pittioni, R. (1959) Die spektrographische Untersuchung des Helmes vom Pass Lueg. (The spectrographic investigation of a helmet from the Pass Lueg). Jahresschrift des Salzburger Museums Carolino-Augusteum, 21-31.

3146 Neuninger, H. and Pittioni, R. (1962) Bemerkungen über zwei Methoden der spektralanalytischen Untersuchung urzeitlicher Kupfer- und Bronzeobjekte. (Remarks on two methods of spectrographic investigation of prehistoric copper and bronze objects). Archaeologia austriaca 31:96-102.

3147 Neuninger, H. and Pittioni, R. (1964) Das Kupfer der Ossarner Metallgeräte. (The copper of the Ossarn metal objects). Archaeologia austriaca 35:96-97.

3148 Neuninger, H. and Pittioni, R. (1966) Spektrographische Untersuchungen von urnenfelderzeitlichen Hortfunden der Steiermark. (Spectrographic analysis of Urnfield period hoard finds of Styria). Archaeologia austriaca 39:81-86.

3149 Otto, H. (1941) Die Anwendung der Spektralanalyse für kulturhistorische Fragen. (The application of spectrographic analysis for cultural-historical questions). Spectrochimica acta 1(5):381-399.

3150 Otto, H. (1953) Analyse der Metallbeigaben aus schnurkeramischen Gräbern von Niederkaina, Kreis Bautzen. (Analysis of metals from Corded Ware graves from Niederkaina, Bautzen district). Arbeits- und Forschungsberichte zur sächsischen Bodendenkmalpflege 3:40-47.

3151 Otto, H. (1958) Neue Metallanalysen von frühbronzezeitlichen "Bronzen" aus mitteldeutschen Hortfunden. (New metal analyses of early Bronze Age "bronzes" from central German hoard finds). Jahresschrift für Mitteldeutsche Vorgeschichte 41/42:315-329.

3152 Patay, P. et al. (1963) Spektrographische und metallographische Untersuchungen kupfer- und frühbronzezeitlicher Funde. (Spectrographic and metallographic investigations of Copper Age and early Bronze Age finds). Acta archaeologica academiae scientiarum hungaricae 15:37-64.

3153 Payne, J. C. (1966) Spectrographic analysis of some Egyptian pottery of the Eighteenth Dynasty. Journal of Egyptian archaeology 52:176-178.

3154 Piccardi, G. (1952) Spettroscopia, archeologia e metallurgia. Spectrochimica acta 5:73-76.

3155 Pigeat, G. (1967) Analyse spectrale des objets trouvés à Port-Bail. Annales de Normandie 17(4):345-350.

3156 Pittioni, R. (1949) Spektralanalytische Untersuchungen von Bronzen aus Hallstatt, O.-Ö. (Spectrographic investigations of bronzes from Hallstatt, upper Austria). Mitteilungen der prähistorischen Kommission 1944 (Wien), 103-125.

3157 Pittioni, R. (1957) Urzeitlicher Bergbau auf Kupfererz und Spurenanalyse. Beiträge zum Problem der Relation Lagerstätte--Fertigobjekt. (Prehistoric mining of copper ore and trace element analysis. Contributions to the problem of the relationship of ore deposit to finished object). Archaeologia austriaca, Beiheft 1.

3158 Pittioni, R. (1959) Zweck und Ziel spektralanalytischer Untersuchungen für die Urgeschichte des Kupferbergwesens. (The object and limitation of spectrographic investigations for prehistory of copper mining). Archaeologia austriaca 26:67-95.

3159 Pittioni, R. (1966) Weitere Spektralanalysen von Funden aus dem Altersee, Oberösterreich. (Further spectrographic analyses of finds from the Altersee, upper Austria). Archaeologia austriaca 39:93.

3160 Prag, A. J. N. W. et al. (1974) Hellenistic glazed wares from Athens and southern Italy: analytical techniques and implications. Archaeometry 16(2): 153-187.

3161 Preuschen, E., Neuninger, H. and Pittioni, R. (1973) Spektralanalytische Untersuchungen von Erzen und urzeitlichen Schlacken aus dem Trentino und Südtirol. (Spectrographic investigations of ores and prehistoric slags from the Trentino and southern Tirol). Archaeologia austriaca 53:47-56.

3162 Renfrew, C. (1967) Cycladic metallurgy and the Aegean early Bronze Age. American journal of archaeology 71(1):1-20.

3163 Richards, E. E. (1959) Spectrographic investigation of some Romano-British mortaria: analytical results. Archaeometry 2:23-31.

3164 Richards, E. E. (1960) Further work on some Romano-British pottery. Archaeometry 3:25-28.

3165 Richards, E. E. and Aitken, M. J. (1959) Spectrographic and magnetic examination of some baked clay slab-moulds. Archaeometry 2:53-57.

3166 Richards, E. E. and Blin-Stoyle, A. E. (1961) A study of the homogeneity in composition of an Irish thick-butted axe. Archaeometry 4:53-55.

3167   Richards, E. E. and Hartley, K. F. (1960) Spectro-
       graphic analysis of Romano-British pottery. Nature
       185:194-196.

3168   Ruzanov, V. D. (1980) K voprosu o metalloobrabotke u
       plemen čustskoj kul'tury. (On the question of metal
       processing among the tribes of the Čustskij culture).
       Sovetskaja arkheologija 4:55-64.

3169   Sangmeister, E. (1961) Neue Ergebnisse spektral-
       analytischer Untersuchungen von Bodenfunden der
       Kupfer- und Frühbronzezeit in Europa. (New results
       of spectrographic investigations of finds from the
       Copper and Bronze Ages in Europe). Berichte über den
       V. internationalen Kongress für Vor- und Früh-
       geschichte. Berlin, 710-713.

3170   Sangmeister, E. (1971) Spektralanalyse in der Er-
       forschung ur- und frühgeschichtlicher Metallurgie.
       (Spectrographic analysis in the investigation of
       prehistoric and early historic metallurgy).
       Informationsblätter zu den Nachbarwissenschaften der
       Ur- und Frühgeschichte, Metallurgie (Göttingen)
       2:1-8.

3171   Sangmeister, E. (1973) Die Bronzen des Hortfund-
       horizontes von Opalyi. Ergebnisse der spektral-
       analytischen Untersuchungen. (The bronzes of the
       hoard horizon from Opályi. Results of the spectro-
       graphic investigations). In: A. Mozsolics, Bronze-
       und Goldfunde des Karpatenbeckens. Depotfundhori-
       zonte von Forró und Opályi. Budapest, 215-249.

3172   Sangmeister, E. and Otto, H. (1973) Archaeology and
       metal analysis. Antiquity 47:217-221.

3173   Sauter, F. and Rossmanith, K. (1967) Chemische Unter-
       suchung frühgeschichtlicher Glasperlen. (Chemical
       investigation of early historic glass beads).
       Archaeologia austriaca 42:59-64.

3174   Scacciati, G. and D'Este, A. (1959) Analisi spetto-
       grafiche di oggetti metallici antichi. Instituto
       Lombardo. Academia di scienze e lettere. Rendiconti
       sciennze matematiche, fisiche, chimiche e geologiche
       (Mailand) A93:213-218.

3175 Ščapova, JU. L. (1963) O khimičeskom sostave polivy. (On the chemical composition of the coating). In: Bližnevostočnaja i zolotoordynskaja polivnaja keramika iz raskopok v Novgorode. Materialy i issledovanija po arkheologii SSSR 117:285-286.

3176 Ščapova, JU. L. (1963) Rezul'taty spektral'nogo analiza stekljannykh izdelij iz Pantikapeja. (Results of spectrographic analysis of glass objects from Pantikapej). Materialy i issledovanija po arkheologii SSSR 103:237-240.

3177 Ščapova, JU. L. (1963) Spektral'nyj analiz stekljannykh sosudov iz antičnykh sloev Tamanskogo gorodišča. (Spectrographic analysis of glass vessels from the early historic levels of the town of Tamanskij). In: Keramika i steklo drevnej Tmutarakani. Moskva, 171-174.

3178 Ščapova, JU. L. (1963) Stekljannye izdelija drevnego Novgoroda. (Glass objects of ancient Novgorod). Materialy i issledovanija po arkheologii SSSR 117: 104-163.

3179 Ščapova, JU. L. (1965) Rezul'taty spektral'nogo analiza bus i brasleta s gorodišča Titčikha. (Results of spectrographic analysis of glass beads and bracelets from the town of Titčikha). In: A. N. Moskalendo, Gorodišče Titčikha. Voronež, 267-269.

3180 Ščapova, JU. L. (1965) Rezul'taty spektral'nogo analiza stekla iz Tanaisa. (Results of spectrographic analysis of glass from Tanais). Materialy i issledovanija po arkheologii SSSR 127:249-255.

3181 Ščapova, JU. L. (1965) Spektral'nyj analiz i istorija stekla (Kievskoj Rusi). (Spectrographic analysis and the history of glass, Kievan Russia). Materialy i issledovanija po arkheologii SSSR 129:111-118.

3182 Schubert, F. and Schubert, E. (1963) Spektralanalytische Untersuchung der Hortfunde von Opályi und Nyírbéltek. (Spectrographic investigation of the hoard finds at Opályi and Nyírbéltek). Acta archaeologica academiae scientiarum hungaricae 15:82-83.

3183 Schubert, F. and Schubert, E. (1967) Spektralanalytische Untersuchungen von Hort- und Einzelfunden der
Periode B III. (Spectrographic investigations of
hoard and isolated finds of period B III). In: A.
Mozsolics, Bronzefunde des Karpatenbeckens. Budapest,
185-203.

3184 Schubert, F. and Schubert, E. (1968) Über die spektralanalytische Untersuchung des Bronzegefässes von Smig.
(On the spectrographic investigation of the bronze
vessel from Smig). Berichte der Römisch-Germanischen
Kommission 46/47:74-76.

3185 Selimkhanov, I. R. (1960) Istoriko-khimičeskie i
analitičeskie issledovanija drevnikh predmetov iz
mednykh splavov (na materiale ėneolita Azerbajdžana).
(Historical-chemical and analytical investigations of
ancient objects from copper alloys, based on
Eneolithic material from Azerbaidzhan). Baku.

3186 Selimkhanov, I. R. (1960) Spektral'noe issledovanie
metalličeskikh predmetov iz arkheologičeskikh
pamjatnikov Kavkaza i ustanovlenie ikh ėpokhi (III-II
tys. do n. ė.). (Spectrographic investigations of
metal objects from archaeological sites of the
Caucasus and the establishment of their dating, 3rd-
2nd millennium B. C.). Izvestija Akademii Nauk
Azerbajdžanskoj SSR, serija geologo-geografičeskikh
nauk (Baku) 1:105-121.

3187 Selimchanow, I. R. (1960) Spektralanalytische Untersuchungen von Metallfunden des 3. und 2. Jahrtausends aus dem östlichen Transkaukasien--
Aserbaidshan. (Spectrographic investigations of metal
finds of the 3rd and 2nd millennia B.C. from the
eastern Transcaucasus--Azerbaidzhan). Archaeologia
austriaca 28:71-79.

3188 Selimkhanov, I. R. (1962) Spectral analysis of metal
articles from archaeological monuments of the
Caucasus. Proceedings of the prehistoric society
28:68-79.

3189 Selimkhanov, I. R. (1965) K spektral'nomu opredeleniju
olova i drugikh ėlementov v drevnikh mednykh splavakh
putëm isparenija opilok proby. (On the spectrographic
determination of tin and other elements in ancient
copper alloys by evaporation of powdered samples).

314

Sovetskaja arkheologija 1:265-269.

3190   Selimkhanov, I. R. (1965) O praktike spektral'nogo
       analiza v Institute istorii AN AzSSR. (On spectro-
       graphic analysis at the Institute of History,
       Academy of Sciences, Azerbaidzhan Soviet Socialist
       Republic). Izvestija Akademii Nauk Azerbajdžanskoj
       SSR (Baku), serija obščestv. nauk 6:138-142.

3191   Selimchanow, I. R. (1966) Ergebnisse spektral-
       analytischer Untersuchungen an Metallgegenständen des
       vierten und dritten Jahrtausends aus Transkaukasien.
       (Results of spectrographic investigations on metal
       objects of the 4th and 3rd millennia B.C. from the
       Transcaucasus). Germania 44:221-233.

3192   Selimchanow, I. R. (1966) Zur spektralanalytischen
       Bestimmung von Zinn und anderen Elementen in
       ältesten Kupferlegierungen mittels Verdampfung des
       durch Bohrung der Proben erzeugten Metallpulvers.
       (On the spectrographic determination of tin and other
       elements in the oldest copper alloys by the
       evaporation of metal powder obtained by boring).
       Archaeologia austriaca 39:87-92.

3193   Selimchanow, I. R. and Maréchal, J.-R. (1968) Früh-
       etappen der vorgeschichtlichen Kupfermetallurgie auf
       dem Gebiet Europas und des Kaukasus im Lichte neuer
       Erkenntnisse und Analysenergebnisse. (The early
       periods of prehistoric copper metallurgy in Europe
       and the Caucasus in light of new knowledge and
       analytical results). Slovenská archaeológia 16(2):
       461-472.

3194   Shaw, T. (1965) Spectrographic analyses of the Igbo and
       other Nigerian bronzes. Archaeometry 8:86-95.

3195   Shaw, T. (1966) Spectrographic analyses of the Igbo and
       other Nigerian bronzes; postscript. Archaeometry
       9:148-150.

3196   Shaw, T. (1967) Further spectrographic analyses of
       Nigerian bronzes. Archaeometry 11:85-93.

3197   Sinay, G. (1963) Spektrographische und metallo-
       graphische Untersuchung kupfer- und frühbronzezeit-
       licher Funde. (Spectrographic and metallographic
       investigation of Copper Age and early Bronze Age

finds). Acta archaeologica academiae scientiarum
hungaricae 15(1-4):37-64.

3198 Slater, E. and Charles, J. (1970) Archaeological
classification by metal analysis. Antiquity 44:
207-213.

3199 Stone, J. F. S. and Thomas, L. C. (1957) The use and
distribution of faience in the ancient East and prehistoric Europe, with notes on the spectrochemical
analysis of faience. Proceedings of the prehistoric
society 22:37-84.

3200 Waterbolk, H. T. and Butler, J. J. (1965) Comments on
the use of metallurgical analysis in prehistoric
studies. Helinium 5:227-251.

3201 Werner, O. (1970) Spektralanalytische Untersuchungen
antiker Kupferlegierungen. (Spectrographic investigations of ancient copper alloys). Fresenius'
Zeitschrift für analytische Chemie 250(1):17-23.

3202 Werner, O. (1972) Spektralanalytische und metallurgische Untersuchungen an indischen Bronzen. (Spectrographic and metallurgical investigations on Indian
bronzes). Leiden: Brill.

3203 Werner, O. (1977) Analysen mittelalterlicher Bronzen
und Messinge I. (Analyses of medieval bronzes and
brasses I). Archäologie und Naturwissenschaften
1:144-220.

3204 Werner, O. (1978) Metallurgische Untersuchungen der
Benin-Messinge des Museums der Völkerkunde Berlin.
Teil II. Beitrag zur Frage der Datierung der
Messinge und der Herkunft des Rohmaterials. (Metallurgical investigations of Benin brasses of the
Museum der Völkerkunde Berlin. Part II. Contribution
to the question of dating of the brasses and the
source of the raw material). Baessler-Archiv
27(7):333-439.

3205 Werner, O. and Willett, F. (1975) The composition of
brasses from Ife and Benin. Archaeometry 17(2):
141-156.

3206 Willett, F. (1964) Spectrographic analysis of Nigerian
bronzes. Archaeometry 7:81-83.

3207 Winkler, J. (1933) Die qualitative und quantitative
      Spektralanalyse vorgeschichtlicher Legierungen. (The
      qualitative and quantitative spectrographic analyses
      of prehistoric alloys). Nachrichtenblatt für deutsche
      Vorzeit 9(6):86-89.

3208 Winkler, J. (1935) Quantitative spektralanalytische
      Untersuchungen an Kupferlegierungen zur Analyse vor-
      geschichtlicher Bronzen. (Quantitative spectrographic
      investigations on copper alloys in addition to
      analyses of prehistoric bronzes). Veröffentlichungen
      der Landesanstalt für Volkheitskunde (Halle), no. 7.

      b) Atomic absorption spectrophotometry (AAS)

3209 Agrawal, D. P., Krishnamurthy, R. V. and Kusumgar, S.
      (1979) Fresh chemical data and the cultural
      affiliation of the Daimabad bronzes. Archaeo-Physika
      10:8-13.

3210 Bower, N. W., Bromund, R. H. and Smith, R. H. (1975)
      Atomic absorption for the archaeologist: an
      application to pottery from Pella of the Decapolis.
      Journal of field archaeology 2:389-398.

3211 Gilmore, G. R. and Ottaway, B. S. (1980) Micromethods
      for the determination of trace elements in copper-
      based metal artifacts. Journal of archaeological
      science 7(3):241-254.

3212 Hughes, M. J. (1979) British middle and late Bronze
      Age metalwork: some reanalyses. Archaeometry 21(2):
      195-202.

3213 Hughes, M. J., Cowell, M. R. and Craddock, P. T. (1976)
      Atomic absorption techniques in archaeology.
      Archaeometry 18(1):19-37.

3214 Le Tensorer, J. M. (1977) L'analyse chimique des
      remplissages des grottes et abris. Principes et
      limites. Approche écologique de l'homme fossile.
      Paris: Université Pierre et Marie Curie, 47:23-27.

3215 Riederer, J. (1977) Metallanalysen chinesischer
      Spiegel. (Metal analyses of Chinese mirrors).
      Berliner Beiträge zur Archäometrie 2:6-16.

3216 Riederer, J. (1977) Die Zusammensetzung der Bronze-
      geschütze des Heeresgeschichtlichen Museums im
      Wiener Arsenal. (The composition of bronze cannons
      of the Heeresgeschichtliches Museum in the Vienna
      arsenal). Berliner Beiträge zur Archäometrie 2:27-40.

3217 Riederer, J. (1978) Metallanalysen der Randleistenbeile
      eines Hortfundes von Bennewitz. (Metal analyses of
      the flanged axes of a hoard find from Bennewitz).
      Berliner Beiträge zur Archäometrie 3:43-49.

3218 Riederer, J. (1978) Die naturwissenschaftliche Unter-
      suchung der Bronzen des Ägyptischen Museums
      Stiftung Preussischer Kulturbesitz, Berlin. (The
      natural science investigation of bronzes of the
      Ägyptisches Museum Stiftung Preussicher Kulturbe-
      sitz, Berlin). Berliner Beiträge zur Archäometrie
      3:5-42.

3219 Riederer, J. and Bandi, H. G. (1977) Die metallurgische
      Untersuchung bronzener Schuppenpanzer der Eskimos.
      (The metallurgical investigation of Eskimo bronze
      plate armour). Berliner Beiträge zur Archäometrie
      2:17-26.

3220 Waldron, H. A., Mackie, A. and Townshend, A. (1976)
      The lead content of some Romano-British bones.
      Archaeometry 18(2):221-227.

3221 Walthall, J. A., Stow, S. H. and Karson, M. J. (1980)
      Copena galena: source identification and analysis.
      American antiquity 45(1):21-42.

3222 Wheeler, M. E. and Clark, D. W. (1977) Elemental
      characterisation of obsidian from the Koyukuk River,
      Alaska, by atomic absorption spectrophotometry.
      Archaeometry 19(1):15-31.

c) X-ray fluorescence spectrometry (XRF)

3223 Allan, J. W., Llewellyn, L. R. and Schweizer, F. (1973)
      The history of so-called Egyptian faience in Islamic
      Persia: investigations into Abu'l-Qasim's treatise.
      Archaeometry 15(2):165-173.

318

3224   Ankner, D. (1977) L'application de l'analyse en
        fluorescence X au Römisch-Germanisches Zentralmuseum
        à Mayence. PACT 1:47-60.

3225   Banks, M., Elphinstone, N. and Hall, E. T. (1963)
        Bristol blue glass. Archaeometry 6:26-30.

3226   Banks, M. and Hall, E. T. (1963) X-ray fluorescent
        analysis in archaeology: the 'milliprobe'.
        Archaeometry 6:31-36.

3227   Banks, M. and Merrick, J. M. (1967) Further analysis of
        Chinese blue-and-white. Archaeometry 10:101-103.

3228   Barrandon, J. N. (1977) Étude comparative de la
        fluorescence X et des méthodes nucléaires dans
        leur application à l'archéologie. PACT 1:61-75.

3229   Bateson, J. D. and Hedges, R. E. M. (1975) The
        scientific analysis of a group of Roman-age
        enamelled brooches. Archaeometry 17(2):177-190.

3230   Birgül, O., Dikšić, M. and Yaffe, L. (1979) X-ray
        fluorescence analysis of Turkish clays and pottery.
        Archaeometry 21(2):203-218.

3231   Brown, P. D. C. and Schweizer, F. (1963) X-ray
        fluorescent analysis of Anglo-Saxon jewellery.
        Archaeometry 15(2):175-192.

3232   Cabral, J. M. P., Possolo, A. and Marques, M. G. (1979)
        Non-destructive analysis of reais and fortes of Dom
        Fernando of Portugal by X-ray spectrometry.
        Archaeometry 21(2):219-231.

3233   Carlson, J. H. (1977) X-ray fluorescence analysis of
        pewter: English and Scottish measures. Archaeometry
        19(2):147-155.

3234   Carter, G. F. (1964) Preparation of ancient coins for
        accurate X-ray fluorescence analysis. Archaeometry
        7:106-113.

3235   Carter, G. F. (1964) X-ray fluorescence analysis of
        Roman coins. Analytical chemistry 36:1264-1268.

3236 Carter, G. F. (1977) Reproducibility of X-ray fluorescence analyses of Septimius Severus denarii. Archaeometry 19(1):67-73.

3237 Carter, G. F. (1978) Precision in the X-ray fluorescence analysis of sixty-one Augustan Quadrantes. Journal of archaeological science 5:293-300.

3238 Carter, G. F. and Carter, W. H. (1974) Chemical compositions of ten Septimius Severus denarii. Archaeometry 16(2):201-209.

3239 Carter, G. F. and Kimiatek, M. H. (1979) Comparison of surface with interior compositions of eight Roman copper-based coins. Archaeo-Physika 10:82-96.

3240 Catling, K. W. and Jones, R. E. (1977) Analyses of copper and bronze artefacts from the unexplored mansion, Knossos. Archaeometry 19(1):57-66.

3241 Cesareo, R. et al. (1972) Non-destructive analysis of chemical elements in paintings and enamels. Archaeometry 14(1):65-78.

3242 Cesareo, R., Sciuti, S. and Marabelli, M. (1973) Nondestructive analysis of ancient bronzes. Studies in conservation 18(2):64-80.

3243 Cheng, C. F. and Schwitter, C. M. (1957) Nickel in ancient bronzes. American journal of archaeology 61:351-365.

3244 Cowell, M. (1977) Energy dispersive X-ray fluorescence analysis of ancient gold alloys. PACT 1:76-85.

3245 Cox, G. A. and Pollard, A. M. (1977) X-ray fluorescence analysis of ancient glass: the importance of sample preparation. Archaeometry 19(1): 45-54.

3246 Duma, G. and Lengyel, I. (1969) Fluoreszenzanalytische Untersuchungen aus bluthaltigem Ton hergestellter urzeitlicher Gefässe. (Fluorescence analysis of blood containing clay from prehistoric vessels). Archaeologia austriaca 45:1-16.

320

3247 Fabris, G. J. and Treloar, F. E. (1980) X-ray
fluorescence and atomic absorption analysis of
Sarawak gold artifacts. Archaeometry 22(1):93-98.

3248 Filippakis, S. E., Perdikatsis, B. and Assimenos, K.
(1979) X-ray analysis of pigments from Vergina,
Greece (second tomb). Studies in conservation 24:
54-58.

3249 Filippakis, S. E., Perdikatsis, B. and Paradellis, T.
(1976) An analysis of blue pigments from the Greek
Bronze Age. Studies in conservation 21(3):143-153.

3250 Florkowski, T. and Stós, E. (1975) Non-destructive
radio-isotope X-ray fluorescence analysis of old
silver coins. Archaeometry 17(2):165-175.

3251 Fornaseri, M. et al. (1975-1977) Analyses of obsidians
from the late Chalcolithic levels of Arslantepe
(Malatya). Paléorient 3:231-246.

3252 Frankel, R. S. (1970) Detection of art forgeries by
X-ray fluorescence spectroscopy. Isotopes, radiation
and technology 8:65.

3253 Frierman, J. D. et al. (1968) X-ray fluorescence
spectrography: use in field archaeology. Science
164:588.

3254 Hall, E. T. (1959) X-ray fluorescent spectroscopy in
chemical analysis. Endeavour 18(70):83-87.

3255 Hall, E. T. (1960) X-ray fluorescent analysis applied
to archaeology. Archaeometry 3:29-35.

3256 Hall, E. T. (1961) Surface-enrichment of buried metals.
Archaeometry 4:62-66.

3257 Hall, E. T. (1974) A portable X-ray spectrometer for
the analysis of archaeological material. In: Recent
advances in science and technology of materials.
New York: Plenum Press, 3:205-220.

3258 Hall, E. T., Banks, M. S. and Stern, J. M. (1964) Uses
of X-ray fluorescent analysis in archaeology.
Archaeometry 7:84-89.

321

3259 Hall, E. T., Schweizer, F. and Toller, P. A. (1973) X-ray fluorescence analysis of museum objects: a new instrument. Archaeometry 15(1):53-78.

3260 Hanson, V. F. (1973) Quantitative elemental analysis of art objects by energy dispersive X-ray fluorescence spectroscopy. Applied spectroscopy 27(5):309-334.

3261 Hawkes, S. C., Merrick, J. M. and Metcalf, D. M. (1966) X-ray fluorescent analysis of some Dark Age coins and jewellery. Archaeometry 9:98-138.

3262 Hedges, R. E. M. (1976) Pre-Islamic glazes in Mesopotamia-Nippur. Archaeometry 18(2):209-238.

3263 Hedges, R. E. M. (1979) Analysis of the 'Drake Plate': comparison with the composition of Elizabethan brass. Archaeometry 21(1):21-26.

3264 Hedges, R. E. M. and Moorey, P. R. S. (1975) Pre-Islamic ceramic glazes at Kish and Nineveh in Iraq. Archaeometry 17(1):25-43.

3265 Hendy, M. F. and Charles, J. A. (1970) The production techniques, silver content and circulation history of the twelfth-century Byzantine trachy. Archaeometry 12(1):13-21.

3266 Hester, T. R. et al. (1975) X-ray fluorescence of obsidian artifacts from the Rio Grande Plain, southern Texas. Texas journal of science 26(1/2): 286-289.

3267 Higashimura, T. and Warashina, T. (1975) Sourcing of sanukite stone implements by X-ray fluorescence analysis. Journal of archaeological science 2(3): 169-178.

3268 King, C. E. (1977) The alloy content of folles and imitations from the Woodeaton hoard. PACT 1:86-100.

3269 King, C. E. and Hedges, R. E. M. (1974) An analysis of some third-century Roman coins for surface silvering and silver percentage of their alloy content. Archaeometry 16(2):189-200.

3270 Kraay, C. M. (1958) The composition of electrum coinage. Archaeometry 1:21-23.

3271 Lahanier, C. (1973) La microfluorescence X appliquée a l'étude des peintures et des objets de musée. Laboratoire de Recherche de Musées de France, Paris. Annales, 45-58.

3272 Lahanier, C. (1977) Annexe 1. Détermination par élément chimique de l'épaisseur de la couche analysée en fluorescence X. PACT 1:31-40.

3273 Lahanier, C. (1977) Annexe 2. Compositions optimales de la perle au borax pour l'analyse des silicates. PACT 1:41-46.

3274 Lahanier, C. (1977) L'application des methodes de fluorescence X à l'archéologie au laboratoire de recherche des musées de France. PACT 1:101-109.

3275 Lahanier, C. and Rouvier-Jeanlin, M. (1977) Analyse de 120 figurines gallo-romaines en terre cuite blanche. PACT 1:110-130.

3276 Leach, B. F. and Anderson, A. J. (1978) The prehistoric sources of Palliser Bay obsidian. Journal of archaeological science 5:301-307.

3277 McKerrell, H. (1974) The application of non-dispersive X-ray fluorescence to archaeological material. Edinburgh: Nuclear Enterprises, Ltd. Archaeological monograph no. 1.

3278 McKerrell, H. (1977) Non-dispersive XRF applied to ancient metalworking in copper and tin bronze. PACT 1:138-173.

3279 Maes, L. (1977) X-ray fluorescence spectrometric analysis of Etruscan mirrors. PACT 1:131-137.

3280 Maggetti, M. and Galetti, G. (1980) Composition of Iron Age fine ceramics from Châtillon-s-Glâne (Kt. Fribourg, Switzerland) and the Heuneburg (Kr. Sigmaringen, West Germany). Journal of archaeological science 7(1):87-91.

3281 Meeks, N. D. and Tite, M. S. (1980) The analysis of platinum--group element inclusions in gold antiquities. Journal of archaeological science 7(3): 267-275.

3282 Merrick, J. M. and Metcalf, D. M. (1969) Milliprobe analyses of some problematic Burgundian and other gold coins of the early Middle Ages. Archaeometry 11:61-65.

3283 Metcalf, D. M. and Merrick, J. M. (1967) Studies in the composition of early medieval coins. Numismatic chronicle 7:217-231.

3284 Metcalf, D. M. and Schweizer, F. (1970) Milliprobe analyses of some Visigothic, Suevic, and other gold coins of the early Middle Ages. Archaeometry 12(2): 173-188.

3285 Metcalf, D. M. and Schweizer, F. (1971) The metal contents of the silver pennies of William II and Henry I (1087-1135). Archaeometry 13(2):177-190.

3286 Mitchell, J. L. (1980) Notes on trace element analysis of obsidian from Hutchinson and Roberts Counties in the Texas panhandle. Bulletin of the Texas archeological society 51:301-308.

3287 Mommsen, H. et al. (1978) Die Teilchen-induzierte Röntgenfluoreszenz-Analyse als Methode zur Klassifizierung von Feuerstein. (Particle-induced X-ray fluorescent analysis as a method of classifying flint). Bonner Hefter zur Vorgeschichte 17:241-250.

3288 Moorey, P. R. S. and Fleming, S. J. (1979) Re-appraisal of a Syro-Palestinian bronze female figurine. MASCA journal 1(3):73-75.

3289 Moorey, P. R. S. and Schweizer, F. (1972) Copper and copper-alloys in ancient Iraq, Syria and Palestine: some new analyses. Archaeometry 14(2):177-1981

3290 Moorey, P. R. S. and Schweizer, F. (1974) Copper and copper alloys in ancient Turkey: some new analyses. Archaeometry 16(1):112-115.

324

3291 Nelson, D. E., D'Auria, J. M. and Bennett, R. B. (1975) Characterization of Pacific northwest coast obsidian by X-ray fluorescence analysis. Archaeometry 17(1): 85-97.

3292 Newton, R. G. (1971) A preliminary examination of a suggestion that pieces of strongly coloured glass were articles of trade in the Iron Age in Britain. Archaeometry 13(1):11-16.

3293 Newton, R. G. and Hedges, R. E. M. (1974) Analysis of weathered glass from York Minster. Archaeometry 16(2):244-245.

3294 Ogilvie, R. E. (1974) Applications of the solid state X-ray detector to the study of art objects. In: Recent advances in science and technology of materials. New York: Plenum Press, 3:221-230.

3295 Olsen, E. J. (1962) Copper artifact analysis with the X-ray spectrometer. American antiquity 28(2):234-238.

3296 Picon, M., Vichy, M. and Meille, E. (1971) Composition of the Lezoux, Lyon and Arezzo Samian ware. Archaeometry 13(2):191-208.

3297 Pigeat, G. (1971) Application de la spectrométrie X à l'étude de trois objets d'or découverts à Hérouvillette. Archéologie médiévale 1:153-159.

3298 Poole, A. B. and Finch, L. R. (1972) The utilization of trace chemical composition to correlate British post-medieval pottery with European kiln site materials. Archaeometry 14(1):79-91.

3299 Profi, S., Perdikatsis, B. and Filippakis, S. E. (1977) X-ray analysis of Greek Bronze Age pigments from Thera (Santorini). Studies in conservation 22(3): 107-115.

3300 Profi, S., Weier, L. and Filippakis, S. E. (1974) X-ray analysis of Greek Bronze Age pigments from Mycenae. Studies in conservation 19(2):105-112.

3301 Profi, S., Weier, L. and Filippakis, S. E. (1976) X-ray analysis of Greek Bronze Age pigments from Knossos. Studies in conservation 21(1):34-39.

3302 Riederer, J. (1977) X-ray fluorescence at the Rathgen Research Laboratory in Berlin. PACT 1:174-180.

3303 Schneider, G. (1976) Anwendung der Röntgenfluoreszenz-analyse und statistischer Methoden bei der Untersuchung von Terra Sigillata. (The use of X-ray fluorescence analysis and statistical methods for the investigation of terra sigillata). Informations-blätter zu den Nachbarwissenschaften der Ur- und Frühgeschichte (Göttingen) 7; Physik 3:1-14.

3304 Schneider, G. (1978) Anwendung quantitativer Material-analysen auf Herkunftsbestimmungen antiker Keramik. (The use of quantitative materials analysis for determining the source of ancient ceramics). Berliner Beiträge zur Archäometrie 3:63-122.

3305 Schneider, G. and Hoffmann, B. (1976) Bestimmung der Herkunft antiker Keramik (Terra Sigillata) mit Hilfe von Röntgenfluoreszenzanalysen. (Determining the origin of ancient ceramics, Terra Sigillata, with the aid of X-ray fluorescence analysis). Berichte der deutschen keramischen Gesellschaft 53(12):417-422.

3306 Schneider, G., Hoffmann, B. and Wirz, E. (1979) Significance and dependability of reference groups for chemical determinations of provenance of ceramic artifacts. Archaeo-Physika 10:269-283.

3307 Schweizer, F. and Friedman, A. M. (1972) Comparison of methods of analysis of silver and gold in silver coins. Archaeometry 14(1):103-107.

3308 Stern, W. B. and Descoeudres, J.-P. (1977) X-ray fluorescence analysis of archaic Greek pottery. Archaeometry 19(1):73-86.

3309 Stevenson, D. P., Stross, F. H. and Heizer, R. F. (1971) An evaluation of X-ray fluorescence analysis as a method for correlating obsidian artifacts with source location. Archaeometry 13(1):17-25.

3310 Stós-Fertner, Z., Fertner, A. and Florkowski, T. (1977) An attempt at a statistical evaluation of the results of the X-ray fluorescence analysis of the chemical composition of dirhams and their imitations from the 8th-10th c. A.D. PACT 1:191-203.

3311   Stós-Fertner, Z. and Kusiński, J. (1977) The presence
       of mercury in Kufic silver coins. PACT 1:181-190.

3312   Stross, F. H. et al. (1968) Analysis of American
       obsidians by X-ray fluorescence and neutron
       activation analysis. University of California
       archaeological research facility contributions
       5:59-79.

3313   Stross, F. H. et al. (1978) Archaeological and chemical
       studies of Mesoamerican obsidian. In: R. E. Taylor,
       ed., Recent advances in obsidian glass studies. Park
       Ridge, New Jersey: Noyes Press, 240-250.

3314   Todd, J. A. and Charles, J. A. (1977) The analysis of
       non-metallic inclusions in ancient iron. PACT
       1:204-220.

3315   Warashina, T., Kamaki, Y. and Higashimura, T. (1978)
       Sourcing of sanukite implements by X-ray
       fluorescence analysis II. Journal of archaeological
       science 5:283-291.

3316   Weaver, J. R. and Stross, F. H. (1965) Analysis by
       X-ray fluorescence of some American obsidians.
       University of California archaeological research
       facility contributions 1:89-103.

3317   Weinstein, J. R. (1980) Preliminary analyses of copper,
       bronze and silver artifacts from Lapithos, Cyprus.
       MASCA journal 1(4):106-109.

3318   White, J. R. (1977) X-ray fluorescent analysis of an
       early Ohio blast furnace slag. Ohio journal of
       science 77:186-188.

       d) Electron microprobe

3319   Brill, R. H. and Moll, S. (1963) The electron-beam
       probe microanalysis of ancient glass. In: G.
       Thompson, ed., Recent advances in conservation.
       London: Butterworth, 145-151.

3320   Clark, D. E. and Purdy, B. A. (1979) Electron micro-
       probe analysis of weathered Florida chert. American
       antiquity 44(3):517-524.

3321 Frost, F. B. (1970) Electron probe analysis of archaeological glasses. In: R. Cramp, Decorated window glass and millefiori from Monkwearmouth. Antiquaries journal 50:333-335.

3322 Hedges, R. E. M. and Salter, C. J. (1979) Source determination of iron currency bars through analysis of slag inclusions. Archaeometry 21(2):161-175.

3323 Hofmann, U., Theisen, R. and Yetmen, Y. (1966) Die Anwendung der Elektronenmikrosonde und der Röntgenanalyse zur Aufklärung der Chemie der antiken Keramik. (The use of the electron microprobe and X-ray analysis for the determination of the chemistry of ancient ceramics). Berichte der deutschen keramischen Gesellschaft 43(10):607-614.

3324 Hoke, E. and Petrascheck-Heim, I. (1977) Microprobe analysis of gilded silver threads from medieval textiles. Studies in conservation 22(2):49-62.

3325 Hooke, R., Yang, H. and Weiblen, P. W. (1969) Desert varnish: an electron probe study. Journal of geology 77(3):275-288.

3326 Hornblower, A. P. (1962) Archaeological applications of the electron probe microanalyser. Archaeometry 5:108-112.

3327 Hornblower, A. P. (1963) Some examples of work with the electron probe microanalyser. Archaeometry 6:37-42.

3328 Mills, A. A. and Wilson, R. N. (1978) A sampling stylus for use with the electron probe. Archaeometry 20(1):101-102.

3329 Newesely, H. (1977) Biogene Materialien als Objekte archäometrischen Interesses. (Biogenic materials as objects of archaeometric interest). Archäologie und Naturwissenschaften 1:81-84.

3330 Notis, M. R. (1979) Study of Japanese mokumē techniques by electron microprobe analysis. MASCA journal 1(3): 67-69.

3331 Schaaber, O. (1977) Metallkundliche Untersuchungen zur
Frühgeschichte der Metallurgie. (Investigations of
metals for the early history of metallurgy).
Archäologie und Naturwissenschaften 1:221-268.

3332 Tylecote, R. F., Ghaznavi, H. A. and Boydell, P. J.
(1977) Partitioning of trace elements between the
ores, fluxes, slags, and metal during the smelting
of copper. Journal of archaeological science
4:305-333.

3333 Whitmore, F. E. and Young, W. J. (1973) Application of
the laser microprobe and electron microprobe in the
analysis of platiniridium inclusions in gold. In:
W. J. Young, ed., Application of science in the
examination of works of art. Boston: Museum of Fine
Arts, 88-95.

3334 Willgallis, A. et al. (1976) Untersuchungen der
Glanztonschicht von Terra Sigillata mit der
Elektronenmikrosonder. (Investigation of the glaze-
clay layer of terra sigillata with the electron
microprobe). Informationsblätter zu den Nachbarwissenschaften der Ur- und Frühgeschichte
(Göttingen) 7; Physik 6:1-6.

e) Neutron activation analysis (NAA)

3335 Aitken, M. J., Emeleus, V. M. and Hall, E. T. (1962)
Neutron activation analysis of silver coins. Radio-
isotopes in the physical sciences and industry.
Wien: International Atomic Energy Agency, 2:261.

3336 Al Kital, R. A., Chan, L.-H. and Sayre, E. V. (1969)
Neutron activation analysis of pottery from Hajar
Bin Humeid and related areas. Appendix II in: G. W.
van Beek, Hajar Bin Humeid: investigations at a
pre-Islamic site in South Arabia. Baltimore: Johns
Hopkins Press, 387-398.

3337 Allen, R. O., Luckenbach, A. H. and Holland, C. G.
(1975) The application of instrumental neutron
activation analysis to a study of prehistoric
steatite artifacts and source materials.
Archaeometry 17(1):69-83.

3338 Arnold, D. E. et al. (1978) Neutron activation analysis of contemporary pottery and pottery materials from the Valley of Guatemala. In: The ceramics of Kaminaljuyu, Guatemala. University Park: Pennsylvania State University Press, 543-586.

3339 Artzy, M. and Asaro, F. (1979) Origin of Tell El-Yahudiyah ware found in Cyprus. Report of the department of antiquities (Nicosia), 135-150.

3340 Asaro, F., Perlman, I. and Dothan, M. (1971) An introductory study of Mycenaean IIIC1 ware from Tel Ashdod. Archaeometry 13(2):169-175.

3341 Ashworth, M. J. and Abeles, T. P. (1966) Neutron activation analysis and archaeology. Nature 210:9-11.

3342 Aspinall, A. et al. (1972) Neutron activation analysis of faience beads. Archaeometry 14(1):27-40.

3343 Aspinall, A. et al. (1972) Obsidian-identification of source of Aegean artefacts by neutron activation analysis. Nature 237(5354):333.

3344 Aspinall, A. and Feather, S. W. (1972) Neutron activation analysis of prehistoric flint mine products. Archaeometry 14(1):41-53.

3345 Aspinall, A. and Feather, S. W. (1978) Neutron activation analysis of Aegean obsidians. In: Thera and the Aegean world. London: Thera and the Aegean World, 517-521.

3346 Aspinall, A., Feather, S. W. and Renfrew, C. (1972) Neutron activation analysis of Aegean obsidians. Nature 237:333-334.

3347 Aspinall, A., Slater, D. N. and Mayes, P. (1968) Neutron activation analysis of medieval ceramics. Nature 217:388.

3348 Attas, M. et al. (1979) Early Bronze Age ceramics from Lerna in Greece: radiochemical studies. Archaeo-Physika 10:14-28.

3349 Attas, M., Yaffe, L. and Fossey, J. M. (1977) Neutron activation analysis of early Bronze Age pottery from Lake Vouliagmeni, Perakhora, central Greece. Archaeometry 19(1):33-43.

3350 Banterla, G. et al. (1973) Characterization of Samian ware sherds by means of neutron activation analysis. Archaeometry 15(2):209-220.

3351 Bard, J. C., Asaro, F. and Heizer, R. F. (1978) Perspectives on the dating of prehistoric Great Basin petroglyphs by neutron activation analysis. Archaeometry 20(1):85-88.

3352 Barrandon, J. N., Callu, J. P. and Brenot, C. (1977) The analysis of Constantinian coins (A.D. 313-40) by non-destructive Californium 252 activation analysis. Archaeometry 19(2):173-186.

3353 Barrandon, J. N. and Irigoin, J. (1979) Papiers de Hollande et papiers d'Angoumois de 1650 à 1810. Leur differenciation au moyen de l'analyse par analyse par activation neutronique. Archaeometry 21(1):101-106.

3354 Becker, M. J. (1976) Neutron activation analysis of rare earth elements in steatite and related rocks: application to archaeological problems throughout the world. MASCA newsletter 12(2):1-2.

3355 Bennyhoff, J. A. and Heizer, R. F. (1965) Neutron activation analysis of some Cuicuilco and Teotihuacan pottery: archaeological interpretation of results. American antiquity 30:348-349.

3356 Birgül, O., Dikšić, M. and Yaffe, L. (1977) Activation analysis of Turkish and Canadian clays and Turkish pottery. Journal of radioanalytical chemistry 39:45-62.

3357 Bluyssen, H. and Smith, P. B. (1962) Determination of the silver content of Greek coins by neutron activation. Archaeometry 5:113-118.

3358 Bowman, H. R., Asaro, F. and Perlman, I. (1973) Compositional variations in obsidian sources and archaeological implications. Archaeometry 15(1):123-7.

331

3359 Brown, G. and Tindall, A. S. (1979) The measurement of the silver concentrations of coins using a small neutron source. Archaeometry 21(1):27-46.

3360 Czerny, W. and Winkler, G. (1977) Non-destructive activation analysis of ancient pottery by 14 MeV neutrons. Journal of radioanalytical chemistry 40:165.

3361 Davidson, T. E. and McKerrell, H. (1976) Pottery analysis and Halaf period trade in the Khabur headwaters region. Iraq 38:45-56.

3362 De Bruin, M. et al. (1972) The use of non-destructive activation analysis and pattern recognition in study of flint artefacts. Archaeometry 14(1):55-63.

3363 Emeleus, V. M. (1958) The technique of neutron activation analysis as applied to trace element determination in pottery and coins. Archaeometry 1:6-15.

3364 Emeleus, V. M. (1960) Neutron activation analysis of Samian ware sherds. Archaeometry 3:16-19.

3365 Emeleus, V. M. and Simpson, G. (1960) Neutron activation analysis of ancient Roman potsherds. Nature 185:196.

3366 Ericson, J. E. and Kimberlin, J. (1977) Obsidian sources, chemical characterization and hydration rates in west Mexico. Archaeometry 19(2):157-166.

3367 Farnsworth, M., Perlman, I. and Asaro, F. (1977) Corinth and Corfu: a neutron activation study of their pottery. American journal of archaeology 81:455-468.

3368 Filbert, E. W., Rowe, M. W. and Shaefer, H. J. (1980) Uranium in Hueco and Guadalupe Mountain Indian ceramics. Archaeometry 22(1):107-110.

3369 Fontes, P. et al. (1979) Analytical study of three Gallo-Roman white figurine workshops. Archaeo-Physika 10:101-112.

3370 Franklin, U. M. and Hancock, R. G. V. (1979) The effect of heat on some samples of Halaf pottery. Archaeo-Physika 10:113-118.

3371 Frison, G. et al. (1968) Neutron activation analysis of obsidian: an example of its relevance to north-western Plains archaeology. Plains anthropologist 13(41):209-217.

3372 Gilmore, G. R. (1976) Analysis of ancient copper alloys using epithermal activation techniques. Proceedings of the international conference: modern trends in activation analysis, 2:1187-1192.

3373 Gordus, A. A. (1967) Quantitative non-destructive neutron activation analysis of silver in coins. Archaeometry 10:78-86.

3374 Gordus, A. A. (1968) Activation analysis, artefacts and art. New scientist (17 October), 128-131.

3375 Gordus, A. A. (1968) Neutron activation analysis of almost any old thing. Chemistry 41(5):8-15.

3376 Gordus, A. A. (1970) Neutron activation analysis of archaeological artifacts. Philosophical transactions of the Royal Society of London A269:165-174.

3377 Gordus, A. A. et al. (1967) Identification of the geologic origins of archaeological artifacts: an automated method of Na and Mn neutron activation analysis. Archaeometry 10:87-96.

3378 Gordus, A. A., Wright, G. A. and Griffin, J. B. (1968) Obsidian sources characterized by neutron activation analysis. Science 161:382-384.

3379 Griffin, J. B., Gordus, A. A. and Wright, G. A. (1969) Identification of the sources of Hopewellian obsidian in the middle west. American antiquity 34:1-14.

3380 Grimanis, A. P. et al. (1980) Neutron activation and X-ray analysis of "Thapsos Class" vases. An attempt to identify their origin. Journal of archaeological science 7(3):227-239.

3381 Gruel, K. et al. (1979) Typological and analytical study of Celtic coins from the Trebry hoard. Archaeo-Physika 10:50-67.

3382 Hallam, B. R., Warren, S. E. and Renfrew, C. (1976) Obsidian in the western Mediterranean: characterization by neutron activation and optical emission spectroscopy. Proceedings of the prehistoric society 42:85-110.

3383 Hammond, N., Harbottle, G. and Gazard, T. (1976) Neutron activation and statistical analysis of Maya ceramics and clays from Lubaantun, Belize. Archaeometry 18(2):147-168.

3384 Hancock, R. G. V. (1976) Low flux multielement instrumental neutron activation analysis in archaeometry. Analytical chemistry 48:1443-1445.

3385 Hansen, B. A. et al. (1977) Comparison of medieval decorated floor-tiles with clay and tile fragments from the kilns at Bistrup. Preliminary results of neutron activation analysis. Proceedings of the Nordic conference on thermoluminescence dating and other archaeometric methods. Risø National Laboratory, 134-142.

3386 Hansen, B. A. et al. (1979) Provenance study of medieval decorated floor-tiles carried out by means of neutron activation analysis. Archaeo-Physika 10:119-140.

3387 Harbottle, G. (1970) Neutron activation analysis of potsherds from Knossos and Mycenae. Archaeometry 12(1):23-34.

3388 Harbottle, G. (1975) Activation analysis study of ceramics from the Capacha (Colima) and Openo (Michoacan) phases of west Mexico. American antiquity 40:453-458.

3389 Houtman, J. P. W. and Turkstra, J. (1965) Neutron activation analysis and its possible application for age determinations of paintings. Radiochemical methods of analysis. Wien: International Atomic Energy Agency, 1:85-103.

334

3390   Ives, D. J. (1975) Trace element analyses of archaeo-
       logical materials. American antiquity 40:235-236.

3391   Kerr, S. A., Spyrou, N. M. and Clark, A. J. (1979)
       Neutron activation techniques employing short-lived
       isotopes for the elemental analysis of soils for
       archaeological sites. Archaeo-Physika 10:157-171.

3392   Kraay, C. M. (1958) Gold and copper traces in early
       Greek silver. Archaeometry 1:1-5.

3393   Kraay, C. M. (1959) Gold and copper traces in early
       Greek silver. Archaeometry 2:1-16.

3394   Lenihan, J. M. A. (1959) Radioactive analysis. Nature
       184:951.

3395   Mahdavi, A. and Bovington, C. (1972) Neutron activation
       analysis of some obsidian samples from geological and
       archaeological sites. Iran 10:148-151.

3396   Meyers, P. (1968) Some applications of non-destructive
       activation analysis. Rotterdam: Bronder-Offset. 83p.

3397   Meyers, P. (1969) Non-destructive activation analysis
       of ancient coins using charged particles and fast
       neutrons. Archaeometry 11:67-85.

3398   Michel, H. V. and Asaro, F. (1979) Chemical study of
       the Plate of Brass. Archaeometry 21(1):3-19.

3399   Michel, H. V., Frierman, J. D. and Asaro, F. (1976)
       Chemical composition patterns of ceramic wares from
       Fustat, Egypt. Archaeometry 18(1):85-92.

3400   Neutron activation analysis of soapstone artifacts.
       (1973) MASCA newsletter 9(2):2-3.

3401   Ortega, R. F. and Lee, B. K. (1970) Neutron activation
       study of ancient pigments from murals of Cholula and
       Teotihuacan. Archaeometry 12(2):197-202.

3402   Ottaway, B. S. (1979) Analysis of earliest metal finds
       from Gomolava. Rad Vojvodjanskih Muzeja 25:53-59.

3403   Perlman, I. and Asaro, F. (1969) Pottery analysis of
       neutron activation. Archaeometry 11:21-52.

3404 Perlman, I. and Asaro, F. (1970) Neutron-activation
analysis of pottery. In: I. U. Olsson, ed., Radiocarbon variations and absolute chronology.
Stockholm: Almqvist & Wiksell; New York: J. Wiley,
141-158.

3405 Perlman, I. and Asaro, F. (1973) Provenience studies
of Mycenaean pottery employing neutron activation
analysis. Acts of the international archaeological
symposium, The Mycenaeans in the eastern
Mediterranean. Nicosia, Cyprus, 213-224.

3406 Ravetz, A. (1963) Neutron activation analysis of silver in some late Roman copper coins. Archaeometry
6:46-55.

3407 Ricq, J. C. and Diebolt, J. (1977) An attempt to
select suitable elements to characterize an ancient
ceramic by neutron activation analysis. Journal of
radioanalytical chemistry 39:9-20.

3408 Sayre, E. V. (1963) Methods and applications of
activation analysis. Annual review of nuclear
science 13:145-162.

3409 Sayre, E. V. (1972) Activation analysis applications
in art and archaeometry. In: Advances in
activation analysis. New York: Academic Press,
2:157-184.

3410 Sayre, E. V. (1976) Neutron activation analysis: an
emerging technique for conservation/preservation.
Technology and conservation of art, architecture,
and antiquities 1(3):26-31.

3411 Sayre, E. V. and Dodson, R. W. (1957) Neutron activation study of Mediterranean potsherds. American
journal of archaeology 61:35-41

3412 Schubiger, P. A. and Müller, O. (1976) Trace elements
in ancient silver coins by neutron activation and
solvent extraction with bismuth diethyldithio-
carbamate. Radiochemical and radioanalytical letters
24:353-362.

3413 Schubiger, P. A., Müller, O. and Gentner, W. (1977)
Neutron activation analysis on ancient Greek silver

coins and related materials. Journal of radioanalytical chemistry 39:99-112.

3414 Schwabe, R. (1980) Neutronaktivierungs analytische
Spurelementbestimmung und Anwendung der Cluster-
analyse an archäologischer Keramik aus Peru. (Neutron activation analysis for trace element determination and application of cluster analysis on
archaeological ceramics from Peru). Baessler-Archiv
(Berlin) 27(2):285-324.

3415 Simpson, G. (1960) Notes on Gaulish Samian pottery and
its analysis by neutron activation. Archaeometry
3:20-24.

3416 Stross, F. H. et al. (1977) Sources of some obsidian
flakes from a Paleoindian site in Guatemala.
American antiquity 42(1):114-118.

3417 Stross, F. H. et al. (1978) Mayan obsidian: source
correlation for southern Belize artifacts.
Archaeometry 20(1):89-93.

3418 Sutherland, C. H. V. and Harold, M. R. (1961) The
silver content of Diocletian's early post-reform
copper coins. Archaeometry 4:56-61.

3419 Thiele, R. W., Aung Khin, U. and Kyaw, U. (1972)
Neutron activation analysis of ancient Burmese
silver coins with a low flux Americium/Beryllium
neutron source. Archaeometry 14(2):199-219.

3420 Thompson, M. (1960) Gold and copper traces in late
Athenian silver. Archaeometry 3:10-15.

3421 Tobia, S. K. and Sayre, E. V. (1974) An analytical
comparison of various Egyptian soils, clays, shales
and some ancient pottery by neutron activation. In:
A. Bishay, ed., Recent advances in science and
technology of materials. New York: Plenum Press,
3:99-127.

3422 Warren, S. E. (1973) Geometrical factors in the neutron
activation analysis of archaeological specimens.
Archaeometry 15(1):115-122.

3423 Wesson, G. et al. (1977) Characterisation of archaeological bone by neutron activation analysis.
Archaeometry 19(1):200-205.

3424 Widemann, F. et al. (1975) A Lyons branch of the
pottery-making firm of Ateius of Arezzo.
Archaeometry 17(1):45-59.

3425 Widemann, F. et al. (1979) Analytical and typological
study of Gallo-Roman workshops producing amphorae in
the area of Narbonne. Archaeo-Physika 10:317-341.

3426 Williams, O. and Nandris, J. (1977) The Hungarian and
Slovak sources of archaeological obsidian: an
interim report on further fieldwork, with a note on
tektites. Journal of archaeological science 4:207-
219.

3427 Wright, G. A. (1969) Obsidian analyses and prehistoric
Near Eastern trade: 7500-3500 B.C. Museum of
Anthropology, University of Michigan. Anthropological
papers, no. 37. 92p.

3428 Wright, G. A. and Gordus, A. A. (1969) Source areas
for obsidian revovered at Munhata, Beisamoun,
Hazorea and el-Khiam. Israel exploration exploration
journal 19(2):79-88.

3429 Wyttenbach, A. and Hermann, H. (1966) The quantitative
non-destructive analysis of silver coins by neutron
activation. Archaeometry 9:139-147.

3430 Wyttenbach, A. and Schubiger, P. A. (1973) Trace
element content of Roman lead by neutron activation
analysis. Archaeometry 15(2):199-207.

3431 Yellin, J. et al. (1978) Comparison of neutron activation analysis from the Lawrence Berkeley Laboratory
and the Hebrew University. Archaeometry 20(1):95-100.

f) Other methods of elemental analysis

3432 Ahlberg, M. et al. (1976) Gold traces on wedge-shaped
artefacts from the late Neolithic of southern
Scandinavia analysed by proton-induced X-ray emission
spectroscopy. Archaeometry 18(1):39-49.

338

3433 Emeleus, V. M. (1960) Beta ray backscattering: a simple method for the quantitative determination of lead oxide in glass, glaze and pottery. Archaeometry 3:5-9.

3434 Fink, D. et al. (1978) Lithium und Bor in antiker Keramik. (Lithium and boron in ancient ceramics). Berliner Beitrage zur Archäometrie 3:51-61.

3435 Fishman, B. and Fleming, S. J. (1980) A bronze figure of Tutankhamun: technical studies. Archaeometry 22(1):81-86.

3436 Fleming, S. J. and Crowfoot-Payne, J. (1979) PIXE analyses of some Egyptian bronzes of the late period. MASCA journal 1(2):46-47.

3437 Lambert, J. B., McLaughlin, C. D. and Leonard, A. (1978) X-ray photoelectron spectroscopic analysis of the Mycenaean pottery from Megiddo. Archaeometry 20(2):107-122.

3438 Lambert, J. B. and McLaughlin, C. D. (1976) X-ray photoelectron spectroscopy: a new analytical method for the examination of archaeological artifacts. Archaeometry 18(2):169-180.

3439 Mancini, C. et al. (1976) Identification of ancient silver-plated coins by means of neutron absorption. Archaeometry 18(2):214-217.

3440 Mommsen, H. et al. (1980) Analysis of a silver statuette of Mercury from Bonn. Archaeometry 22(1): 87-92.

3441 Mommsen, H., Bauer, K. G. and Fazly, Q. (1979) PIXE-analysis of Klippen and coins from Bonn and Jülich. Archaeo-Physika 10:348-359.

3442 Nielson, K. K. et al. (1976) Elemental analysis of obsidian artifacts by proton-induced X-ray emission. Analytical chemistry 48(13):1947-1950.

3443 Radcliffe, C. D. et al. (1980) Gold analysis by differential absorption of gamma rays. Archaeometry 22(1):47-55.

3444 Reimers, P., Lutz, G. J. and Segebade, C. (1977) The
non-destructive determination of gold, silver and
copper by photon activation analysis of coins and
art objects. Archaeometry 19(1):167-172.

3445 Segebade, C. and Lutz, G. J. (1976) Simultane instru-
mentelle Multielementbestimmung in antiker Keramik
(Terra Sigillata) durch Aktivierungsanalyse mit
hochenegetischen Photonen. (Simultaneous instrumental
multielement determination in ancient ceramics
(terra sigillata) through activation analysis with
high energy photons). Journal of radioanalytical
chemistry 834:345-363.

3446 Segebade, C. and Riemers, P. (1979) The contribution
of photon activation analysis (PAA) to archaeometry.
Archaeo-Physika 10:284-285.

3447 Thompson, B. A. and Lutz, G. J. (1972) Characterization
of ancient bronze artifacts by neutron and photon
activation analysis. Radiochemical and radioanalytical letters 9:343-350.

3. Isotopic analysis

3448 Alfsen, B. E. and Christie, O. H. J. (1978) Massen-
spektrometrische Analysen von Specksteinfunden aus
Haithabu und Wikingerzeitlichen Steinbrüchen in
Norden. (Mass spectroscopy analyses of steatite
finds from Haithabu and Viking period quarries in
the north). Berichte über die Ausgrabungen in
Haithabu. Schleswig.

3449 Brill, R. H. and Shields, W. R. (1972) Lead isotopes
in ancient coins. Royal Numismatic Society, London.
Special publication no. 8:279-303.

3450 Brill, R. H. and Wampler, J. M. (1967) Isotope studies
of ancient lead. American journal of archaeology
71(1):63-77.

3451 Coleman, M. and Walker, S. (1979) Stable isotope
identification of Greek and Turkish marbles.
Archaeometry 21(1):107-112.

340

3452 Craig, H. and Craig, V. (1972) Greek marbles: determination of provenance by isotopic analysis. Science 176:401-403.

3453 Eiseman, C. J. (1978) The Porticello shipwreck: lead isotope data. MASCA journal 1:18.

3454 Farquhar, R. M. and Fletcher, I. R. (1980) Lead isotope identification of sources of galena from some prehistoric Indian sites in Ontario, Canada. Science 207(4431):640-643.

3455 Gale, N. H. (1978) Lead isotopes and Aegean metallurgy. In: Thera and the Aegean world. London: Thera and the Aegean World, 529-545.

3456 Gale, N. H. (1979) Lead isotopes and archaic Greek silver coins. Archaeo-Physika 10:194-208.

3457 Gale, N. H. and Stós-Fertner, S. (1978) Lead isotope composition of Egyptian artifacts. MASCA journal 1:19-21.

3458 Gentner, W. et al. (1978) Silver sources of archaic Greek coinage. Die Naturwissenschaften 65:273-284.

3459 Germann, K., Holzmann, G. and Winkler, F. J. (1980) Determination of marble provenance: limits of isotopic analysis. Archaeometry 22(1):99-106.

3460 Grögler, N. et al. (1966) Isotopenuntersuchungen zur Bestimmung der Herkunft römischer Bleirohre und Bleibarren. (Isotopic investigations for determining the origin of Roman lead pipes and lead ingots). Zeitschrift für Naturforschung 21a:1167-1172.

3461 Herz, N. and Wenner, D. B. (1978) Assembly of Greek marble inscriptions by isotopic methods. Science 199:1070-1072.

3462 Letolle, R. (1976) Isotopes stables: application en archéometrie. Colloque 1. IX Congrès, Union internationale des sciences préhistoriques et protohistoriques. Nice, 129-132.

3463 Manfra, L., Masi, U. and Turi, B. (1975) Carbon and oxygen isotope ratios of marbles from some ancient quarries of western Anatolia and their archaeological significance. Archaeometry 17(2):215-221.

3464 Müller, O. and Gentner, W. (1979) On the composition and silver sources of Aeginetan coins from the Asyut hoard. Archaeo-Physika 10:176-193.

3465 Shackleton, N. J. (1973) Oxygen isotope analysis as a means of determining season of occupation of prehistoric midden sites. Archaeometry 15:133-141.

3466 Smith, A. W. (1978) Stable carbon and oxygen isotope ratios of malachite from the patinas of ancient bronze objects. Archaeometry 20(2):123-133.

3467 Stós-Fertner, Z. and Gale, N. H. (1979) Chemical and lead isotope analysis of ancient Egyptian gold, silver and lead. Archaeo-Physika 10:299-314.

3468 Vogel, J. C. and Merwe, N. J. van der (1977) Isotopic evidence for early maize cultivation in New York state. American antiquity 42:238-242.

3469 Žirov, K. K. et al. (1970) Opyt primenenija izotopii svintsa v arkheologii. (Application of lead isotopes in archaeology). Geokhimija 1:120-123.

E. Properties of materials

1. Specific gravity

3470 Caley, E. R. (1944) The specific gravity and fineness of Persian darics. Numismatic review 2(1):21-23.

3471 Caley, E. R. (1946) On the occurrence of abnormally low weight and specific gravity in ancient coins. Numismatic review 3(2):51-53.

3472 Caley, E. R. (1949) Validity of the specific gravity method for determination of the fineness of gold objects. Ohio journal of science 49(2):73-82.

3473 Caley, E. R. (1952) Estimation of composition of
      ancient metal objects. Analytical chemistry
      24:676-681.

3474 Das, H. A. and Zonderhus, J. (1964) The analysis of
      electrum coins. Archaeometry 7:90-97.

3475 Hall, E. T. and Roberts, G. (1962) Analysis of the
      Moulsford torc. Archaeometry 5:28-37.

3476 Hughes, M. J. and Oddy, W. A. (1970) A reappraisal of
      the specific gravity method for the analysis of gold
      alloys. Archaeometry 12(1):1-11.

3477 Kushelevsky, A. P. (1975) A simple instrument for
      measuring the density of solid objects. Archaeometry
      17(1):99-101.

3478 Oddy, W. A. (1972) The analysis of gold coins--a
      comparison of results obtained by non-destructive
      methods. Archaeometry 14(1):109-117.

3479 Oddy, W. A. (1979) Coin forgers at work. MASCA
      journal 1(3):80-81.

3480 Oddy, W. A. and Blackshaw, S. M. (1974) The accuracy
      of the specific gravity method for the analysis of
      gold alloys. Archaeometry 16(1):81-90.

2. Thermal properties

3481 Enriquez, C. R., Danon, J. and Beltrão, M. (1979)
      Differential thermal analysis of some Amazonian
      archaeological pottery. Archaeometry 21(2):183-186.

3482 Fleet, R. J. (1974) The use of specific heat in the
      non-destructive analysis of silver/copper alloy
      coins. Archaeometry 17(1):101-106.

3483 Fleet, R. J. (1976) The application of specific heat
      in the detection of debasement in ancient silver/
      copper alloy coins. Archaeometry 18(1):117-120.

3484 Freeth, S. J. (1967) A chemical study of some Bronze
      Age pottery sherds. Archaeometry 10:104-119.

3485 Kingery, W. D. (1974) A note on the differential
      thermal analysis of archaeological ceramics.
      Archaeometry 16(1):109-112.

3486 Meacham, W. and Solheim, W. G. (1979) Determination of
      the original firing temperature of ceramics from
      Non Nok Tha and Phimai, Thailand. Journal of the
      Hong Kong archaeological society 7:114-118.

3487 Roberts, J. P. (1963) Determination of the firing
      temperature of ancient ceramics by measurement of
      thermal expansion. Archaeometry 6:21-25.

3488 Roberts, J. P. (1963) Some experiments on Romano-
      British colour-coated ware. Archaeometry 6:18-20.

3489 Tite, M. S. (1969) Determination of the firing
      temperature of ancient ceramics by measurement of
      thermal expansion: reassessment. Archaeometry
      11:131-143.

3490 Tite, M. S. (1969) Determination of the firing tem-
      perature of ancient ceramics by measurement of
      thermal expansion. Nature 222(5188):81.

3. Porosimetry

3491 Goodyear, F. H. (1971) Initial firing temperature,
      composition and provenance of pottery. Science and
      archaeology 6:12-14.

3492 Heimann, R. B. (1977) A simple method for estimation
      of the macroporosity of ceramic sherds by a replica
      technique. Archaeometry 19(1):55-56.

3493 Matson, F. R. (1941) Porosity studies of ancient
      pottery. Papers of the Michigan Academy of Sciences,
      Arts and Letters 26:469-477.

3494 Morariu, V. V., Bogdan, M. and Ardelean, I. (1977)
      Ancient pottery: its pore structure. Archaeometry
      19(2):187-192.

3495 Plant, R. J. (1970) A study of the moisture absorbed by
      biscuit pottery as a means of determining the ap-
      proximate firing temperature. Science and
      archaeology 4:19-20.

3496   Sanders, H. P. (1973) Pore-size distribution deter-
        minations in Neolithic, Iron Age, Roman, and other
        pottery. Archaeometry 15(1):159-161.

4. Other properties

3497   Goodman, M. E. (1944) The physical properties of stone
        tool materials. American antiquity 9:415-433.

3498   Hultgren, A. (1931) The hardness of Columbian tools
        made from copper-gold-silver alloys. Appendix to:
        E. Nordenskiöld, ed., Origin of the Indian
        civilizations in South America. Comparative
        ethnographical studies (Göteborg) 9:108-112.

3499   Shackley, M. L. (1972) The use of textural parameters
        in the analysis of cave sediments. Archaeometry
        14(1):133-145.

VI. DATA MANAGEMENT

A. General studies

3500 Borillo, M., Fernandez de la Vega, W. and Guenoche, A.
(1977) Raisonnement et méthodes en archéologie.
Paris.

3501 Borko, H. (1962) Computer applications in the
behavioral sciences. Englewood Cliffs, New Jersey:
Prentice-Hall.

3502 Doran, J. E. and Hodson, F. R. (1975) Mathematics and
computers in archaeology. Edinburgh: Edinburgh
Univ. Press.

3503 Floud, R. (1973) An introduction to quantitative
methods for historians. London: Methuen.

3504 Gardin, J.-C., ed. (1970) Archéologie et calculateurs.
Problèmes sémiologiques et mathématiques. Paris:
Centre National de la Recherche Scientifique.

3505 Hodder, I. and Orton, C. (1976) Spatial analysis in
archaeology. Cambridge: Cambridge Univ. Press.

3506 Hodson, F. R. and Kendall, D. G. (1971) Mathematics in
archaeology and history. Antiquity 45:55-56.

3507 Hodson, F. R., Kendall, D. G. and Tautu, P. (1971)
Mathematics in the archaeological and historical
sciences. Edinburgh: Edinburgh Univ. Press.

3508 Hymes, D., ed. (1965) The use of computers in
anthropology. The Hague: Mouton.

345

3509 Ihm, P., Lüning, J. and Zimmerman, A. (1978) Statistik
in der Archäologie. (Statistics in archaeology).
Archaeo-Physika 9. 619p.

3510 Metropolitan Museum of Art (1968) Computers and their
potential applications in museums. New York: Arno
Press.

3511 Renfrew, C. and Cooke, K. L., eds. (1979) Trans-
formations: mathematical approaches to culture
change. New York: Academic Press.

B. Statistical analysis and computerization

3512 Albrecht, G., Hahn, J. and Torke, W. G. (1972) Merk-
malanalyse von Geschossspitzen des mittleren Jung-
pleistozäns in Mittel- und Osteuropa. (Classification
of projective points of the middle to late Pleistocene in central and eastern Europe). Archaeologica
venatoria 2. Stuttgart, Berlin, Köln, and Mainz:
Verlag W. Kohlhammer. 107p.

3513 Aldrich, F. T. (1979) Comments on computer graphics
applications in archaeology. Computer graphics in
archaeology. Anthropological research paper (Tempe,
Arizona) 15:145-148.

3514 Allsworth Jones, P. (1975) The early Upper Palaeolithic
in Central Europe: a cluster analysis of some
Aurignacian and some Szeletian assemblages. Computer
applications in archaeology 1975. Birmingham:
Computer Centre Univ. of Birmingham, 81-92.

3515 Allsworth-Jones, P. and Wilcock, J. D. (1974) A
computer-assisted study of European Palaeolithic
"leafpoints". Science and archaeology 11:25-46.

3516 Alvey, R. C. and Laxton, R. R. (1974) Analysis of some
Nottingham clay pipes. Science and archaeology
13:3-12.

3517 Alvey, R. C. and Laxton, R. R. (1977) Further analysis
of some Nottingham clay pipes. Science and
archaeology 19:20-29.

3518 Angell, I. O. (1977) Are sone circles circles? Science and archaeology 19:16-19.

3519 Angell, I. O. (1978) On fitting certain closed convex curves to archaeological point data using an interactive graphics terminal. Journal of archaeological science 5:309-313.

3520 Angell, I. O. (1979) The megalithic yard: fact or fiction? MASCA journal 1(3):82-84.

3521 Angell, I. O. and Barber, J. (1977) An algorithm for fitting circles and ellipses to metalithic stone rings. Science and archaeology 20:11-16.

3522 Aniol, R. W. (1980) Kartierung mit dem Fortran-Programm KARTE. (Preparation of survey sheets with the fortran program KARTE). Archaeo-Physika 7:121-145.

3523 Arnold, J. B. (1975) A marine archeological application of automated data acquisition and processing. Newsletter of computer archaeology (Tempe, Arizona) 9(1):5-12.

3524 Arnold, J. B. (1979) Archaeological applications of computer-drawn contour and three dimensional perspective plots. Computer graphics in archaeology. Anthropological research paper (Tempe, Arizona) 15:1-15.

3525 Arnold, J. B. and Ford, A. (1980) A statistical examination of settlement patterns at Tikal, Guatemala. American antiquity 45(4):713-726.

3526 Ascher, M. (1959) A mathematical rationale for graphical seriation. American antiquity 25(2): 212-214.

3527 Baillie, M. G. L. and Pilcher, J. R. (1973) A simple crossdating program for tree-ring research. Tree-ring bulletin 33:7-14.

3528 Barker, P. C. (1975) An exact method of describing iron weapon points. Computer applications in archaeology 1975. Birmingham: Computer Centre Univ. of Birmingham, 3-8.

3529 Bettinger, R. L. (1979) Multivariate statistical analysis of a regional subsistence-settlement model for Owens Valley. American antiquity 44(3):455-470.

3530 Bieber, A. M. et al. (1976) Application of multivariate techniques to analytical data on Aegean ceramics. Archaeometry 18(1):59-74.

3531 Biek, L. (1979) Comparative pictorial graphics within the LERNIE concept. Archaeo-Physika 10:541-553.

3532 Bietti, A., Rambaldi, A. and Zanello, I. (1978) Un programma FORTRAN di "cluster analysis" per applicazioni archeologiche, paletnologiche e paleoecologiche. Quaternaria (Roma) 20:49-85.

3533 Bishop, S. and Wilcock, J. D. (1976) Archaeological context sorting by computer: the STRATA program. Science and archaeology 17:3-12.

3534 Botinger, E. and Davidson, I. (1977) Radiocarbon age and depth: a statistical treatment of two sequences of dates from Spain. Journal of archaeological science 4:231-243.

3535 Bohmers, A. and Wouters, A. (1956) Statistics and graphs in the study of flint assemblages. Palaeohistoria 5:1-38.

3536 Borgogno, I. (1980) Computer typology--pro and con. In: Adaptive radiations in prehistoric Panama. Peabody Museum, Harvard University. Monographs 5:394-403.

3537 Bowman, R. et al. (1975) A statistical study of the impurity occurrences in copper ores and their relationship to ore types. Archaeometry 17(2):157-163.

3538 Bromund, R. H., Bower, N. W. and Smith, R. H. (1976) Inclusions in ancient ceramics: an approach to the problem of sampling for chemical analysis. Archaeometry 18(2):218-221.

3539 Buckland, P. (1973) An experiment in the use of a computer for on-site recording of finds. Science and archaeology 9:22-25.

3540 Burton, J. (1980) Making sense of waste flakes: new methods for investigating the technology and economics behind chipped stone assemblages. Journal of archaeological science 7(2):131-148.

3541 Burton, R. J. (1977) ARCHSAMP: a general purpose sampling simulation program. Newsletter of computer archaeology (Tempe, Arizona) 13(2):1-24.

3542 Cavagnaro Vanoni, L. (1967) L'uso del calcolatore elettronico in archeologia. Palatino 11(2):191-193

3543 Celoria, F. S. C. and Wilcock, J. D. (1975) A computer-assisted classification of British Neolithic axes and a comparison with some Mexican and Guatemalan axes. Science and archaeology 16:11-29.

3544 Chantrew, D. F., Wilcock, J. D. and Celoria, F. S. C. (1975) The sorting of archaeological materials by man: an interdisciplinary study in pottery classification. Science and archaeology 14:5-31.

3545 Chenhall, R. G. (1966) Education in the use of computers. Newsletter of computer archaeology (Tempe, Arizona) 2(2):2-4.

3546 Chenhall, R. G. (1971) Computers in anthropology and archeology. New York: IBM Corporation. 71p.

3547 Christie, O. H. J., Brenna, J. A. and Straume, E. (1979) Multivariate classification of Roman glasses found in Norway. Archaeometry 21(2):233-241.

3548 Clack, P. (1975) The information retrieval system of the Northern Archaeological Survey. Computer applications in archaeology 1975. Birmingham: Computer Centre Univ. of Birmingham, 9-17.

3549 Clarke, D. L. (1962) Matrix analysis and archaeology with special reference to British Beaker pottery. Proceedings of the prehistoric society 28:371-382.

3550 Clark, G. A. (1979) Spatial association at Liencres, an early Holocene open site on the Santander Coast, north-central Spain. Computer graphics in archaeology. Anthropological research paper (Tempe, Arizona) 15:121-143.

350

3551 Clark, R. M. and Renfrew, C. (1972) A statistical approach to the calibration of floating tree-ring chronologies using radiocarbon dates. Archaeometry 14:5-19.

3552 Clark, R. M. and Sowray, A. (1973) Further statistical methods for the calibration of floating tree-rings chronologies. Archaeometry 15(2):255-266.

3553 Copp, S. A. (1977) A quick plotting program for archaeological data. Newsletter of computer archaeology (Tempe, Arizona) 13(1):17-24.

3554 Cowgill, G. L. (1967) Computer applications in archaeology. Computers and the humanities 2(1):17-23.

3555 Cowgill, G. L. (1968) Archaeological applications of factor, cluster, and proximity analysis. American antiquity 33:367-375.

3556 Dally, C. W. (1973) Was there a Neolithic yard? Science and archaeology 10:7-8.

3557 Daniels, S. G. H. (1965) Statistical determination of pottery types from the recently excavated site at Dambwa, near Livingstone, northern Rhodesia. In: G. J. Snowball, ed., Science and medicine in central Africa. Oxford: Pergamon Press, 591-610.

3558 Daniels, S. G. H. (1966) An operational scheme for the analysis of large assemblages of archaeological material. Archaeometry 9:151-154.

3559 Dean, J. S. and Robinson, W. J. (1979) Computer cartography and the reconstruction of dendroclimatic variability in the American Southwest, A. D. 680 to 1970. Computer graphics in archaeology. Anthropological research paper (Tempe, Arizona) 15:79-94.

3560 De Bruin, M. et al. (1976) The use of trace element concentrations in the identification of objects. Archaeometry 18(1):75-83.

3561 Dempsey, P. and Baumhoff, M. (1963) The statistical use of artifact distributions to establish chronological sequence. American antiquity 28(4):496-509.

3562 Deopik, V. B. (1977) Sootnošenie statističeskikh metodov, klassifikatsij i kul'turno-stratigrafičeskikh kharakteristik v arkheologičeskom issledovanii. (The correlation of statistical methods, classification, and cultural-stratigraphic characteristics in archaeological investigations). Kratkie soobščenija Instituta Arkheologii 148:3-9.

3563 De Souza, P. and Houghton, P. (1977) The mean measure of divergence and the use of non-metric data in the estimation of biological distances. Journal of archaeological science 4(2):163-169.

3564 Doran, J. E. (1970) Systems theory, computer simulations and archaeology. World archaeology 1(3): 289-298.

3565 Doran, J. E. (1979) Fitting models and studying process: some comments on the role of computer simulation in archaeology. Institute of Archaeology, Univ. of London. Bulletin 16:81-93.

3566 Doran, J. E. and Hodson, F. R. (1966) A digital computer analysis of Palaeolithic flint assemblages. Nature 210(5037):688-689.

3567 Drager, D. L. (1978) Automated data processing of digital aerial imagery in cultural resources survey. In: Remote sensing and non-destructive archeology. Washington, D.C.: National Park Service, 35-51.

3568 Duncan, J. M. and Main, P. L. (1977) The drawing of archaeological sections and plans by computer. Science and archaeology 20:17-26.

3569 Effland, R. W. (1979) Statistical distribution cartography and computer graphics. Computer graphics in archaeology. Anthropological research paper (Tempe, Arizona) 15:17-29.

3570 Feder, K. L. (1979) Geographic patterning of tool types as elicited by trend surface analysis. Computer graphics in archaeology. Anthropological research paper (Tempe, Arizona) 15:95-102.

3571 Ferguson, J. (1975) Statistical analysis of flint trace element data. Second international symposium on flint, Nederlandse Geol. Vereniging. Staringia 3:46-47.

3572 Ferguson, J. (1980) Application of data coding to the differentiation of British flint mine series. Journal of archaeological science 7(3):277-286.

3573 Fischer, A. and Mortensen, B. N. (1978) Report on the use of computers for description and analysis of Palaeolithic and Mesolithic occupation areas. Studies in Scandinavian prehistory and early history 1:7-22.

3574 Fisher, C. (1979) Discriminant analysis and classification of projectile points from eastern New York. Man in the northeast (Rindge, New Hampshire) 17: 145-158.

3575 Frankel, D. (1980) Contour-plans and surface plotting: aids for the field archaeologist. Journal of field archaeology 7(3):367-372.

3576 Friedman, B. D. (1980) Artifact distribution at Real Alto, Ecuador: computer generated plots. MASCA journal 1(5):134-135.

3577 Fritts, H. C. (1963) Computer programs for tree-ring research. Tree-ring bulletin 25(3/4):2-7.

3578 Fritts, H. C., Mosimann, J. E. and Bottorff, C. (1969) A revised computer program for standardizing tree-ring series. Tree-ring bulletin 29(1/2):15-20.

3579 Fritz, M. C. (1977) Understanding variability in Cantabrian Magdalenian bone assemblages by means of cluster analysis techniques. In: Colloques internationaux du centre national de la recherche scientifique. Paris, no. 568:143-160.

3580 Froom, F. R. (1973) A metrical technique for flint blades and similar artefacts. Proceedings of the prehistoric society 39:456-460.

3581 Gaines, S. W. (1970) Computer ceramics. Newsletter of computer archaeology (Tempe, Arizona) 5(3):2-4.

3582 Gaines, S. W. (1971) Computer utilization for archaeological field problems. Science and archaeology 8:6-7.

3583 Gaines, S. W. (1974) Computer use at an archaeological field location. American antiquity 39:454-465.

3584 Gaines, S. W. (1978) Computer application of SARG data: an evaluation. Investigations of the Southwestern Anthropological Research Group. Bulletin of the Museum of Northern Arizona (Flagstaff) 50:119-138.

3585 Gaines, S. W. (1979) Computing in archaeology: an era in retrospect. Newsletter of computer archaeology (Tempe, Arizona) 14:1-5.

3586 Gaines, S. W. and Gaines, W. M. (1980) Future trends in computer applications. American antiquity 45(3):462-471.

3587 Galloway, P. (1978) Restoring the map of medieval Trondheim: a computer-aided investigation into the nightwatchmen's itinerary. Journal of archaeological science 5:153-165.

3588 Gardin, J.-C. (1962) Projet de code pour l'analyse des formes de poteries (sur cartes perforées). Centre d'Analyse Documentaire pour l'Archéologie. Paris: Centre National de la Recherche Scientifique.

3589 Gardin, J.-C. (1967) Methods for the descriptive analysis of archaeological material. American antiquity 32(1):13-30.

3590 Gelfand, A. E. (1971) Seriation methods for archaeological materials. American antiquity 36(3):263-274.

3591 Gening, V. F. (1973) Programma statističeskoj obrabotki keramiki iz arkheologičeskikh raskopok. (A program of statistical processing of ceramics from archaeological excavations). Sovetskaja arkheologija 1:114-136.

3592 Gifford, D. P. and Crader, D. C. (1977) A computer coding system for archaeological faunal remains. American antiquity 42:225-237.

3593 Graham, I. (1980) Spectral analysis and distance
methods in the study of archaeological distributions.
Journal of archaeological science 7(2):105-129.

3594 Graham, I., Galloway, P. and Scollar, I. (1975) Model
studies in seriation techniques. Computer applications in archaeology 1975. Birmingham: Computer
Centre Univ. of Birmingham, 18-24.

3595 Graham, I., Galloway, P. and Scollar, I. (1976) Model
studies in computer seriation. Journal of
archaeological science 3:1-30.

3596 Graham, I. and Saunders, A. (1978) A multivariate
statistical analysis of small mammal bones. Institute
of Archaeology, London. Occasional publication 3:
59-67.

3597 Graham, J. M. and Roe, D. (1970) Discrimination of
British Lower and Middle Palaeolithic handaxe groups
using canonical variates. World archaeology 1(3):
321-342.

3598 Grayson, D. K. (1979) On the quantification of vertebrate archaeofaunas. Advances in archaeological
method and theory (New York) 2:200-237.

3599 Green, D. F. (1975) Testing a traditional typology
using cluster analysis. Computer applications in
archaeology 1975. Birmingham: Computer Centre Univ.
of Birmingham, 25-32.

3600 Hall, J. A. and Hewson, A. D. (1977) On-line computing
and radiocarbon dating at the British Museum.
Journal of archaeological science 4(1):89-94.

3601 Hamlin, C. L. (1977) Machine processing of LANDSAT
data, an introduction for anthropologists and
archaeologists. MASCA newsletter 13(1/2):1-11.

3602 Harris, E. C. (1975) Stratigraphic analyses and the
computer. Computer applications in archaeology 1975.
Birmingham: Computer Centre Univ. of Birmingham,
33-40.

3603 Hewson, A. D. (1980) The Ashanti weights--a statistical evaluation. Journal of archaeological science 7(4):363-370.

3604 Hietala, H. J. and Close, A. E. (1979) Testing hypotheses of independence on symmetrical artifacts. Journal of archaeological science 6(1):85-92.

3605 Hietala, H. J. and Larson, P. A. (1979) SYMAP analyses in archeology: intrasite assumptions and a comparison with TREND analysis. Norwegian archaeological review 12(1):57-64.

3606 Hodder, I. R. (1979) Trend surfaces in archaeology. Computer graphics in archaeology. Anthropological research paper (Tempe, Arizona) 15:149-153.

3607 Hodder, I. R. and Reece, R. (1980) An analysis of the distribution of coins in the western Roman Empire. Archaeo-Physika 7:179-192.

3608 Hodson, F. R. (1969) Searching for structure within multivariate archaeological data. World archaeology 1(1):90-105.

3609 Hodson, F. R. (1970) Cluster analysis and archaeology: some new developments and applications. World archaeology 1(3):299-320.

3610 Hodson, F. R., Sneath, P. H. A. and Doran, J. E. (1966) Some experiments in the numerical analysis of archaeological data. Biometrika 53:311-324.

3611 Hole, F. and Shaw, M. (1967) Computer analysis of chronological seriation. Rice University studies 53(3):1-166.

3612 Holzhausen, H. and Röttlander, R. C. A. (1970) Standardization of provincial Roman pottery IV: the origin of standardization. Archaeometry 12(2):189-195.

3613 Ihm, P. (1961) Classification automatique des objets de l'âge du bronze. Compte-rendus du séminaire sur les modèles mathématiques dans les sciences sociales 1960-1961. Paris: École Pratique des Hautes Études, 3:28-33.

3614   Ihm, P. (1980) Poisson- und negative Binomialver-
       teilung. (Poisson and negative binomial distribution).
       Archaeo-Physika 7:95-106.

3615   Ihm, P. (1980) Seriation mittels des Goldmann-
       Verfahrens. (Seriation with the aid of the Goldmann
       method). Archaeo-Physika 7:107-120

3616   Jedrzejewska, H. (1972) Sampling precautions in the
       analysis of antiquities. Studies in conservation
       7:27-32.

3617   Jelinek, A. J. (1962) Use of the cumulative graph in
       temporal ordering. American antiquity 28:241-243.

3618   Jermann, J. V. and Dunnell, R. C. (1979) Some limita-
       tions of isopleth mapping in archaeology. Computer
       graphics in archaeology. Anthropological research
       paper (Tempe, Arizona) 15:31-60.

3619   Kendall, D. G. (1963) A statistical approach to
       Flinders Petrie's sequence dating. Bulletin of the
       international statist. institute 40:657-680.

3620   Kendall, D. G. (1969) Incidence matrices, interval
       graphs, and seriation in archaeology. Pacific
       journal of mathematics 28(3):565-570.

3621   Kendall, D. G. (1969) Some problems and methods in
       statistical archaeology. World archaeology 1:68-76.

3622   Kendall, D. G. (1971) Abundance matrices and seriation
       in archaeology. Zeitschrift für Wahrscheinlichkeits-
       theorie 17:104-112.

3623   Kendall, D. G. (1971) A mathematical approach to
       seriation. Philosophical transactions of the Royal
       Society, London A269:125-135.

3624   Kenworthy, J. B., Stapleton, J. R. and Thurston, J. H.
       (1975) The Fife archaeological index--a computer
       implementation. Computer applications in archaeology
       1975. Birmingham: Computer Centre Univ. of
       Birmingham, 41-48.

3625 Kerrich, J. E. (1967) Relevance of cumulative frequency graphs for comparison of prehistoric artefact percentages. In: W. W. Bishop and J. D. Clark, eds., Background to evolution in Africa. Chicago: Univ. of Chicago Press, 761-763.

3626 Kerrich, J. E. and Clarke, D. L. (1967) Notes on the possible mis-use and errors of cumulative frequency graphs for the comparison of prehistoric artefact assemblages. Proceedings of the prehistoric society 33:57-69.

3627 Kovalevskaja (Deopik), V. B. (1965) Primenenie statistiĉeskikh metodov k izuĉeniju massovogo arkheologiĉeskogo materiala. (The application of statistical methods to the study of mass archaeological material). Materialy i isslodovanija po arkheologii SSSR 129:286-301.

3628 Kovalevskaja (Deopik), V. B., Pogoĵev, N. B. and Pogoĵeva, A. I. (1974) Quantitative methods for evaluating the degree of closeness between sites by percentage analysis of mass materials. Soviet anthropology and archaeology 13(2):33-56.

3629 Kroeber, A. L. (1940) Statistical classification. American antiquity 6(1):29-44.

3630 Kromholz, A. H. (1975) A generalized information system for archaeological use. Computer applications in archaeology 1975. Birmingham: Computer Centre Univ. of Birmingham, 49-55.

3631 Krug, G. K. and Krug, O. JU. (1965) Matematiĉeskij metod klassifikatsii drevnej keramiki. (A mathematical method for the classification of ancient ceramics. Materialy i issledovanija po arkheologii SSSR 129:318-325.

3632 Laflin, S. (1973) Computer system for county gazetteers. Science and archaeology 9:26-28.

3633 Laflin, S. (1979) Similarity coefficients for cluster analysis. Archaeo-Physika 10:556-565.

3634 Laplace-Jaurètche, G. (1954) Application des méthodes statistique à l'étude du Mesolitique. Bulletin de la société préhistorique de France 51:127-139.

3635 Leach, B. F. (1972) Multi-sampling and absolute dating methods: a problem of statistical combination for archaeologists. New Zealand archaeological association newsletter 15(3):113-113.

3636 Leblanc, J. et al. (1979) Attempt to reconstitute the original organisation of blocks belonging to dismantled monuments. Application to the Gallo-Roman monuments of Narbonne. Archaeo-Physika 10:566-579.

3637 Lehmer, D. J. (1951) Robinson's coefficient of agreement--a critique. American antiquity 17(2):151.

3638 Lengyel, A. (1975) Computer application in classical archaeology (pottery). Computer applications in archaeology 1975. Birmingham: Computer Centre Univ. of Birmingham, 56-62.

3639 Linington, R. E. (1967) Ancora sull'uso del calcolatore elettronico in archeologia. Palatino 11(3/4):409-414.

3640 Linington, R. E. (1968) The Rome computer system for treating archaeological survey results. First part. Prospezioni archeologiche 3:19-36.

3641 Linington, R. E. (1969) The Rome computer system for treating archaeological survey results. Second part. Prospezioni archeologiche 4:9-58.

3642 Linington, R. E. (1970) A first use of linear filtering techniques on archaeological prospecting results. Prospezioni archeologiche 5:43-54.

3643 Linington, R. E. (1971) Further tests on non-symmetrical filtering system. Prospezioni archeologiche 6:9-20.

3644 Lord, K. J. (1977) Numerical analysis of faunal remains of the Little Bethlehem (41AU38) and Leonard K (41AU37) sites. Plains anthropologist 22:291-298.

3645 Lukesh, S. S. (1975) Excavation recording: Buccino, south Italy. Computer applications in archaeology 1975. Birmingham: Computer Centre Univ. of Birmingham, 63-68.

3646 Lynch, B. M. and Donahue, R. (1980) A statistical analysis of two rock-art sites in northwest Kenya. Journal of field archaeology 7(1):75-85.

3647 McArdle, J. (1975-1977) A numerical (computerized) method for quantifying zooarchaeological comparisons. Paléorient 3:181-190.

3648 McNett, C. W. (1979) Computer graphics in the analysis of an eastern Paleo-Indian site. Computer graphics in archaeology. Anthropological research paper (Tempe, Arizona) 15:69-77.

3649 Matson, R. G. (1975) SAMSIM: a sampling simulation program. Newsletter of computer archaeology (Tempe, Arizona) 9(1):1-4.

3650 Matthews, J. (1963) Application of matrix analysis to archaeological problems. Nature 198:930-934.

3651 Meadow, R. H. (1978) "Bonecode"--a system of numerical coding for faunal data from Middle Eastern sites. In: Approaches to faunal analysis in the Middle East. Peabody Museum bulletin 2:169-186.

3652 Mertz, R., Melson, W. and Levenbach, G. (1979) Exploratory data analysis of Mycenaean ceramic compositions and provenances. Archaeo-Physika 10:580-596.

3653 Newell, R. R. (1975) A proposed attribute analysis of archaeological ground-features: an expansion of the automatic artifact registration system. Computer applications in archaeology 1975. Birmingham: Computer Centre Univ. of Birmingham, 69-80.

3654 Newell, R. R. and Vroomans, A. P. J. (1972) Automated artifact registration and systems for archaeological analysis with the Philips P1100 computer: a Mesolithic test case. Anthropological publications, Oosterhout, Netherlands. 102p.

3655 Nichol, R. K. and Creak, G. A. (1979) Matching paired
elements among archaeological bone remains: a
computer procedure and some practical limitations.
Newsletter of computer archaeology (Tempe, Arizona)
14:6-16.

3656 Nielsen, H. and Nielsen, K. (1978) Module search by
means of a computer--an aid for analysis of historical architecture, etc. Studies in Scandinavian
prehistory and early history 1:23-45.

3657 Nunley, R. E. and Fischer, M. A. (1979) A preliminary
simulation of a non-steady state process of
expansion of urban impact on the U.S. countryside:
an example of work in spatial models and interactive
computer graphics. Computer graphics in archaeology.
Anthropological research paper (Tempe, Arizona)
15:103-119.

3658 Olshan, A. F., Hantman, J. L. and Lightfoot, K. G.
(1977) The use of high-dimensional plotting in the
analysis of multivariate archaeological data.
Newsletter of computer archaeology (Tempe, Arizona)
12(4):1-13.

3659 Orton, C. R. (1970) The production of pottery from a
Romano-British kiln site: a statistical investigation. World archaeology 1(3):343-358.

3660 Orton, C. R. (1973) The tactical use of models in
archaeology--the SHERD project. In: C. Renfrew,
ed., The explanation of culture change: models in
prehistory. London: Duckworth, 137-139.

3661 Orton, C. R. (1975) Quantitative pottery studies;
some progress, problems and prospects. Science and
archaeology 16:30-35.

3662 Ottaway, B. S. (1973) Dispersion diagrams: a new
approach to the display of carbon-14 dates.
Archaeometry 15(1):5-12.

3663 Ottaway, B. S. (1974) Cluster analysis of impurity
patterns in Armorico-British daggers. Archaeometry
16(2):221-231.

3664 Ottaway, B. S. (1979) Interpretation of prehistoric metal artifacts with the aid of cluster analysis. Archaeo-Physika 10:597-606.

3665 Palmer, R. (1977) A computer method for transcribing information graphically from oblique aerial photographs to maps. Journal of archaeological science 4:283-290.

3666 Picon, M. et al. (1975) Composition of the La Graufesenque, Banassac and Montans terra sigillata. Archaeometry 17(2):191-199.

3667 Pitts, M. W. and Jacobi, R. M. (1979) Some aspects of change in flaked stone industries of the Mesolithic and Neolithic in southern Britain. Journal of archaeological science 6(2):163-177.

3668 Pryor, R. A. (1973) A general scheme for local inventories. Science and archaeology 9:7-16.

3669 Redding, R. W., Pires-Ferreira, J. C. W. and Zeder, M. A. (1975-1977) A proposed system for computer analysis of identifiable faunal material from archaeological sites. Paléorient 3:191-205.

3670 Redding, R. W., Zeder, M. A. and McArdle, J. (1978) "Bonesort II"--a system for the computer processing of identifiable faunal material. In: Approaches to faunal analysis in the Middle East. Peabody Museum bulletin 2:135-147.

3671 Robertson, W. S. (1976) A quantitative morphological study of the evolution of some post-medieval wine bottles. Science and archaeology 17:13-20.

3672 Schauffler, W. (1979) Computerized data base management systems in archaeological research: a SELGEM case study. MASCA journal 1(2):50-52.

3673 Scheitlin, T. E. and Clark, G. A. (1978) Three dimensional surface representations of lithic categories at Lencres. Newsletter of computer archaeology 13(3/4):1-13.

3674 Schwarz, G. T. (1964) Dating Roman masonry by statistical analysis (teichography). Archaeometry 7:63-66.

362

3675 Scollar, I. (1968) Program package for the interpretation of magnetometer data. Prospezioni
archeologiche 3:9-18.

3676 Scollar, I. (1969) A program for the simulation of
magnetic anomalies of archaeological origin in a
computer. Prospezioni archeologiche 4:59-83.

3677 Scollar, I. (1970) Fourier transform methods for the
evaluation of magnetic maps. Prospezioni
archeologiche 5:9-41.

3678 Scollar, I. (1978) Computer image processing for
archaeological air photographs. Field techniques and
research design. World archaeology 10(1):71-87.

3679 Scollar, I. and Krückeberg, F. (1966) Computer treatment of magnetic measurements from archaeological
sites. Archaeometry 9:61-71.

3680 Shackley, M. L. (1973) Computers and sediment
analysis in archaeology. Science and archaeology
9:29-30.

3681 Shennan, S. J. and Wilcock, J. D. (1975) Shape and
style variation in central German Bell Beakers: a
computer-assisted study. Science and archaeology
15:17-31.

3682 Smith, L. D. (1977) Programmable pocket calculators:
some archeological applications. Newsletter of
computer archaeology (Tempe, Arizona) 12(3):1-26.

3683 Spaulding, A. C. (1953) Statistical techniques for the
discovery of artifact types. American antiquity
18(4):305-313.

3684 Stehli, P. and Zimmerman, A. (1980) Zur Analyse
neolithischer Gefässformen. (On the analysis of
Neolithic vessel forms). Archaeo-Physika 7:147-177.

3685 Steuer, H. (1971) Zur "statistischen" Auswertung früh-
mittelalterlicher Keramik im Nordseeküstenbereich.
(On the "statistical" evaluation of early Medieval
ceramics in the North Sea coast area). Nachrichten
aus Niedersachsens Urgeschichte 40:1-27.

3686 Stones, C. J. and Williamson, J. B. (1970) Sevres porcelain and its incised marks. Science and archaeology 4:15-18.

3687 Thomas, D. H. (1971) On the use of cumulative curves and numerical taxonomy. American antiquity 36(2): 206-209.

3688 Thomas, D. H. (1980) The gruesome truth about statistics in archaeology. American antiquity 45(2): 344-345.

3689 Tout, R. E., Gilboy, W. B. and Clark, A. J. (1979) The use of computerised X-ray tomography for the non-destructive examination of archaeological objects. Archaeo-Physika 10:608-616.

3690 Uerpmann, H.-P. (1978) The "KNOCOD" system for processing data on animal bones from archaeological sites. In: Approaches to faunal analysis in the Middle East. Peabody Museum bulletin 2:149-167.

3691 Urbańczyk, P. (1980) Some problems of formal methods and computer science application against the background of contemporary archaeological theory and methodology. Archaeologia Polona 19:97-114.

3692 Vark, G. N. van (1974) The investigation of human cremated skeletal material by multivariate statistical methods. I. Methodology. Ossa 1:63-95.

3693 Vark, G. N. van (1975) The investigation of human cremated skeletal material by multivariate statistical methods. II. Measures. Ossa 2(1):47-68.

3694 Voorrips, A. (1980) On the use of statistics for testing archaeological hypotheses. Current anthropology 21(4):529-532.

3695 Wagner, N. (1971) Computerised pottery analysis. Newsletter of computer archaeology (Tempe, Arizona) 7(2):2.

3696 Walker, I. C. (1967) Statistical methods for dating clay pipe fragments. Post-medieval archaeology 1:90-101.

3697 Walker, M. J. (1970) An analysis of British petroglyphs. Science and archaeology 2/3:30-61.

3698 Walker, M. J. (1973) T-tests on prehistoric and
modern charred grain measurements. Science and
archaeology 10:11-32.

3699 Ward, G. K. (1974) A systematic approach to the
definition of sources of raw material. Archaeometry
16(1):41-53.

3700 Webb, E. (1979) Problems in the use of the cumulative
frequency graph for the comparison of lithic
assemblages. Archaeo-Physika 10:617-631.

3701 Whallon, R. (1971) Type: a computer program for mono-
thetic subdivisive classification in archaeology.
Museum of Anthropology, Univ. of Michigan. Technical
reports no. 1.

3702 Whallon, R. (1972) The computer in archaeology: a
critical survey. Computers and the humanities 7(1):
29-45.

3703 Whallon, R. (1973) Spatial analysis of occupation
floors, I: application of dimensional analysis of
variance. American antiquity 38:266-278.

3704 Whallon, R. (1974) Spatial analysis of occupation
floors, II: the application of nearest neighbor
analysis. American antiquity 39:16-34.

3705 Wilcock, J. D. (1968) A comparison of computer graphic
techniques for the automatic reduction of archaeomagnetic field observations. Prospezioni
archeologiche 3:87-90.

3706 Wilcock, J. D. (1969) Computer analysis of proton magnetometer readings from South Cadbury 1969--a long-
distance exercise. Prospezioni archeologiche 4:85-93.

3707 Wilcock, J. D. (1970) Petroglyphs by computer. Science
and archaeology 2/3:27-29.

3708 Wilcock, J. D. (1970) Prospecting at South Cadbury:
an exercise in computer archaeology. Science and
archaeology 1:9-11.

3709 Wilcock, J. D. (1970) Some developments in the portrayal of magnetic anomalies by digital incremental plotter. Prospezioni archeologiche 5:55-58.

3710 Wilcock, J. D. (1973) A general survey of computer application in archaeology. Science and archaeology 9:17-21.

3711 Wilcock, J. D. (1974) The facilities of the PLUTARCH system. Science and archaeology 11:16-24.

3712 Wilcock, J. D. (1975) Archaeological context sorting by computer. Computer applications in archaeology 1975. Birmingham: Computer Centre Univ. of Birmingham, 93-97.

3713 Wilcock, J. D. (1975) Presentation of computer classification results: a comparison of graphical methods. Science and archaeology 15:32-37.

3714 Wilcock, J. D. and Shennan, S. J. (1975) The computer analysis of pottery shapes with application to Bell Beaker pottery. Computer applications in archaeology 1975. Birmingham: Computer Centre Univ. of Birmingham, 98-106.

3715 Wilkinson, E. M. (1974) Techniques of data analysis. Seriation theory. Archaeo-Physika 5:1-42.

3716 Wobst, H. M. (1979) Computers and coordinates: strategies for the analysis of Paleolithic stratigraphy. Computer graphics in archaeology. Anthropological research paper (Tempe, Arizona) 15:61-67.

VII. ADDENDA

3717 Ascenzi, A. (1979) A problem in paleopathology. The origin of thalassemia in Italy. Virchows Archiv 384:121-130.

3718 Bakkevig, S. (1980) Phosphate analysis in archaeology--problems and recent progress. Norwegian archaeological review 13(2):73-100.

3719 Bell, W. H. and King, C. J. (1944) Methods for the identification of the leaf fibers of mescal (Agave), yucca (Yucca), beargrass (Nolina), and sotol (Dasylirion). American antiquity 10:150-160.

3720 Briuer, F. L. (1976) New clues to stone tool function: plant and animal residues. American antiquity 41(4): 478-484.

3721 Brugam, R. B. (1978) Pollen indicators of land-use change in southern Connecticut. Quaternary research (New York) 9(3):349-362.

3722 Buczko, C. M. and Vas, L. (1977) Effect of climate on chemical composition of fossil bones. Nature 269:792-793.

3723 Burleigh, R. and Clutton-Brock, J. (1980) The survival of Myotragus balearicus Bate, 1909, into the Neolithic on Mallorca. Journal of archaeological science 7(4):385-388.

3724 Cann, J. R. and Renfrew, C. (1964) The characterization of obsidian and its application to the Mediterranean region. Proceedings of the prehistoric society 30:111-131.

367

3725 Clason, A. T. (1979) The farmers of Gomolava in the
      Vinča and La Tène period. Rad Vojvodjanskih Muzeja
      25:60-114.

3726 Cubuk, G. A. et al. (1977/1978) Altsteinzeitliche
      Funde und eiszeitliche Faunenreste von Rockenberg,
      Wetteraukreis. (Palaeolithic finds and ice age
      faunal remains from Rockenberg, Wetterau district).
      Fundberichte aus Hessen (Bonn) 17/18:37-64.

3727 Dering, J. P. (1977) Plant macrofossil study: a
      progress report. In: Archeological and botanical
      studies at Hinds Cave, Val Verde County, Texas.
      Texas A & M University Anthropology Laboratory
      special series no. 1.

3728 De Roever-Bonnet, H. et al. (1979) Helminth eggs and
      gregarines from coprolites from the excavations at
      Swifterbant: Swifterbant contribution 10. Helinium
      (Wetteren, Belgium) 19(1):7-12.

3729 Dixon, J. E., Cann, J. R. and Renfrew, C. (1968)
      Obsidian and the origins of trade. Scientific
      American 218(3):38-46.

3730 Ericson, J. E., Shirahata, H. and Patterson, C. C.
      (1979) Skeletal concentrations of lead in ancient
      Peruvians. New England journal of medicine 300:
      946-951.

3731 Fornaciari, G. and Mallegni, F. (1980) Iperostosi
      porotica verosimilmente talassemica in due
      scheletri rinvenuti in un gruppo di tombe del III
      secolo a.c. di San Giovenale (Viterbo). Quaderni di
      scienze antropologiche (Padova) 4:21-50.

3732 Glass, B. et al. (1967) Geomagnetic reversals and
      Pleistocene chronology. Nature 216:437-442.

3733 Grandjean, P., Nielson, O. V. and Shapiro, I. M. (1979)
      Lead retention in ancient Nubian and contemporary
      populations. Journal of environmental pathology and
      toxicology (Park Forest South, Illinois) 2:781-787.

3734 Guilday, J. E. (1967) The climatic significance of the
      Hosterman's Pit local fauna, Centre County,
      Pennsylvania. American antiquity 32:231-232.

3735 Gulliksen, S. (1980) Calibration of radiocarbon dates: a review. Norwegian archaeological review 13(2):101-109.

3736 Hassan, F. A. (1979) Geoarchaeology: the geologist and archaeology. American antiquity 44(2):267-270.

3737 Hesse, A. (1973) Applications des méthodes géophysiques de prospection à l'étude des sites préhistoriques. Paléorient 1:11-20.

3738 Ispol'zovanie metodov estestvennykh nauk v arkheologii. (Utilization of the methods of the natural sciences in archaeology). (1978) Kiev: Akademija Nauk Ukrainskoj SSR. Institut Arkheologii. 130p.

3739 Jones, M. (1980) Carbonized cereals from Grooved Ware contexts. Proceedings of the prehistoric society 46:61-63.

3740 Kolčin, B. A., ed. (1972) Problemy absoljutnogo datirovanija v arkheologii. (Problems of absolute dating in archaeology). Moskva: Akademija Nauk SSSR. 147p.

3741 Mallegni, F. and Fornaciari, G. (1980) Studio antropologico e paleopatologico di un gruppo di scheletri rinvenuti nella villa romana di Settefinestre (Grosseto). Quaderni di scienze antropologiche (Padova) 4:63-77.

3742 Mellars, P. A. and Wilkinson, M. R. (1980) Fish otoliths as indicators of seasonality in prehistoric shell middens: the evidence from Oronsay (Inner Hebrides). Proceedings of the prehistoric society 46:19-44.

3743 Mills, J. S. and White, R. (1977) Natural resins of art and archaeology: their sources, chemistry and identification. Studies in conservation 22(1):12-31.

3744 Monk, M. A. and Fasham, P. J. (1980) Carbonised plant remains from two Iron Age sites in central Hampshire. Proceedings of the prehistoric society 46:321-344.

3745 Moseley, J. E. (1965) The paleopathologic riddle of "symmetrical osteoporosis". American journal of roentgenology, radium therapy and nuclear medicine 95:135-142.

3746 Oeschger, H. (1980) Radiokarbon-Alterbestimmungen zum süddeutschen Mesolithikum und deren Vergleich mit der vegetationsgeschichtlichen Datierung. (Carbon-14 age determinations for the south German Mesolithic and their comparison with the dating of vegetation history). Tübinger Monographien zur Urgeschichte (Stuttgart) 5(2):15-19.

3747 Renfrew, C., Cann, J. R. and Dixon, J. E. (1965) Obsidian in the Aegean. Annual of the British School of Archaeology at Athens 60:225-251.

3748 Renfrew, C., Dixon, J. E. and Cann, J. R. (1966) Obsidian and early cultural contact in the Near East. Proceedings of the prehistoric society 32:30-72.

3749 Renfrew, C., Dixon, J. E. and Cann, J. R. (1968) Further analysis of Near East obsidian. Proceedings of the prehistoric society 34:319-331.

3750 St. Joseph, J. K. S. (1980) Aerial reconnaissance: recent results, 50. Antiquity 54(211):132-135.

3751 Schmid, E. (1980) Relative Alterbestimmung einiger Knochenreste von einer Steinzeitlichen Fundstelle auf der Kleinen Kalmit bei Arzheim, Stadt Landau (Pfalz). (Relative age determination of some bone remains from a stone age site on the Kleinen Kalmit near Arzheim, city of Landau, Palatinate). Tübinger Monographien zur Urgeschichte 5(2):127-128.

3752 Shafer, H. J. and Bryant, V. M., eds. (1977) Archeological and botanical study of Hinds Cave, Val Verde County, Texas. Texas A & M University Anthropology Laboratory special series no. 1.

3753 Shafer, H. J. and Holloway, R. G. (1977) Organic residue analysis and stone tool function from Hinds Cave, Val Verde County, Texas: a progress statement. In: Archeological and botanical study of Hinds Cave, Val Verde County, Texas. Texas A & M University Anthropology Laboratory special series no. 1.

3754 Théorêt, M. A. (1980) Side-scan sonar in Lake
     Champlain, Vermont, U.S.A. International journal of
     nautical archaeology 9(1):35-41.

3755 Wehmiller, J. F. and Belknap, D. F. (1978) Alternative
     kinetic models for the interpretation of amino acid
     encantiometric ratios in Pleistocene mollusks:
     examples from California, Washington, and Florida.
     Quaternary research (New York) 9(3):330-348.

Zambia, 1870

METHOD INDEX

Aerial surveying, 108, 1419, 3567, 3665, 3678, 3750
Amino acid racemization, 2582, 3755
Archaeomagnetic dating, 379, 380, 530, 739, 3165, 3732, 3738
Atomic absorption spectrophotometry (AAS), 1434, 2760, 2825,
    3247, 3398
Beta-ray backscattering, 3433
Blood typing, 2491-2494, 2553, 2554, 2557, 2580, 2649, 2693,
    2697, 2705, 2706
Chromatography, 2942, 2947, 2948, 2950, 2953, 2955, 2966,
    2973, 2974, 2979, 2983, 2997
Coprolite analysis, 1538, 2082, 2287, 2400, 2681, 2709, 2723
Data management, 320, 501, 838, 3303, 3310, 3362, 3414
Dendrochronology, 358, 363, 389, 392, 393, 401, 402, 443,
    444, 447-449, 457, 467, 485, 489, 503, 506, 529, 536,
    538, 542, 570, 1482, 1483, 1489, 1496-1505, 1508, 1511-
    1515, 1522, 1525, 1526, 1530, 1531, 3527, 3551, 3552,
    3559, 3577, 3578, 3740
Differential thermal analysis (DTA), 674, 790, 3481, 3485
Electromagnetic surveying, 54
Electron microprobe analysis, 426, 2780, 2848, 2850, 2874,
    3652
Electron microscopy, 791, 2091, 2103, 2207, 2367, 2850, 2851,
    2867, 2874, 2885, 2886, 3005, 3329
Electron spin resonance (ESR), 806, 1374-1376
Energy dispersive X-ray analysis (EDAX), 3314, 3317
Faunal analysis, 1418, 1507, 2037, 2118, 2163, 2187, 2418,
    2428, 3011, 3592, 3596, 3598, 3644, 3647, 3651, 3655,
    3669, 3670, 3690, 3723, 3725, 3726, 3734, 3738, 3742
Flotation, 2307, 2387
Fluorine-uranium-nitrogen dating (FUN), 3722
Gamma-ray absorption, 3443
Granulometric analysis, 1470, 3499
Hardness determinations, 3497, 3498

MATERIALS INDEX

Amber, 2924, 3020-3028, 3031, 3035
Antimony, 2963
Bone, 350, 368, 378, 385, 426, 427, 429, 440, 459, 462, 483, 520, 549, 554, 609, 612, 613, 615-617, 705, 730, 731, 733, 736, 2430, 2437, 2438, 2582, 2596, 2599, 2626, 2813, 2921, 2937, 3011, 3017, 3220, 3329, 3423, 3512, 3579, 3692, 3693
Ceramics, 633, 669, 674, 676, 678, 680, 685, 694, 696, 702, 704, 706, 708, 710, 711, 713, 715, 716, 719, 744, 745, 747, 749, 753, 756, 757, 759, 767, 772, 775, 781, 788, 792, 793, 796, 798, 800, 802, 804, 815, 817, 820, 821, 830, 832, 835, 842, 853, 885, 895, 908, 921, 925, 2239, 2312, 2352, 2742, 2744, 2752, 2754-2756, 2760, 2761, 2764, 2765, 2769, 2772, 2773, 2777, 2779, 2785, 2786, 2788-2790, 2792, 2803, 2806, 2807, 2811, 2815, 2816, 2820, 2826, 2839-2842, 2844, 2845, 2928, 2933-2935, 2939, 2954, 2957, 2967, 2976, 2981, 2984, 2987, 2999, 3001, 3002, 3005, 3006, 3010, 3012, 3013, 3016, 3039-3049, 3051, 3057, 3072-3074, 3076-3079, 3100, 3119, 3123, 3137, 3138, 3140, 3151, 3152, 3157, 3160, 3163, 3164, 3167, 3210, 3227, 3230, 3246, 3273, 3275, 3280, 3296, 3298, 3303-3306, 3308, 3323, 3334, 3336, 3338-3340, 3347-3350, 3355, 3356, 3360, 3361, 3363-3365, 3367-3370, 3380, 3383, 3387, 3388, 3399, 3403-3405, 3407, 3411, 3414, 3415, 3421, 3424, 3425, 3433, 3434, 3437, 3445, 3481, 3485-3496, 3530, 3538, 3544, 3549, 3588, 3591, 3612, 3631, 3638, 3652, 3659-3661, 3666, 3681, 3684-3686, 3695, 3714
Copper, 2865-2867, 2881, 2895, 2897, 2900, 2907, 2938, 2940, 2970, 3080, 3082, 3083, 3089-3091, 3120, 3124-3128, 3134, 3146, 3147, 3158, 3166, 3169, 3170, 3191, 3193, 3197, 3211, 3239, 3240, 3289, 3290, 3295, 3317, 3330, 3332, 3372, 3392, 3393, 3402, 3406, 3418, 3444
Copper alloys, 707, 726, 787, 822, 837, 2852, 2853, 2866, 2890-2893, 2895, 2902, 2908, 2909, 2952, 2963, 2969, 2970, 2978, 3058, 3061, 3065, 3068, 3080, 3093, 3094, 3098, 3122,

AUTHOR INDEX